My Monster Secret

"Actually, I am..."

2

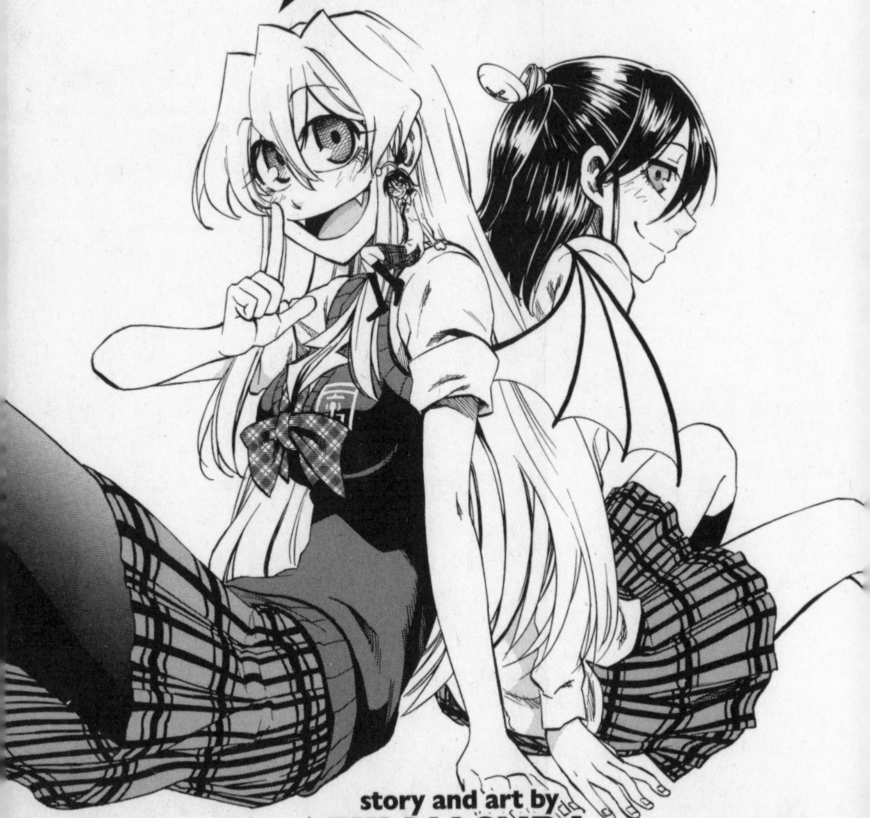

story and art by

EIJI MASUDA

Story & Characters

After school one day, Kuromine Asahi opened the door to his classroom to confess his love to his crush, Shiragami Youko... and discovered that she's actually a vampire! His goal was to tell Shiragami that he loved her, but he instead resolved to keep her secret--as a friend. It means they can continue to go to school together, but their problems are only beginning...

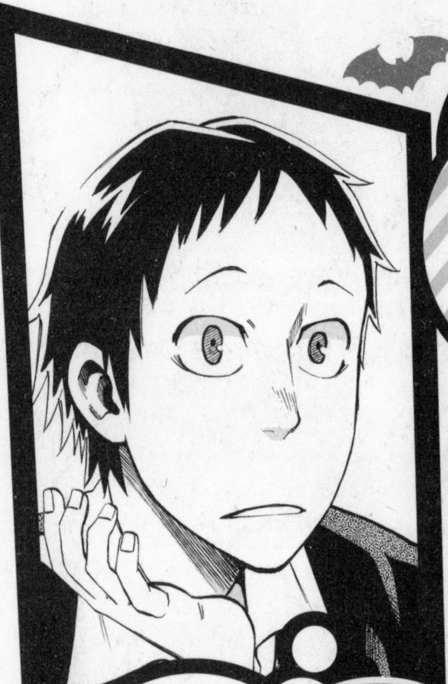

KUROMINE ASAHI

THE HOLEY SIEVE

The man with the worst poker face in the world, he's known as *The Sieve With A Hole In It*...because secrets slide right out of him. Now he has to hide the fact that Shiragami-san--the girl he's in love with--is a vampire.

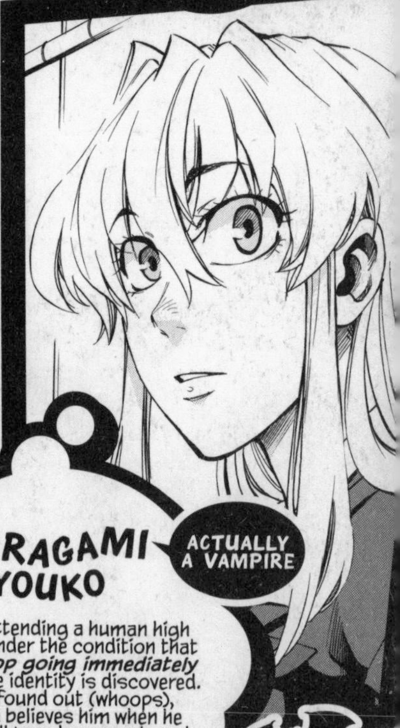

SHIRAGAMI YOUKO

ACTUALLY A VAMPIRE

She's attending a human high school under the condition that she'll ***stop going immediately*** if her true identity is discovered. Asahi found out (whoops), but she believes him when he says he'll keep her secret, and the two are now friends.

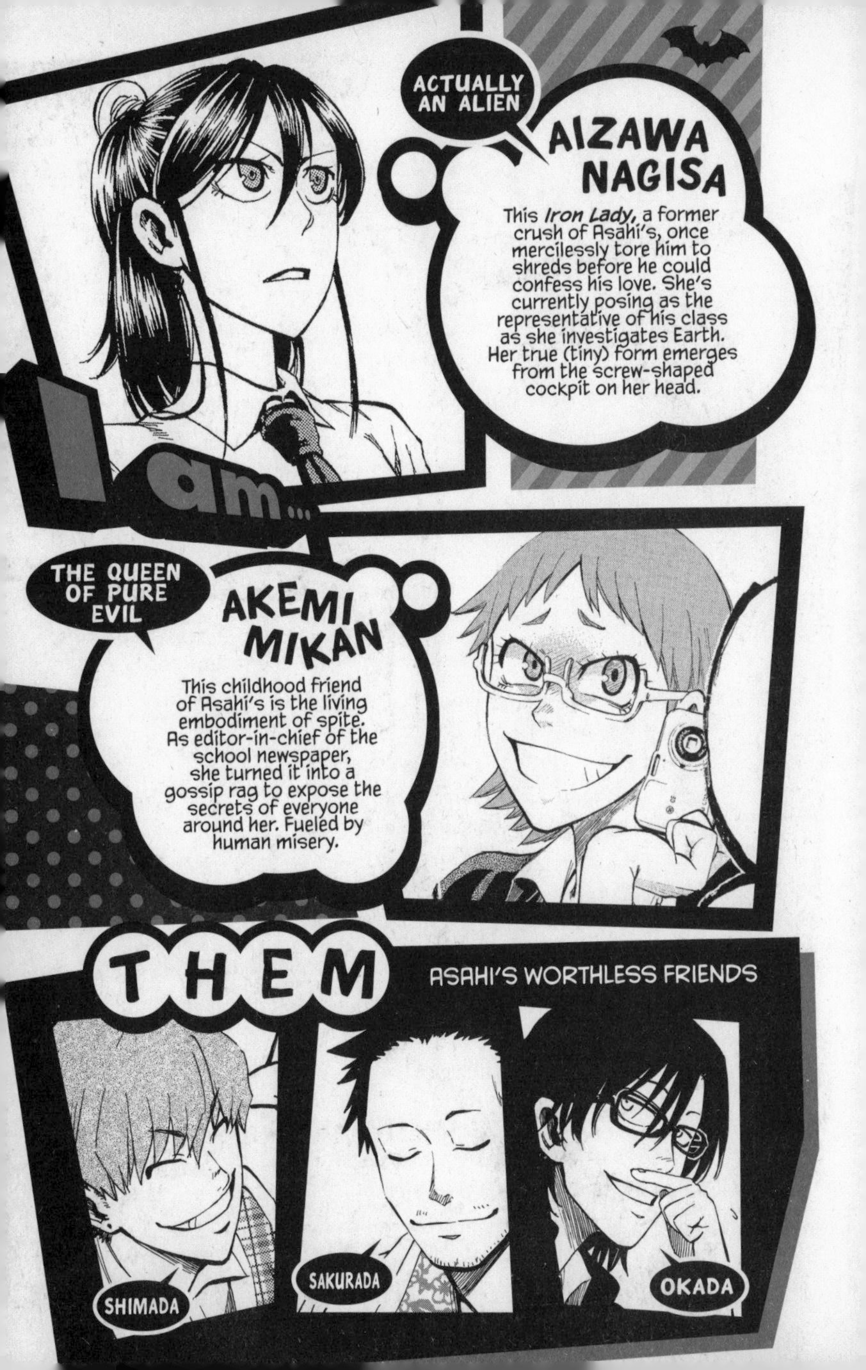
ACTUALLY AN ALIEN
AIZAWA NAGISA
This *Iron Lady*, a former crush of Asahi's, once mercilessly tore him to shreds before he could confess his love. She's currently posing as the representative of his class as she investigates Earth. Her true (tiny) form emerges from the screw-shaped cockpit on her head.
I am...
THE QUEEN OF PURE EVIL
AKEMI MIKAN
This childhood friend of Asahi's is the living embodiment of spite. As editor-in-chief of the school newspaper, she turned it into a gossip rag to expose the secrets of everyone around her. Fueled by human misery.
THEM
ASAHI'S WORTHLESS FRIENDS
OKADA
SAKURADA
SHIMADA

SEVEN SEAS ENTERTAINMENT PRESENTS

My Monster Secret
"Actually, I am..."

story and art by Eiji Masuda

VOLUME 2

TRANSLATION
Alethea and Athena Nibley

ADAPTATION
Lianne Sentar

LETTERING AND LAYOUT
Annaliese Christman

LOGO DESIGN
Karis Page

COVER DESIGN
Nicky Lim

PROOFREADER
Shanti Whitesides

PRODUCTION MANAGER
Lissa Pattillo

EDITOR-IN-CHIEF
Adam Arnold

PUBLISHER
Jason DeAngelis

JITSUHA WATASHIHA Volume 2
© EIJI MASUDA 2013
Originally published in Japan in 2013 by Akita Publishing Co., Ltd.
English translation rights arranged with Akita Publishing Co., Ltd.
through TOHAN CORPORATION, Tokyo.

Seven Seas books may be purchased in bulk for educational, business, or
promotional use. For information on bulk purchases, please contact Macmillan
Corporate & Premium Sales Department at 1-800-221-7945 (ext 5442)
or write specialmarkets@macmillan.com.

Seven Seas and the Seven Seas logo are trademarks of
Seven Seas Entertainment, LLC. All rights reserved.

ISBN: 978-1-626922-59-4

Printed in Canada

First Printing: April 2016

10 9 8 7 6 5 4 3 2 1

FOLLOW US ONLINE: *www.gomanga.com*

READING DIRECTIONS

This book reads from *right to left*, Japanese style. If
this is your first time reading manga, you start
reading from the top right panel on each page and
take it from there. If you get lost, just follow the
numbered diagram here. It may seem backwards at
first, but you'll get the hang of it! Have fun!!

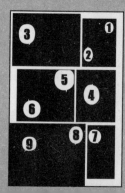

Chapter 8: "Let's Prevent Tanning!"

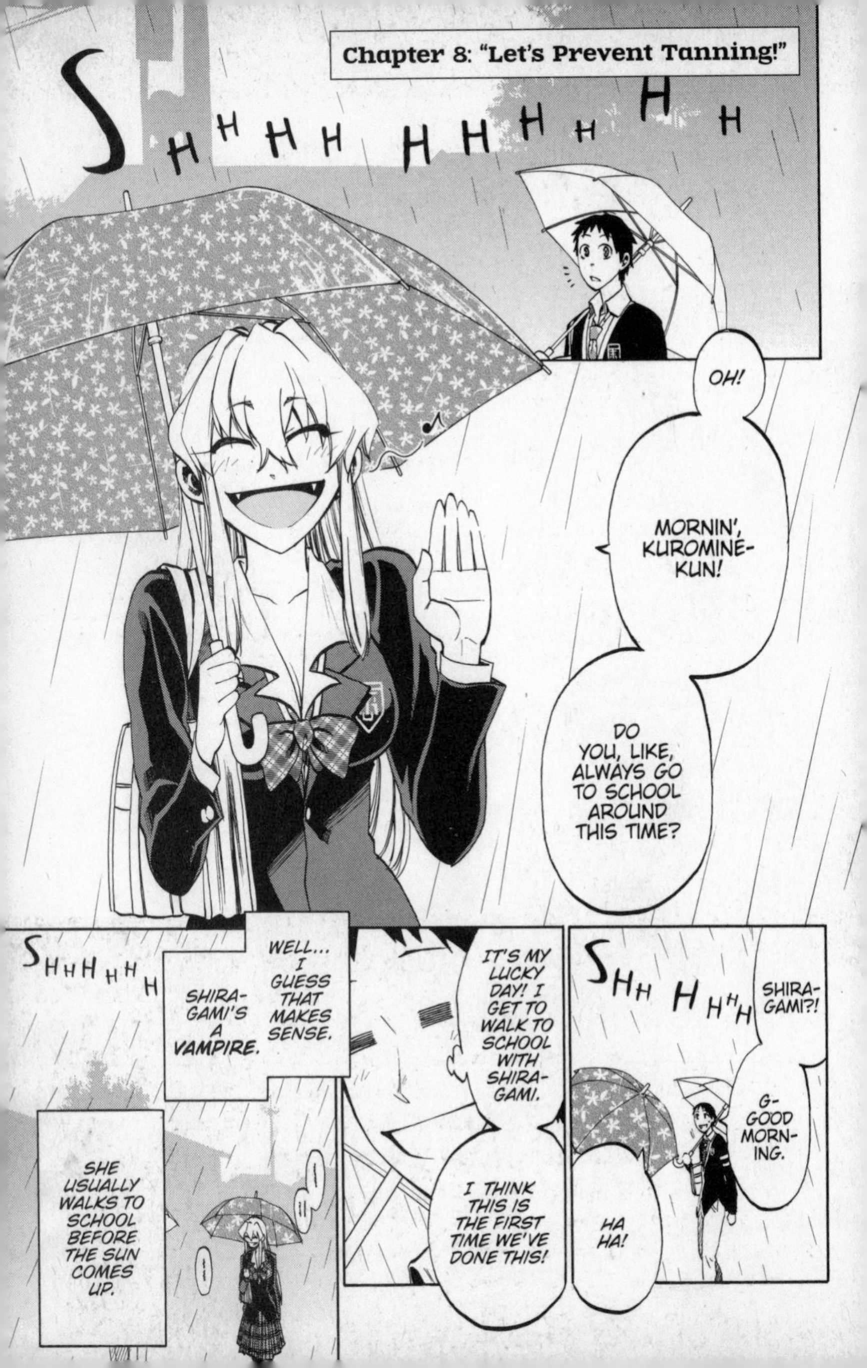
SHHHHHHHHHHH
OH!
MORNIN', KUROMINE-KUN!
DO YOU, LIKE, ALWAYS GO TO SCHOOL AROUND THIS TIME?
SHH HHHH
SHIRA-GAMI?!
G-GOOD MORN-ING.
HA HA!
IT'S MY LUCKY DAY! I GET TO WALK TO SCHOOL WITH SHIRA-GAMI.
I THINK THIS IS THE FIRST TIME WE'VE DONE THIS!
SHHHHHH
WELL... I GUESS THAT MAKES SENSE.
SHIRA-GAMI'S A **VAMPIRE**.
SHE USUALLY WALKS TO SCHOOL BEFORE THE SUN COMES UP.

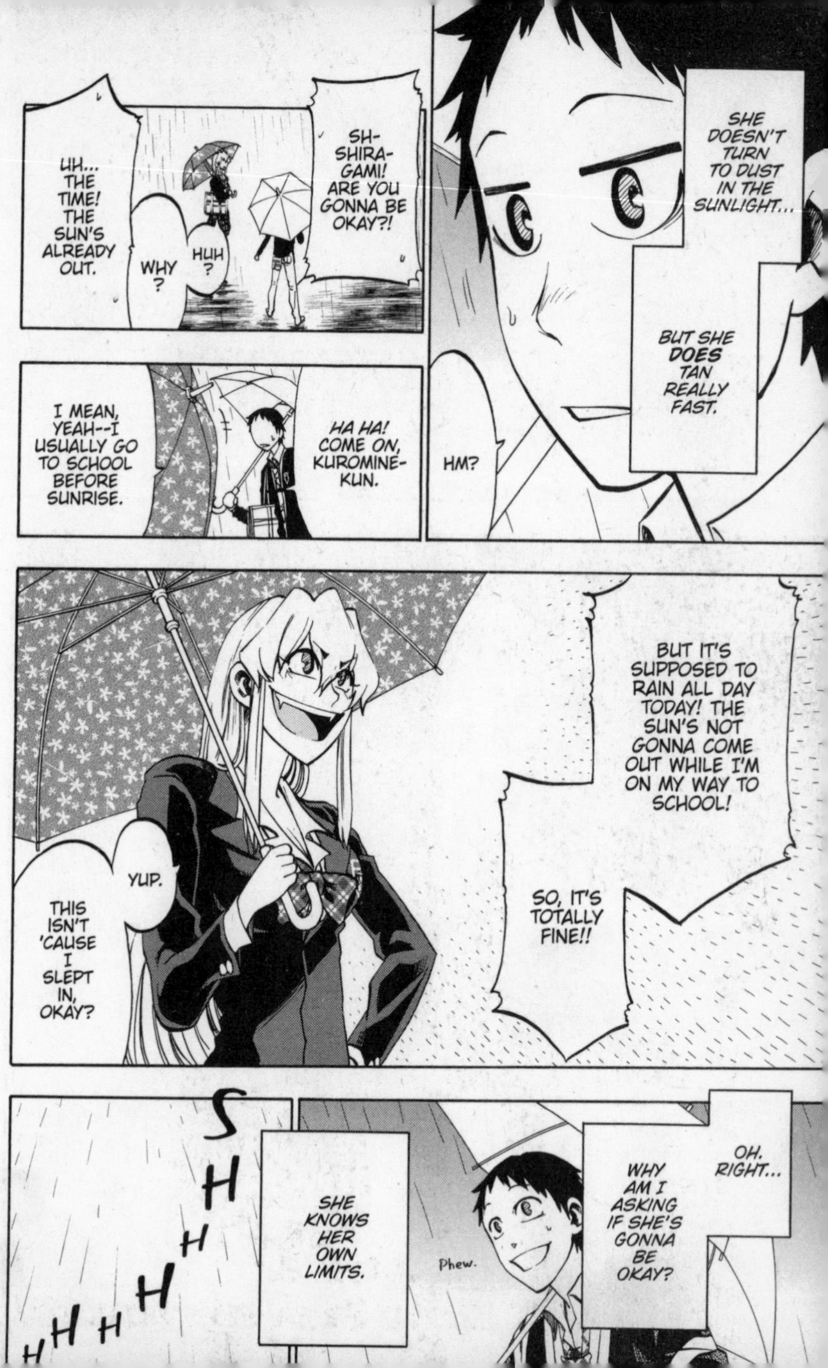
SHE DOESN'T TURN TO DUST IN THE SUNLIGHT...
BUT SHE **DOES** TAN REALLY FAST.
HM?
SH-SHIRA-GAMI! ARE YOU GONNA BE OKAY?!
HUH?
WHY?
UH... THE TIME! THE SUN'S ALREADY OUT.
HA HA! COME ON, KUROMINE-KUN.
I MEAN, YEAH--I USUALLY GO TO SCHOOL BEFORE SUNRISE.
BUT IT'S SUPPOSED TO RAIN ALL DAY TODAY! THE SUN'S NOT GONNA COME OUT WHILE I'M ON MY WAY TO SCHOOL!
SO, IT'S TOTALLY FINE!!
YUP.
THIS ISN'T 'CAUSE I SLEPT IN, OKAY?
OH. RIGHT...
WHY AM I ASKING IF SHE'S GONNA BE OKAY?
Phew.
SHE KNOWS HER OWN LIMITS.
SHHHHHHHH

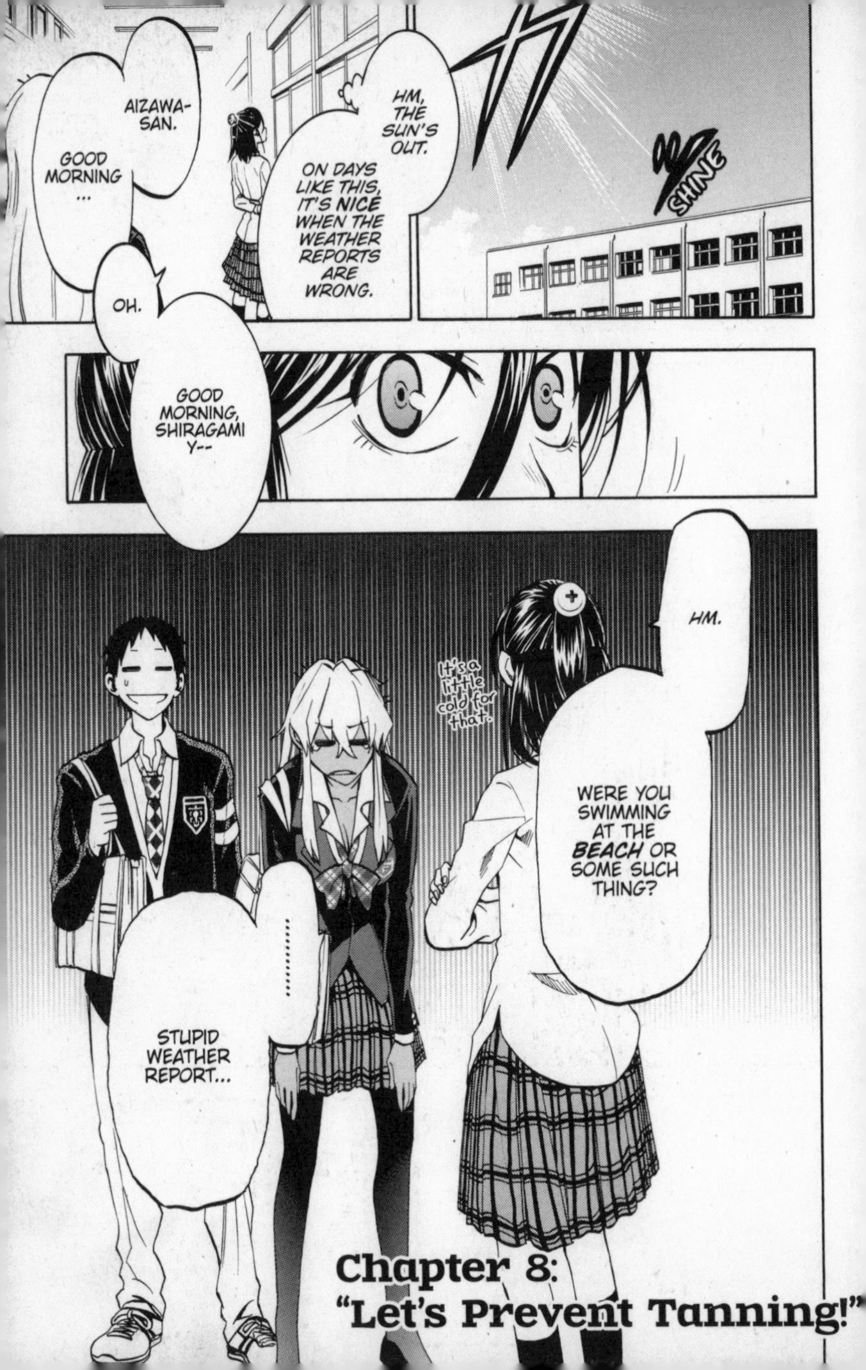
SHINE
HM, THE SUN'S OUT.
ON DAYS LIKE THIS, IT'S **NICE** WHEN THE WEATHER REPORTS ARE WRONG.
AIZAWA-SAN.
GOOD MORNING ...
OH.
GOOD MORNING, SHIRAGAMI Y--
HM.
It's a little cold for that.
WERE YOU SWIMMING AT THE *BEACH* OR SOME SUCH THING?
......
STUPID WEATHER REPORT...

Chapter 8: "Let's Prevent Tanning!"

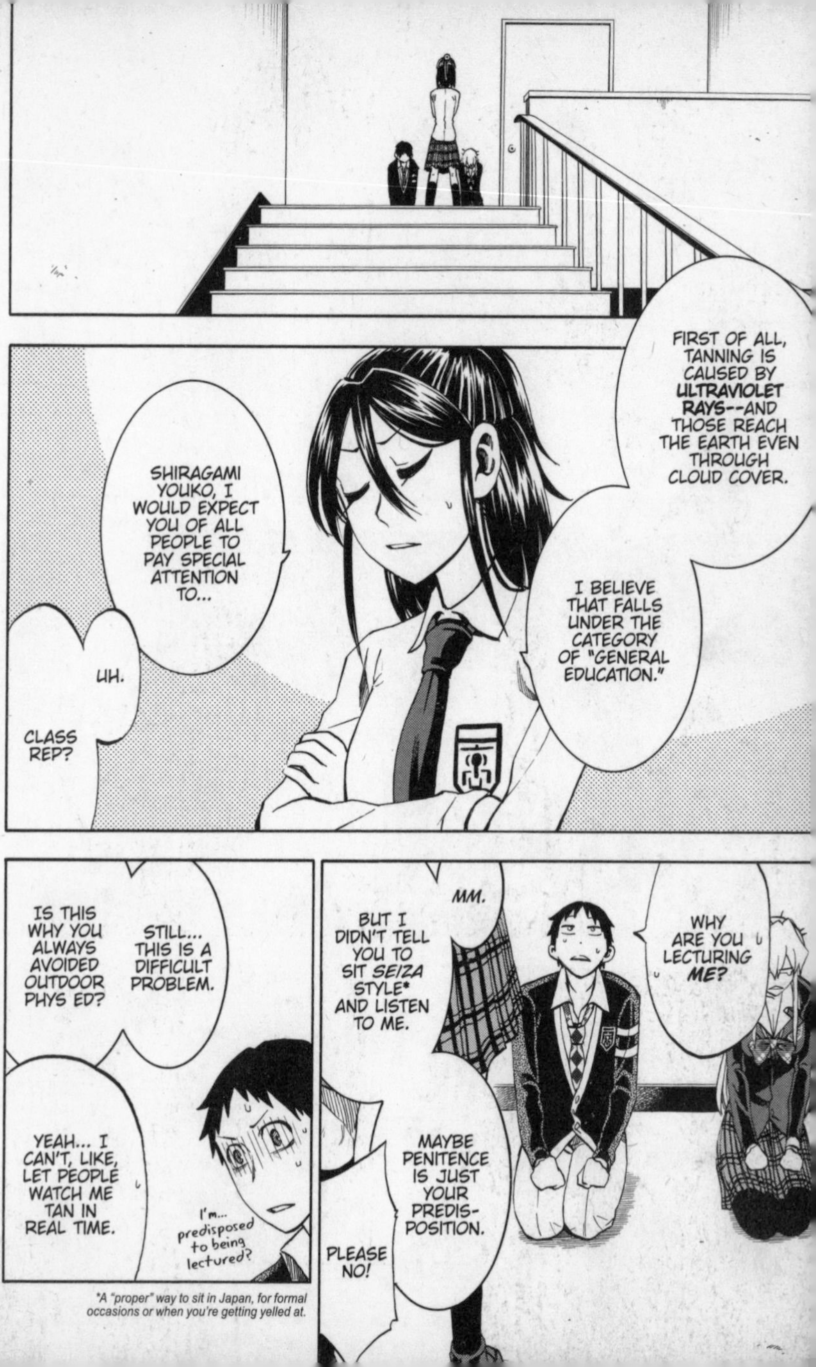
FIRST OF ALL, TANNING IS CAUSED BY **ULTRAVIOLET RAYS**--AND THOSE REACH THE EARTH EVEN THROUGH CLOUD COVER.
I BELIEVE THAT FALLS UNDER THE CATEGORY OF "GENERAL EDUCATION."
SHIRAGAMI YOUKO, I WOULD EXPECT YOU OF ALL PEOPLE TO PAY SPECIAL ATTENTION TO...
UH.
CLASS REP?
WHY ARE YOU LECTURING *ME?*
MM.
BUT I DIDN'T TELL YOU TO SIT *SEIZA* STYLE* AND LISTEN TO ME.
MAYBE PENITENCE IS JUST YOUR PREDIS-POSITION.
PLEASE NO!
STILL... THIS IS A DIFFICULT PROBLEM.
IS THIS WHY YOU ALWAYS AVOIDED OUTDOOR PHYS ED?
YEAH... I CAN'T, LIKE, LET PEOPLE WATCH ME TAN IN REAL TIME.
I'm... predisposed to being lectured?

**A "proper" way to sit in Japan, for formal occasions or when you're getting yelled at.*

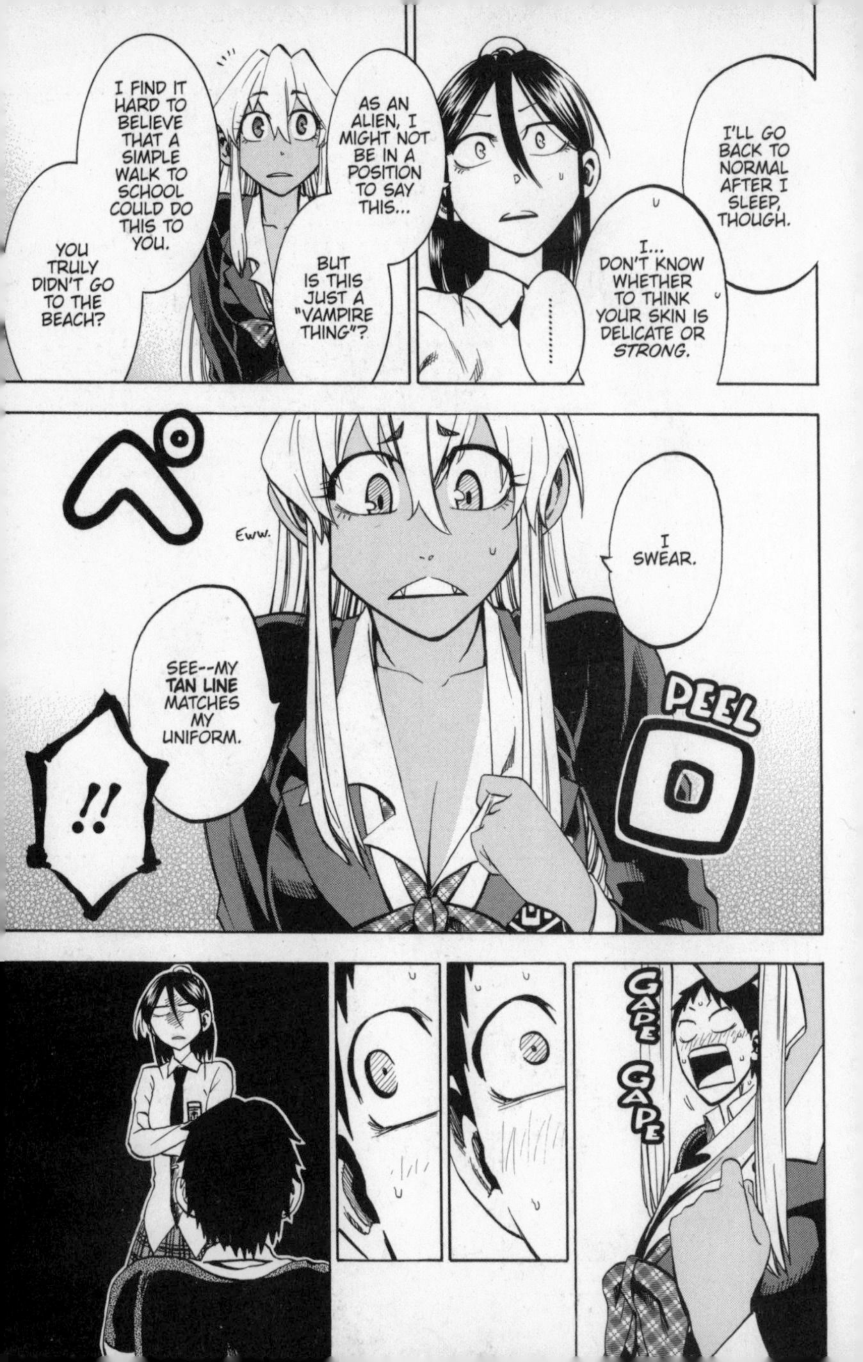
I'LL GO BACK TO NORMAL AFTER I SLEEP, THOUGH.
I... DON'T KNOW WHETHER TO THINK YOUR SKIN IS DELICATE OR *STRONG*.
......
AS AN ALIEN, I MIGHT NOT BE IN A POSITION TO SAY THIS...
BUT IS THIS JUST A "VAMPIRE THING"?
I FIND IT HARD TO BELIEVE THAT A SIMPLE WALK TO SCHOOL COULD DO THIS TO YOU.
YOU TRULY DIDN'T GO TO THE BEACH?
I SWEAR.
ぺ
Eww.
PEEL
SEE--MY **TAN LINE** MATCHES MY UNIFORM.
!!
GAPE GAPE

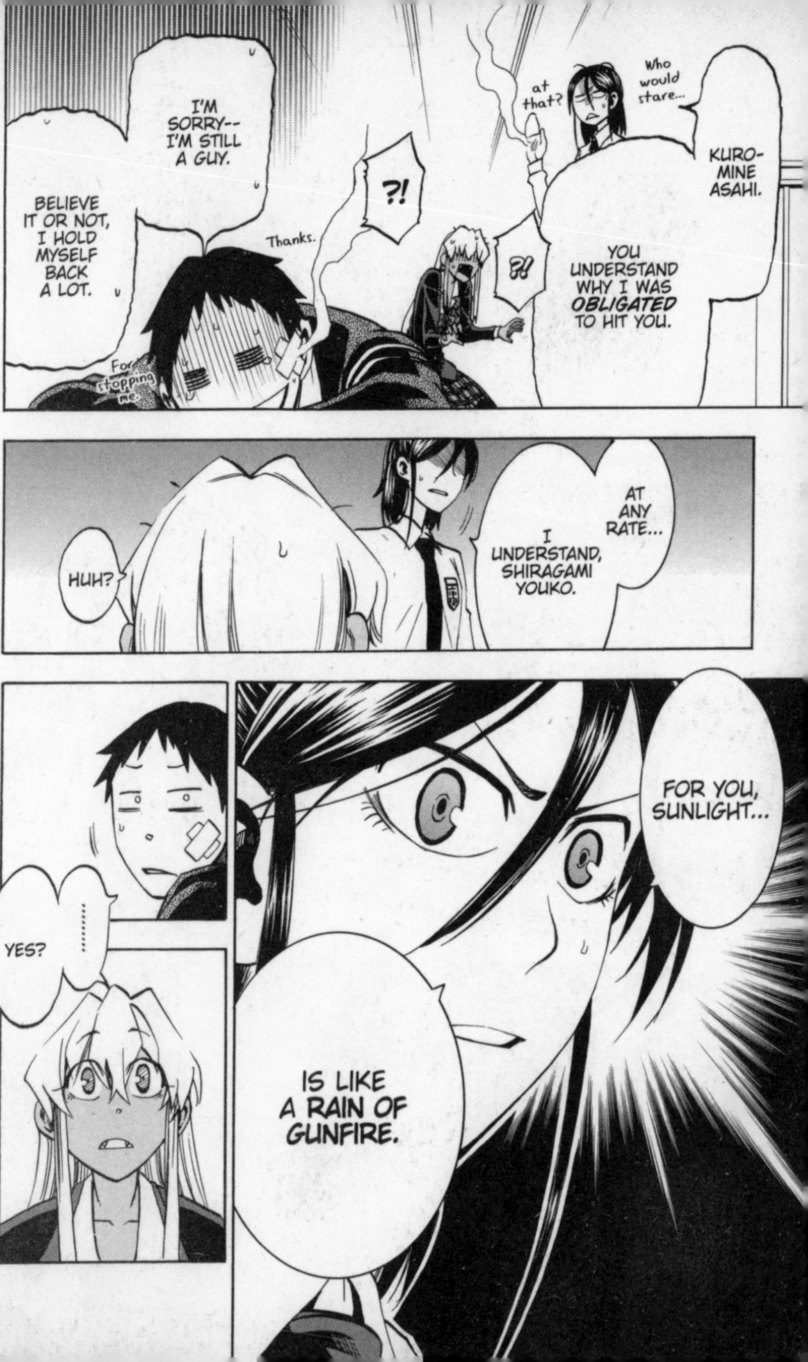
Who would stare...
at that?
KURO-MINE ASAHI.
YOU UNDERSTAND WHY I WAS OBLIGATED TO HIT YOU.
?!
?!
Thanks.
I'M SORRY-- I'M STILL A GUY.
BELIEVE IT OR NOT, I HOLD MYSELF BACK A LOT.
For stopping me.
AT ANY RATE...
I UNDERSTAND, SHIRAGAMI YOUKO.
HUH?
FOR YOU, SUNLIGHT...
IS LIKE A RAIN OF GUNFIRE.
......
YES?

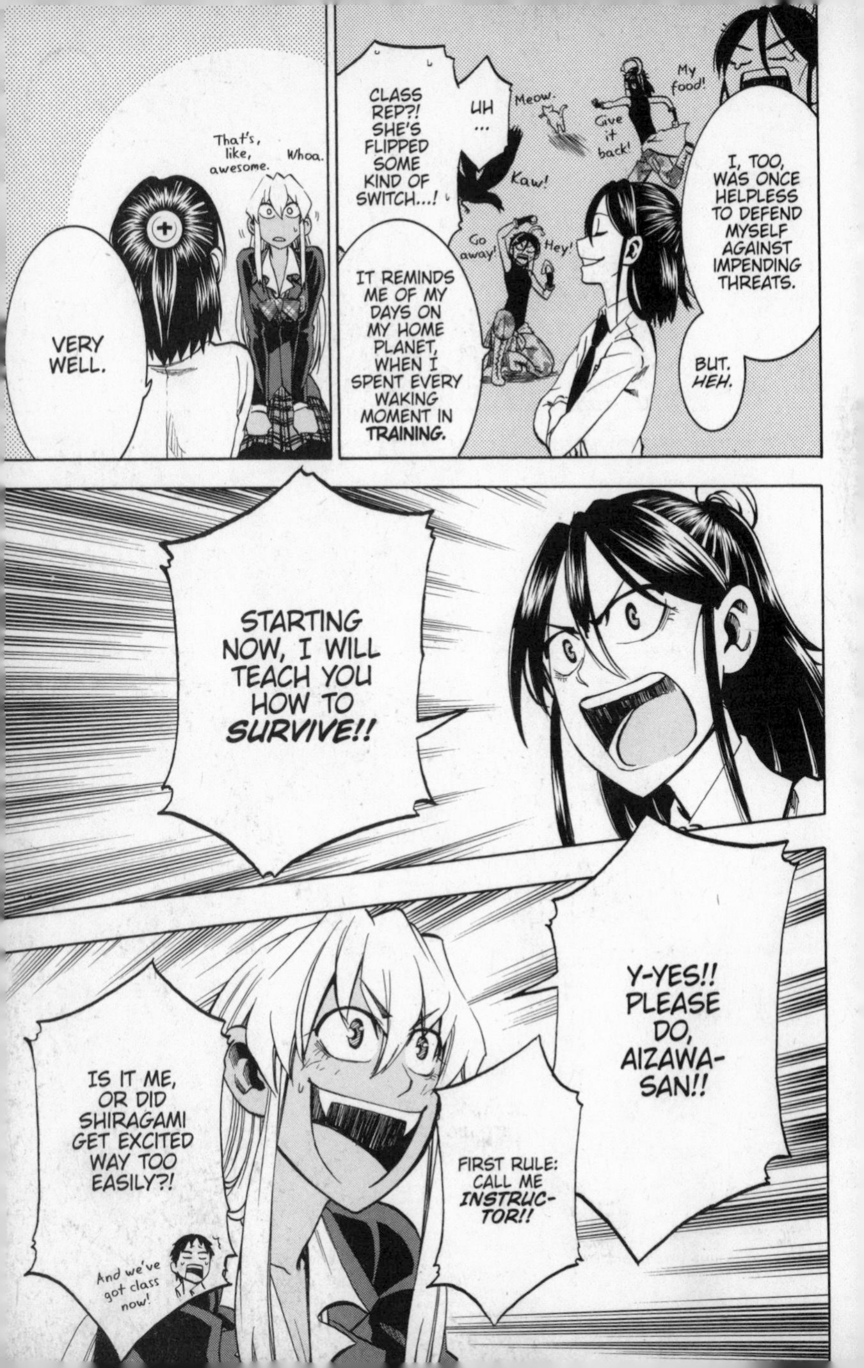
I, TOO, WAS ONCE HELPLESS TO DEFEND MYSELF AGAINST IMPENDING THREATS.
BUT. *HEH.*
My food!
Give it back!
Meow.
UH ...
Kaw!
CLASS REP?! SHE'S FLIPPED SOME KIND OF SWITCH...!
Hey!
Go away!
IT REMINDS ME OF MY DAYS ON MY HOME PLANET, WHEN I SPENT EVERY WAKING MOMENT IN **TRAINING.**
Whoa.
That's, like, awesome.
VERY WELL.
STARTING NOW, I WILL TEACH YOU HOW TO ***SURVIVE!!***
Y-YES!! PLEASE DO, AIZAWA-SAN!!
FIRST RULE: CALL ME ***INSTRUCTOR!!***
IS IT ME, OR DID SHIRAGAMI GET EXCITED WAY TOO EASILY?!
And we've got class now!

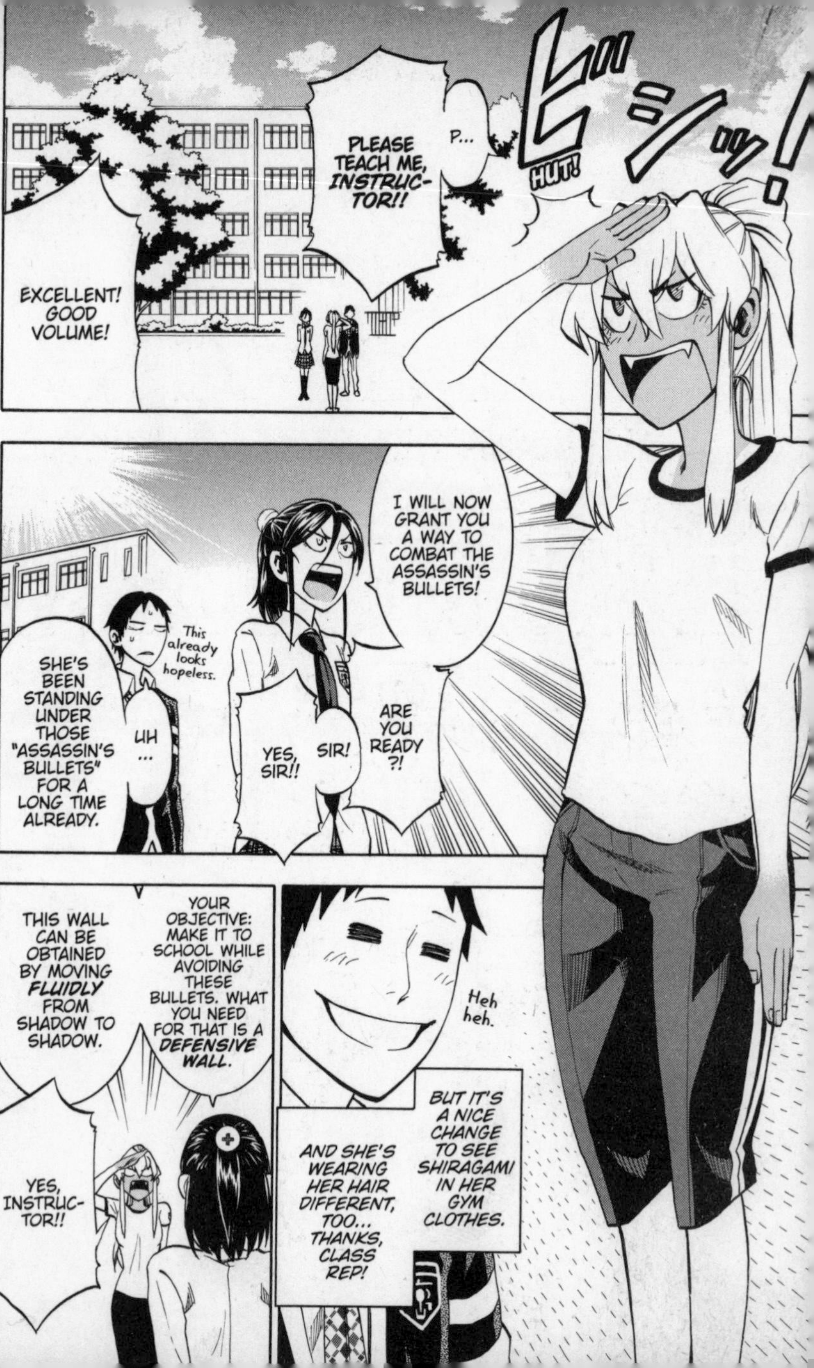
HUT!
P...
PLEASE TEACH ME, INSTRUCTOR!!
EXCELLENT! GOOD VOLUME!
I WILL NOW GRANT YOU A WAY TO COMBAT THE ASSASSIN'S BULLETS!
ARE YOU READY ?!
SIR!
YES, SIR!!
This already looks hopeless.
UH ...
SHE'S BEEN STANDING UNDER THOSE "ASSASSIN'S BULLETS" FOR A LONG TIME ALREADY.
BUT IT'S A NICE CHANGE TO SEE SHIRAGAMI IN HER GYM CLOTHES.
AND SHE'S WEARING HER HAIR DIFFERENT, TOO... THANKS, CLASS REP!
Heh heh.
YOUR OBJECTIVE: MAKE IT TO SCHOOL WHILE AVOIDING THESE BULLETS. WHAT YOU NEED FOR THAT IS A DEFENSIVE WALL.
THIS WALL CAN BE OBTAINED BY MOVING FLUIDLY FROM SHADOW TO SHADOW.
YES, INSTRUCTOR!!

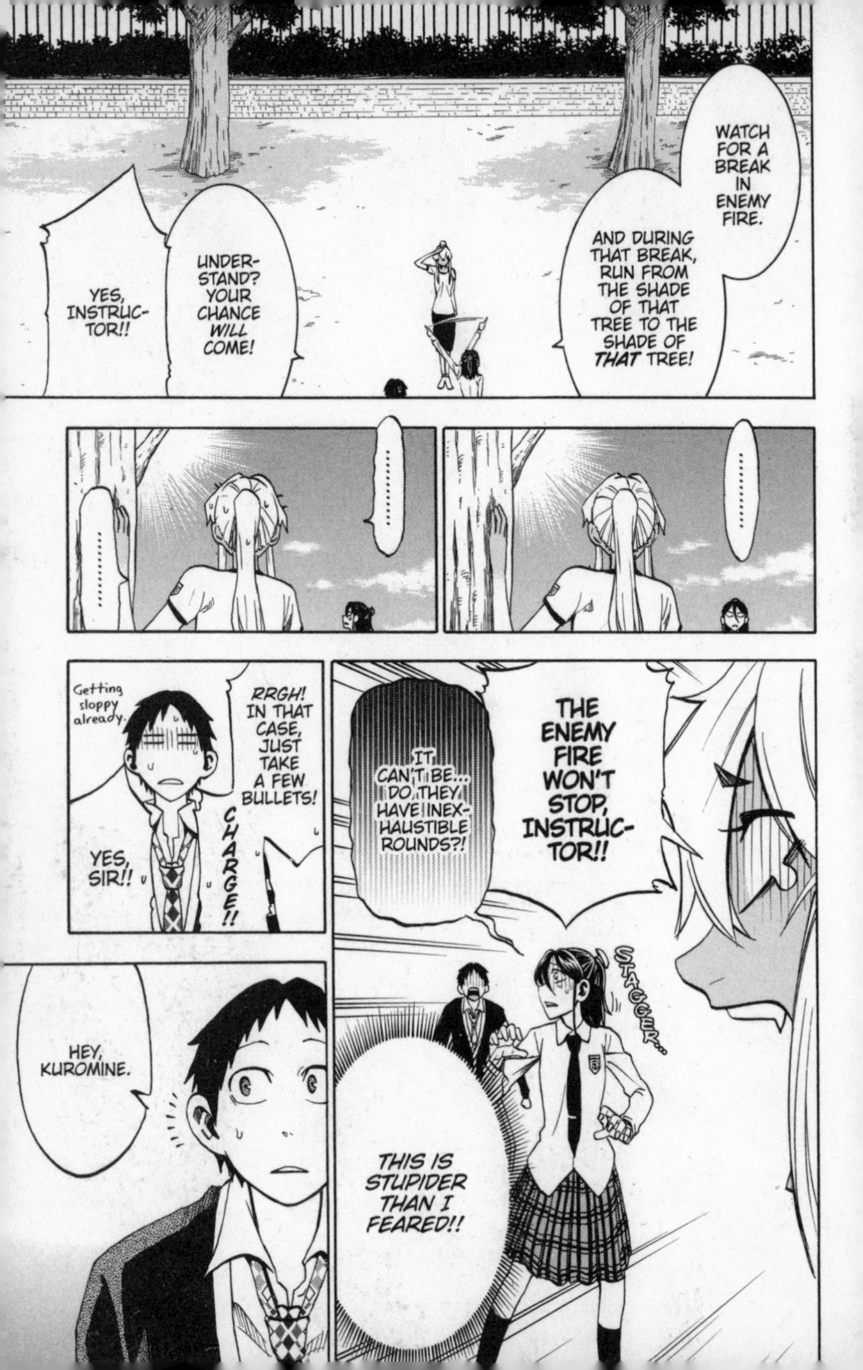
WATCH FOR A BREAK IN ENEMY FIRE.
AND DURING THAT BREAK, RUN FROM THE SHADE OF THAT TREE TO THE SHADE OF *THAT* TREE!
UNDER-STAND? YOUR CHANCE *WILL* COME!
YES, INSTRUC-TOR!!
......
......
......
THE ENEMY FIRE WON'T STOP, INSTRUC-TOR!!
IT CAN'T BE... DO THEY HAVE INEX-HAUSTIBLE ROUNDS?!
STAGGER...
THIS IS STUPIDER THAN I FEARED!!
RRGH! IN THAT CASE, JUST TAKE A FEW BULLETS!
CHARGE!!
YES, SIR!!
Getting sloppy already.
HEY, KUROMINE.

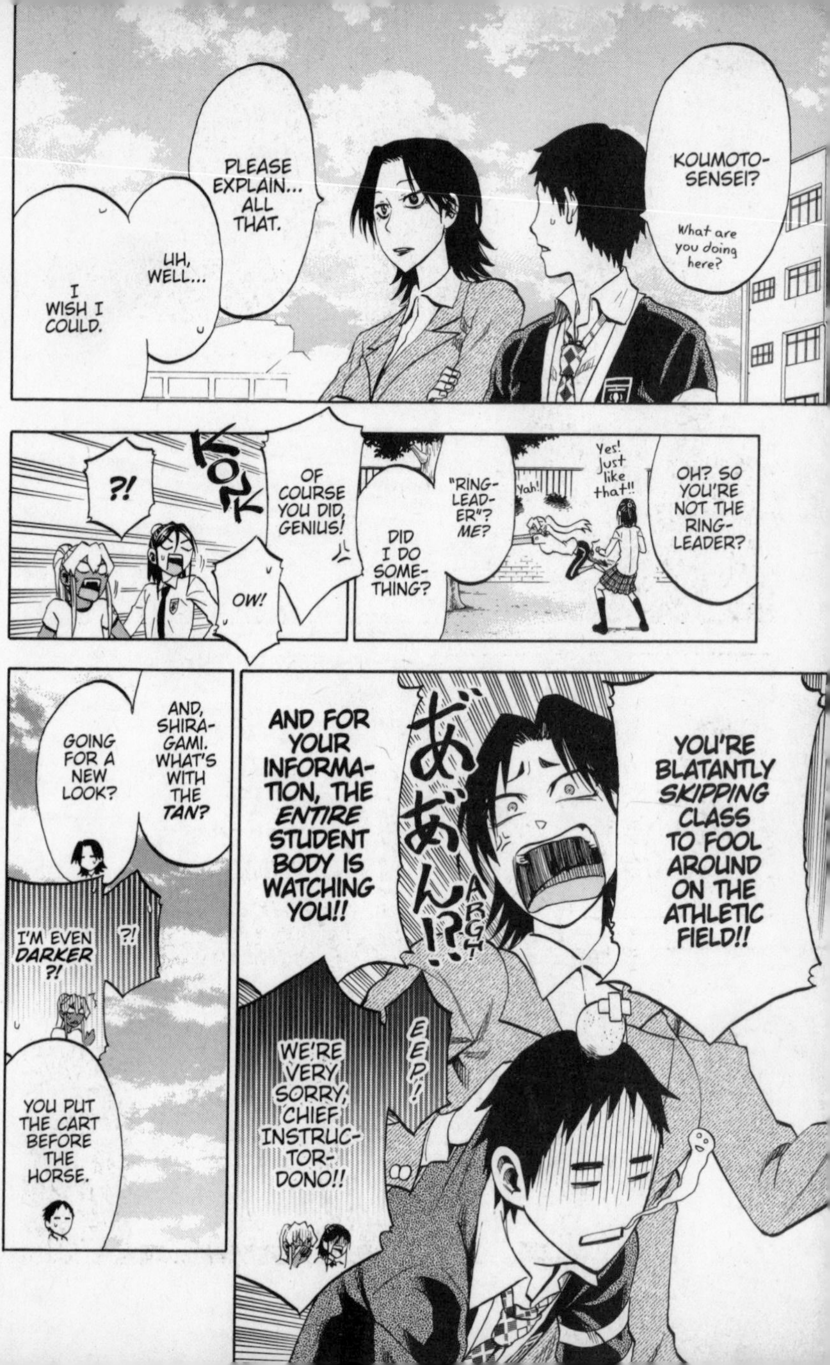
KOUMOTO-SENSEI?
What are you doing here?
PLEASE EXPLAIN... ALL THAT.
UH, WELL...
I WISH I COULD.
OH? SO YOU'RE NOT THE RING-LEADER?
Yes! Just like that!!
Yah!
"RING-LEADER"? ME?
DID I DO SOMETHING?
OF COURSE YOU DID, GENIUS!
KONK
?!
OW!
YOU'RE BLATANTLY SKIPPING CLASS TO FOOL AROUND ON THE ATHLETIC FIELD!!
あ゛あん!?
ARGH!
AND FOR YOUR INFORMATION, THE ENTIRE STUDENT BODY IS WATCHING YOU!!
EEP!
WE'RE VERY SORRY, CHIEF INSTRUCTOR-DONO!!
AND, SHIRAGAMI. WHAT'S WITH THE TAN?
GOING FOR A NEW LOOK?
?!
I'M EVEN DARKER?!
YOU PUT THE CART BEFORE THE HORSE.

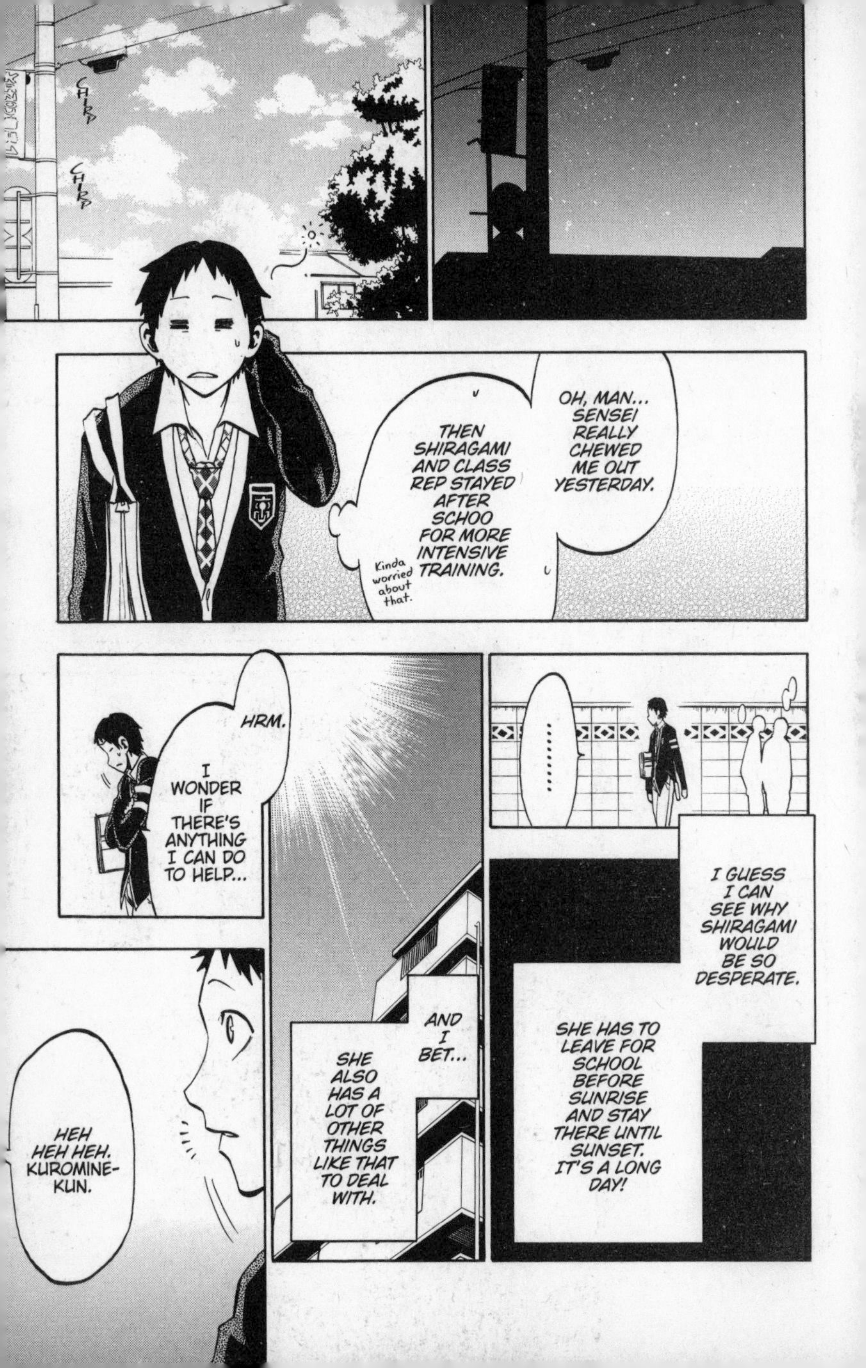
CHIRP
CHIRP
OH, MAN... SENSEI REALLY CHEWED ME OUT YESTERDAY.
THEN SHIRAGAMI AND CLASS REP STAYED AFTER SCHOO FOR MORE INTENSIVE TRAINING.
Kinda worried about that.
......
HRM.
I WONDER IF THERE'S ANYTHING I CAN DO TO HELP...
I GUESS I CAN SEE WHY SHIRAGAMI WOULD BE SO DESPERATE.
SHE HAS TO LEAVE FOR SCHOOL BEFORE SUNRISE AND STAY THERE UNTIL SUNSET. IT'S A LONG DAY!
AND I BET...
SHE ALSO HAS A LOT OF OTHER THINGS LIKE THAT TO DEAL WITH.
HEH HEH HEH. KUROMINE-KUN.

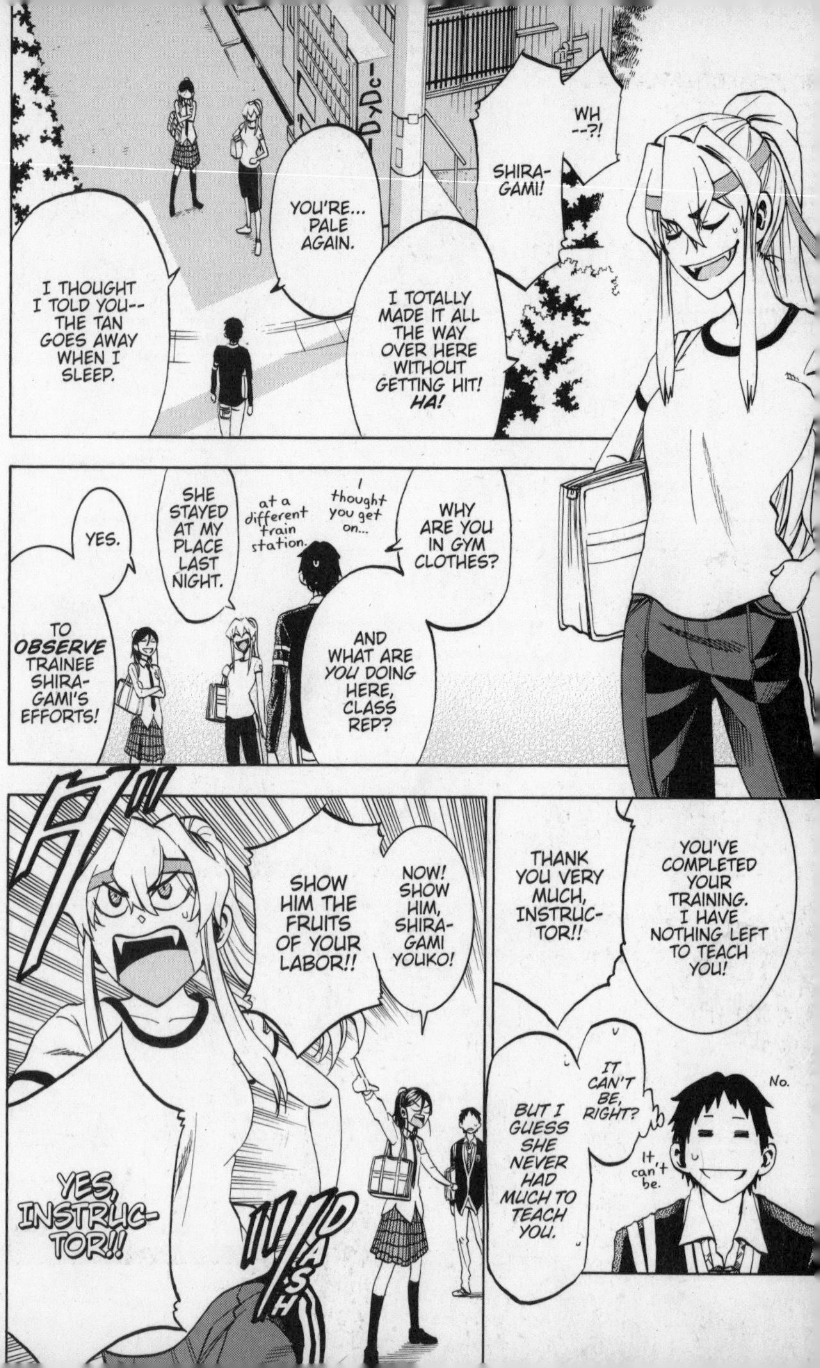
WH--?!
SHIRA-GAMI!
I TOTALLY MADE IT ALL THE WAY OVER HERE WITHOUT GETTING HIT! *HA!*
YOU'RE... PALE AGAIN.
I THOUGHT I TOLD YOU-- THE TAN GOES AWAY WHEN I SLEEP.
WHY ARE YOU IN GYM CLOTHES?
I thought you get on...
at a different train station.
SHE STAYED AT MY PLACE LAST NIGHT.
YES.
AND WHAT ARE *YOU* DOING HERE, CLASS REP?
TO ***OBSERVE*** TRAINEE SHIRA-GAMI'S EFFORTS!
YOU'VE COMPLETED YOUR TRAINING. I HAVE NOTHING LEFT TO TEACH YOU!
THANK YOU VERY MUCH, INSTRUC-TOR!!
IT CAN'T BE, RIGHT?
No.
It can't be.
BUT I GUESS SHE NEVER HAD MUCH TO TEACH YOU.
NOW! SHOW HIM, SHIRA-GAMI YOUKO!
SHOW HIM THE FRUITS OF YOUR LABOR!!
YES, INSTRUC-TOR!!
DASH

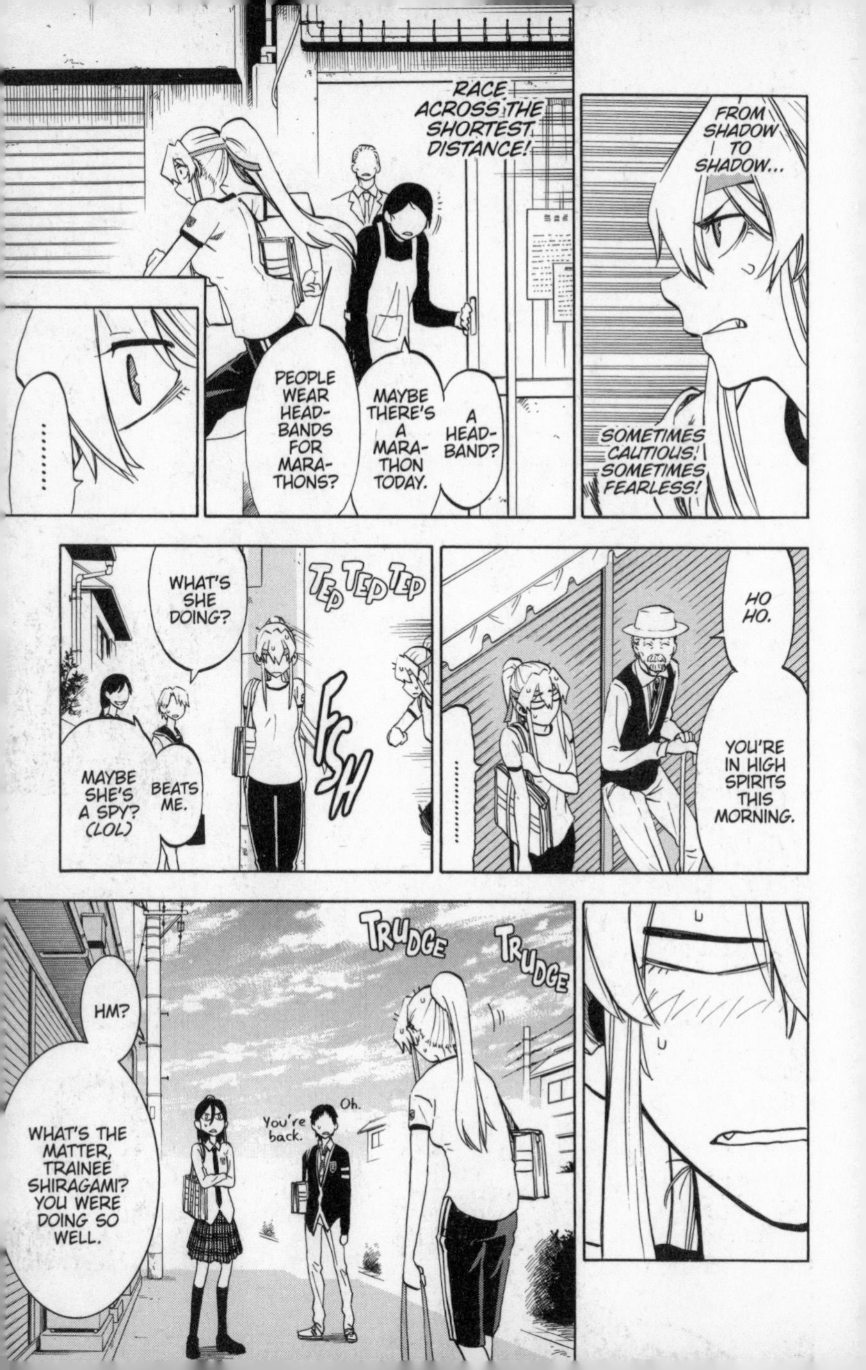
FROM SHADOW TO SHADOW...
SOMETIMES CAUTIOUS! SOMETIMES FEARLESS!
RACE ACROSS THE SHORTEST DISTANCE!
A HEAD-BAND?
MAYBE THERE'S A MARA-THON TODAY.
PEOPLE WEAR HEAD-BANDS FOR MARA-THONS?
......
HO HO.
YOU'RE IN HIGH SPIRITS THIS MORNING.
......
TEP TEP TEP
FSH
WHAT'S SHE DOING?
BEATS ME.
MAYBE SHE'S A SPY? (LOL)
TRUDGE TRUDGE
Oh.
You're back.
HM?
WHAT'S THE MATTER, TRAINEE SHIRAGAMI? YOU WERE DOING SO WELL.

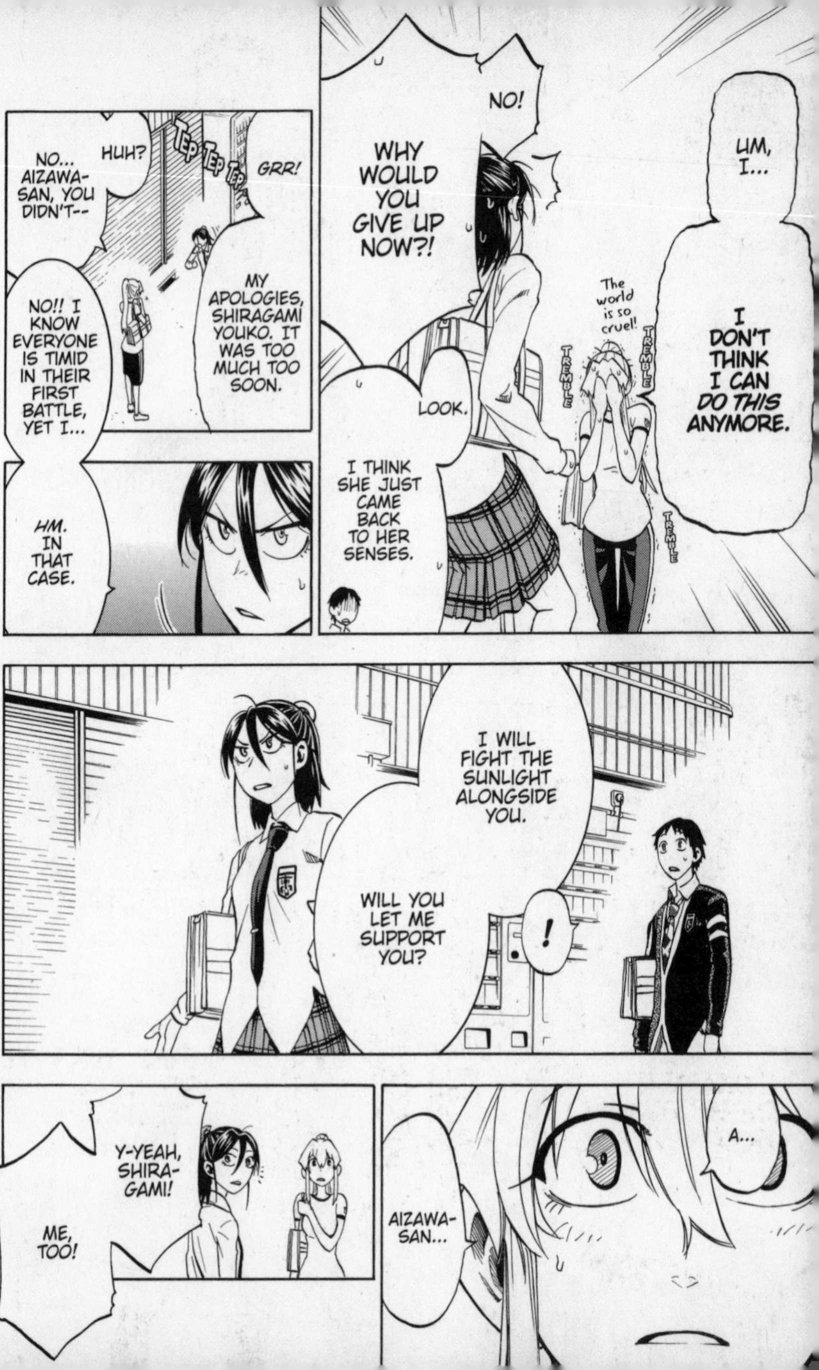
UM, I...
I DON'T THINK I CAN DO THIS ANYMORE.
The world is so cruel!
TREMBLE
TREMBLE
TREMBLE
NO!
WHY WOULD YOU GIVE UP NOW?!
LOOK.
I THINK SHE JUST CAME BACK TO HER SENSES.
GRR!
TEP TEP TEP
HUH?
NO... AIZAWA-SAN, YOU DIDN'T--
MY APOLOGIES, SHIRAGAMI YOUKO. IT WAS TOO MUCH TOO SOON.
NO!! I KNOW EVERYONE IS TIMID IN THEIR FIRST BATTLE, YET I...
HM. IN THAT CASE.
I WILL FIGHT THE SUNLIGHT ALONGSIDE YOU.
WILL YOU LET ME SUPPORT YOU?
!
A...
AIZAWA-SAN...
Y-YEAH, SHIRAGAMI!
ME, TOO!

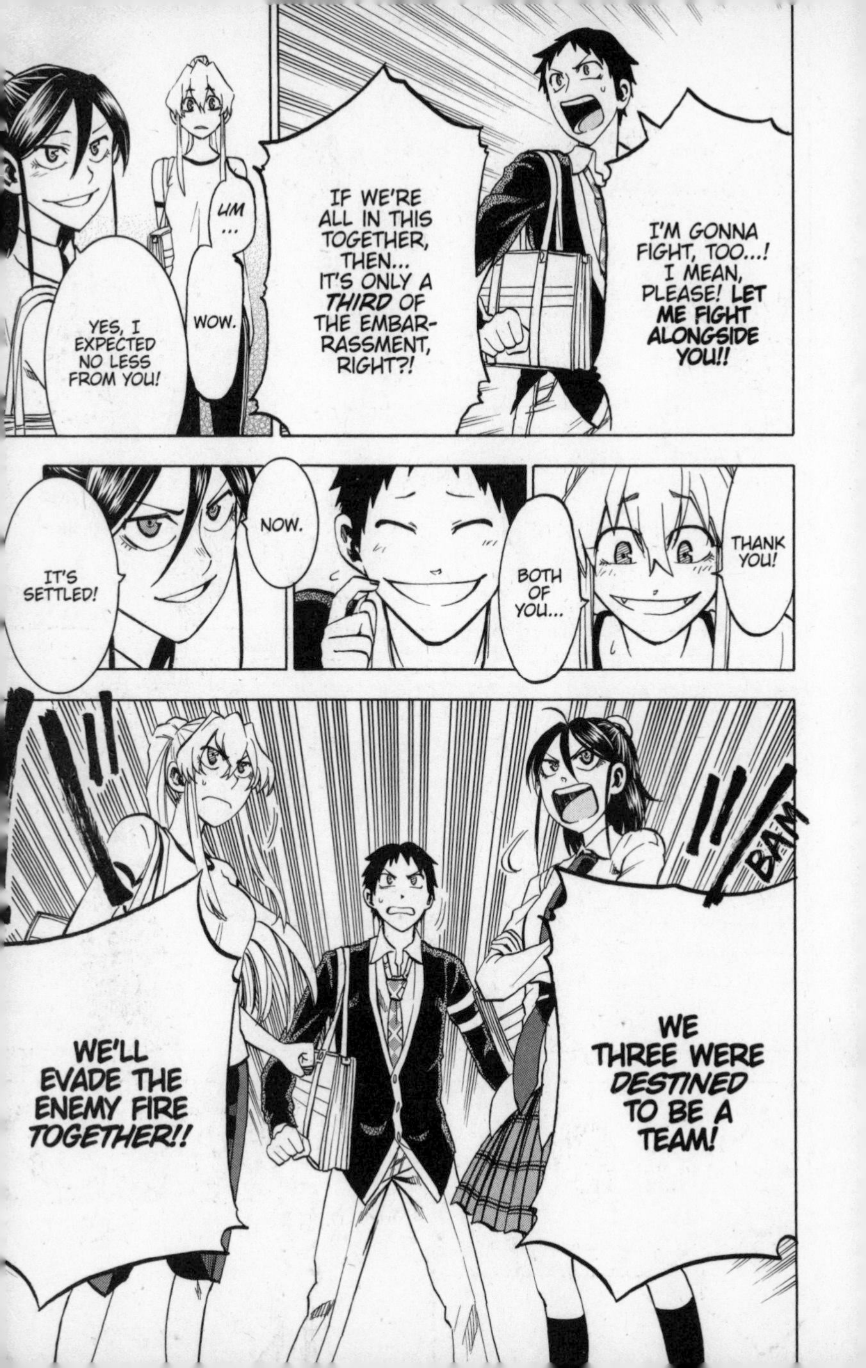
I'M GONNA FIGHT, TOO...! I MEAN, PLEASE! LET ME FIGHT ALONGSIDE YOU!!
IF WE'RE ALL IN THIS TOGETHER, THEN... IT'S ONLY A THIRD OF THE EMBARRASSMENT, RIGHT?!
UM ...
WOW.
YES, I EXPECTED NO LESS FROM YOU!
THANK YOU!
BOTH OF YOU...
NOW.
IT'S SETTLED!
BAM
WE THREE WERE DESTINED TO BE A TEAM!
WE'LL EVADE THE ENEMY FIRE TOGETHER!!

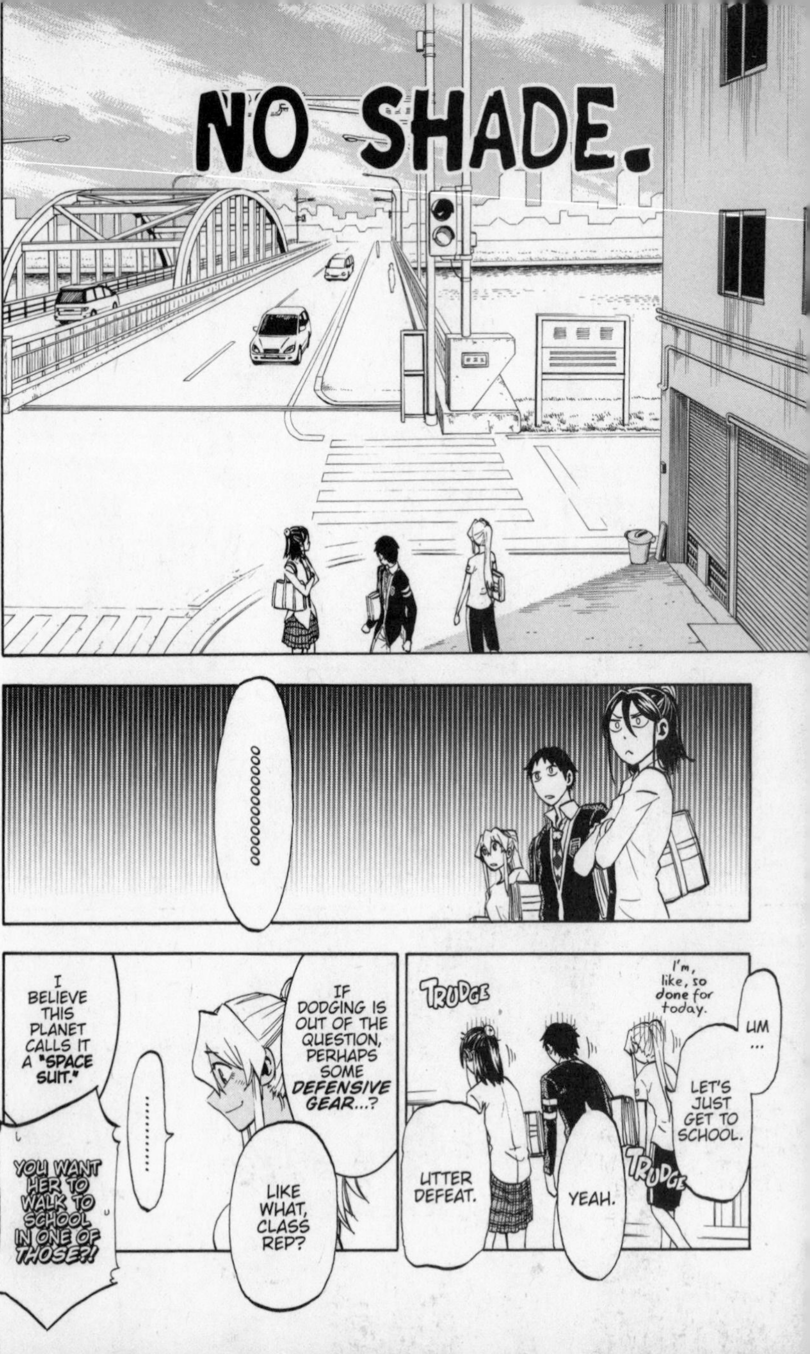
NO SHADE.
OOOOOOOOOOOOO
I'm, like, so done for today.
UM ...
LET'S JUST GET TO SCHOOL.
TRUDGE
YEAH.
TRUDGE
UTTER DEFEAT.
IF DODGING IS OUT OF THE QUESTION, PERHAPS SOME DEFENSIVE GEAR...?
LIKE WHAT, CLASS REP?
......
I BELIEVE THIS PLANET CALLS IT A "SPACE SUIT."
YOU WANT HER TO WALK TO SCHOOL IN ONE OF THOSE?!

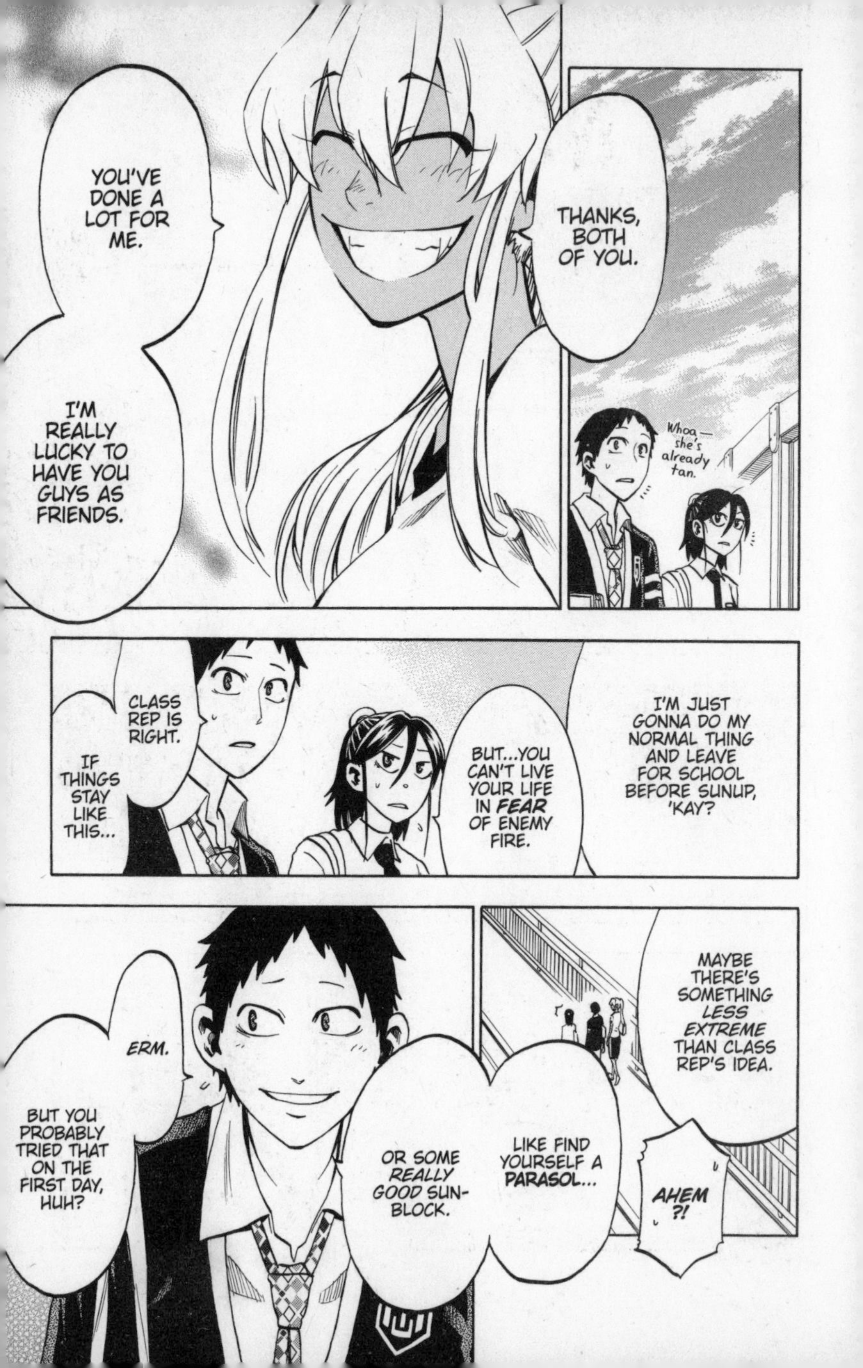
THANKS, BOTH OF YOU.
Whoa— she's already tan.
YOU'VE DONE A LOT FOR ME.
I'M REALLY LUCKY TO HAVE YOU GUYS AS FRIENDS.
I'M JUST GONNA DO MY NORMAL THING AND LEAVE FOR SCHOOL BEFORE SUNUP, 'KAY?
BUT...YOU CAN'T LIVE YOUR LIFE IN *FEAR* OF ENEMY FIRE.
CLASS REP IS RIGHT.
IF THINGS STAY LIKE THIS...
MAYBE THERE'S SOMETHING *LESS EXTREME* THAN CLASS REP'S IDEA.
AHEM ?!
LIKE FIND YOURSELF A **PARASOL**...
OR SOME *REALLY GOOD* SUN-BLOCK.
ERM.
BUT YOU PROBABLY TRIED THAT ON THE FIRST DAY, HUH?

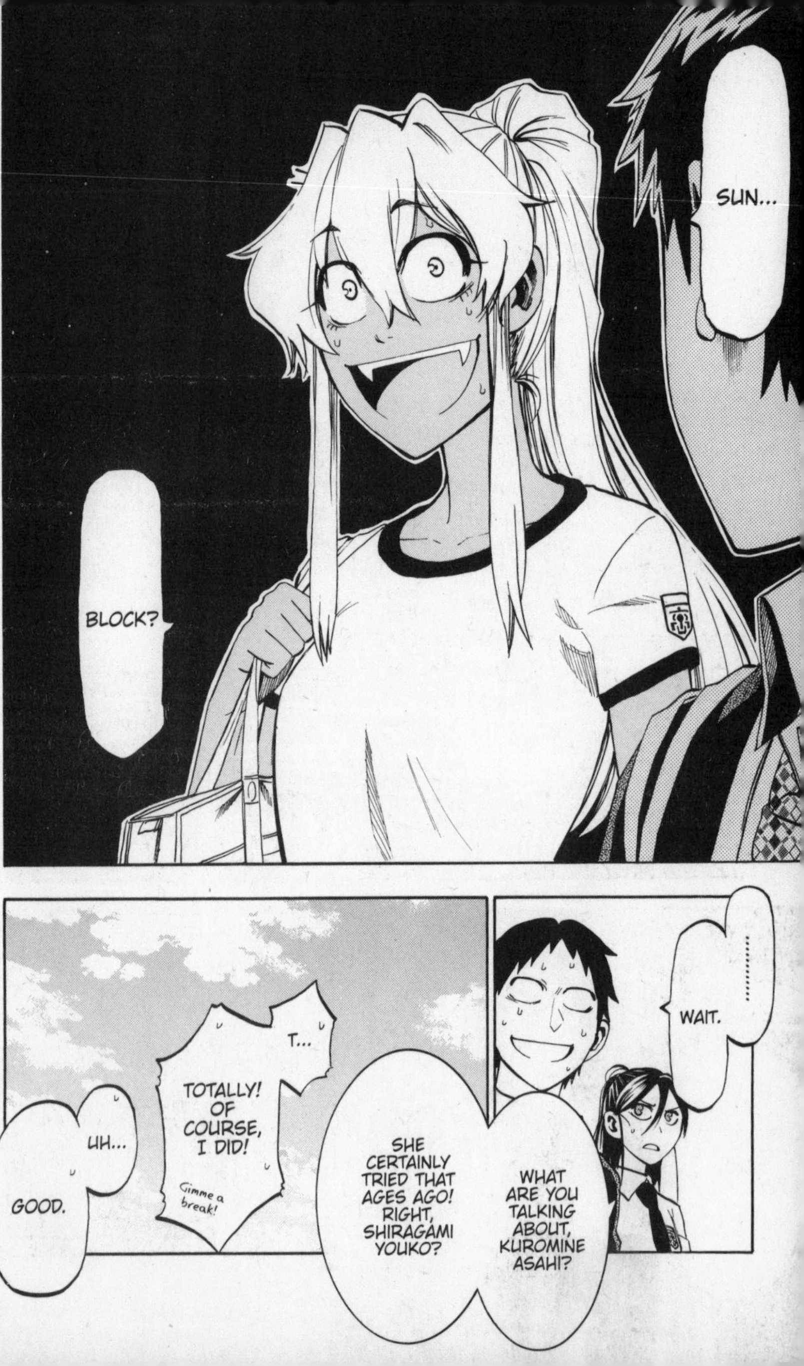
SUN...
BLOCK?
......
WAIT.
WHAT ARE YOU TALKING ABOUT, KUROMINE ASAHI?
SHE CERTAINLY TRIED THAT AGES AGO! RIGHT, SHIRAGAMI YOUKO?
T...
TOTALLY! OF COURSE, I DID!
Gimme a break!
UH...
GOOD.

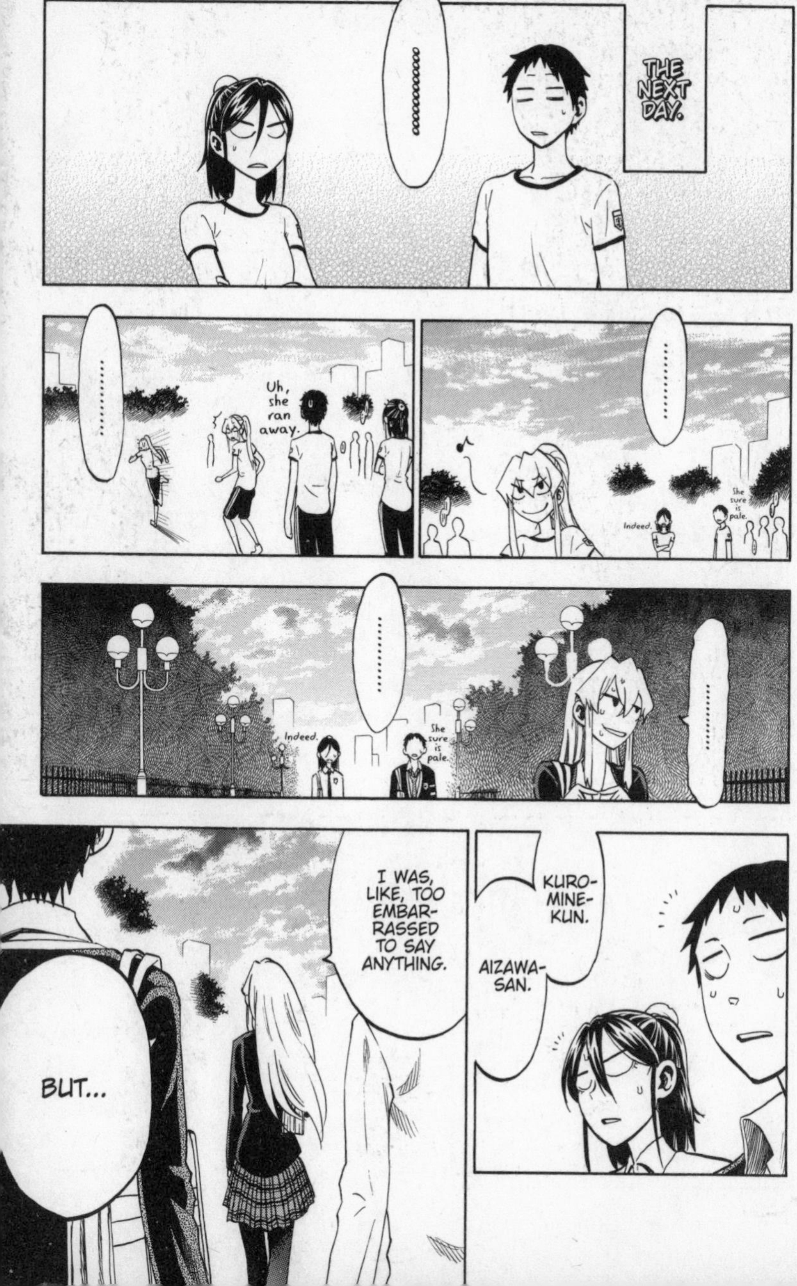
THE NEXT DAY.
....
....
She sure is pale.
Indeed.
Uh, she ran away.
....
....
....
She sure is pale.
Indeed.
KURO-MINE-KUN.
AIZAWA-SAN.
I WAS, LIKE, TOO EMBAR-RASSED TO SAY ANYTHING.
BUT...

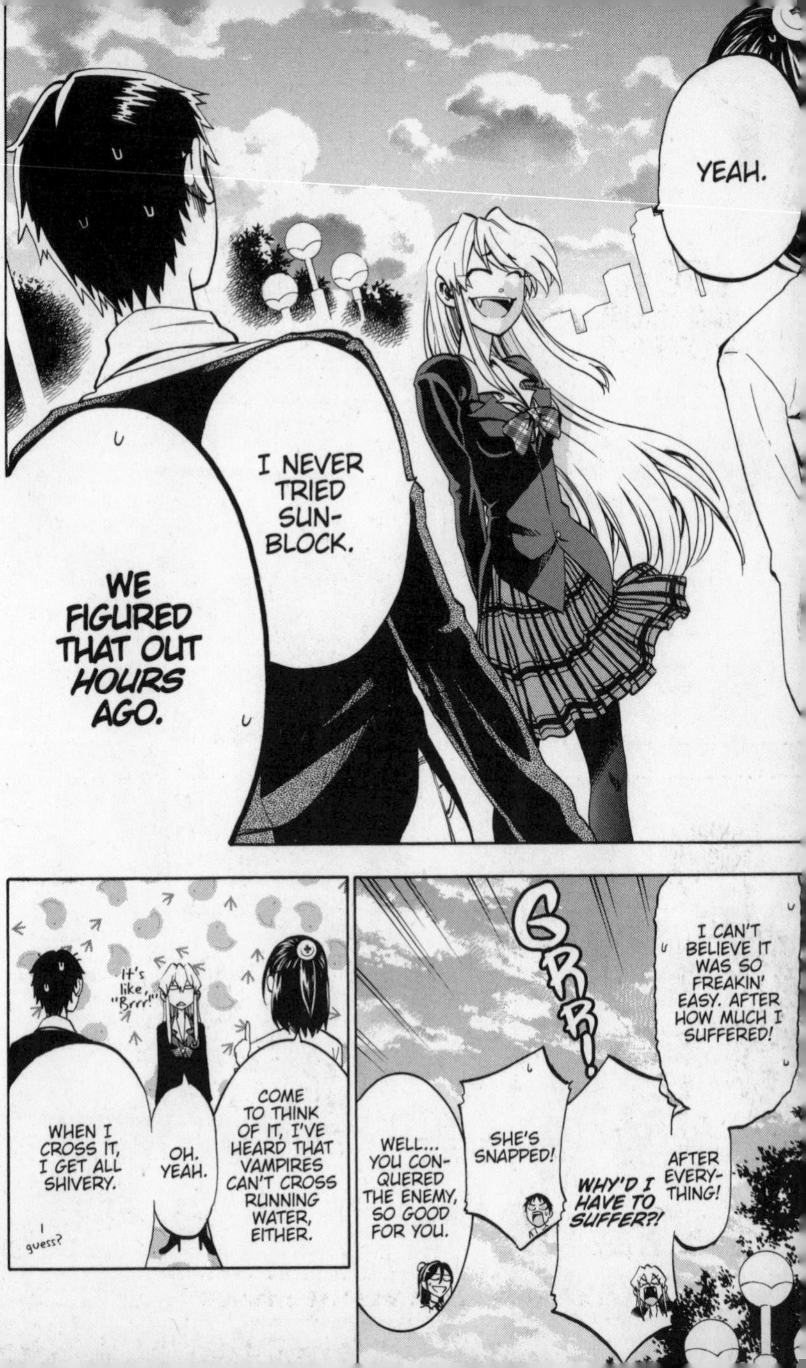
YEAH.
I NEVER TRIED SUN-BLOCK.
WE FIGURED THAT OUT *HOURS* AGO.
I CAN'T BELIEVE IT WAS SO FREAKIN' EASY. AFTER HOW MUCH I SUFFERED!
AFTER EVERYTHING!
WHY'D I HAVE TO SUFFER?!
GRR!
SHE'S SNAPPED!
WELL... YOU CONQUERED THE ENEMY, SO GOOD FOR YOU.
COME TO THINK OF IT, I'VE HEARD THAT VAMPIRES CAN'T CROSS RUNNING WATER, EITHER.
It's like, "Brrr!"
OH. YEAH.
WHEN I CROSS IT, I GET ALL SHIVERY.
I guess?

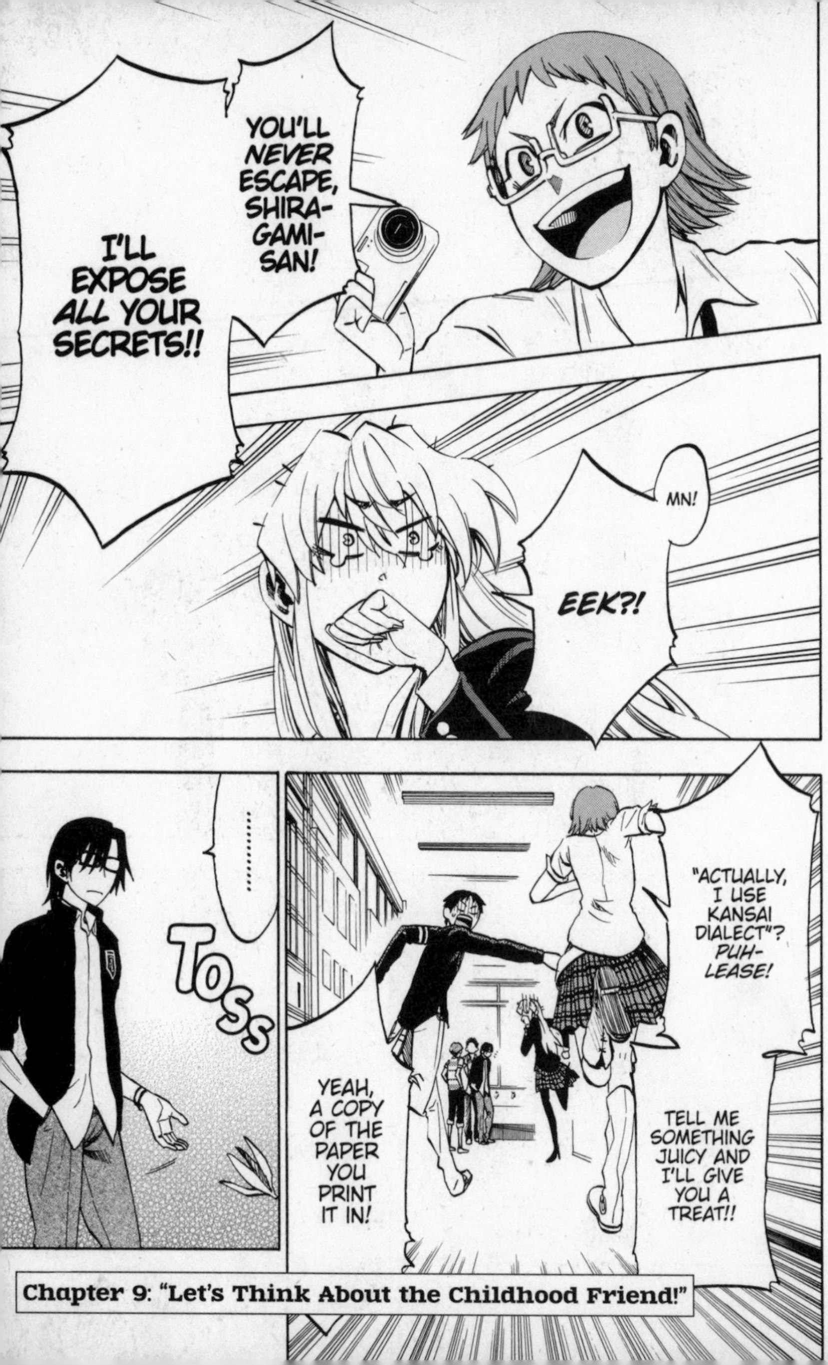
YOU'LL NEVER ESCAPE, SHIRA-GAMI-SAN!
I'LL EXPOSE ALL YOUR SECRETS!!
MN!
EEK?!
"ACTUALLY, I USE KANSAI DIALECT"? PUH-LEASE!
TELL ME SOMETHING JUICY AND I'LL GIVE YOU A TREAT!!
YEAH, A COPY OF THE PAPER YOU PRINT IT IN!
......
TOSS

Chapter 9: "Let's Think About the Childhood Friend!"

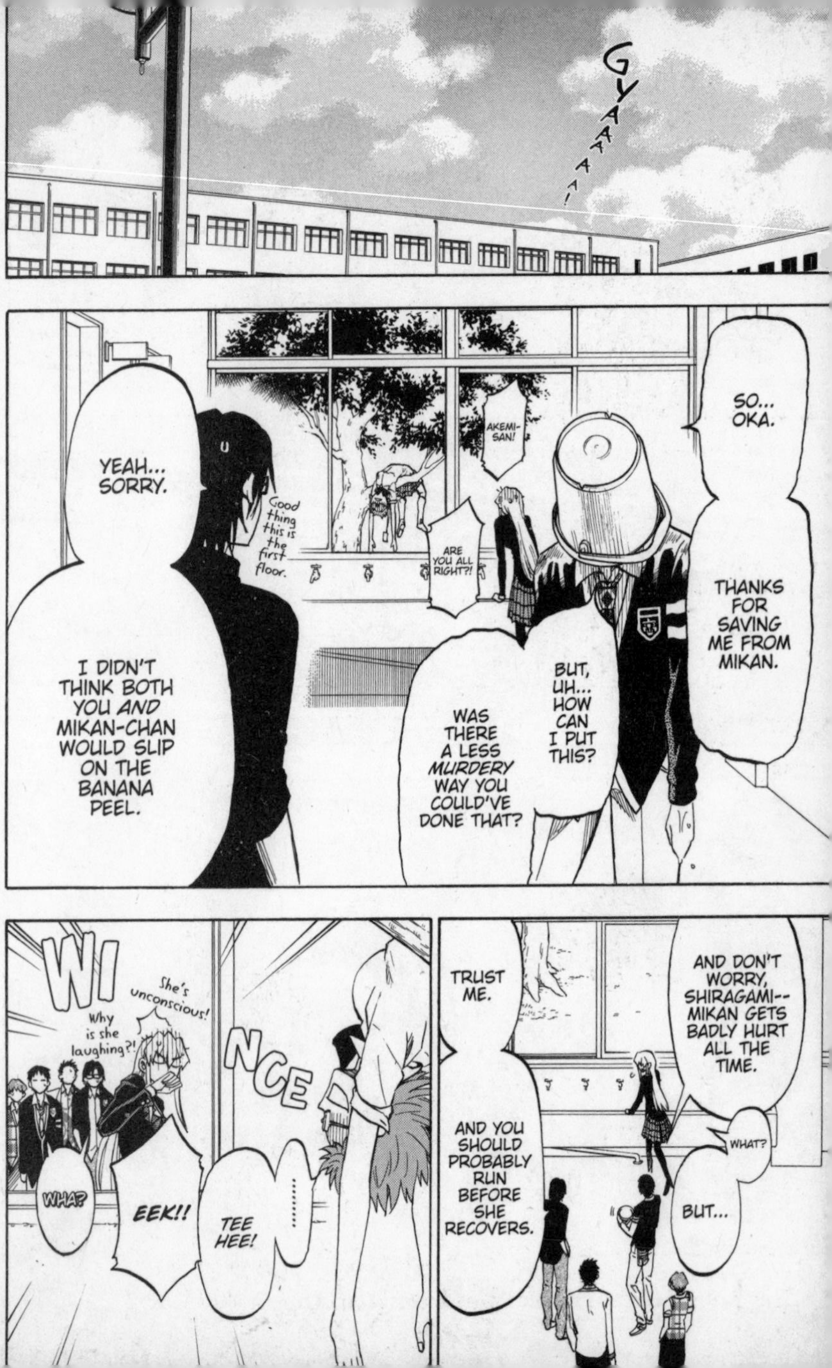
GYAAAAA!
SO... OKA.
THANKS FOR SAVING ME FROM MIKAN.
AKEMI-SAN!
ARE YOU ALL RIGHT?!
BUT, UH... HOW CAN I PUT THIS?
WAS THERE A LESS *MURDERY* WAY YOU COULD'VE DONE THAT?
YEAH... SORRY.
Good thing this is the first floor.
I DIDN'T THINK BOTH YOU *AND* MIKAN-CHAN WOULD SLIP ON THE BANANA PEEL.
AND DON'T WORRY, SHIRAGAMI--MIKAN GETS BADLY HURT ALL THE TIME.
WHAT?
BUT...
TRUST ME.
AND YOU SHOULD PROBABLY RUN BEFORE SHE RECOVERS.
WINCE
....
TEE HEE!
EEK!!
She's unconscious!
Why is she laughing?!
WHA?

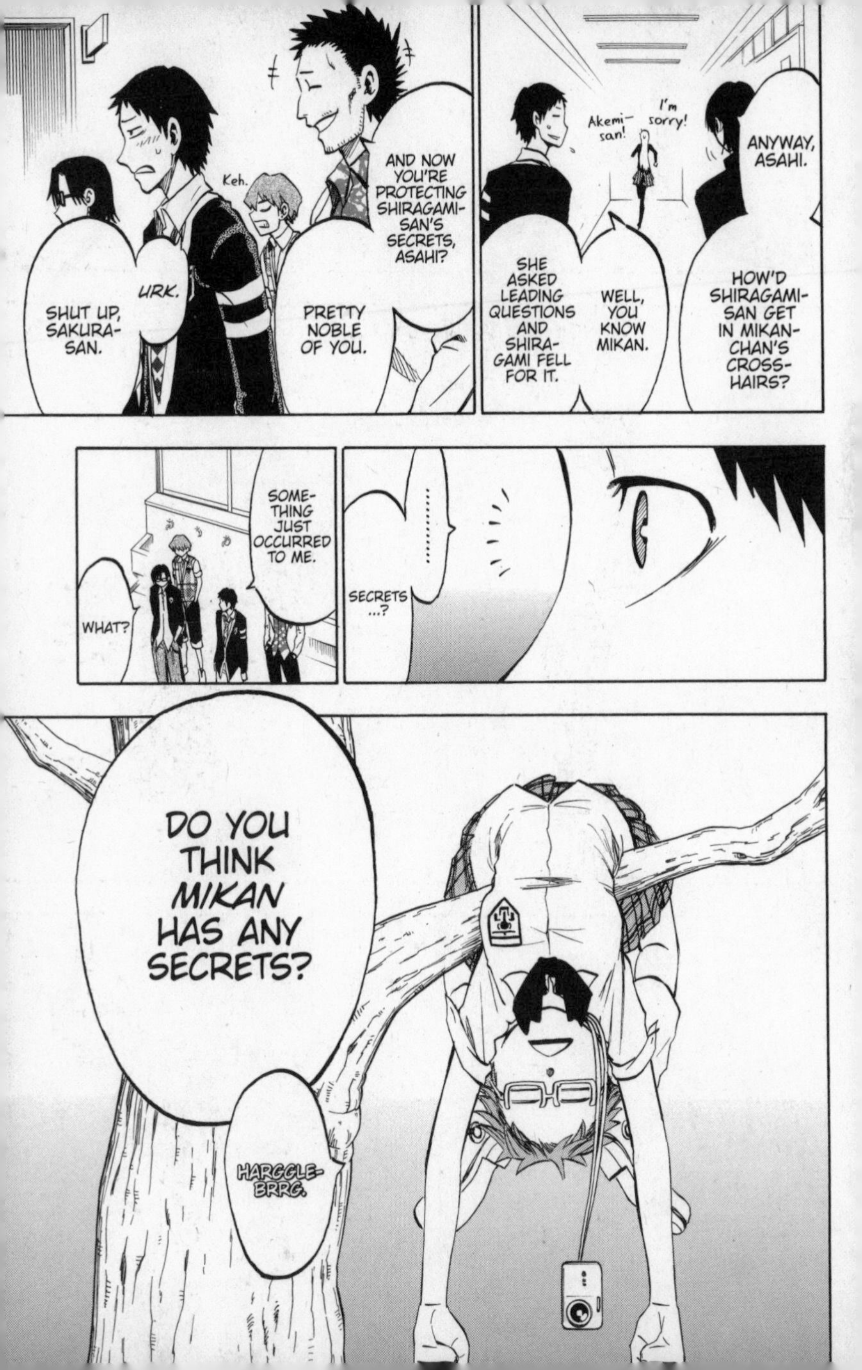
ANYWAY, ASAHI.
HOW'D SHIRAGAMI-SAN GET IN MIKAN-CHAN'S CROSS-HAIRS?
I'm sorry!
Akemi-san!
WELL, YOU KNOW MIKAN.
SHE ASKED LEADING QUESTIONS AND SHIRAGAMI FELL FOR IT.
AND NOW YOU'RE PROTECTING SHIRAGAMI-SAN'S SECRETS, ASAHI?
PRETTY NOBLE OF YOU.
Keh.
URK.
SHUT UP, SAKURA-SAN.
......
SECRETS ...?
SOMETHING JUST OCCURRED TO ME.
WHAT?
DO YOU THINK *MIKAN* HAS ANY SECRETS?
HARGGLE-BRRG.

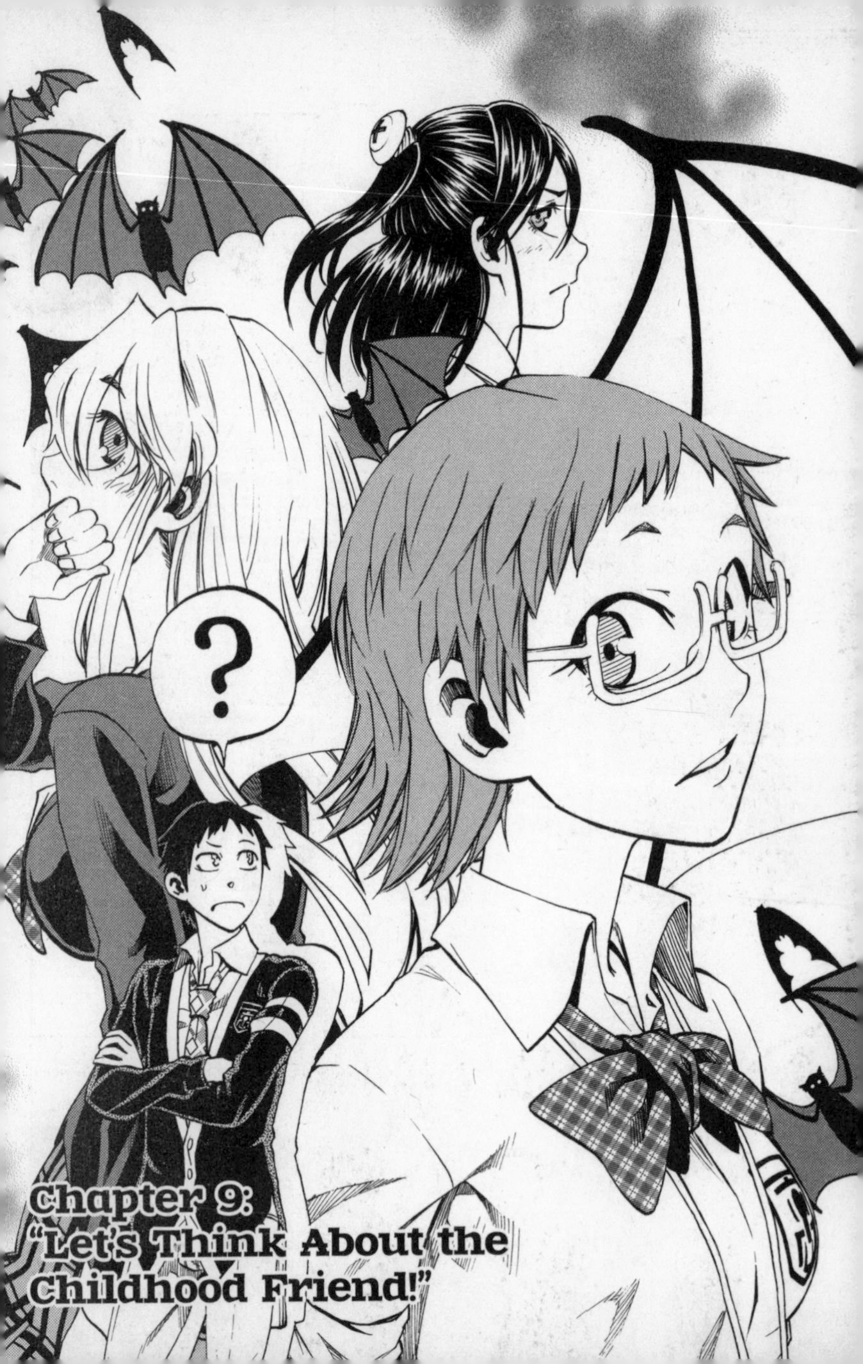
?
Chapter 9:
"Let's Think About the Childhood Friend!"

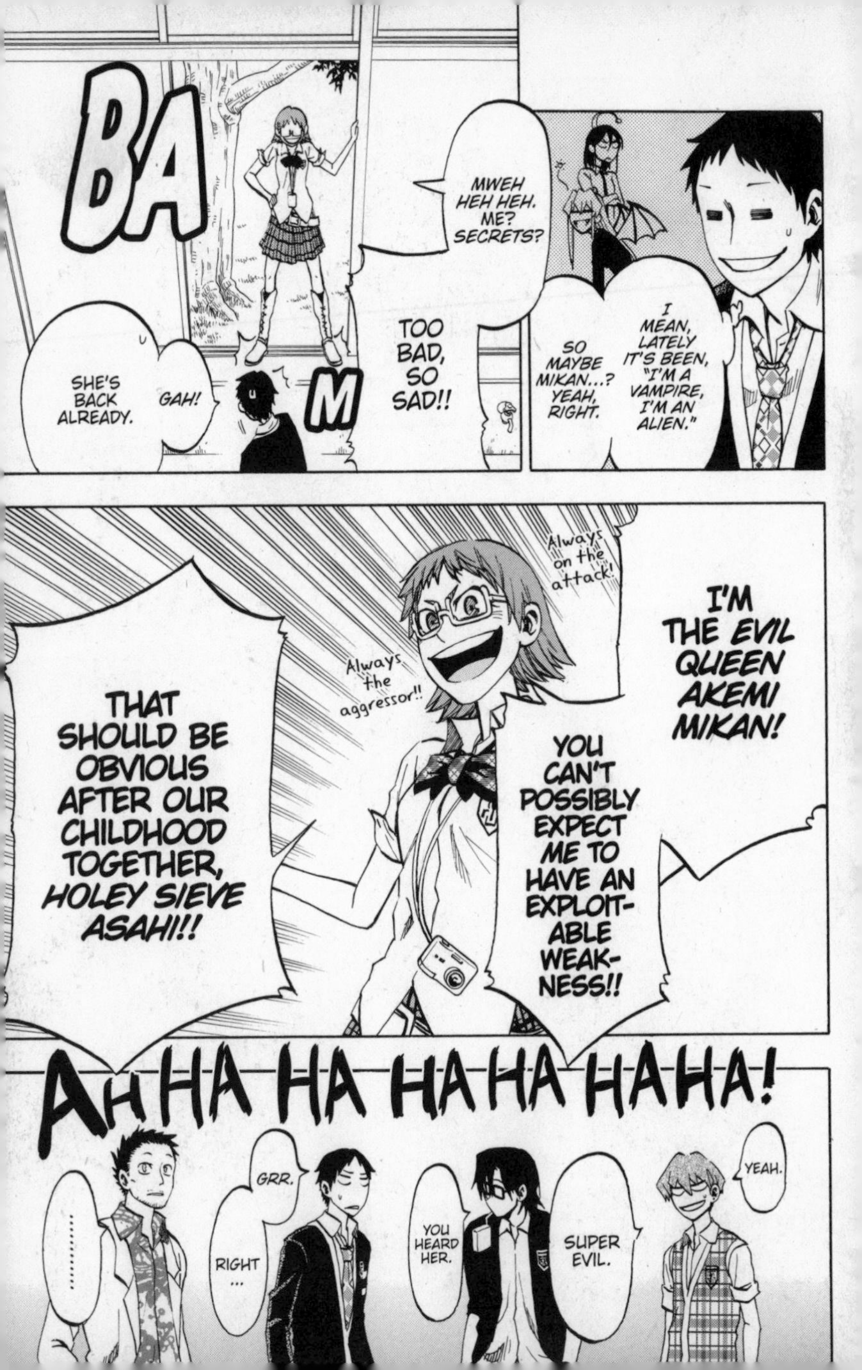
I MEAN, LATELY IT'S BEEN, "I'M A VAMPIRE, I'M AN ALIEN."
SO MAYBE MIKAN...? YEAH, RIGHT.
MWEH HEH HEH. ME? SECRETS?
TOO BAD, SO SAD!!
BAM
GAH!
SHE'S BACK ALREADY.
I'M THE EVIL QUEEN AKEMI MIKAN!
Always on the attack!
YOU CAN'T POSSIBLY EXPECT ME TO HAVE AN EXPLOIT-ABLE WEAK-NESS!!
Always the aggressor!!
THAT SHOULD BE OBVIOUS AFTER OUR CHILDHOOD TOGETHER, HOLEY SIEVE ASAHI!!
AH HA HA HA HA HA HA!
YEAH.
SUPER EVIL.
YOU HEARD HER.
GRR.
RIGHT...
....

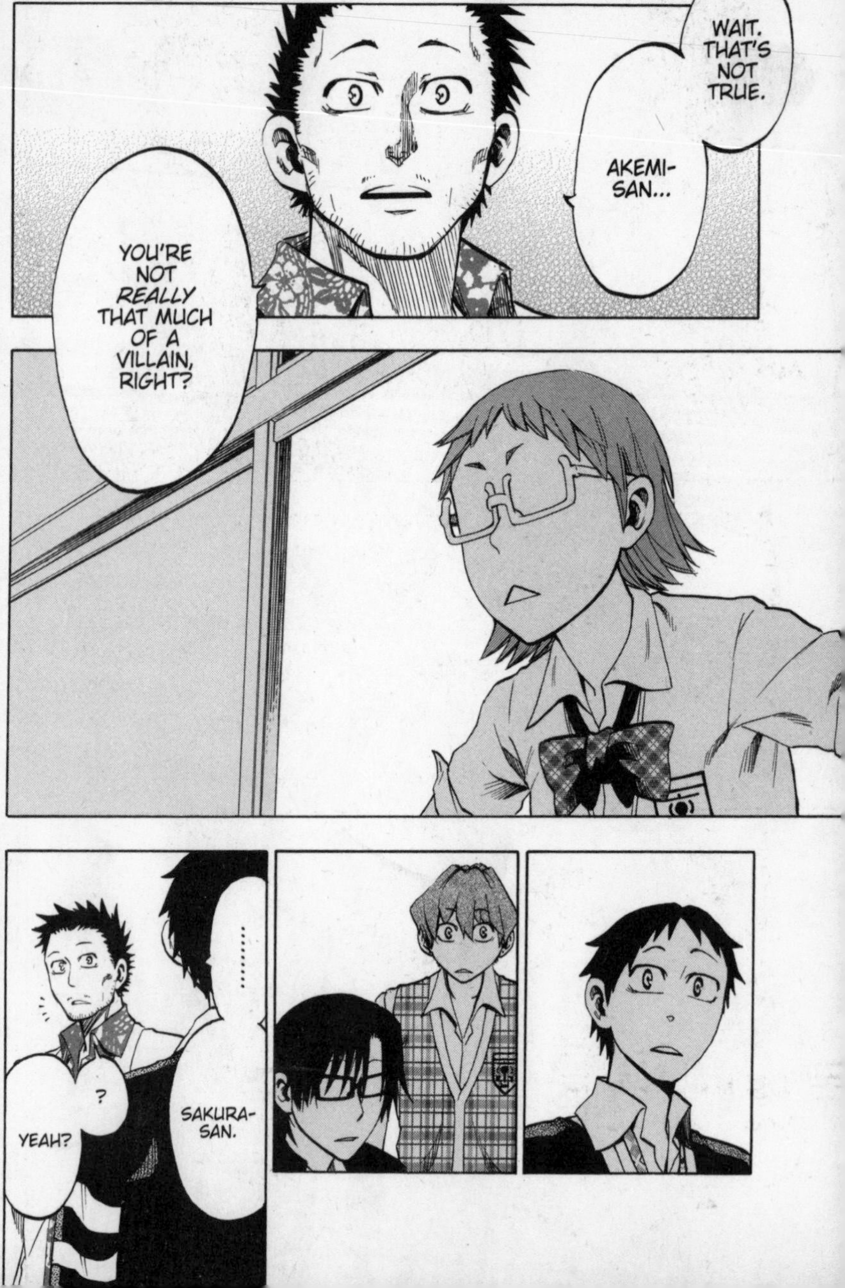
WAIT. THAT'S NOT TRUE.
AKEMI-SAN...
YOU'RE NOT *REALLY* THAT MUCH OF A VILLAIN, RIGHT?
......
SAKURA-SAN.
?
YEAH?

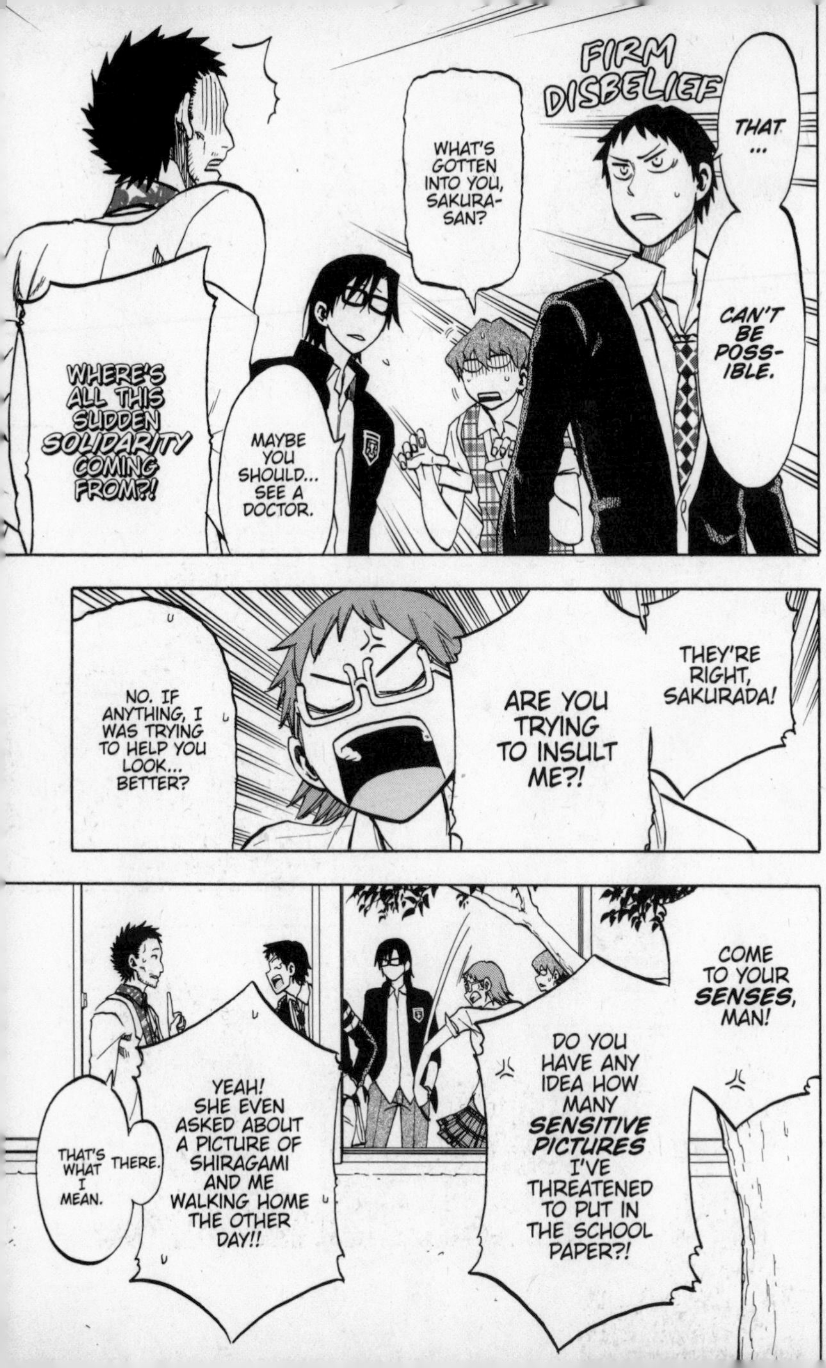
FIRM DISBELIEF
THAT... CAN'T BE POSSIBLE.
WHAT'S GOTTEN INTO YOU, SAKURA-SAN?
MAYBE YOU SHOULD... SEE A DOCTOR.
WHERE'S ALL THIS SUDDEN SOLIDARITY COMING FROM?!
THEY'RE RIGHT, SAKURADA!
ARE YOU TRYING TO INSULT ME?!
NO. IF ANYTHING, I WAS TRYING TO HELP YOU LOOK... BETTER?
COME TO YOUR SENSES, MAN!
DO YOU HAVE ANY IDEA HOW MANY SENSITIVE PICTURES I'VE THREATENED TO PUT IN THE SCHOOL PAPER?!
YEAH! SHE EVEN ASKED ABOUT A PICTURE OF SHIRAGAMI AND ME WALKING HOME THE OTHER DAY!!
THERE.
THAT'S WHAT I MEAN.

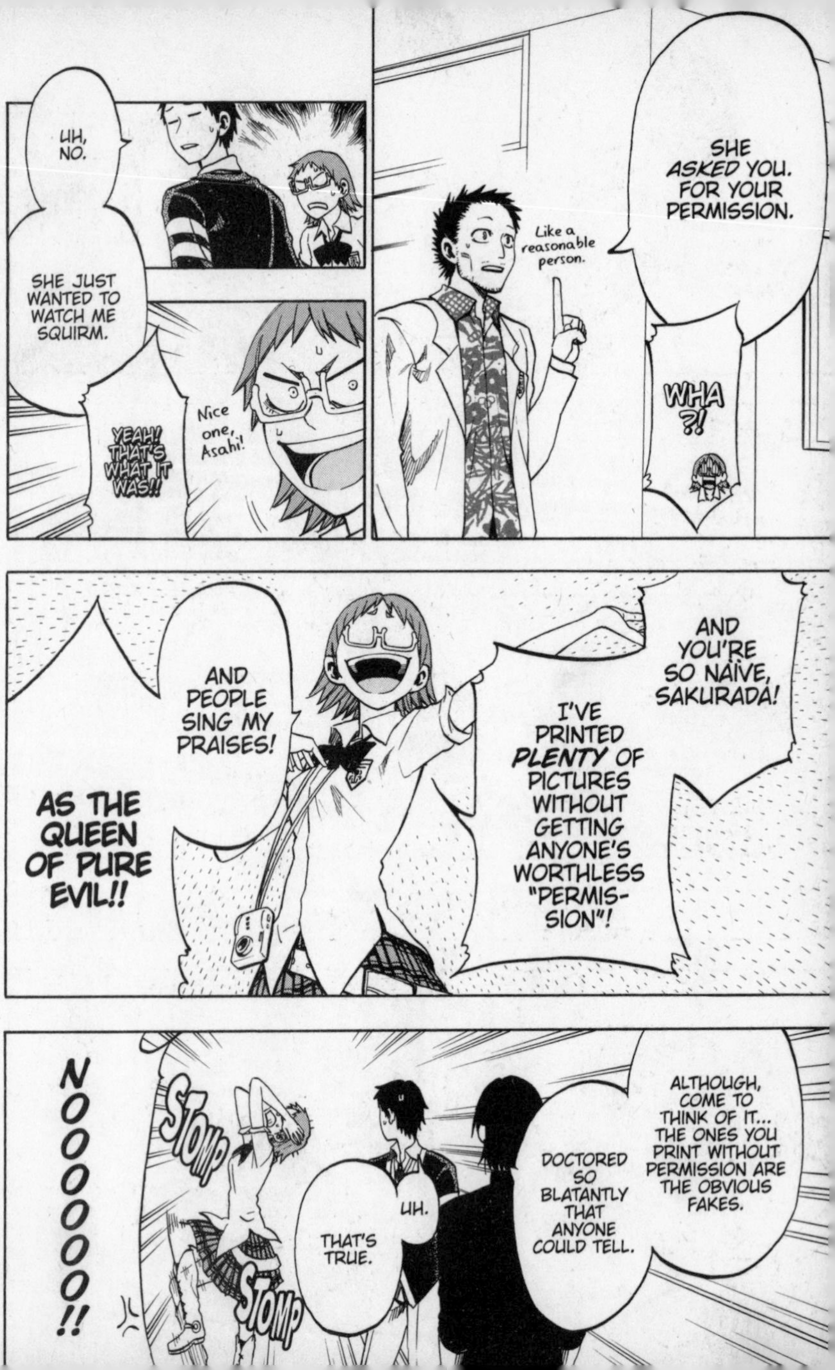
SHE ASKED YOU. FOR YOUR PERMISSION.
Like a reasonable person.
WHA?!
UH, NO.
SHE JUST WANTED TO WATCH ME SQUIRM.
YEAH! THAT'S WHAT IT WAS!!
Nice one, Asahi!
AND YOU'RE SO NAÏVE, SAKURADA!
I'VE PRINTED PLENTY OF PICTURES WITHOUT GETTING ANYONE'S WORTHLESS "PERMIS-SION"!
AND PEOPLE SING MY PRAISES!
AS THE QUEEN OF PURE EVIL!!
ALTHOUGH, COME TO THINK OF IT... THE ONES YOU PRINT WITHOUT PERMISSION ARE THE OBVIOUS FAKES.
DOCTORED SO BLATANTLY THAT ANYONE COULD TELL.
UH.
THAT'S TRUE.
STOMP
STOMP
NOOOOOOOO!!

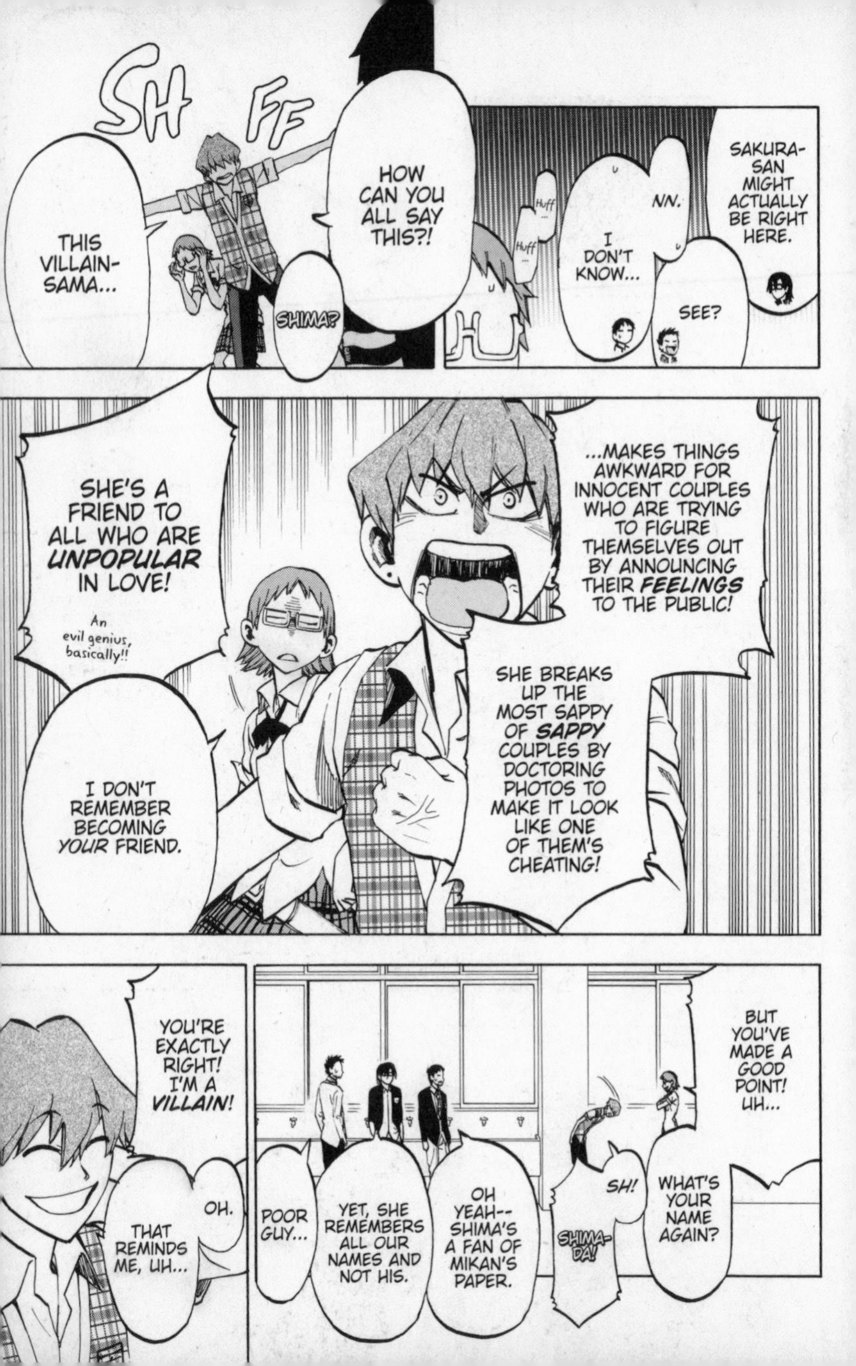
SAKURA-SAN MIGHT ACTUALLY BE RIGHT HERE.
SEE?
NN.
I DON'T KNOW...
Huff... Huff...
HU
HOW CAN YOU ALL SAY THIS?!
SHIMA?
THIS VILLAIN-SAMA...
SH FF
...MAKES THINGS AWKWARD FOR INNOCENT COUPLES WHO ARE TRYING TO FIGURE THEMSELVES OUT BY ANNOUNCING THEIR FEELINGS TO THE PUBLIC!
SHE BREAKS UP THE MOST SAPPY OF SAPPY COUPLES BY DOCTORING PHOTOS TO MAKE IT LOOK LIKE ONE OF THEM'S CHEATING!
SHE'S A FRIEND TO ALL WHO ARE UNPOPULAR IN LOVE!
An evil genius, basically!!
I DON'T REMEMBER BECOMING YOUR FRIEND.
BUT YOU'VE MADE A GOOD POINT! UH...
WHAT'S YOUR NAME AGAIN?
SH!
SHIMA-DA!
OH YEAH-- SHIMA'S A FAN OF MIKAN'S PAPER.
YET, SHE REMEMBERS ALL OUR NAMES AND NOT HIS.
POOR GUY...
YOU'RE EXACTLY RIGHT! I'M A VILLAIN!
OH.
THAT REMINDS ME, UH...

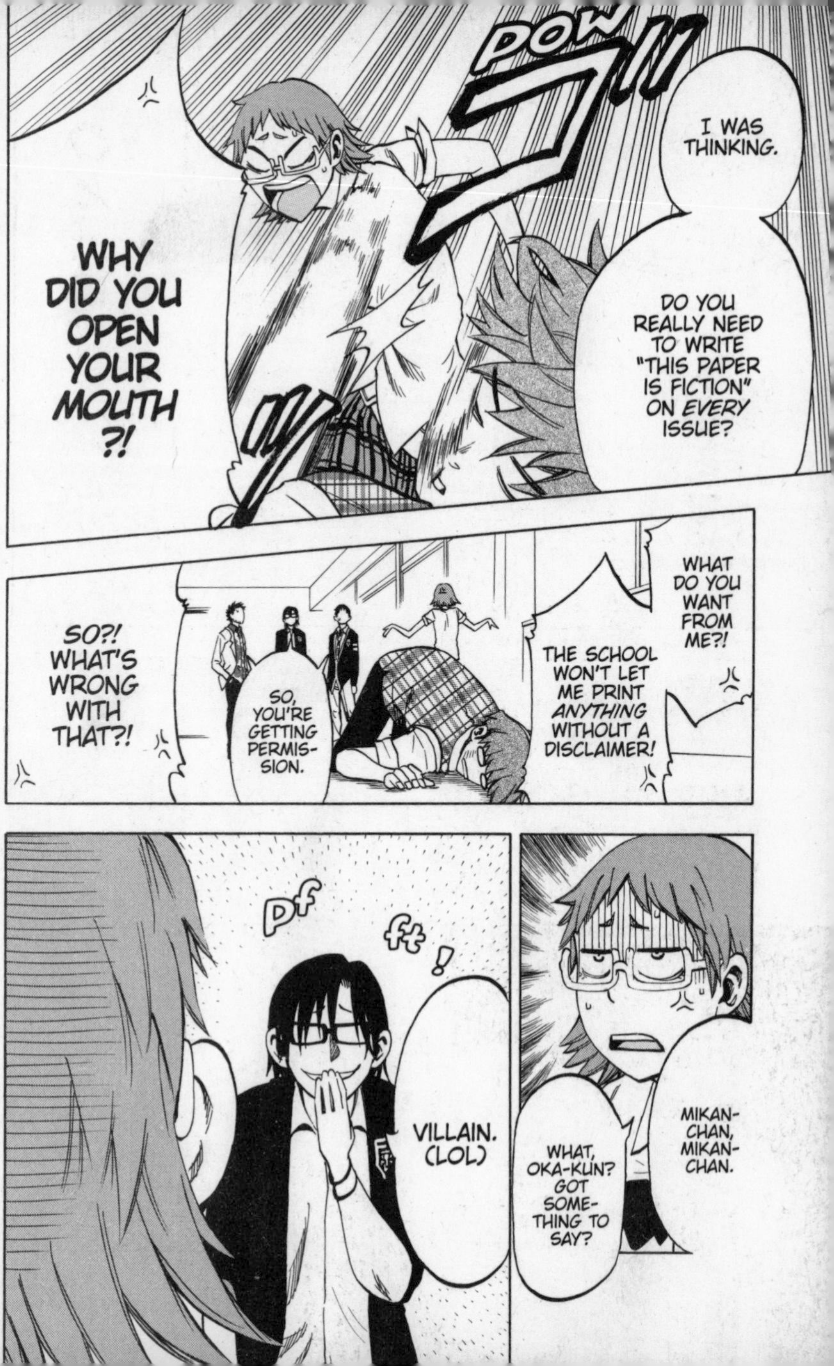
I WAS THINKING.
DO YOU REALLY NEED TO WRITE "THIS PAPER IS FICTION" ON *EVERY* ISSUE?
POW
WHY DID YOU OPEN YOUR MOUTH ?!
WHAT DO YOU WANT FROM ME?!
THE SCHOOL WON'T LET ME PRINT *ANYTHING* WITHOUT A DISCLAIMER!
SO, YOU'RE GETTING PERMISSION.
SO?! WHAT'S WRONG WITH THAT?!
MIKAN-CHAN, MIKAN-CHAN.
WHAT, OKA-KUN? GOT SOMETHING TO SAY?
pf ft!
VILLAIN. (LOL)

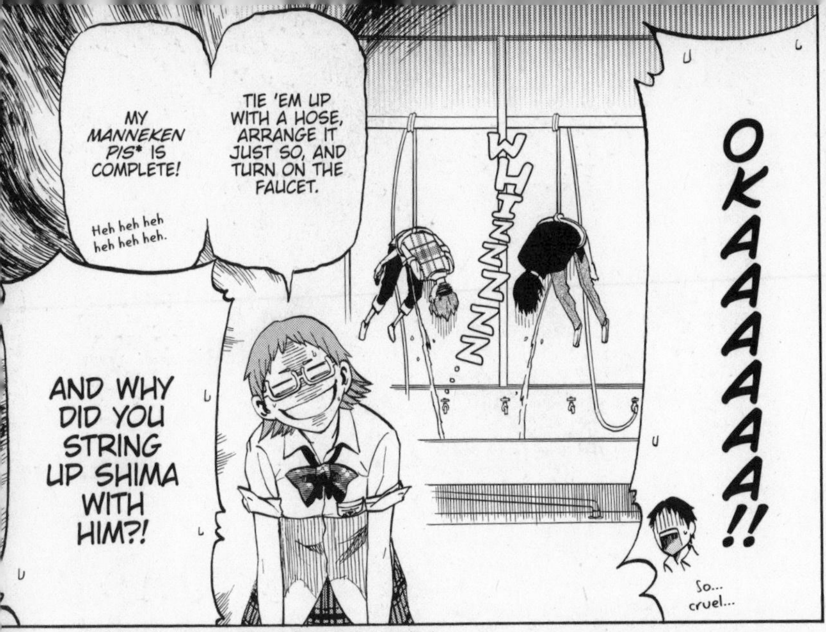
OKAAAAAAA!!
So... cruel...
WHIZZZZZ
TIE 'EM UP WITH A HOSE, ARRANGE IT JUST SO, AND TURN ON THE FAUCET.
MY MANNEKEN PIS* IS COMPLETE!
Heh heh heh heh heh heh.
AND WHY DID YOU STRING UP SHIMA WITH HIM?!

*"Little Man Pee," a famous statue in Brussels of a boy urinating.

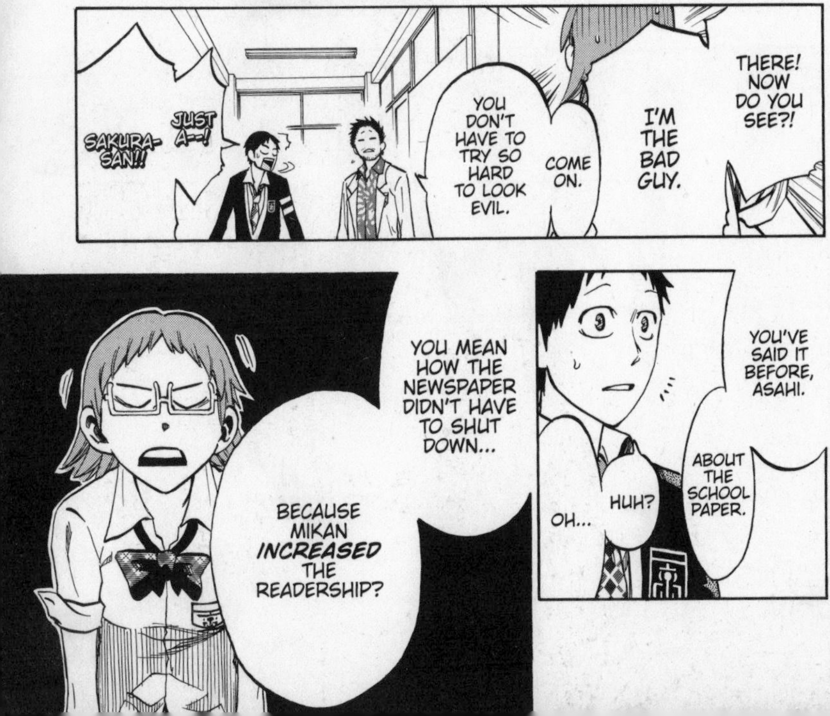
THERE! NOW DO YOU SEE?!
I'M THE BAD GUY.
COME ON.
YOU DON'T HAVE TO TRY SO HARD TO LOOK EVIL.
JUST A--!
SAKURA-SAN!!
YOU'VE SAID IT BEFORE, ASAHI.
ABOUT THE SCHOOL PAPER.
HUH?
OH...
YOU MEAN HOW THE NEWSPAPER DIDN'T HAVE TO SHUT DOWN...
BECAUSE MIKAN INCREASED THE READERSHIP?

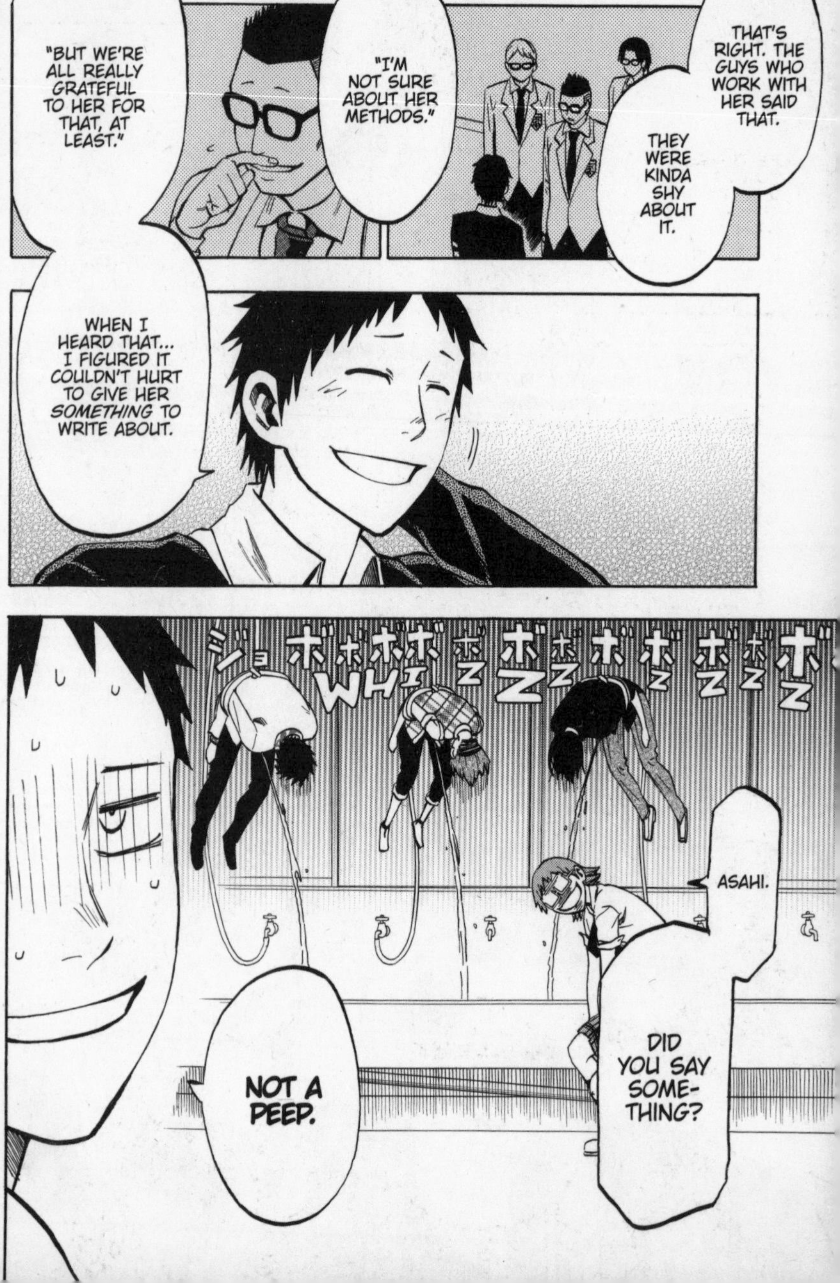
THAT'S RIGHT. THE GUYS WHO WORK WITH HER SAID THAT.
THEY WERE KINDA SHY ABOUT IT.
"I'M NOT SURE ABOUT HER METHODS."
"BUT WE'RE ALL REALLY GRATEFUL TO HER FOR THAT, AT LEAST."
WHEN I HEARD THAT... I FIGURED IT COULDN'T HURT TO GIVE HER *SOMETHING* TO WRITE ABOUT.
WHIZZZZZZ
ASAHI.
DID YOU SAY SOME-THING?
NOT A PEEP.

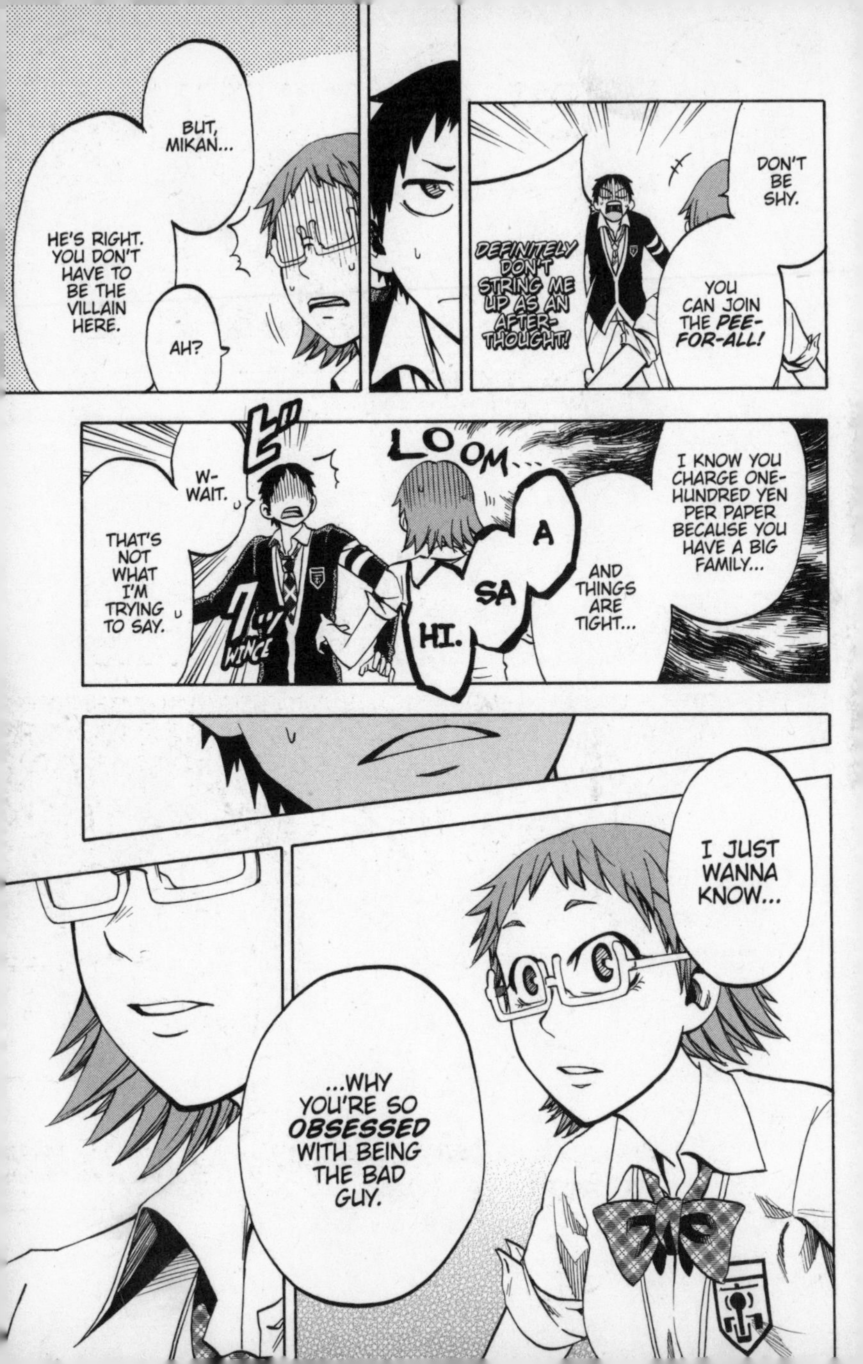
DON'T BE SHY.
YOU CAN JOIN THE *PEE-FOR-ALL!*
DEFINITELY DON'T STRING ME UP AS AN AFTER-THOUGHT!
BUT, MIKAN...
HE'S RIGHT. YOU DON'T HAVE TO BE THE VILLAIN HERE.
AH?
I KNOW YOU CHARGE ONE-HUNDRED YEN PER PAPER BECAUSE YOU HAVE A BIG FAMILY...
AND THINGS ARE TIGHT...
LOOM...
A SA HI.
W-WAIT.
THAT'S NOT WHAT I'M TRYING TO SAY.
WINCE
I JUST WANNA KNOW...
...WHY YOU'RE SO *OBSESSED* WITH BEING THE BAD GUY.

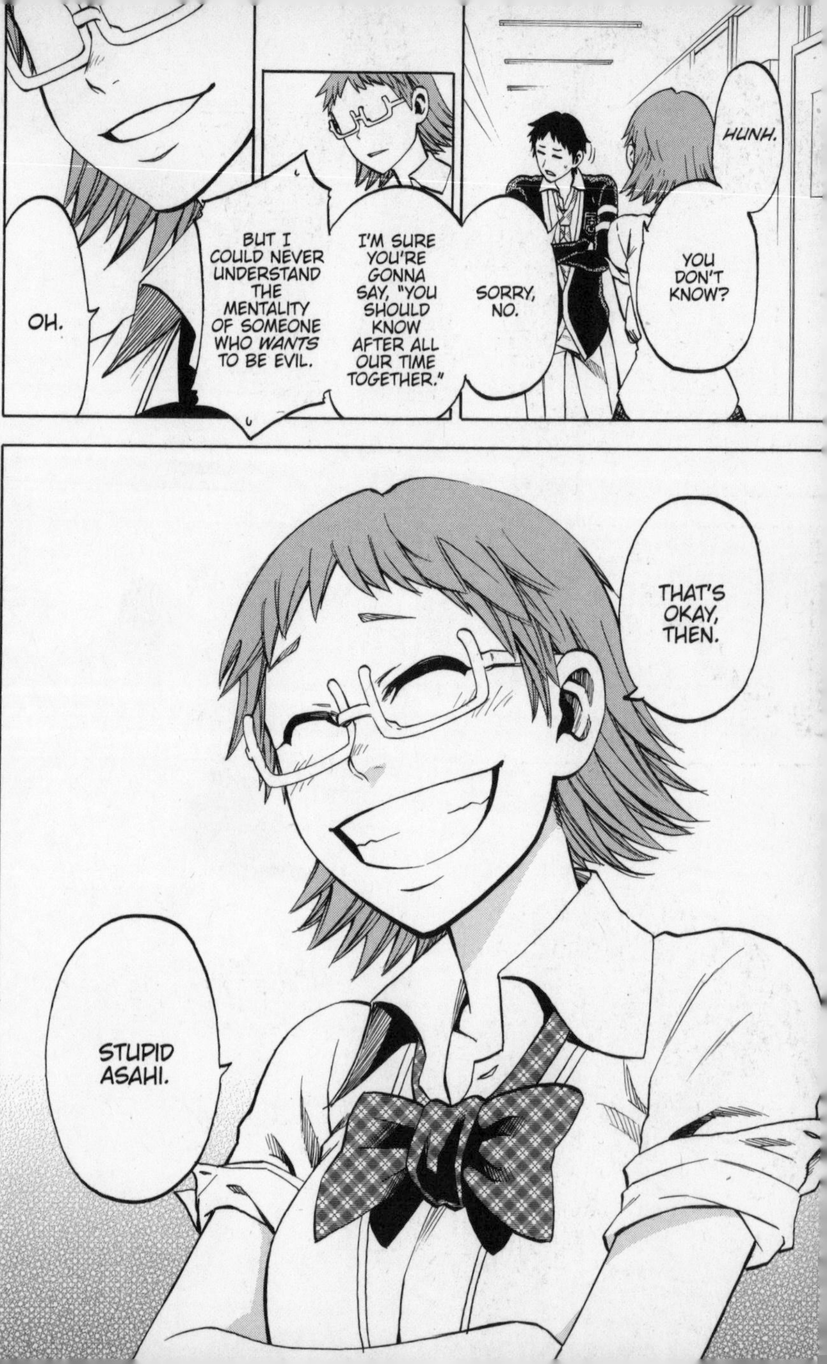
HUNH.
YOU DON'T KNOW?
SORRY, NO.
I'M SURE YOU'RE GONNA SAY, "YOU SHOULD KNOW AFTER ALL OUR TIME TOGETHER."
BUT I COULD NEVER UNDERSTAND THE MENTALITY OF SOMEONE WHO *WANTS* TO BE EVIL.
OH.
THAT'S OKAY, THEN.
STUPID ASAHI.

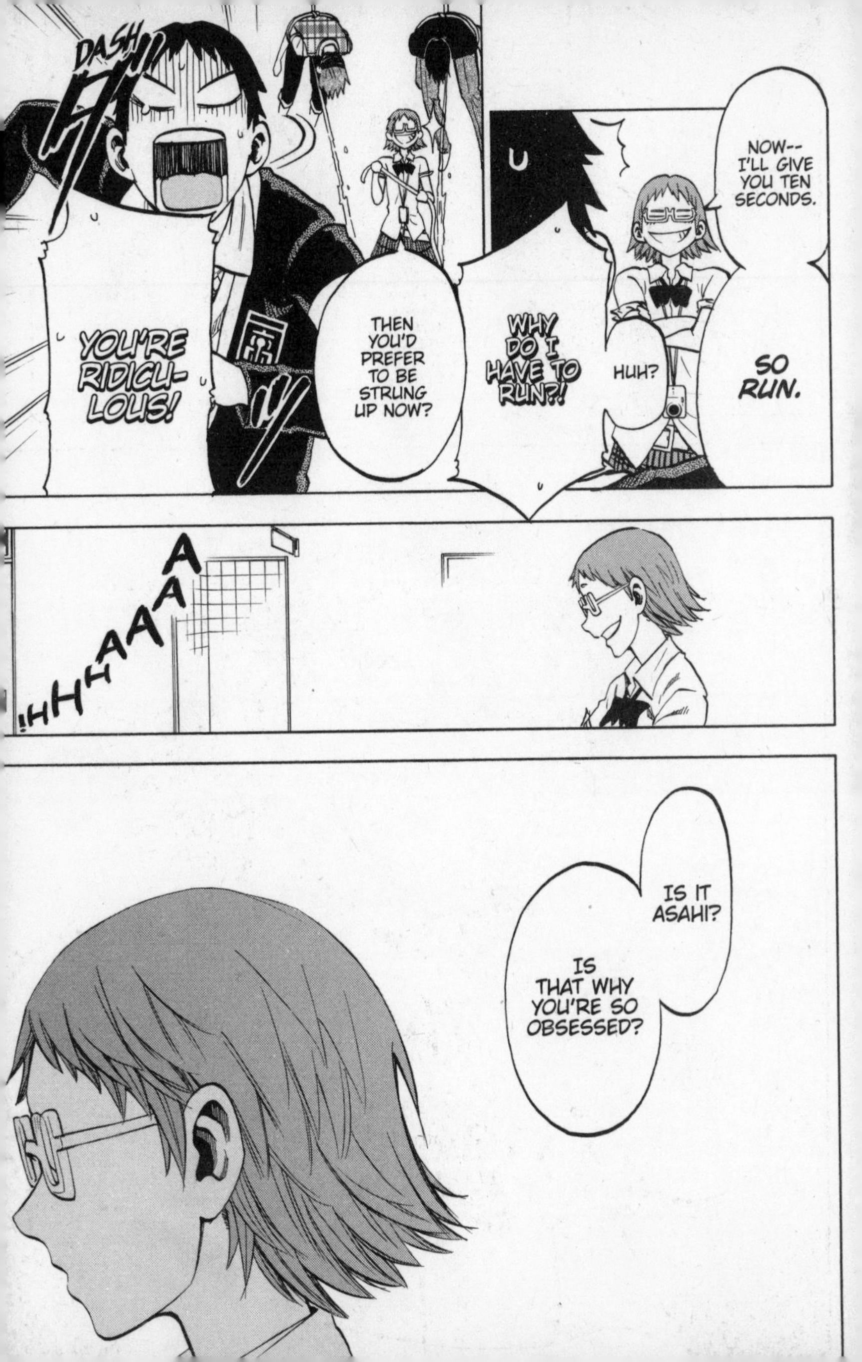
NOW-- I'LL GIVE YOU TEN SECONDS.
SO RUN.
HUH?
WHY DO I HAVE TO RUN?!
THEN YOU'D PREFER TO BE STRUNG UP NOW?
DASH
YOU'RE RIDICULOUS!
AAAAAHHH!!
IS IT ASAHI?
IS THAT WHY YOU'RE SO OBSESSED?

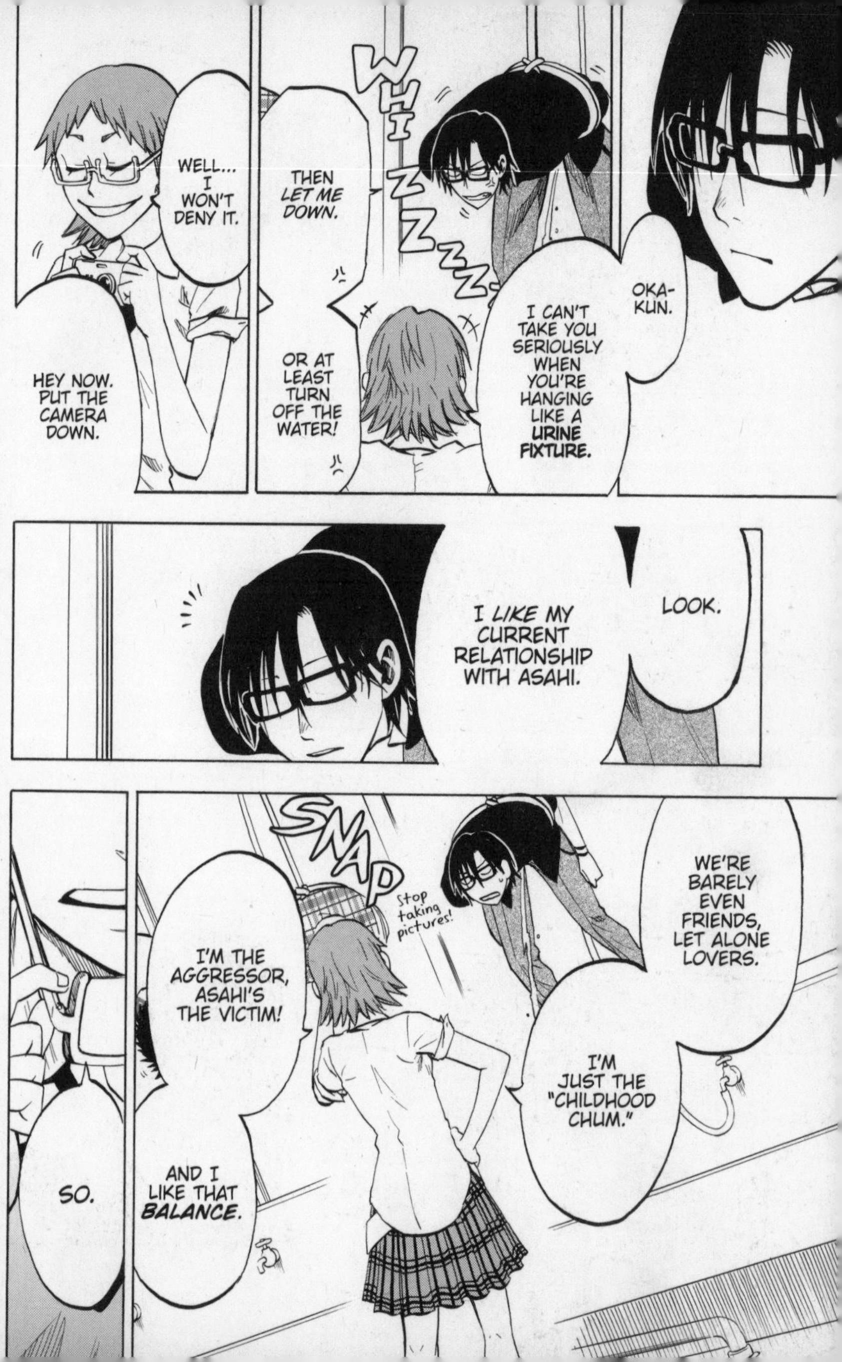
OKA-KUN.
I CAN'T TAKE YOU SERIOUSLY WHEN YOU'RE HANGING LIKE A **URINE FIXTURE.**
WHIZZZZ
THEN *LET ME* DOWN.
OR AT LEAST TURN OFF THE WATER!
WELL... I WON'T DENY IT.
HEY NOW. PUT THE CAMERA DOWN.
LOOK.
I *LIKE* MY CURRENT RELATIONSHIP WITH ASAHI.
WE'RE BARELY EVEN FRIENDS, LET ALONE LOVERS.
I'M JUST THE "CHILDHOOD CHUM."
SNAP
Stop taking pictures!
I'M THE AGGRESSOR, ASAHI'S THE VICTIM!
AND I LIKE THAT ***BALANCE***.
SO.

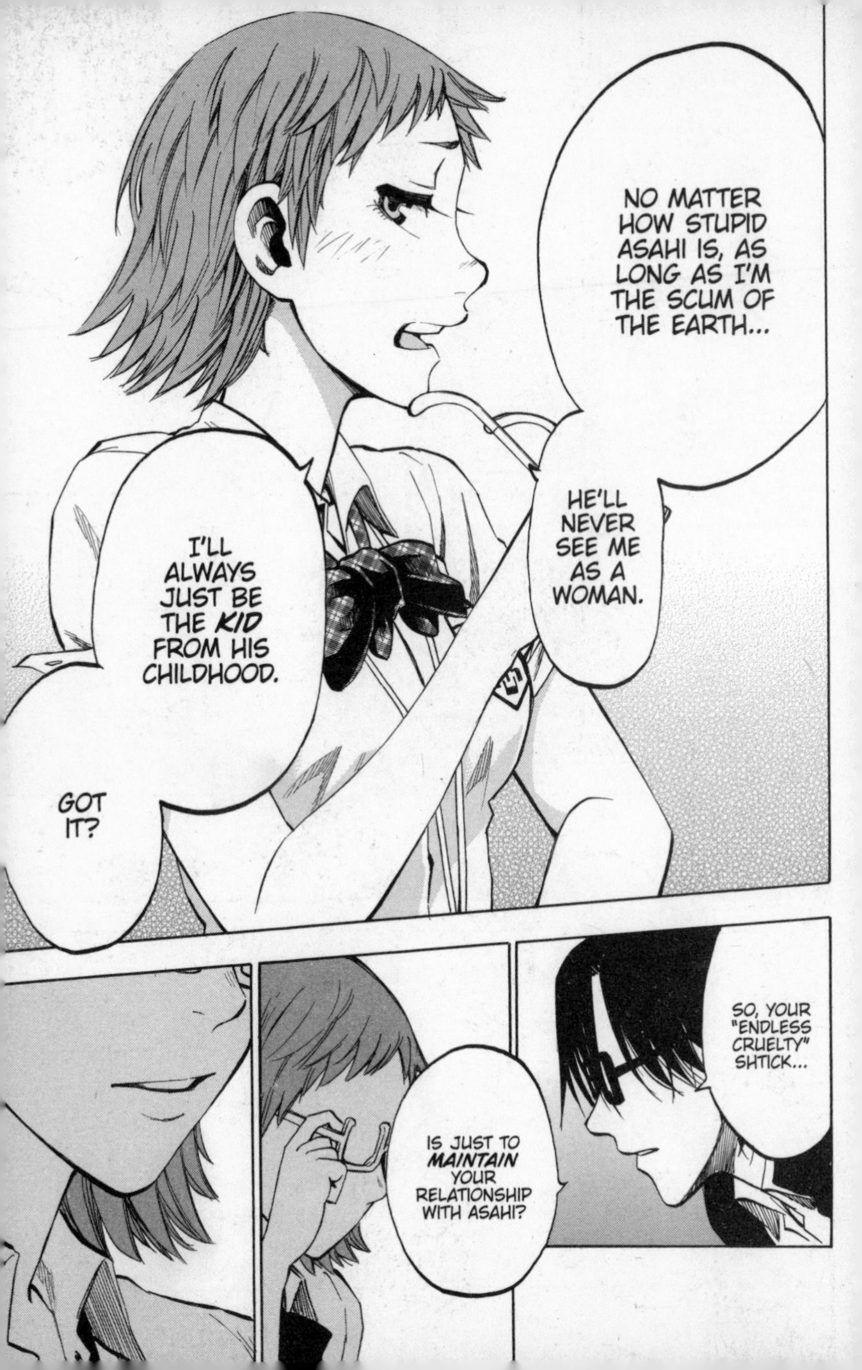
NO MATTER HOW STUPID ASAHI IS, AS LONG AS I'M THE SCUM OF THE EARTH...
HE'LL NEVER SEE ME AS A WOMAN.
I'LL ALWAYS JUST BE THE *KID* FROM HIS CHILDHOOD.
GOT IT?
SO, YOUR "ENDLESS CRUELTY" SHTICK...
IS JUST TO ***MAINTAIN*** YOUR RELATIONSHIP WITH ASAHI?

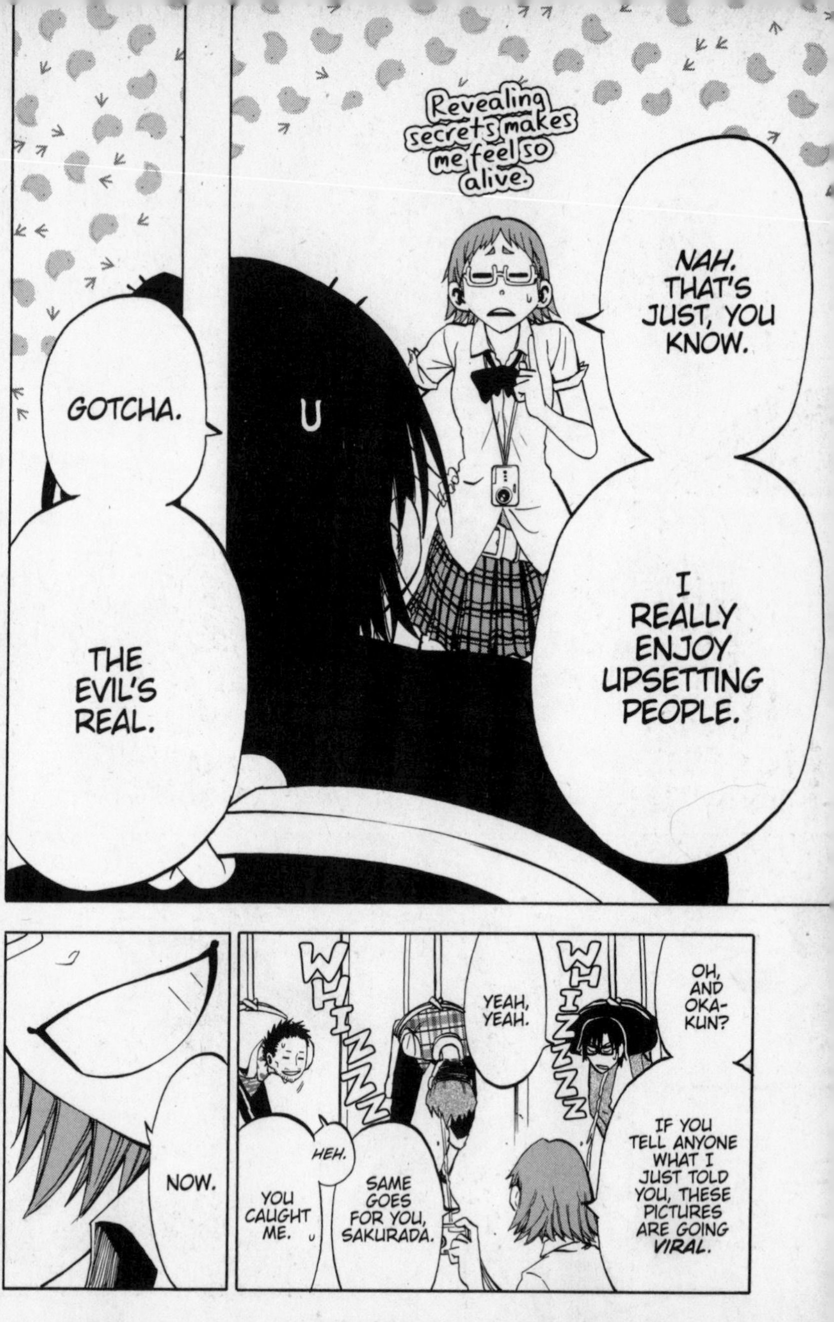
Revealing secrets makes me feel so alive.
NAH. THAT'S JUST, YOU KNOW.
I REALLY ENJOY UPSETTING PEOPLE.
GOTCHA.
THE EVIL'S REAL.
OH, AND OKA-KUN?
IF YOU TELL ANYONE WHAT I JUST TOLD YOU, THESE PICTURES ARE GOING *VIRAL*.
WHIZZZZ
YEAH, YEAH.
WHIZZZ
SAME GOES FOR YOU, SAKURADA.
HEH.
YOU CAUGHT ME.
NOW.

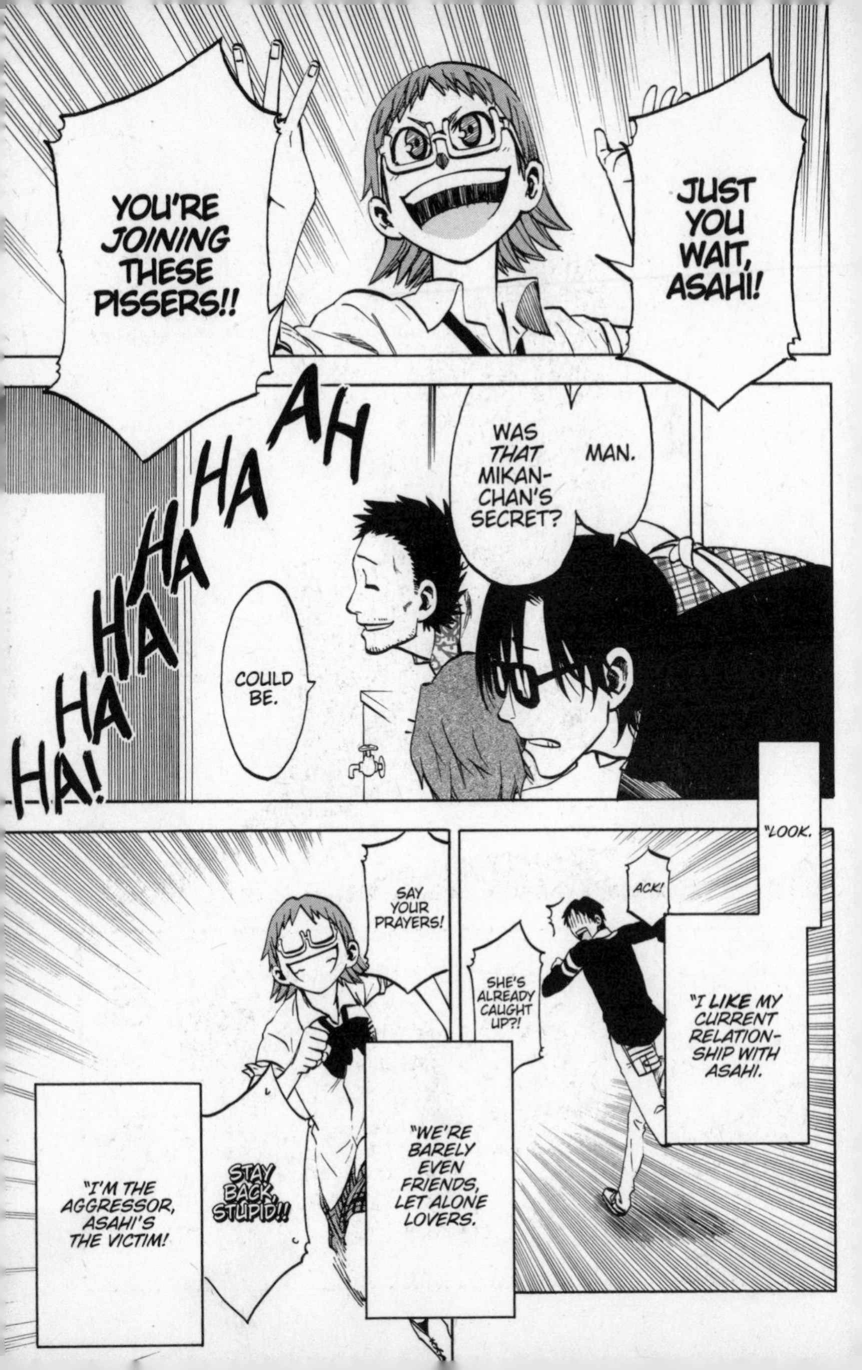
JUST YOU WAIT, ASAHI!
YOU'RE JOINING THESE PISSERS!!
MAN.
WAS THAT MIKAN-CHAN'S SECRET?
COULD BE.
AH HA HA HA HA HA HA!
"LOOK.
ACK!
SHE'S ALREADY CAUGHT UP?!
"I LIKE MY CURRENT RELATIONSHIP WITH ASAHI.
SAY YOUR PRAYERS!
"WE'RE BARELY EVEN FRIENDS, LET ALONE LOVERS.
STAY BACK, STUPID!!
"I'M THE AGGRESSOR, ASAHI'S THE VICTIM!

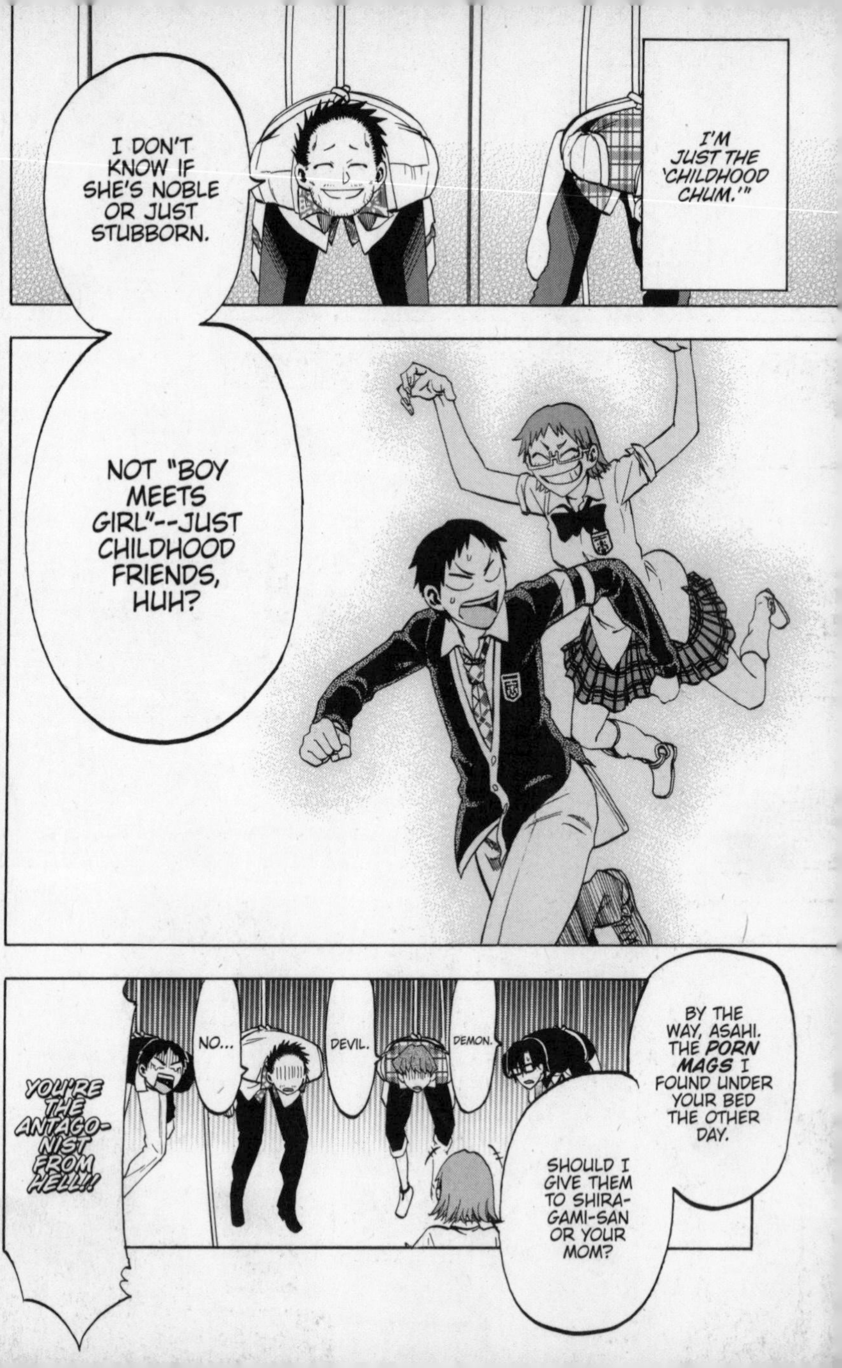
I'M JUST THE 'CHILDHOOD CHUM.'"
I DON'T KNOW IF SHE'S NOBLE OR JUST STUBBORN.
NOT "BOY MEETS GIRL"--JUST CHILDHOOD FRIENDS, HUH?
BY THE WAY, ASAHI. THE PORN MAGS I FOUND UNDER YOUR BED THE OTHER DAY.
SHOULD I GIVE THEM TO SHIRA-GAMI-SAN OR YOUR MOM?
DEMON.
DEVIL.
NO...
YOU'RE THE ANTAGO-NIST FROM HELL!!

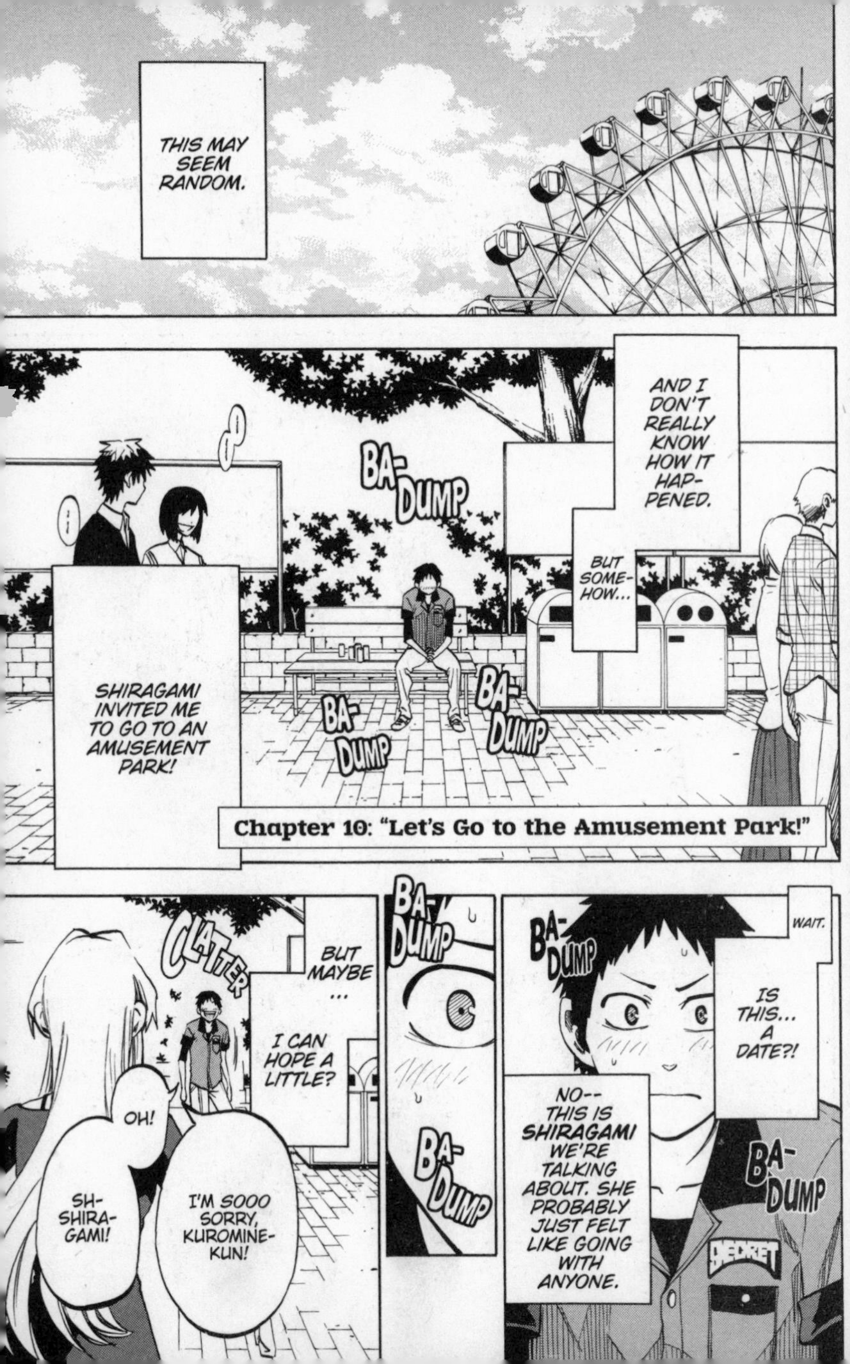
THIS MAY SEEM RANDOM.
AND I DON'T REALLY KNOW HOW IT HAPPENED.
BUT SOMEHOW...
BA-DUMP
BA-DUMP
BA-DUMP
SHIRAGAMI INVITED ME TO GO TO AN AMUSEMENT PARK!
Chapter 10: "Let's Go to the Amusement Park!"
WAIT.
IS THIS... A DATE?!
BA-DUMP
NO-- THIS IS SHIRAGAMI WE'RE TALKING ABOUT. SHE PROBABLY JUST FELT LIKE GOING WITH ANYONE.
BA-DUMP
BA-DUMP
BA-DUMP
BUT MAYBE...
I CAN HOPE A LITTLE?
CLATTER
OH!
I'M SOOO SORRY, KUROMINE-KUN!
SH-SHIRAGAMI!

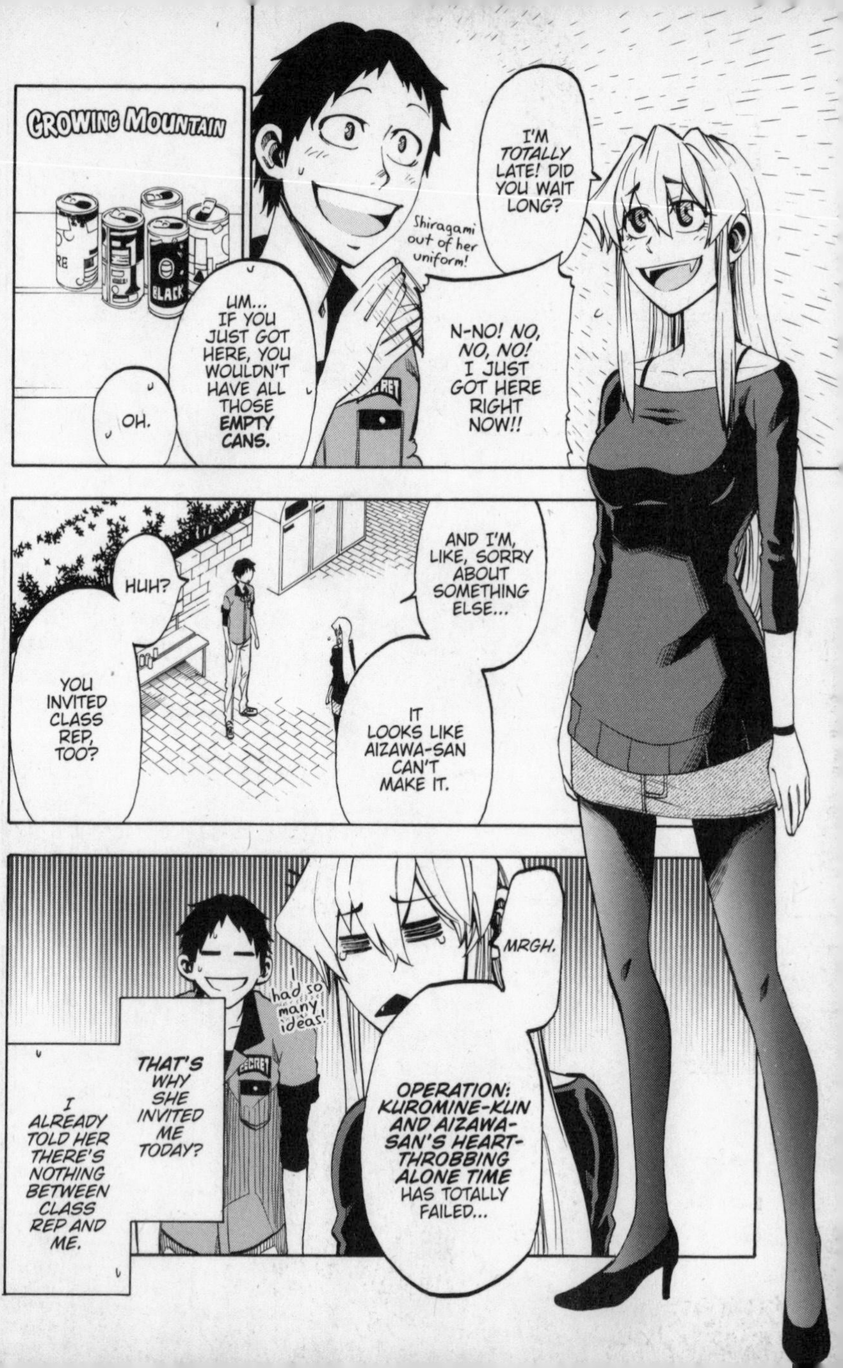
I'M TOTALLY LATE! DID YOU WAIT LONG?
Shiragami out of her uniform!
N-NO! NO, NO, NO! I JUST GOT HERE RIGHT NOW!!
GROWING MOUNTAIN
BLACK
UM... IF YOU JUST GOT HERE, YOU WOULDN'T HAVE ALL THOSE EMPTY CANS.
OH.
AND I'M, LIKE, SORRY ABOUT SOMETHING ELSE...
HUH?
IT LOOKS LIKE AIZAWA-SAN CAN'T MAKE IT.
YOU INVITED CLASS REP, TOO?
MRGH.
OPERATION: KUROMINE-KUN AND AIZAWA-SAN'S HEART-THROBBING ALONE TIME HAS TOTALLY FAILED...
I had so many ideas!
THAT'S WHY SHE INVITED ME TODAY?
I ALREADY TOLD HER THERE'S NOTHING BETWEEN CLASS REP AND ME.

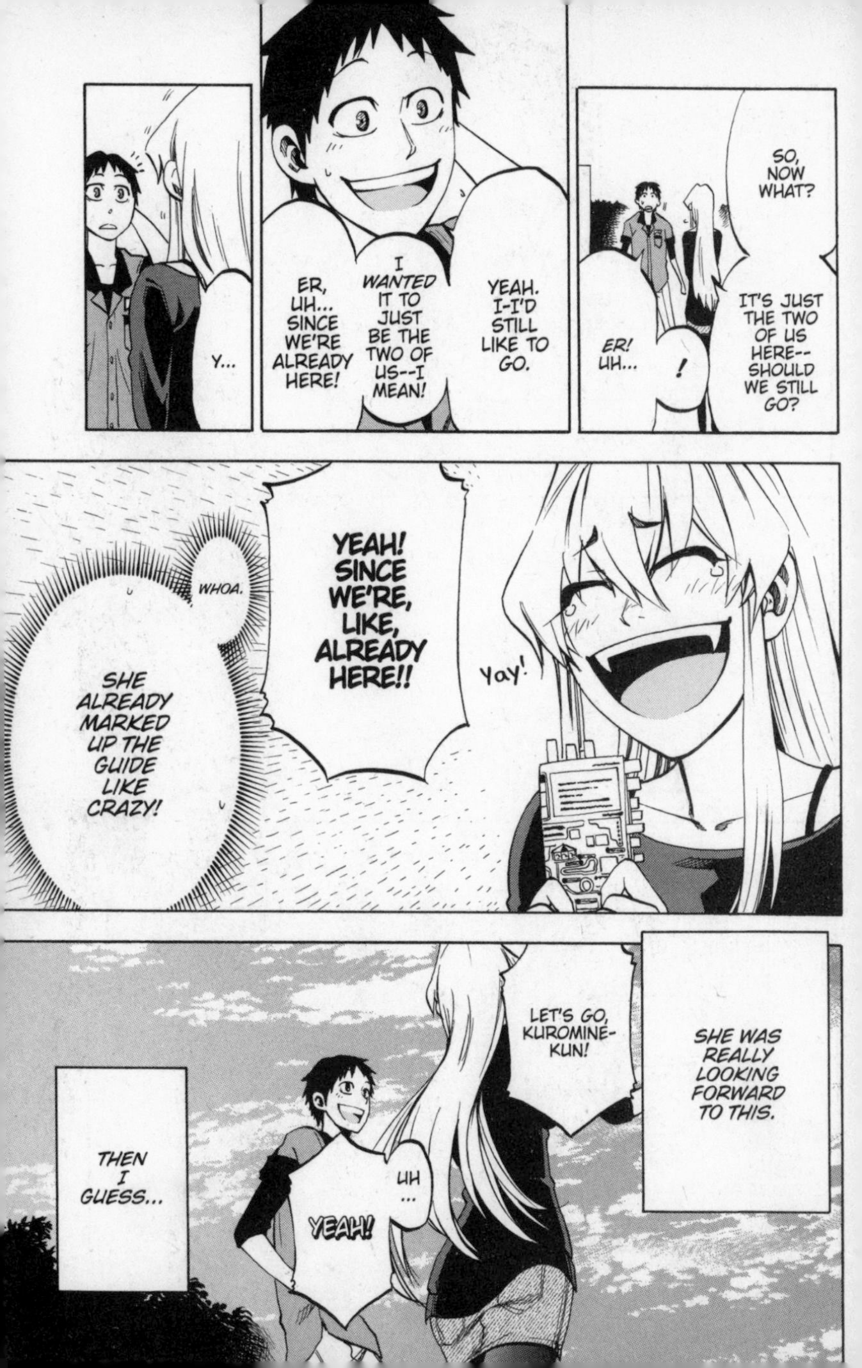
SO, NOW WHAT?
IT'S JUST THE TWO OF US HERE--SHOULD WE STILL GO?
!
ER! UH...
YEAH. I-I'D STILL LIKE TO GO.
I WANTED IT TO JUST BE THE TWO OF US--I MEAN!
ER, UH... SINCE WE'RE ALREADY HERE!
Y...
Yay!
YEAH! SINCE WE'RE, LIKE, ALREADY HERE!!
WHOA.
SHE ALREADY MARKED UP THE GUIDE LIKE CRAZY!
SHE WAS REALLY LOOKING FORWARD TO THIS.
LET'S GO, KUROMINE-KUN!
UH ...
YEAH!
THEN I GUESS...

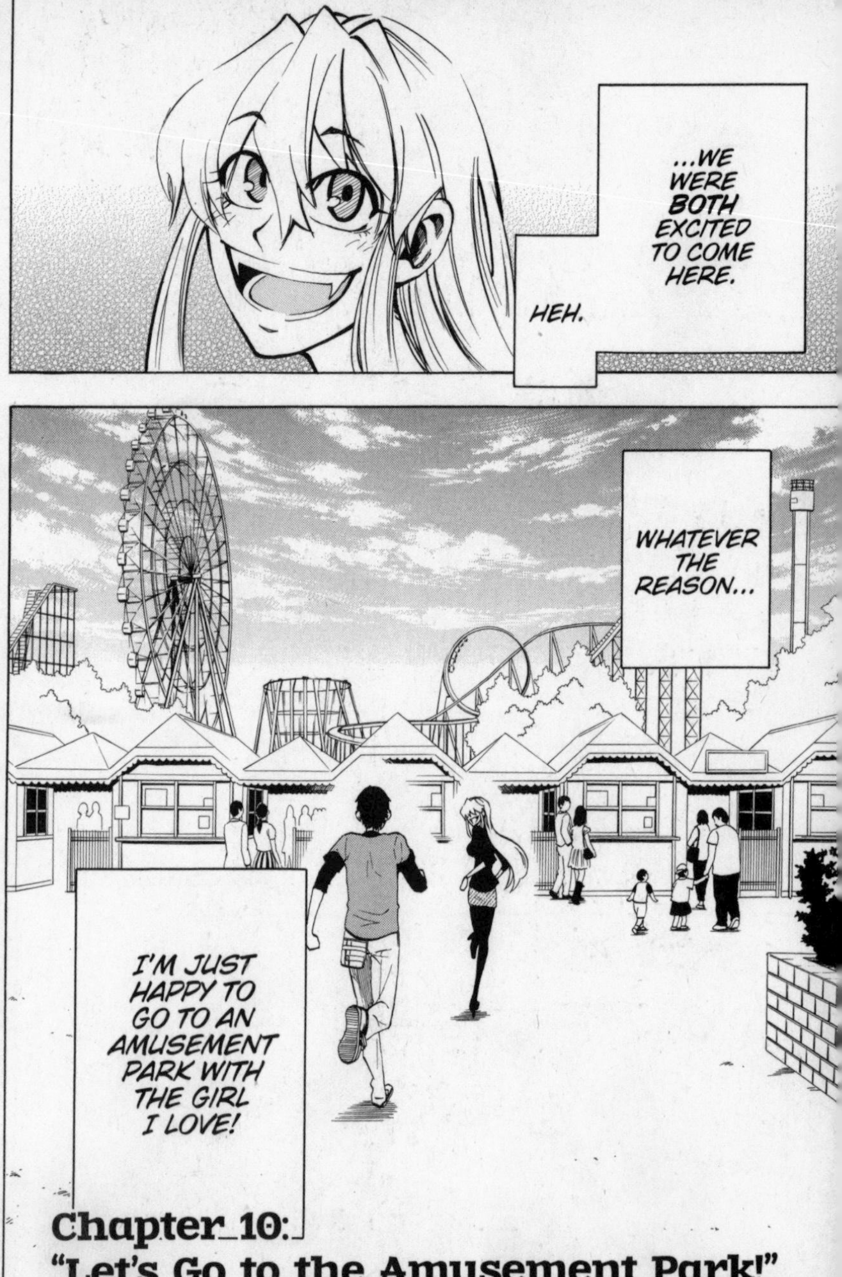
...WE WERE BOTH EXCITED TO COME HERE.
HEH.
WHATEVER THE REASON...
I'M JUST HAPPY TO GO TO AN AMUSEMENT PARK WITH THE GIRL I LOVE!

Chapter 10: "Let's Go to the Amusement Park!"

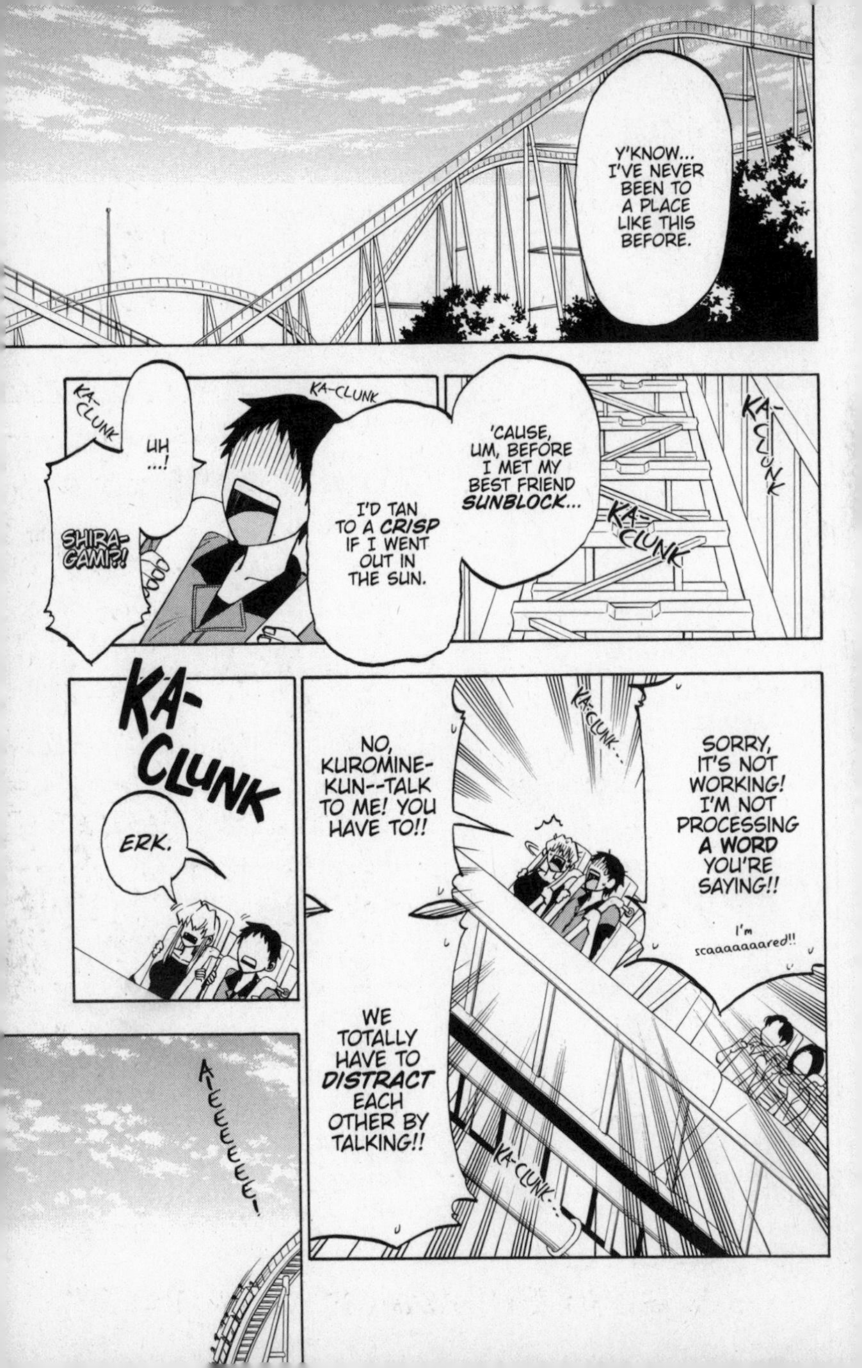
Y'KNOW... I'VE NEVER BEEN TO A PLACE LIKE THIS BEFORE.
KA-CLUNK
'CAUSE, UM, BEFORE I MET MY BEST FRIEND **SUNBLOCK**...
KA-CLUNK
KA-CLUNK
I'D TAN TO A **CRISP** IF I WENT OUT IN THE SUN.
UH ...!
KA-CLUNK
SHIRAGAMI?!
SORRY, IT'S NOT WORKING! I'M NOT PROCESSING **A WORD** YOU'RE SAYING!!
KA-CLUNK...
NO, KUROMINE-KUN--TALK TO ME! YOU HAVE TO!!
I'm scaaaaaaared!!
WE TOTALLY HAVE TO **DISTRACT** EACH OTHER BY TALKING!!
KA-CLUNK...
KA-CLUNK
ERK.
AIEEEEEEE!

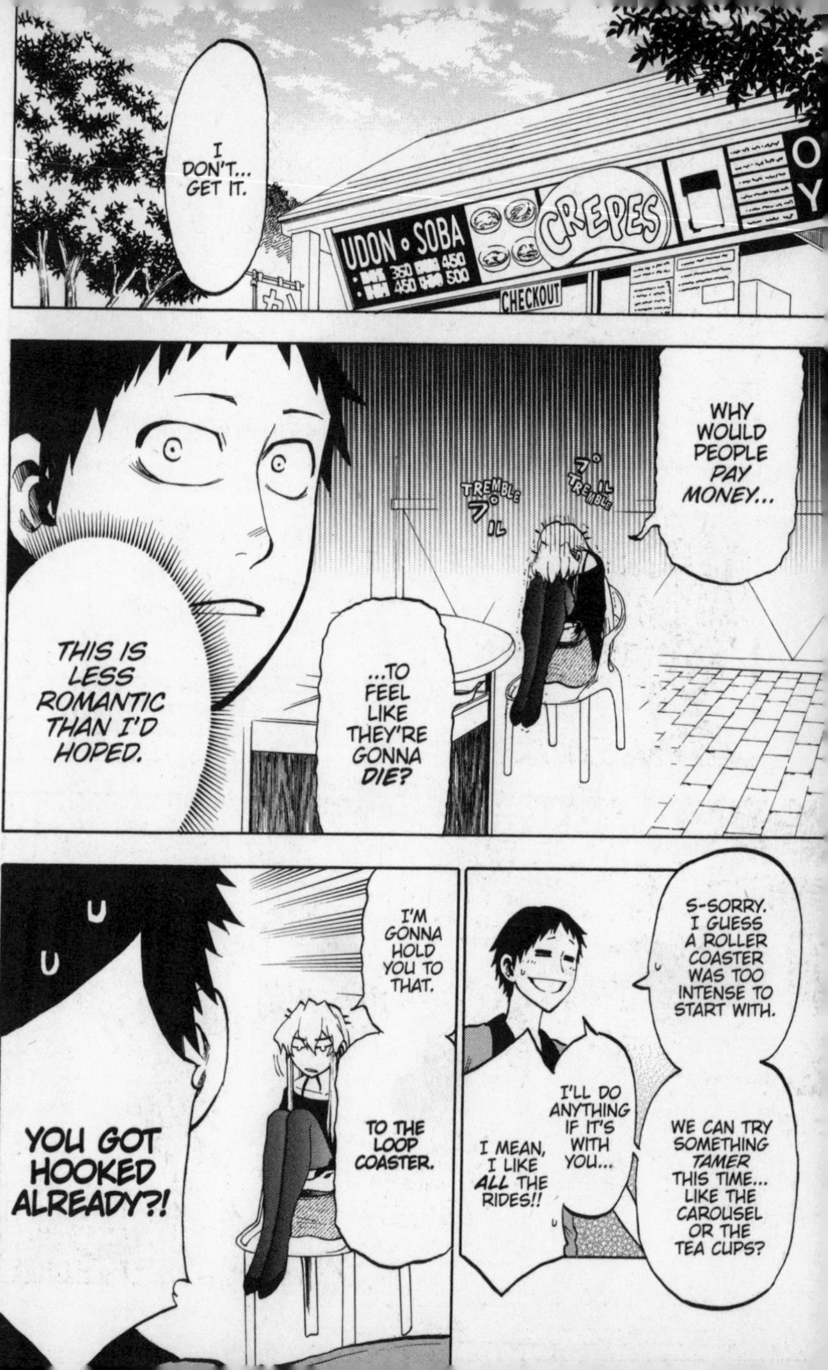
UDON • SOBA
CREPES
CHECKOUT
I DON'T... GET IT.
WHY WOULD PEOPLE PAY MONEY...
TREMBLE
TREMBLE
...TO FEEL LIKE THEY'RE GONNA DIE?
THIS IS LESS ROMANTIC THAN I'D HOPED.
S-SORRY. I GUESS A ROLLER COASTER WAS TOO INTENSE TO START WITH.
WE CAN TRY SOMETHING TAMER THIS TIME... LIKE THE CAROUSEL OR THE TEA CUPS?
I'LL DO ANYTHING IF IT'S WITH YOU...
I MEAN, I LIKE ALL THE RIDES!!
I'M GONNA HOLD YOU TO THAT.
TO THE LOOP COASTER.
YOU GOT HOOKED ALREADY?!

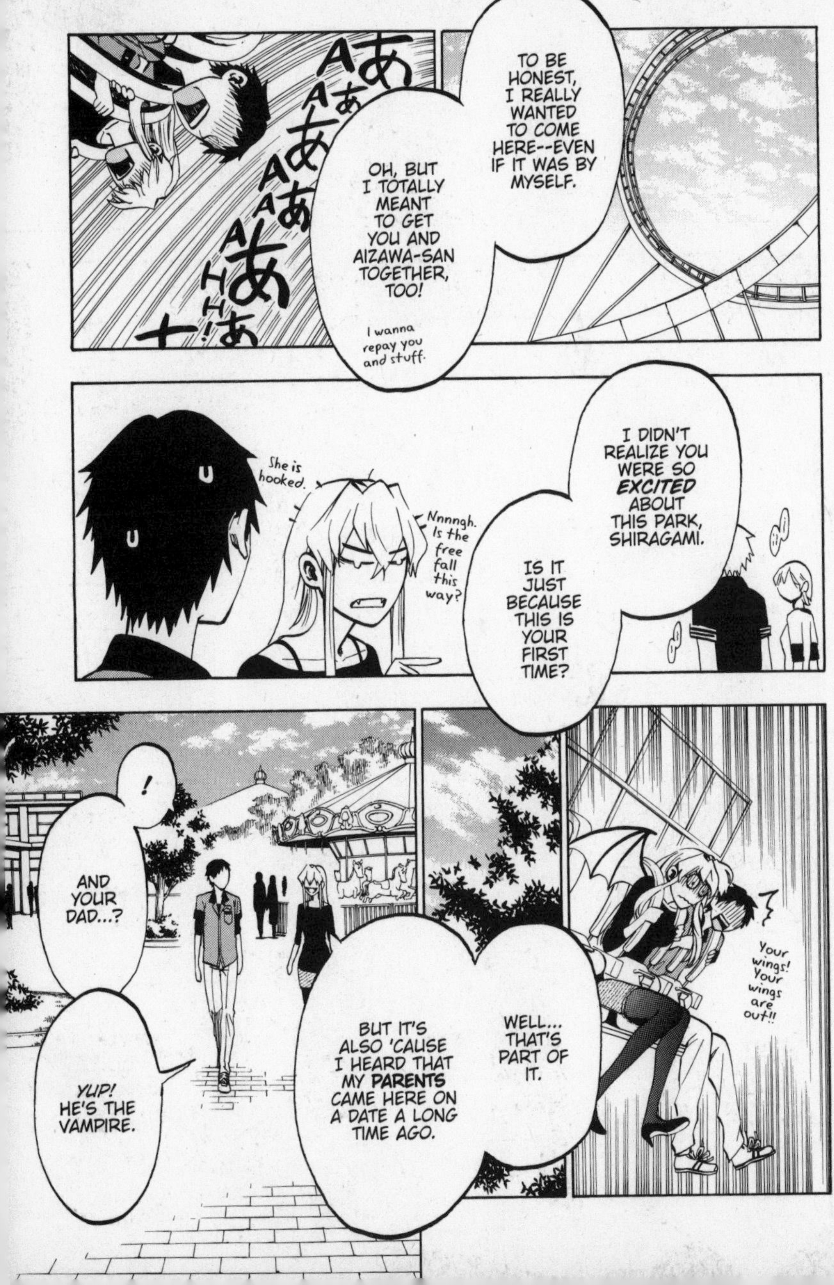
TO BE HONEST, I REALLY WANTED TO COME HERE--EVEN IF IT WAS BY MYSELF.
OH, BUT I TOTALLY MEANT TO GET YOU AND AIZAWA-SAN TOGETHER, TOO!
I wanna repay you and stuff.
AAAAHH!
I DIDN'T REALIZE YOU WERE SO EXCITED ABOUT THIS PARK, SHIRAGAMI.
IS IT JUST BECAUSE THIS IS YOUR FIRST TIME?
Nnnngh. Is the free fall this way?
She is hooked.
WELL... THAT'S PART OF IT.
BUT IT'S ALSO 'CAUSE I HEARD THAT MY PARENTS CAME HERE ON A DATE A LONG TIME AGO.
Your wings! Your wings are out!!
!
AND YOUR DAD...?
YUP! HE'S THE VAMPIRE.

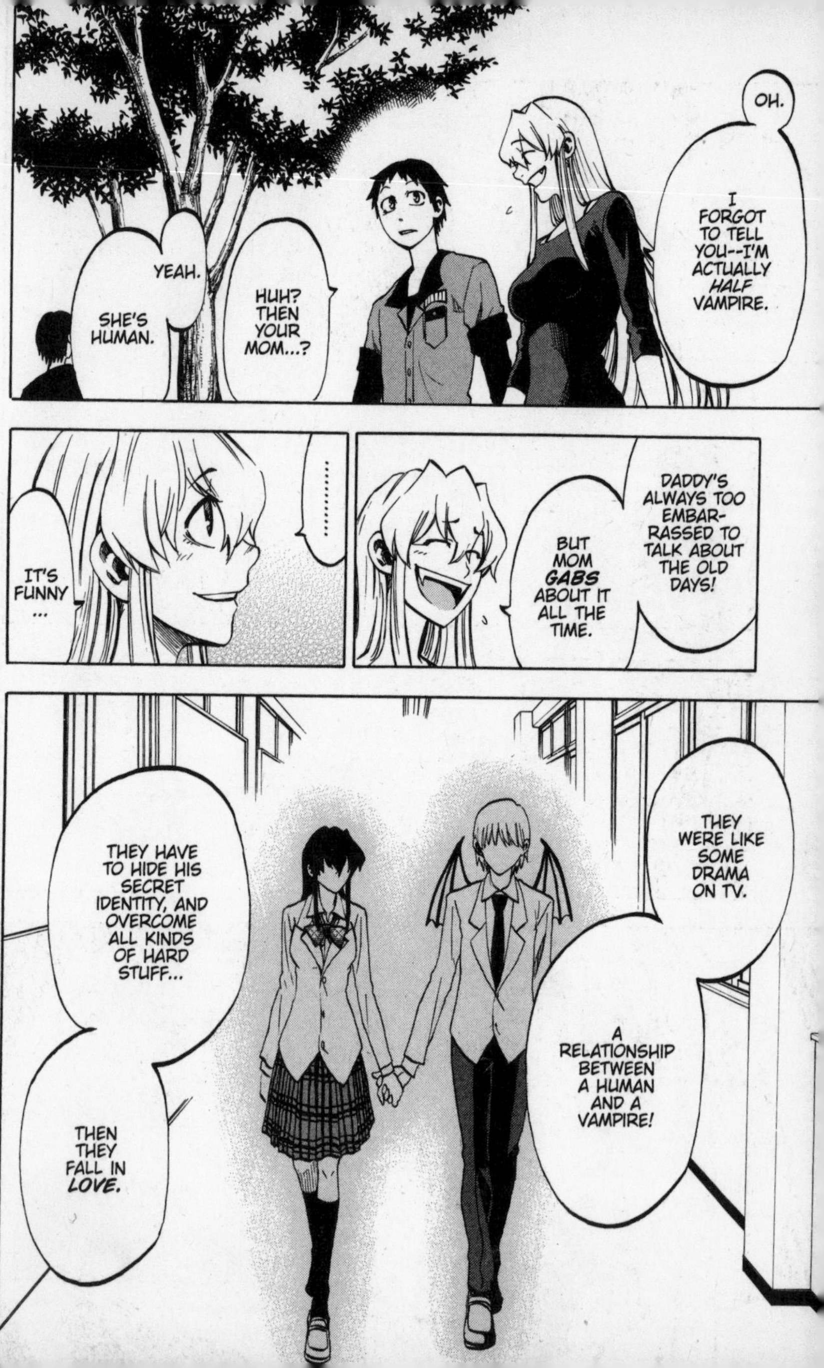
OH.
I FORGOT TO TELL YOU--I'M ACTUALLY *HALF* VAMPIRE.
HUH? THEN YOUR MOM...?
YEAH.
SHE'S HUMAN.
DADDY'S ALWAYS TOO EMBAR-RASSED TO TALK ABOUT THE OLD DAYS!
BUT MOM **GABS** ABOUT IT ALL THE TIME.
......
IT'S FUNNY...
THEY WERE LIKE SOME DRAMA ON TV.
A RELATIONSHIP BETWEEN A HUMAN AND A VAMPIRE!
THEY HAVE TO HIDE HIS SECRET IDENTITY, AND OVERCOME ALL KINDS OF HARD STUFF...
THEN THEY FALL IN ***LOVE***.

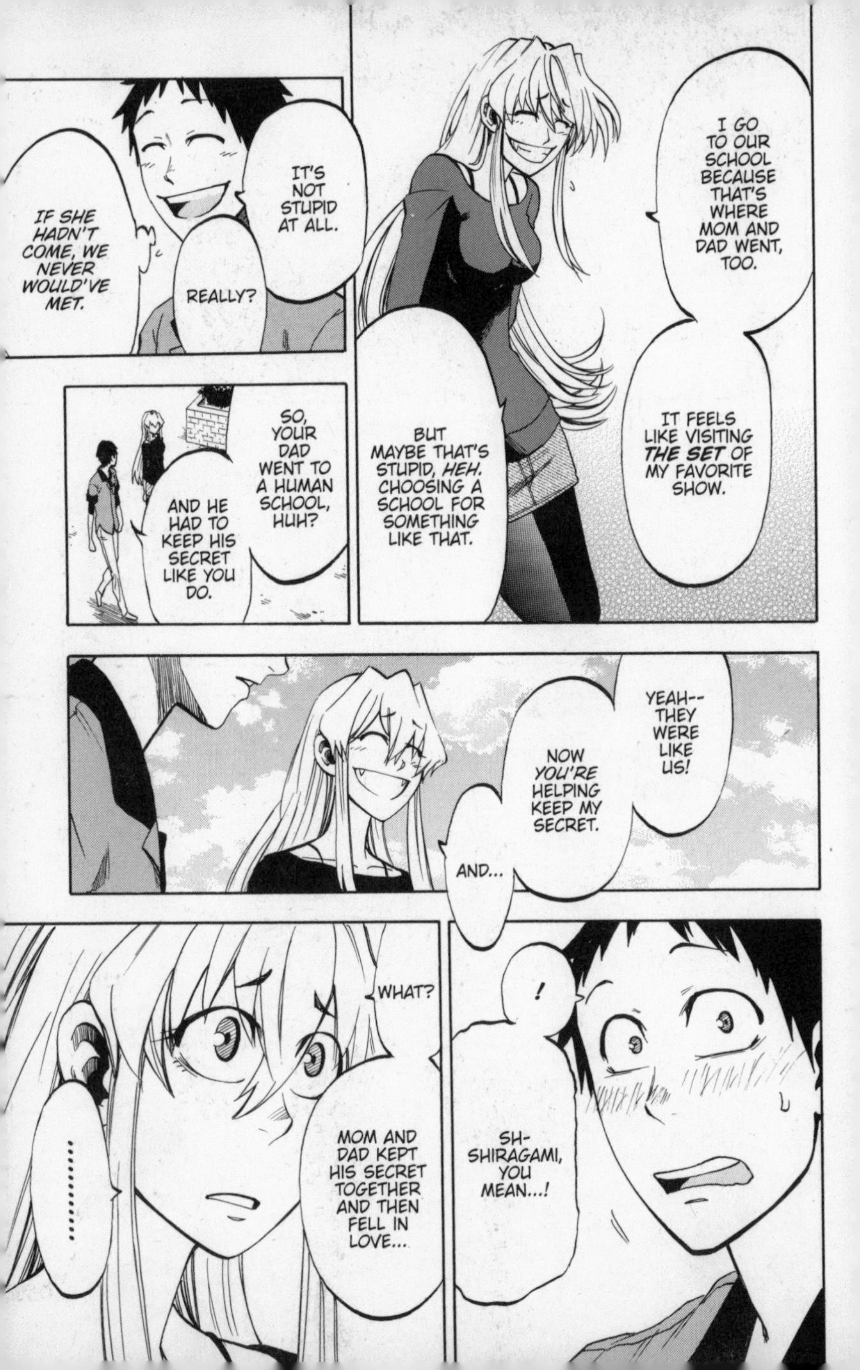
I GO TO OUR SCHOOL BECAUSE THAT'S WHERE MOM AND DAD WENT, TOO.
IT FEELS LIKE VISITING *THE SET* OF MY FAVORITE SHOW.
BUT MAYBE THAT'S STUPID, *HEH.* CHOOSING A SCHOOL FOR SOMETHING LIKE THAT.
IT'S NOT STUPID AT ALL.
REALLY?
IF SHE HADN'T COME, WE NEVER WOULD'VE MET.
SO, YOUR DAD WENT TO A HUMAN SCHOOL, HUH?
AND HE HAD TO KEEP HIS SECRET LIKE YOU DO.
YEAH-- THEY WERE LIKE US!
NOW *YOU'RE* HELPING KEEP MY SECRET.
AND...
!
SH- SHIRAGAMI, YOU MEAN...!
WHAT?
MOM AND DAD KEPT HIS SECRET TOGETHER AND THEN FELL IN LOVE...
....

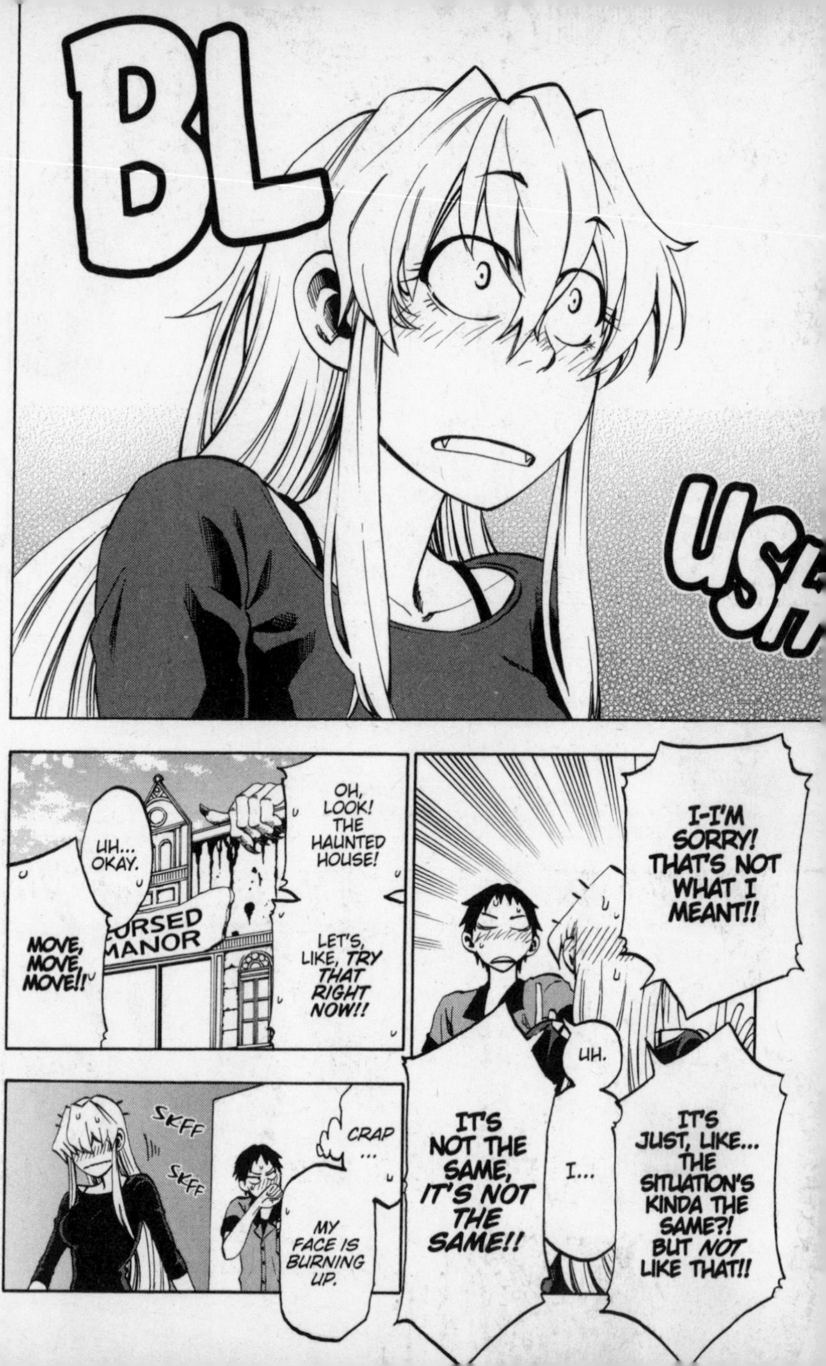
BL
USH
I-I'M SORRY! THAT'S NOT WHAT I MEANT!!
UH.
IT'S JUST, LIKE... THE SITUATION'S KINDA THE SAME?! BUT *NOT* LIKE THAT!!
I...
IT'S NOT THE SAME, *IT'S NOT THE SAME!!*
OH, LOOK! THE HAUNTED HOUSE!
LET'S, LIKE, *TRY THAT RIGHT NOW!!*
UH... OKAY.
CURSED MANOR
MOVE, MOVE, MOVE!!
SKFF
SKFF
CRAP ...
MY FACE IS BURNING UP.

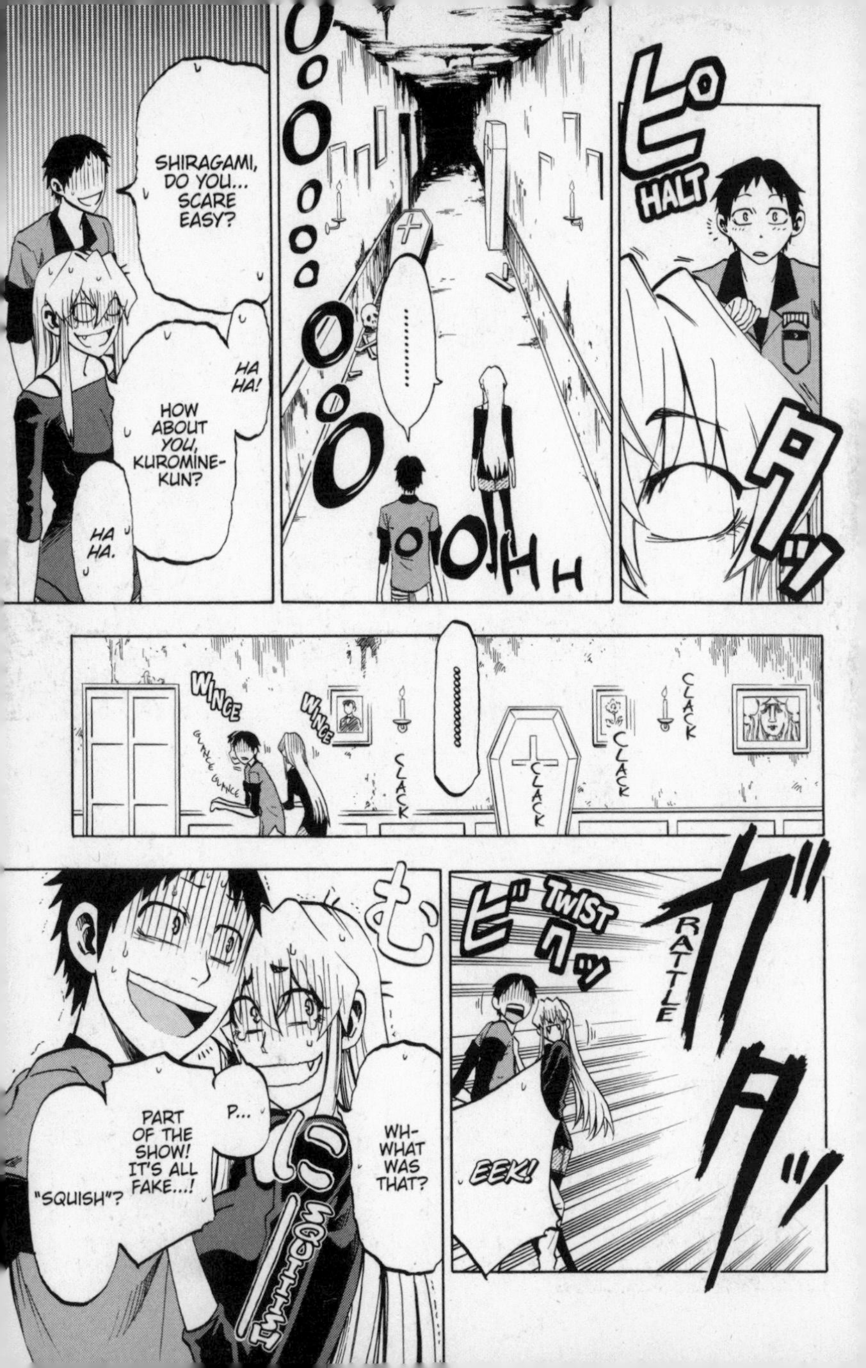
ピ
HALT
タッ
OOOOOOOOOOOOOHH
......
SHIRAGAMI, DO YOU... SCARE EASY?
HA HA!
HOW ABOUT YOU, KUROMINE-KUN?
HA HA.
....
CLACK
CLACK
CLACK
CLACK
WINCE
WINCE
GLANCE GLANCE
ガタッ
RATTLE
ビクッ
TWIST
EEK!
む
WH-WHAT WAS THAT?
P...
PART OF THE SHOW! IT'S ALL FAKE...!
"SQUISH"?
SQUIIIISH

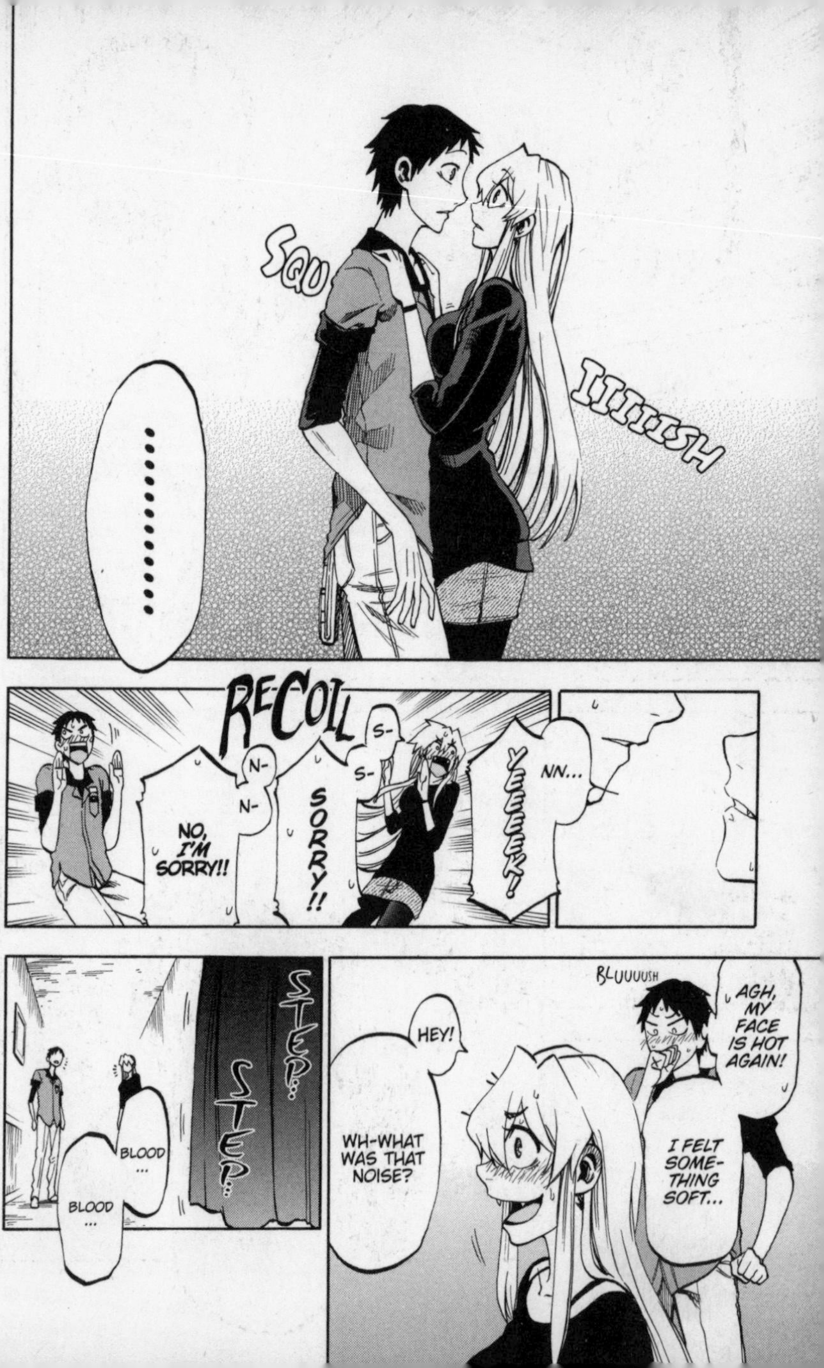
SQU
IIIIISH
....
NN...
YEEEEK!
S- S- SORRY!!
RECOIL
N- N- NO, I'M SORRY!!
BLUUUUSH
AGH, MY FACE IS HOT AGAIN!
I FELT SOMETHING SOFT...
HEY!
WH-WHAT WAS THAT NOISE?
STEP...
STEP...
BLOOD...
BLOOD...

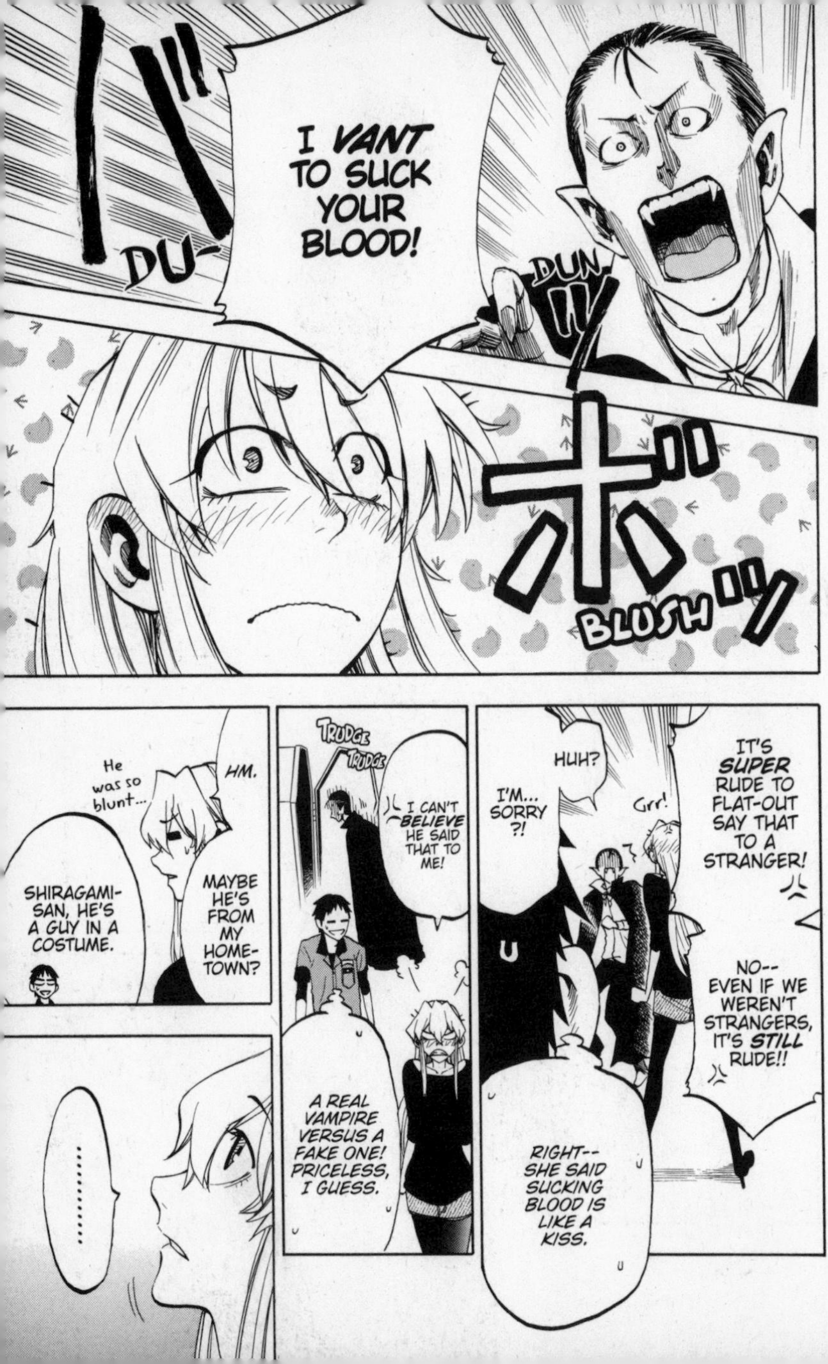
I VANT TO SUCK YOUR BLOOD!
DUN
DU-
BLUSH
IT'S SUPER RUDE TO FLAT-OUT SAY THAT TO A STRANGER!
HUH?
Grr!
I'M... SORRY?!
NO-- EVEN IF WE WEREN'T STRANGERS, IT'S STILL RUDE!!
RIGHT-- SHE SAID SUCKING BLOOD IS LIKE A KISS.
TRUDGE
TRUDGE
I CAN'T BELIEVE HE SAID THAT TO ME!
A REAL VAMPIRE VERSUS A FAKE ONE! PRICELESS, I GUESS.
HM.
He was so blunt...
MAYBE HE'S FROM MY HOME-TOWN?
SHIRAGAMI-SAN, HE'S A GUY IN A COSTUME.
....

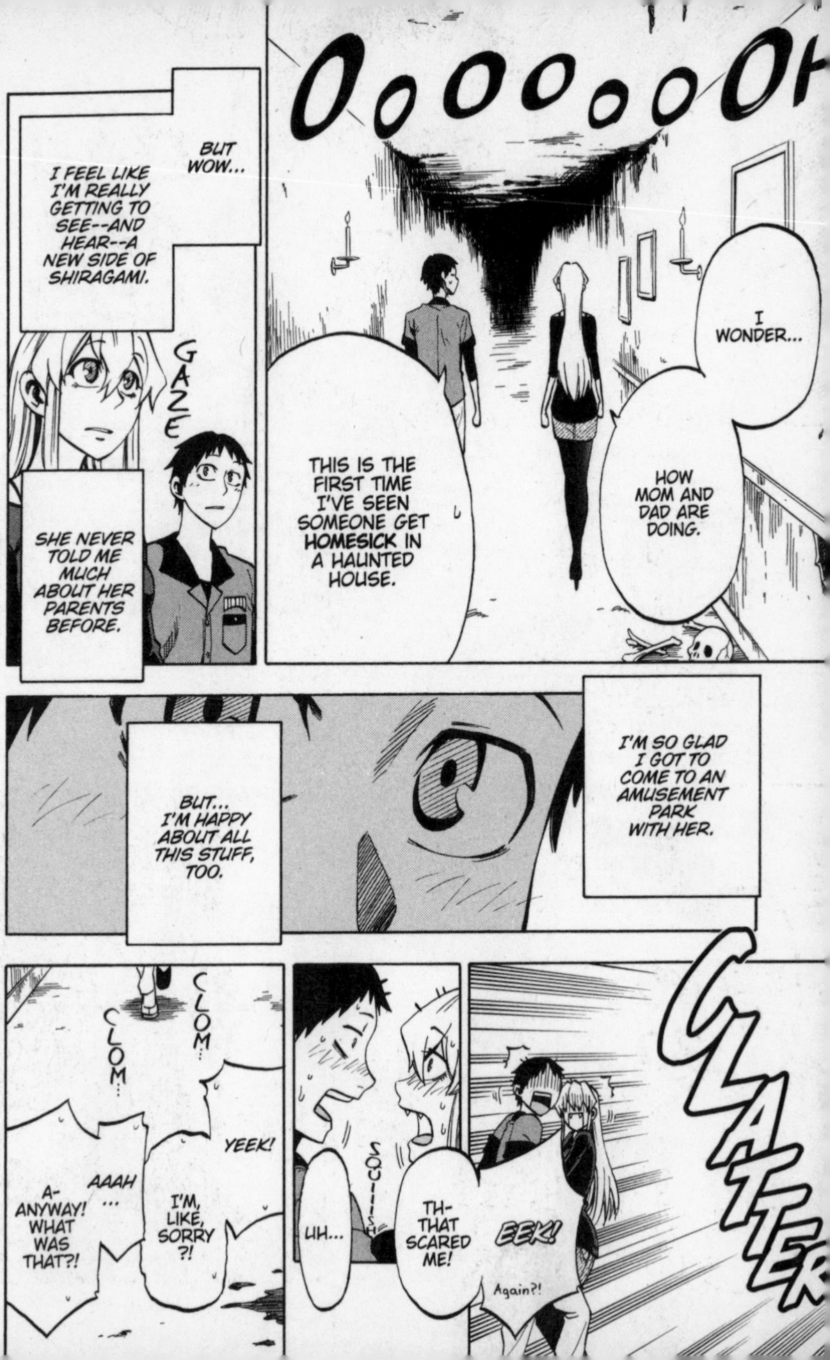
OOOOOOOH
I WONDER...
HOW MOM AND DAD ARE DOING.
THIS IS THE FIRST TIME I'VE SEEN SOMEONE GET HOMESICK IN A HAUNTED HOUSE.
BUT WOW...
I FEEL LIKE I'M REALLY GETTING TO SEE--AND HEAR--A NEW SIDE OF SHIRAGAMI.
GAZE
SHE NEVER TOLD ME MUCH ABOUT HER PARENTS BEFORE.
I'M SO GLAD I GOT TO COME TO AN AMUSEMENT PARK WITH HER.
BUT... I'M HAPPY ABOUT ALL THIS STUFF, TOO.
CLATTER
EEK!
Again?!
TH- THAT SCARED ME!
SQUIISH
UH...
CLOM...
CLOM...
YEEK!
I'M, LIKE, SORRY?!
AAAH...
A- ANYWAY! WHAT WAS THAT?!

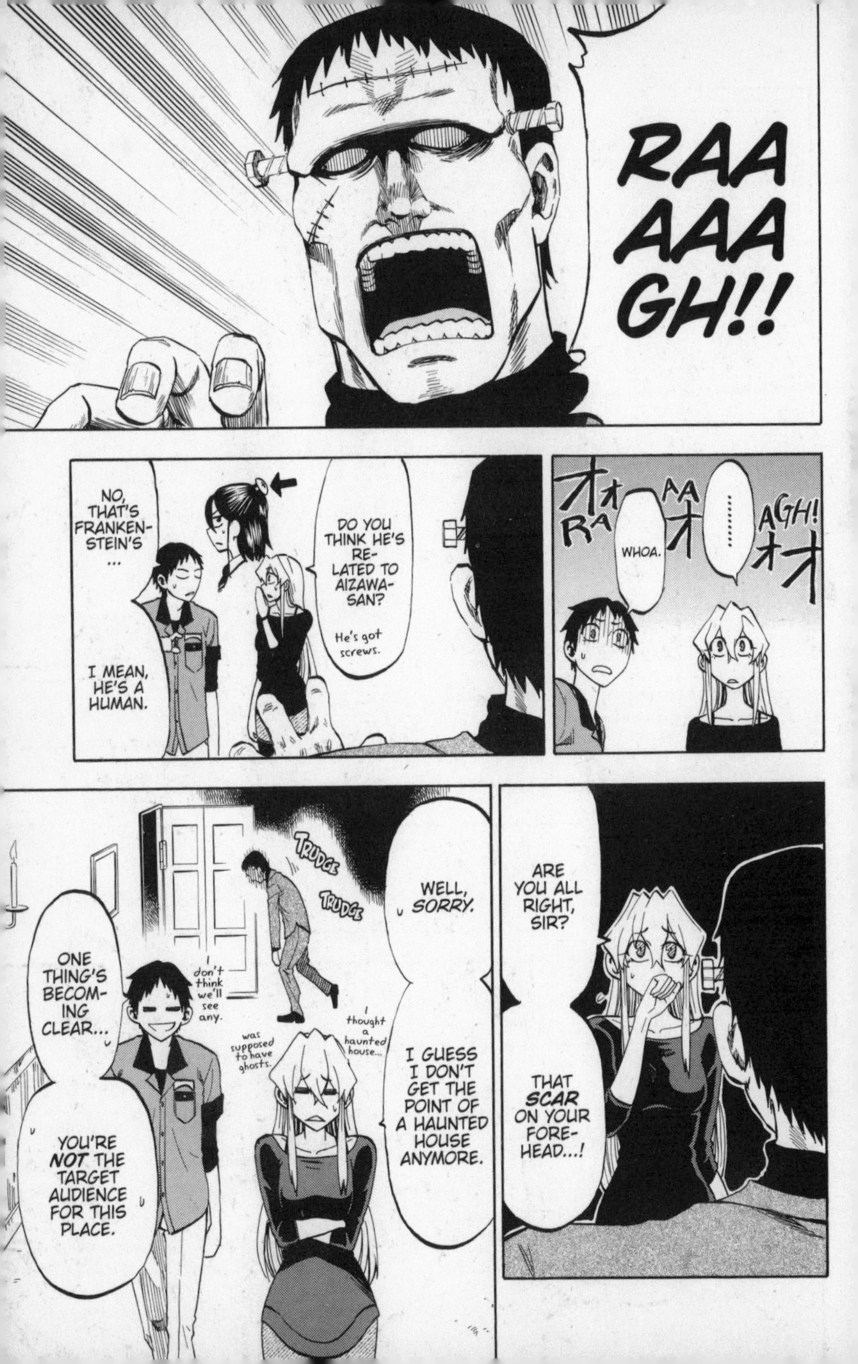
RAA AAA GH!!
RAA AAGH!
......
WHOA.
DO YOU THINK HE'S RE-LATED TO AIZAWA-SAN?
He's got screws.
NO, THAT'S FRANKEN-STEIN'S ...
I MEAN, HE'S A HUMAN.
ARE YOU ALL RIGHT, SIR?
THAT **SCAR** ON YOUR FORE-HEAD...!
WELL, *SORRY.*
TRUDGE
TRUDGE
I GUESS I DON'T GET THE POINT OF A HAUNTED HOUSE ANYMORE.
I thought a haunted house...
was supposed to have ghosts.
I don't think we'll see any.
ONE THING'S BECOM-ING CLEAR...
YOU'RE ***NOT*** THE TARGET AUDIENCE FOR THIS PLACE.

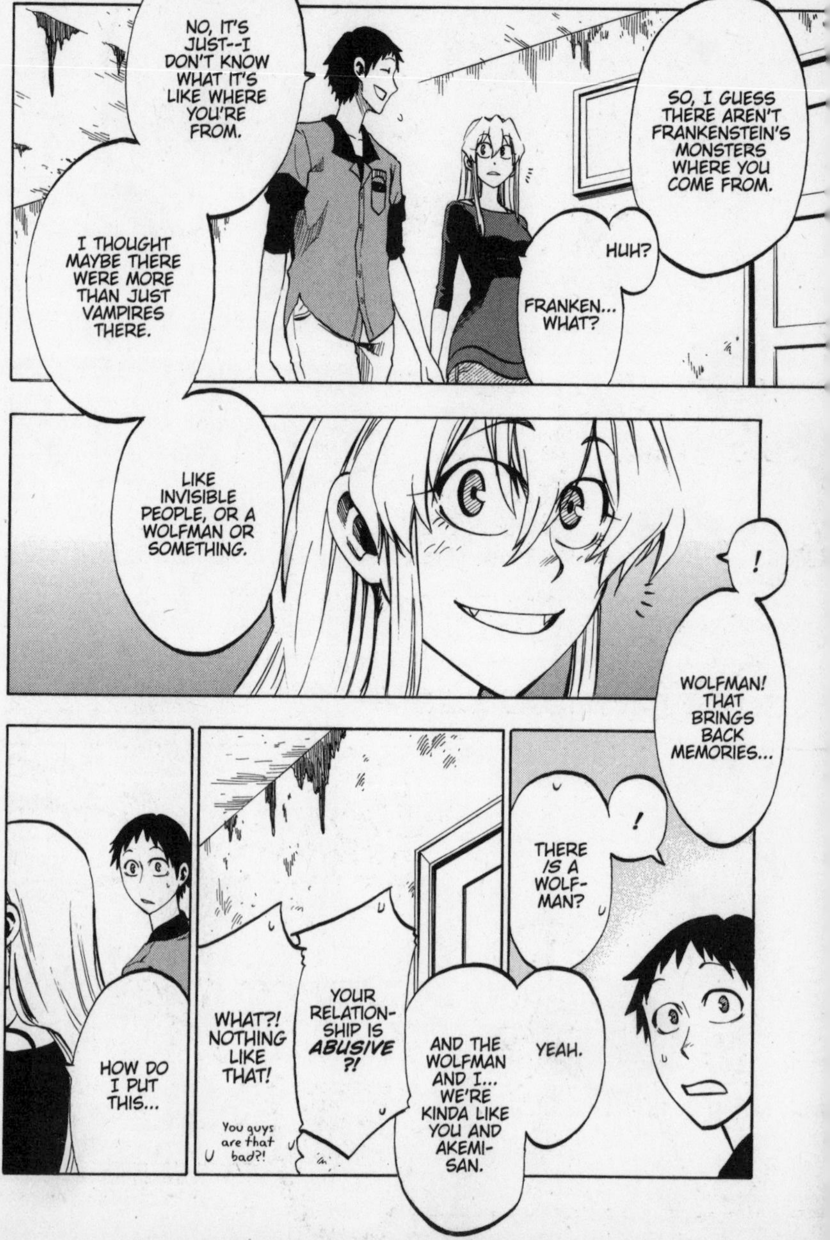
SO, I GUESS THERE AREN'T FRANKENSTEIN'S MONSTERS WHERE YOU COME FROM.
HUH?
FRANKEN... WHAT?
NO, IT'S JUST--I DON'T KNOW WHAT IT'S LIKE WHERE YOU'RE FROM.
I THOUGHT MAYBE THERE WERE MORE THAN JUST VAMPIRES THERE.
LIKE INVISIBLE PEOPLE, OR A WOLFMAN OR SOMETHING.
!
WOLFMAN! THAT BRINGS BACK MEMORIES...
!
THERE *IS* A WOLF-MAN?
YEAH.
AND THE WOLFMAN AND I... WE'RE KINDA LIKE YOU AND AKEMI-SAN.
YOUR RELATIONSHIP IS ***ABUSIVE***?!
WHAT?! NOTHING LIKE THAT!
You guys are that bad?!
HOW DO I PUT THIS...

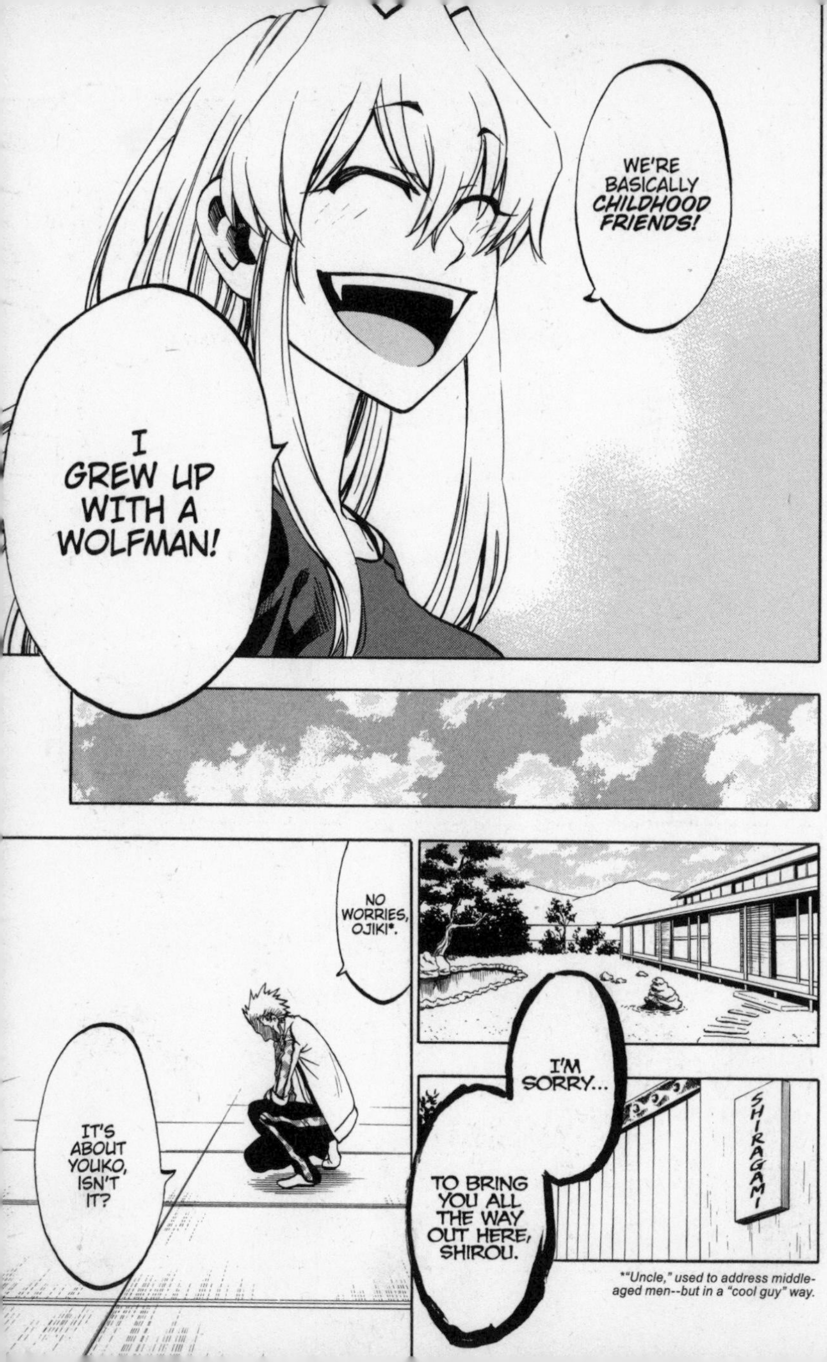
WE'RE BASICALLY CHILDHOOD FRIENDS!
I GREW UP WITH A WOLFMAN!
I'M SORRY...
TO BRING YOU ALL THE WAY OUT HERE, SHIROU.
SHIRAGAMI
NO WORRIES, OJIKI*.
IT'S ABOUT YOUKO, ISN'T IT?

*"Uncle," used to address middle-aged men--but in a "cool guy" way.

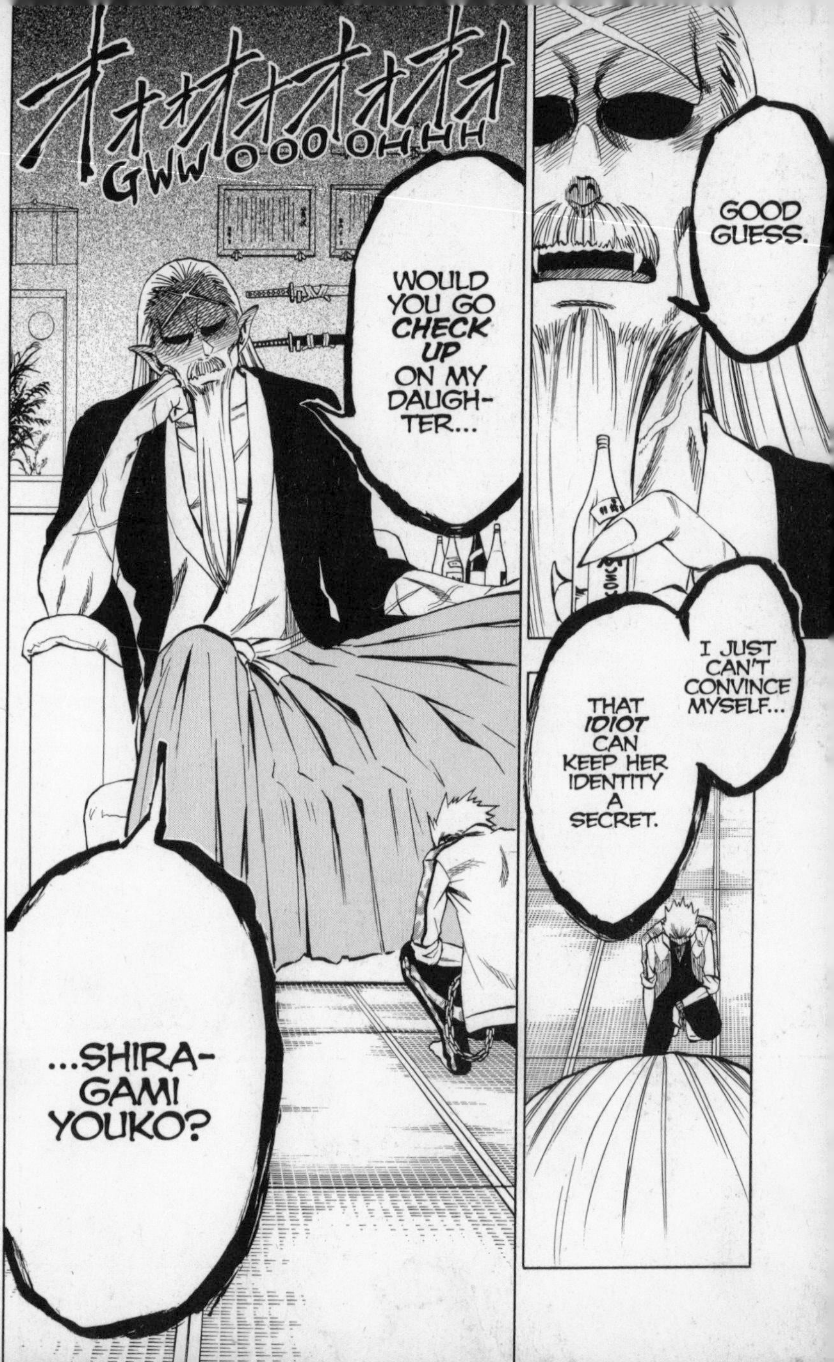
GOOD GUESS.
I JUST CAN'T CONVINCE MYSELF...
THAT *IDIOT* CAN KEEP HER IDENTITY A SECRET.
オォォオォオォオォ
GWWOOOOHHH
WOULD YOU GO *CHECK UP* ON MY DAUGHTER...
...SHIRAGAMI YOUKO?

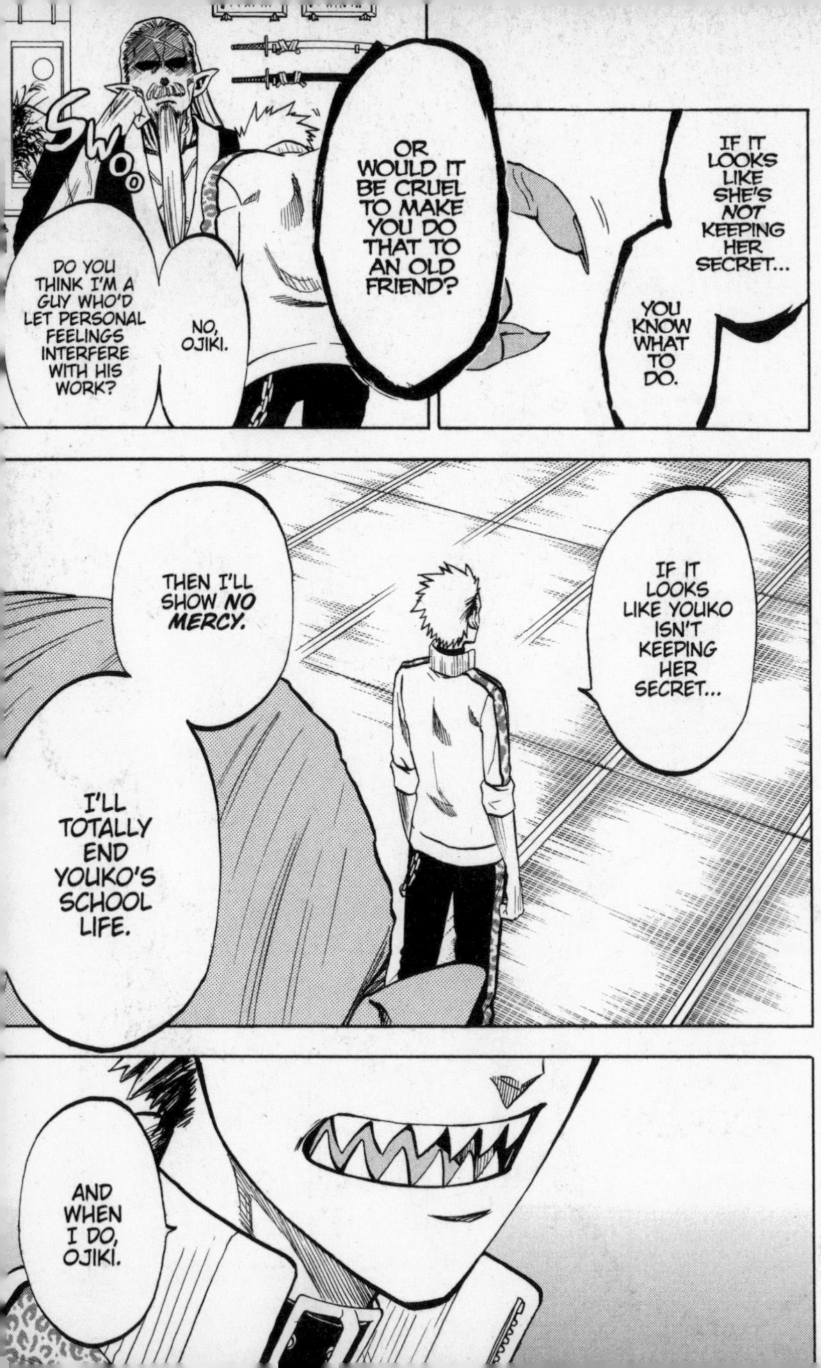
IF IT LOOKS LIKE SHE'S *NOT* KEEPING HER SECRET...
YOU KNOW WHAT TO DO.
OR WOULD IT BE CRUEL TO MAKE YOU DO THAT TO AN OLD FRIEND?
SWOO
NO, OJIKI.
DO YOU THINK I'M A GUY WHO'D LET PERSONAL FEELINGS INTERFERE WITH HIS WORK?
IF IT LOOKS LIKE YOUKO ISN'T KEEPING HER SECRET...
THEN I'LL SHOW ***NO MERCY.***
I'LL TOTALLY END YOUKO'S SCHOOL LIFE.
AND WHEN I DO, OJIKI.

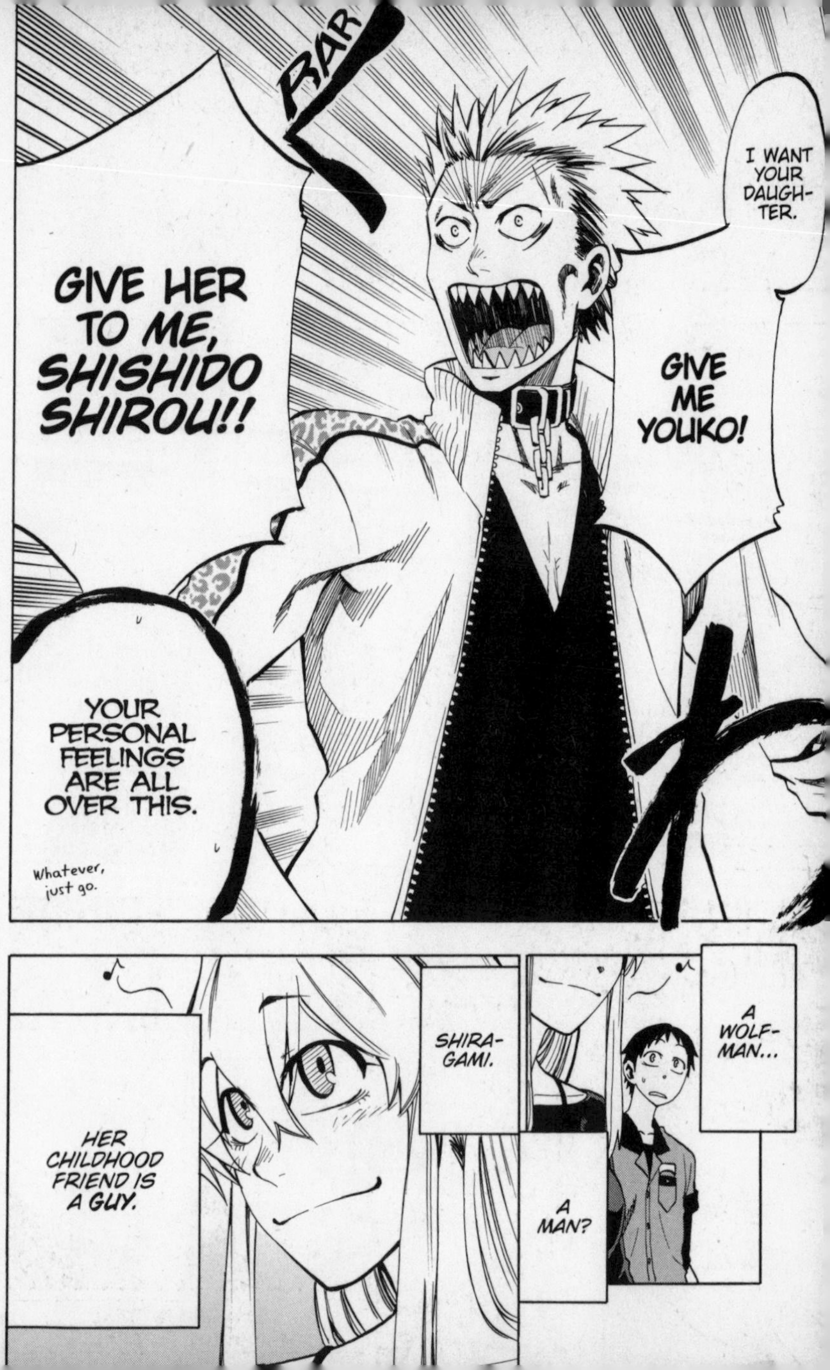
I WANT YOUR DAUGH-TER.
GIVE ME YOUKO!
RAR
GIVE HER TO ME, SHISHIDO SHIROU!!
YOUR PERSONAL FEELINGS ARE ALL OVER THIS.
Whatever, just go.
A WOLF-MAN...
A MAN?
SHIRA-GAMI.
HER CHILDHOOD FRIEND IS A GUY.

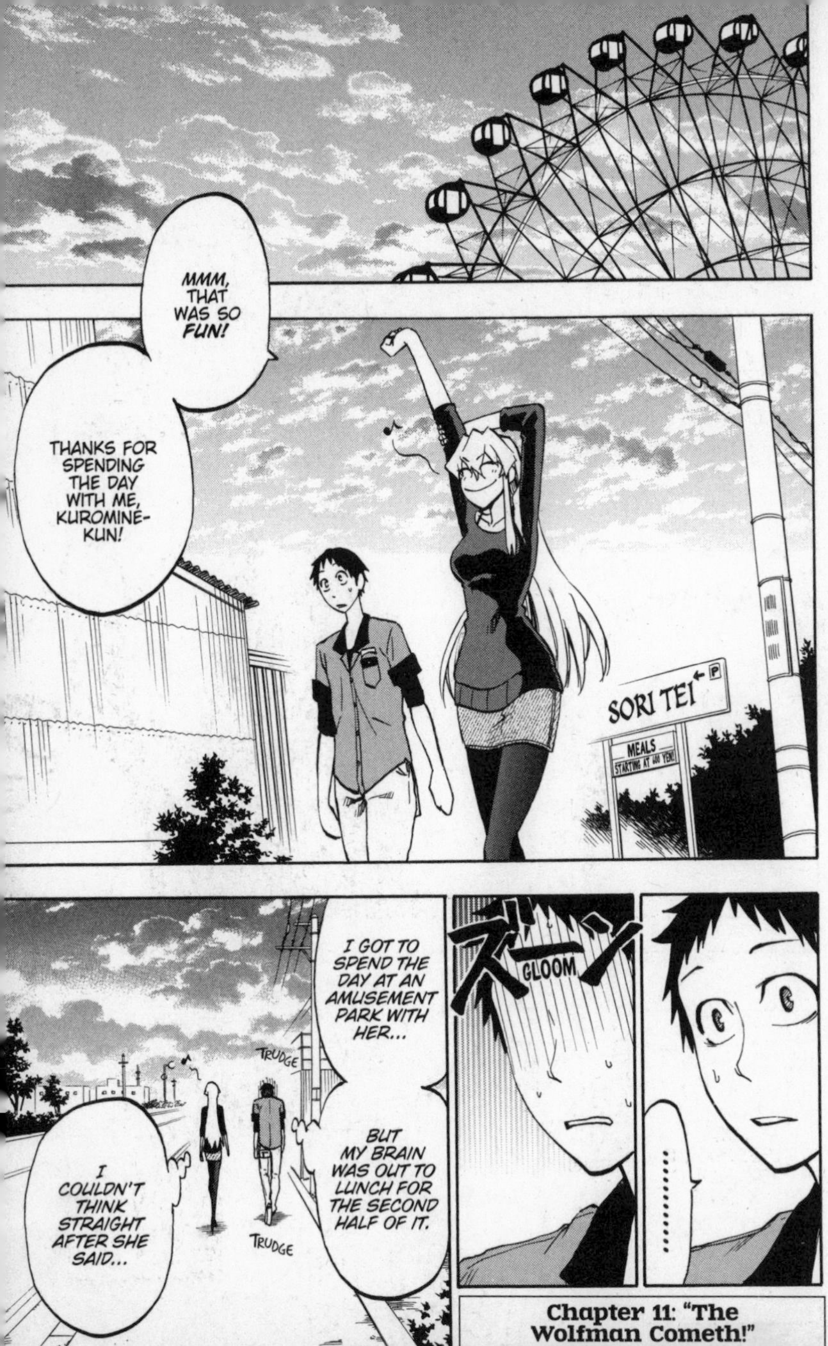
MMM, THAT WAS SO *FUN!*
THANKS FOR SPENDING THE DAY WITH ME, KUROMINE-KUN!
SORI TEI
P
MEALS
......
GLOOM
I GOT TO SPEND THE DAY AT AN AMUSEMENT PARK WITH HER...
BUT MY BRAIN WAS OUT TO LUNCH FOR THE SECOND HALF OF IT.
TRUDGE
TRUDGE
I COULDN'T THINK STRAIGHT AFTER SHE SAID...

Chapter 11: "The Wolfman Cometh!"

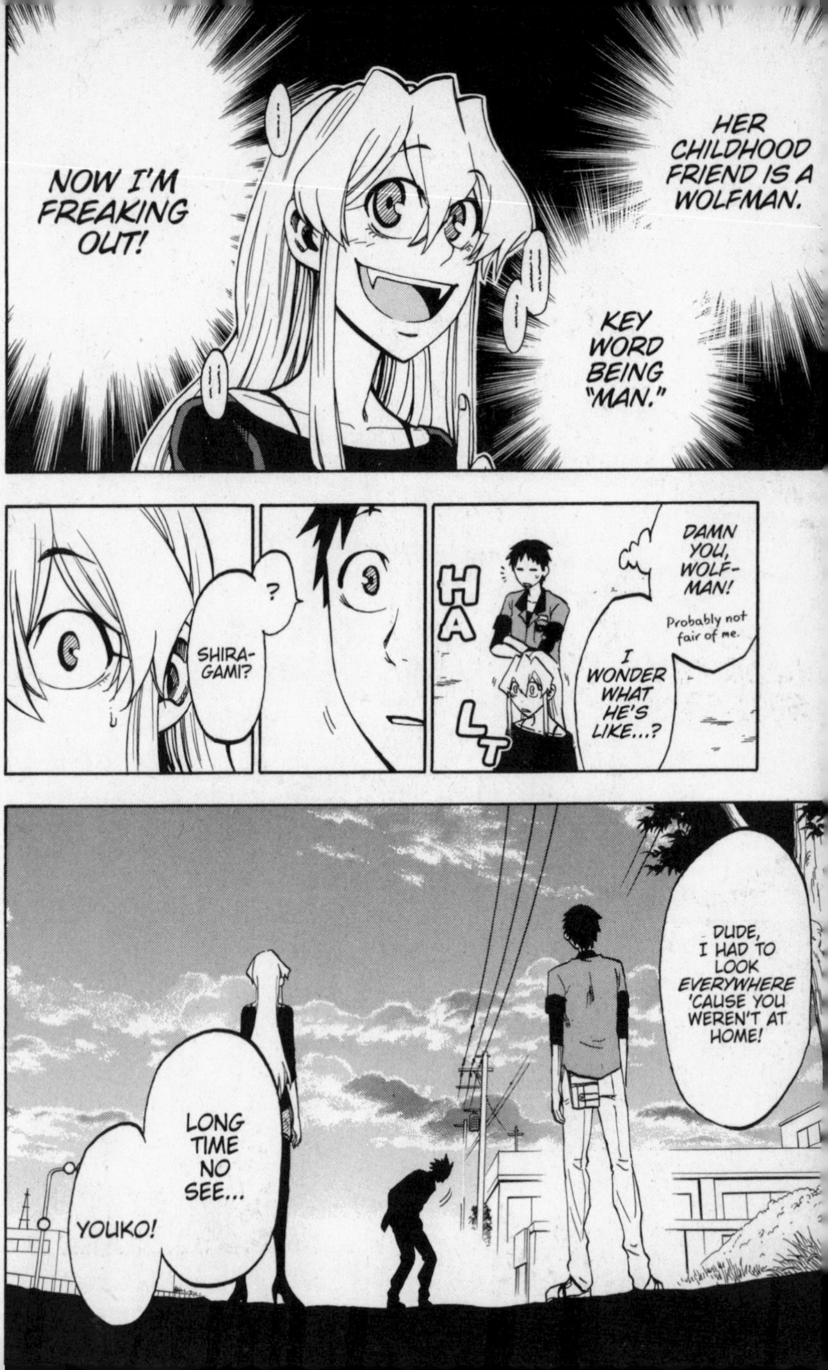
HER CHILDHOOD FRIEND IS A WOLFMAN.
KEY WORD BEING "MAN."
NOW I'M FREAKING OUT!
DAMN YOU, WOLF-MAN!
Probably not fair of me.
I WONDER WHAT HE'S LIKE...?
HALT
?
SHIRA-GAMI?
DUDE, I HAD TO LOOK EVERYWHERE 'CAUSE YOU WEREN'T AT HOME!
LONG TIME NO SEE...
YOUKO!

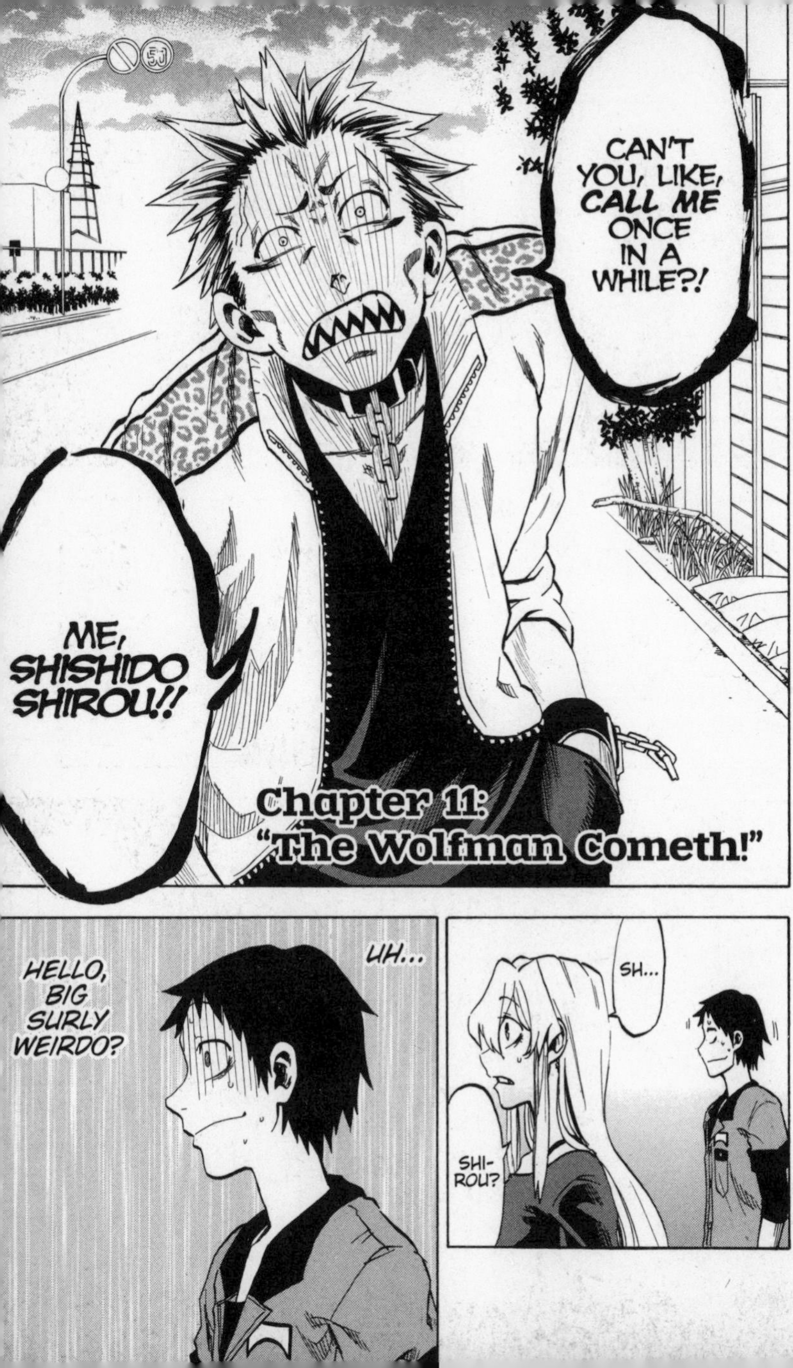
CAN'T YOU, LIKE, CALL ME ONCE IN A WHILE?!
ME, SHISHIDO SHIROU!!
Chapter 11: "The Wolfman Cometh!"
SH...
SHI-ROU?
UH...
HELLO, BIG SURLY WEIRDO?

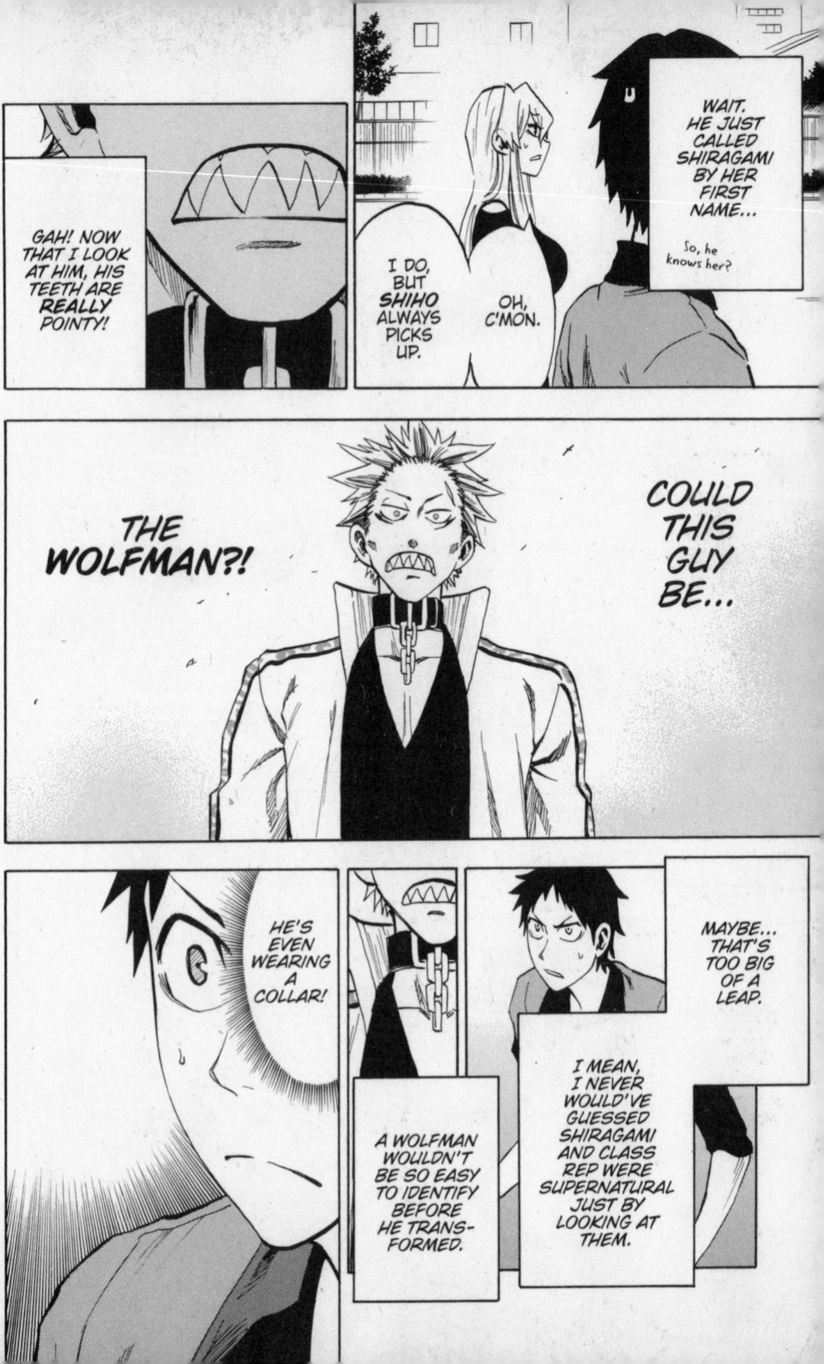

WAIT. HE JUST CALLED SHIRAGAMI BY HER FIRST NAME...
So, he knows her?
OH, C'MON.
I DO, BUT SHIHO ALWAYS PICKS UP.
GAH! NOW THAT I LOOK AT HIM, HIS TEETH ARE REALLY POINTY!
COULD THIS GUY BE...
THE WOLFMAN?!
MAYBE... THAT'S TOO BIG OF A LEAP.
I MEAN, I NEVER WOULD'VE GUESSED SHIRAGAMI AND CLASS REP WERE SUPERNATURAL JUST BY LOOKING AT THEM.
A WOLFMAN WOULDN'T BE SO EASY TO IDENTIFY BEFORE HE TRANSFORMED.
HE'S EVEN WEARING A COLLAR!

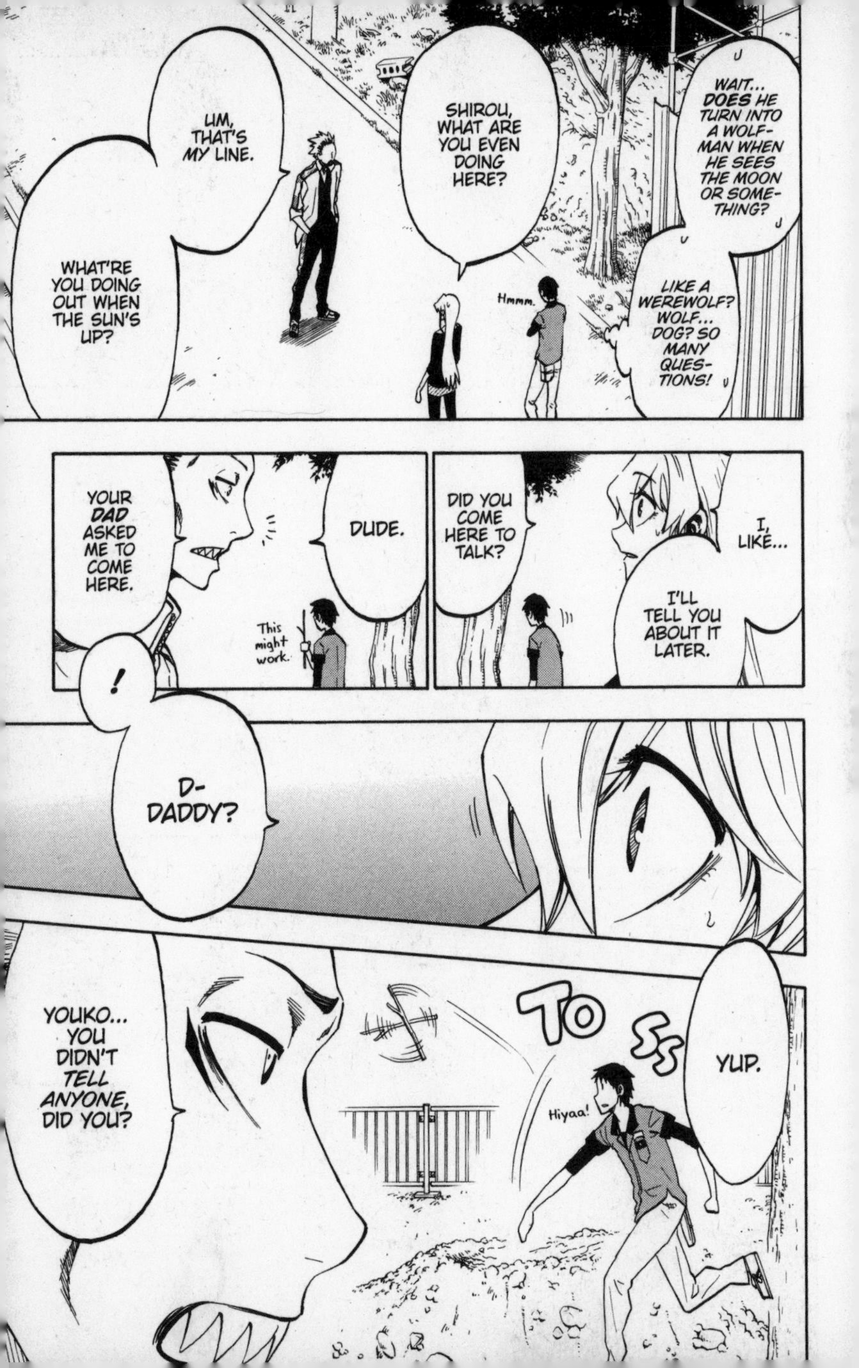
WAIT... DOES HE TURN INTO A WOLF-MAN WHEN HE SEES THE MOON OR SOMETHING?
LIKE A WEREWOLF? WOLF... DOG? SO MANY QUESTIONS!
SHIROU, WHAT ARE YOU EVEN DOING HERE?
Hmmm.
UM, THAT'S MY LINE.
WHAT'RE YOU DOING OUT WHEN THE SUN'S UP?
I, LIKE...
I'LL TELL YOU ABOUT IT LATER.
DID YOU COME HERE TO TALK?
DUDE.
This might work.
YOUR DAD ASKED ME TO COME HERE.
!
D-DADDY?
YUP.
TOSS
Hiyaa!
YOUKO... YOU DIDN'T TELL ANYONE, DID YOU?

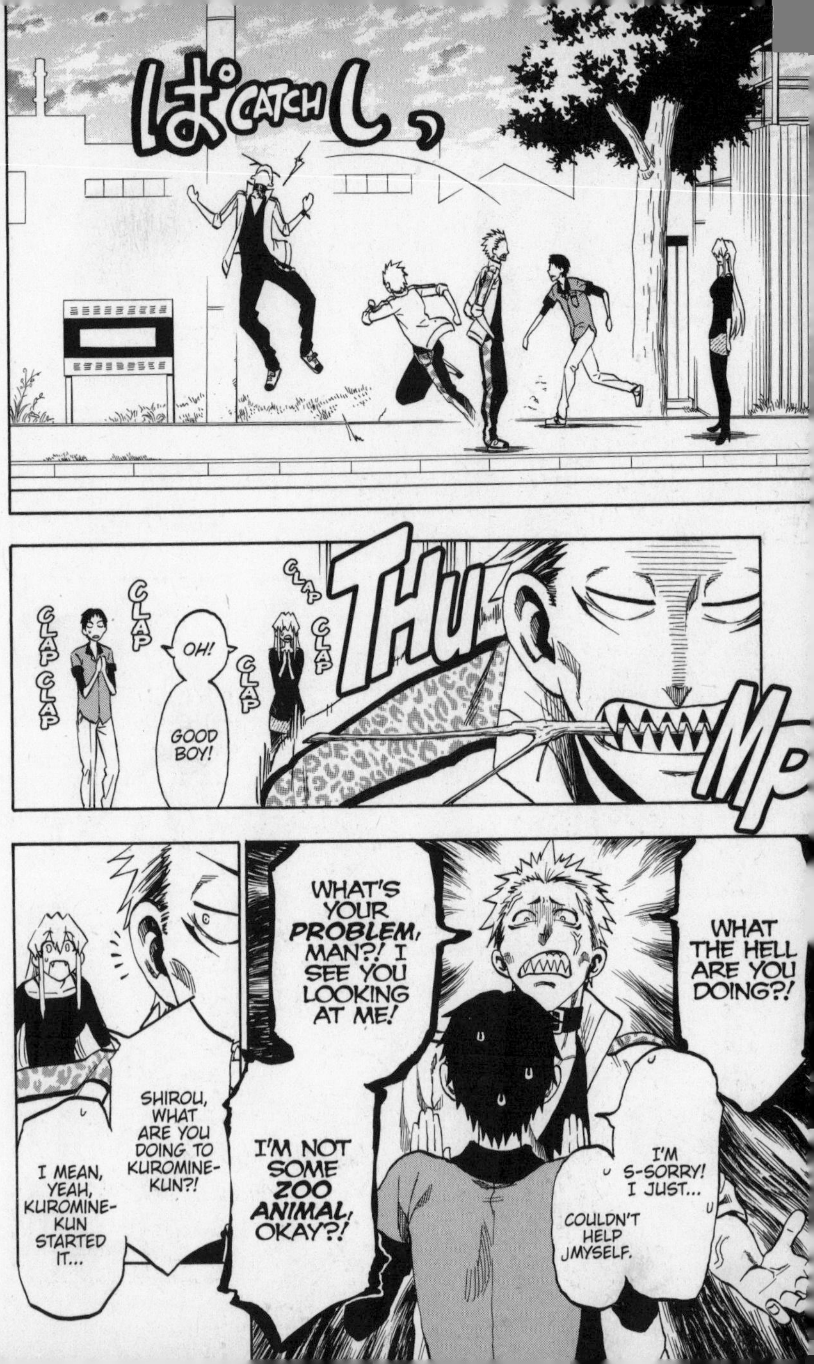
ぱCATCHし、
THUMP
CLAP CLAP
CLAP
OH!
GOOD BOY!
CLAP
CLAP
CLAP CLAP
WHAT THE HELL ARE YOU DOING?!
WHAT'S YOUR PROBLEM, MAN?! I SEE YOU LOOKING AT ME!
I'M S-SORRY! I JUST...
COULDN'T HELP MYSELF.
I'M NOT SOME ZOO ANIMAL, OKAY?!
SHIROU, WHAT ARE YOU DOING TO KUROMINE-KUN?!
I MEAN, YEAH, KUROMINE-KUN STARTED IT...

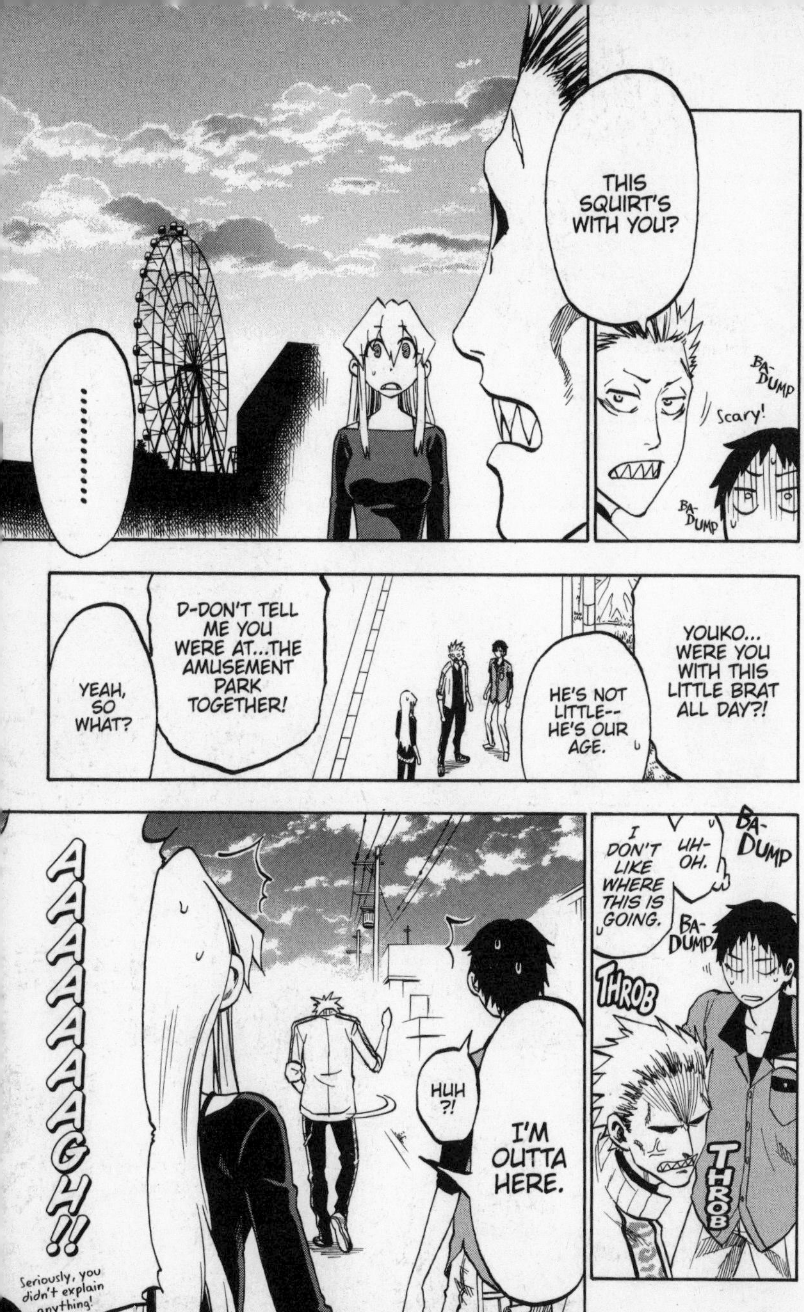
THIS SQUIRT'S WITH YOU?
BA-DUMP
Scary!
BA-DUMP
....
YOUKO... WERE YOU WITH THIS LITTLE BRAT ALL DAY?!
HE'S NOT LITTLE-- HE'S OUR AGE.
D-DON'T TELL ME YOU WERE AT...THE AMUSEMENT PARK TOGETHER!
YEAH, SO WHAT?
BA-DUMP
UH-OH.
I DON'T LIKE WHERE THIS IS GOING.
BA-DUMP
THROB
THROB
I'M OUTTA HERE.
HUH?!
AAAAAAAGH!!
Seriously, you didn't explain anything!

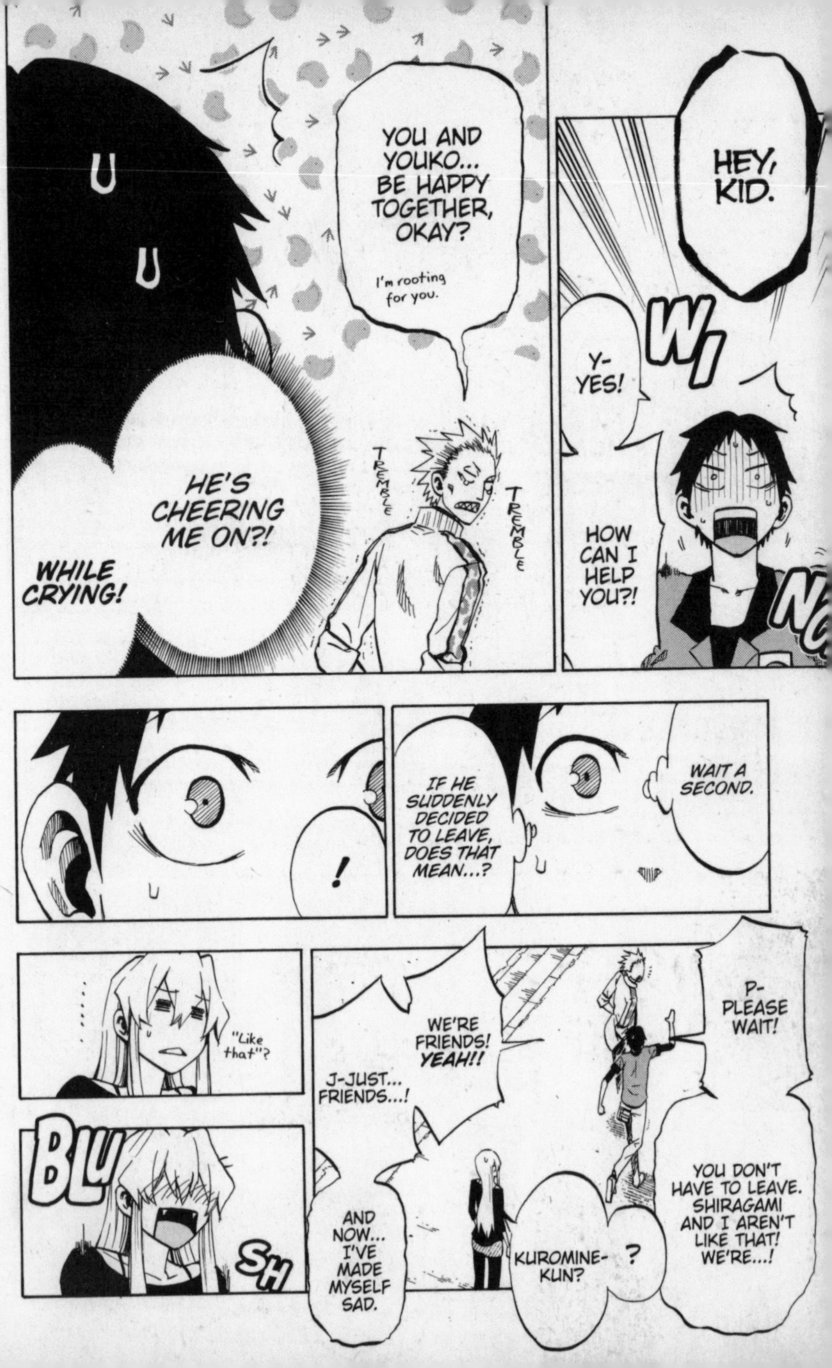
HEY, KID.
WI
Y- YES!
HOW CAN I HELP YOU?!
N
YOU AND YOUKO... BE HAPPY TOGETHER, OKAY?
I'm rooting for you.
TREMBLE
TREMBLE
HE'S CHEERING ME ON?!
WHILE CRYING!
WAIT A SECOND.
IF HE SUDDENLY DECIDED TO LEAVE, DOES THAT MEAN...?
!
P- PLEASE WAIT!
YOU DON'T HAVE TO LEAVE. SHIRAGAMI AND I AREN'T LIKE THAT! WE'RE...!
KUROMINE-KUN?
?
WE'RE FRIENDS! YEAH!!
J-JUST... FRIENDS...!
AND NOW... I'VE MADE MYSELF SAD.
.....
"Like that"?
BLU
SH

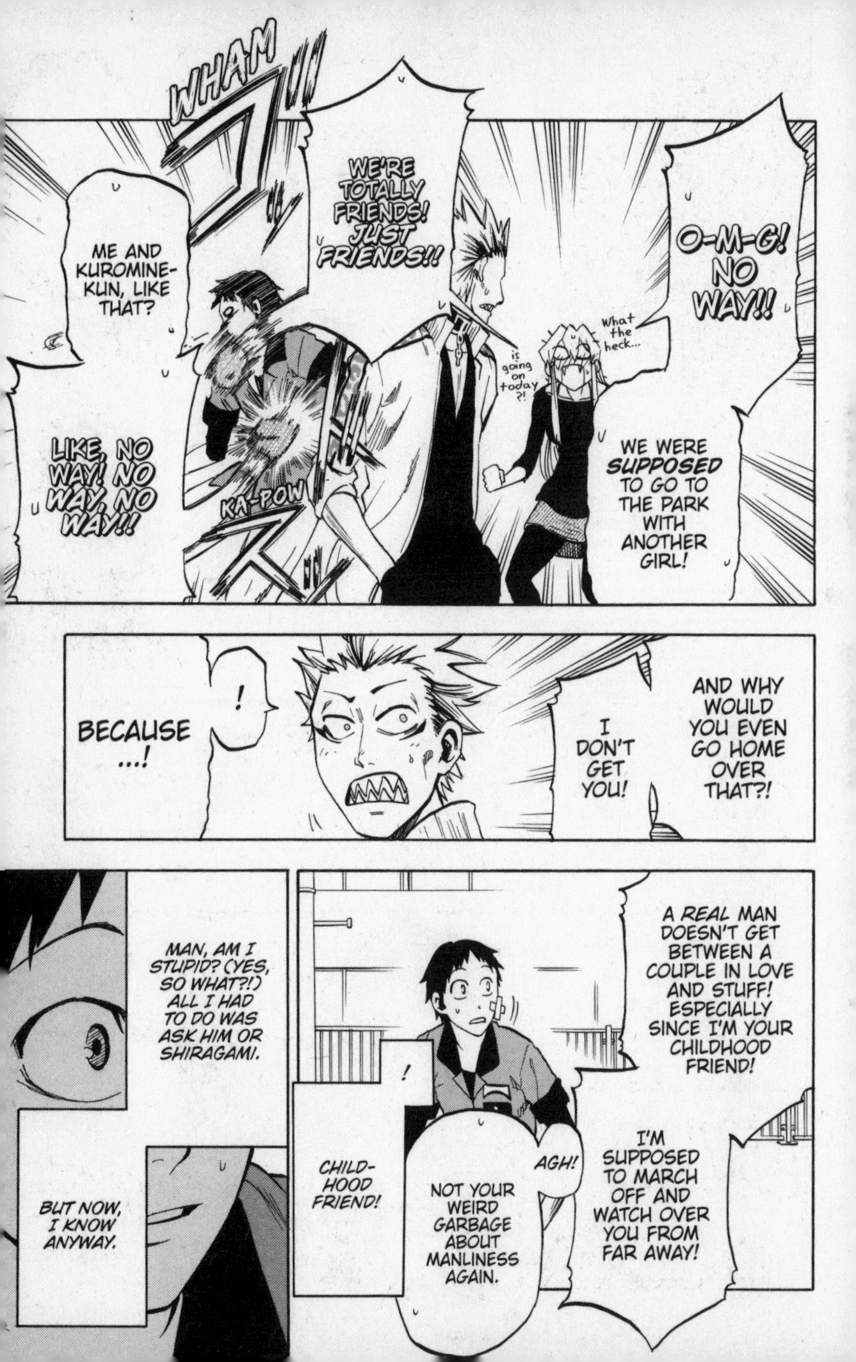
O-M-G! NO WAY!!
WE WERE SUPPOSED TO GO TO THE PARK WITH ANOTHER GIRL!
What the heck... is going on today?!
WE'RE TOTALLY FRIENDS! JUST FRIENDS!!
WHAM
ME AND KUROMINE-KUN, LIKE THAT?
LIKE, NO WAY! NO WAY, NO WAY!!
KA-POW
AND WHY WOULD YOU EVEN GO HOME OVER THAT?!
I DON'T GET YOU!
!
BECAUSE ...!
A REAL MAN DOESN'T GET BETWEEN A COUPLE IN LOVE AND STUFF! ESPECIALLY SINCE I'M YOUR CHILDHOOD FRIEND!
I'M SUPPOSED TO MARCH OFF AND WATCH OVER YOU FROM FAR AWAY!
AGH!
NOT YOUR WEIRD GARBAGE ABOUT MANLINESS AGAIN.
!
CHILD-HOOD FRIEND!
MAN, AM I STUPID? (YES, SO WHAT?!) ALL I HAD TO DO WAS ASK HIM OR SHIRAGAMI.
BUT NOW, I KNOW ANYWAY.

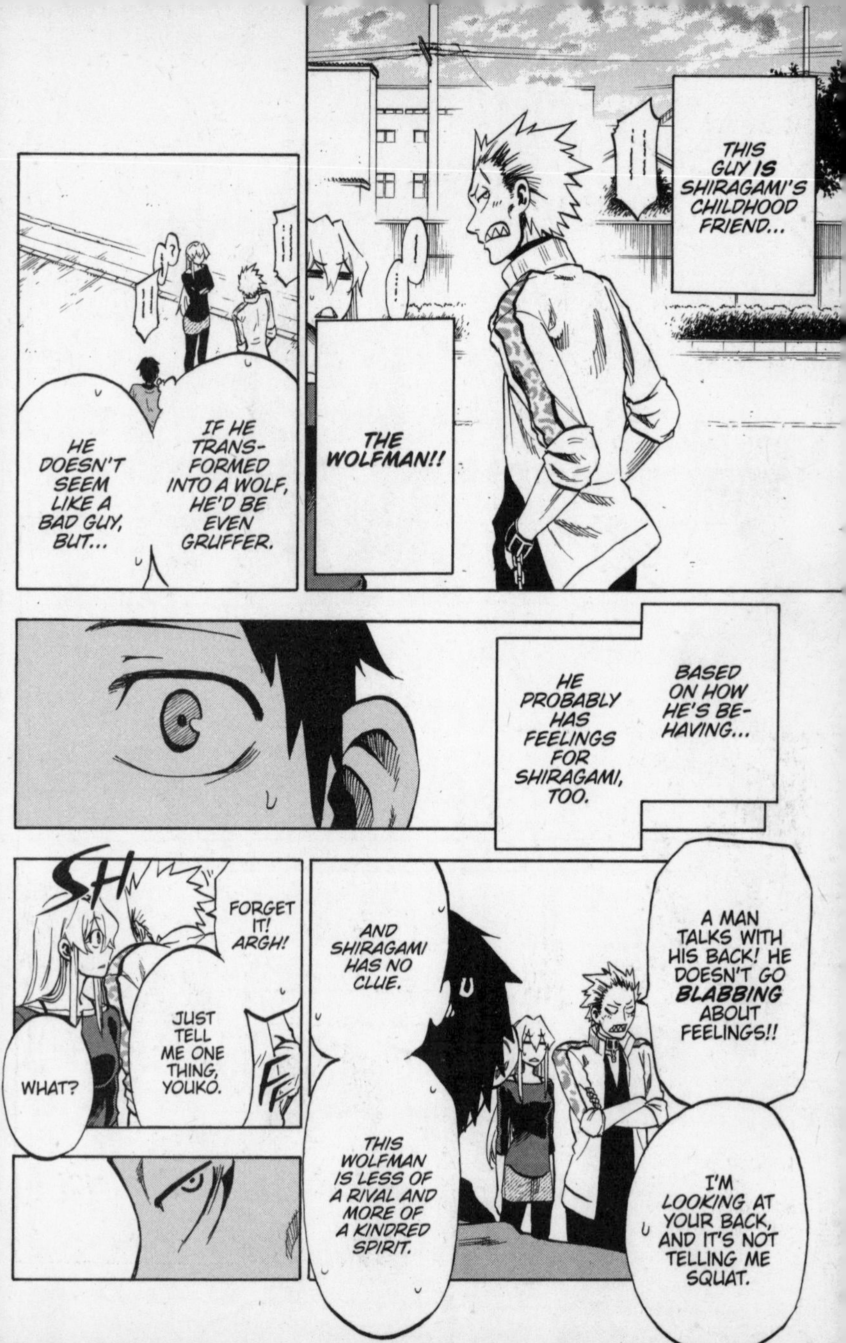
THIS GUY IS SHIRAGAMI'S CHILDHOOD FRIEND...
THE WOLFMAN!!
IF HE TRANS-FORMED INTO A WOLF, HE'D BE EVEN GRUFFER.
HE DOESN'T SEEM LIKE A BAD GUY, BUT...
BASED ON HOW HE'S BE-HAVING...
HE PROBABLY HAS FEELINGS FOR SHIRAGAMI, TOO.
A MAN TALKS WITH HIS BACK! HE DOESN'T GO BLABBING ABOUT FEELINGS!!
AND SHIRAGAMI HAS NO CLUE.
I'M LOOKING AT YOUR BACK, AND IT'S NOT TELLING ME SQUAT.
THIS WOLFMAN IS LESS OF A RIVAL AND MORE OF A KINDRED SPIRIT.
SH
FORGET IT! ARGH!
JUST TELL ME ONE THING, YOUKO.
WHAT?

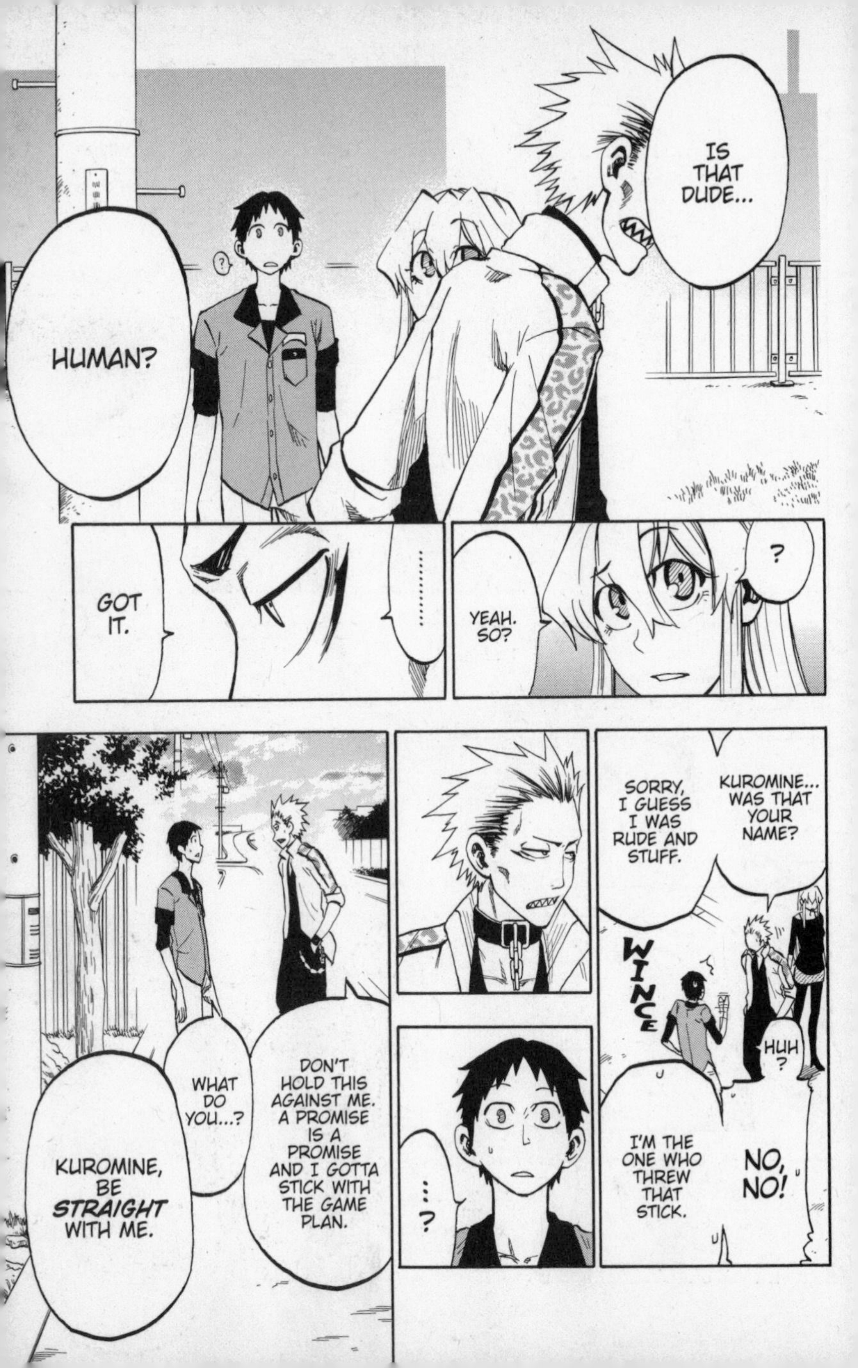
IS THAT DUDE...
HUMAN?
?
YEAH. SO?
......
GOT IT.
KUROMINE... WAS THAT YOUR NAME?
SORRY, I GUESS I WAS RUDE AND STUFF.
WINCE
HUH?
NO, NO!
I'M THE ONE WHO THREW THAT STICK.
...?
DON'T HOLD THIS AGAINST ME. A PROMISE IS A PROMISE AND I GOTTA STICK WITH THE GAME PLAN.
WHAT DO YOU...?
KUROMINE, BE STRAIGHT WITH ME.

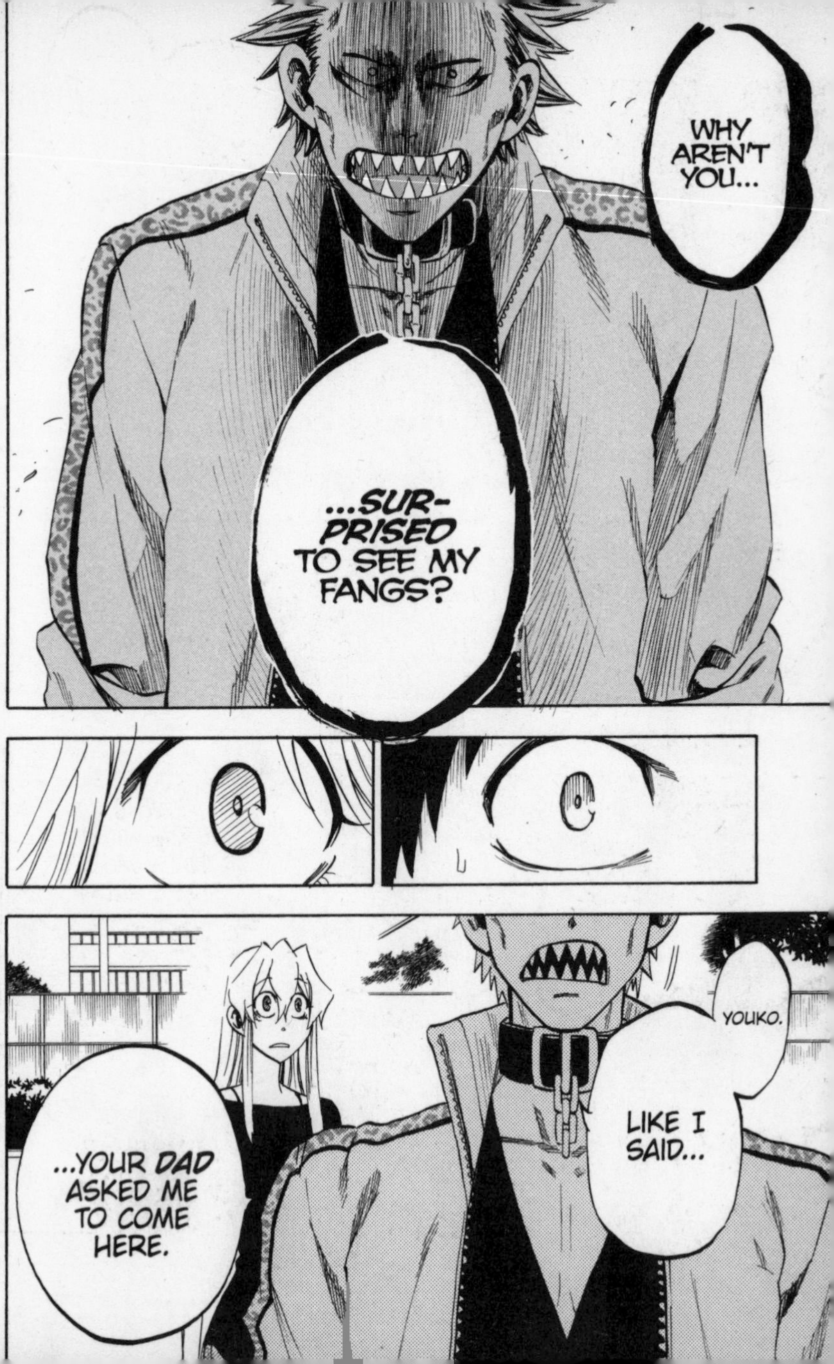
WHY AREN'T YOU...
...SUR-PRISED TO SEE MY FANGS?
YOUKO.
LIKE I SAID...
...YOUR DAD ASKED ME TO COME HERE.

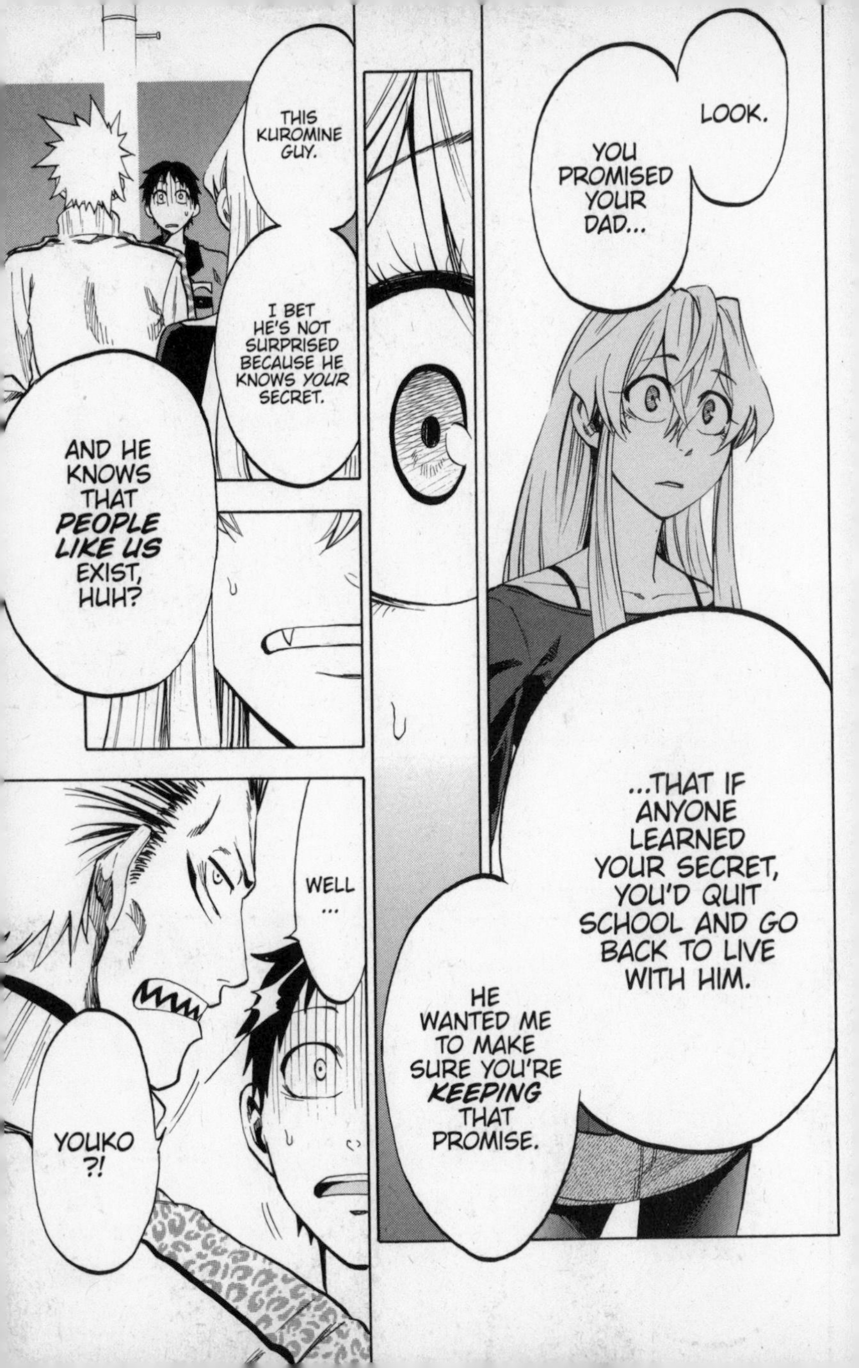
LOOK.
YOU PROMISED YOUR DAD...
...THAT IF ANYONE LEARNED YOUR SECRET, YOU'D QUIT SCHOOL AND GO BACK TO LIVE WITH HIM.
HE WANTED ME TO MAKE SURE YOU'RE *KEEPING* THAT PROMISE.
THIS KUROMINE GUY.
I BET HE'S NOT SURPRISED BECAUSE HE KNOWS *YOUR* SECRET.
AND HE KNOWS THAT ***PEOPLE LIKE US*** EXIST, HUH?
WELL ...
YOUKO ?!

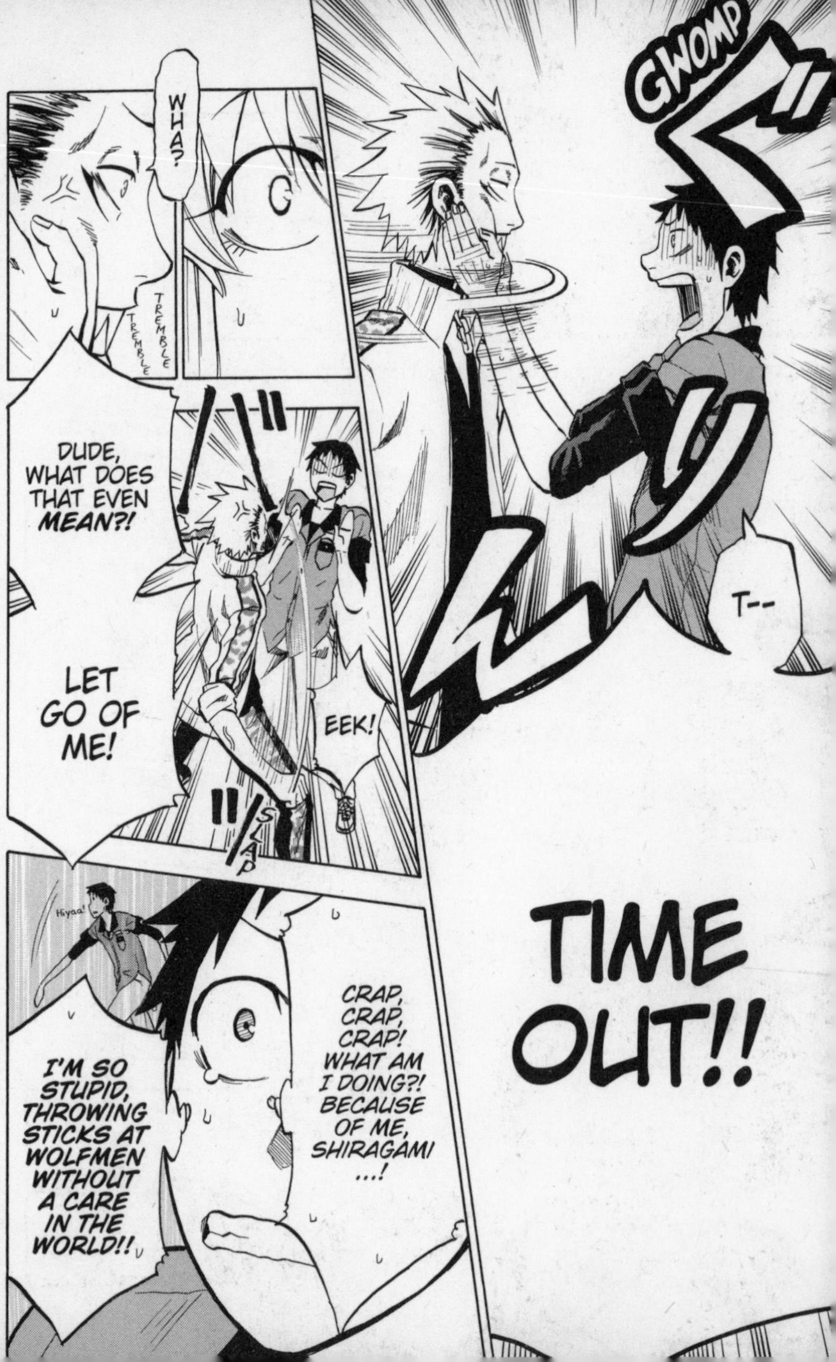
GWOMP
T--
TIME OUT!!
WHA?
TREMBLE TREMBLE
DUDE, WHAT DOES THAT EVEN MEAN?!
LET GO OF ME!
EEK!
SLAP
Hiyaa!
CRAP, CRAP, CRAP! WHAT AM I DOING?! BECAUSE OF ME, SHIRAGAMI ...!
I'M SO STUPID, THROWING STICKS AT WOLFMEN WITHOUT A CARE IN THE WORLD!!

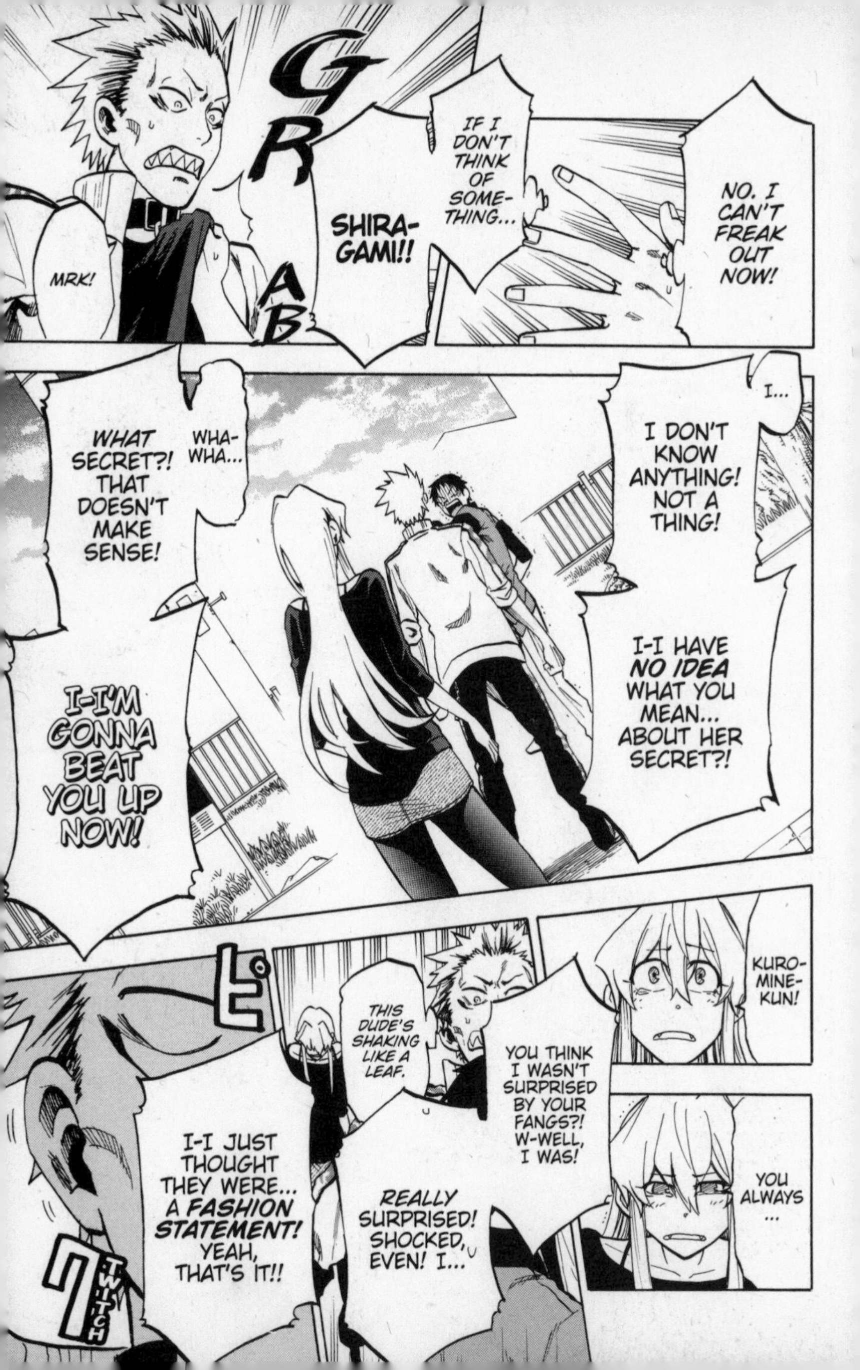
NO. I CAN'T FREAK OUT NOW!
IF I DON'T THINK OF SOME-THING...
SHIRA-GAMI!!
GRAB
MRK!
I...
I DON'T KNOW ANYTHING! NOT A THING!
I-I HAVE NO IDEA WHAT YOU MEAN... ABOUT HER SECRET?!
WHA-WHA...
WHAT SECRET?! THAT DOESN'T MAKE SENSE!
I-I'M GONNA BEAT YOU UP NOW!
KURO-MINE-KUN!
YOU ALWAYS ...
THIS DUDE'S SHAKING LIKE A LEAF.
YOU THINK I WASN'T SURPRISED BY YOUR FANGS?! W-WELL, I WAS!
REALLY SURPRISED! SHOCKED, EVEN! I...
I-I JUST THOUGHT THEY WERE... A FASHION STATEMENT! YEAH, THAT'S IT!!
TWITCH

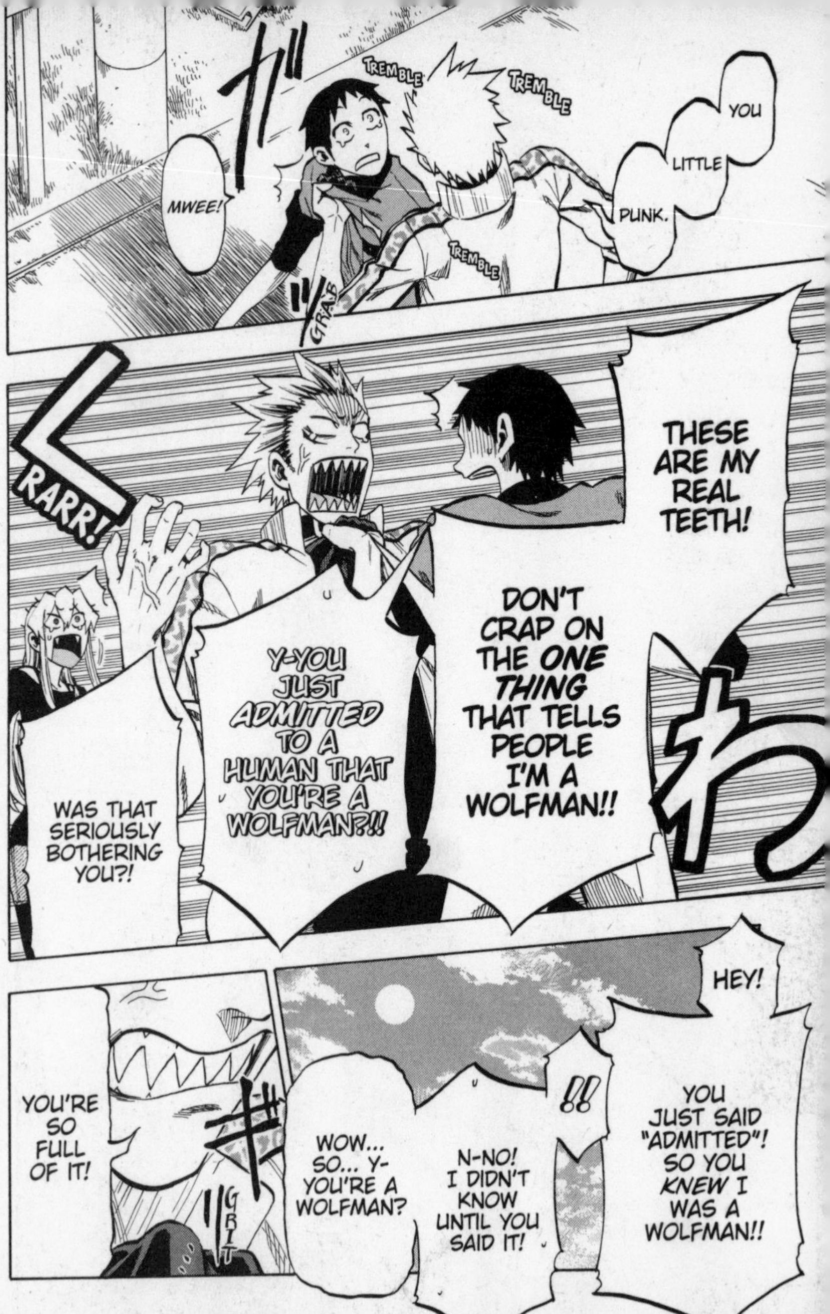
YOU LITTLE PUNK.
TREMBLE
TREMBLE
TREMBLE
MWEE!
GRAB
THESE ARE MY REAL TEETH!
DON'T CRAP ON THE *ONE THING* THAT TELLS PEOPLE I'M A WOLFMAN!!
Y-YOU JUST *ADMITTED* TO A HUMAN THAT YOU'RE A WOLFMAN?!!
RARR!
WAS THAT SERIOUSLY BOTHERING YOU?!
HEY!
YOU JUST SAID "ADMITTED"! SO YOU *KNEW* I WAS A WOLFMAN!!
!!
N-NO! I DIDN'T KNOW UNTIL YOU SAID IT!
WOW... SO... Y-YOU'RE A WOLFMAN?
YOU'RE SO FULL OF IT!
GRIT

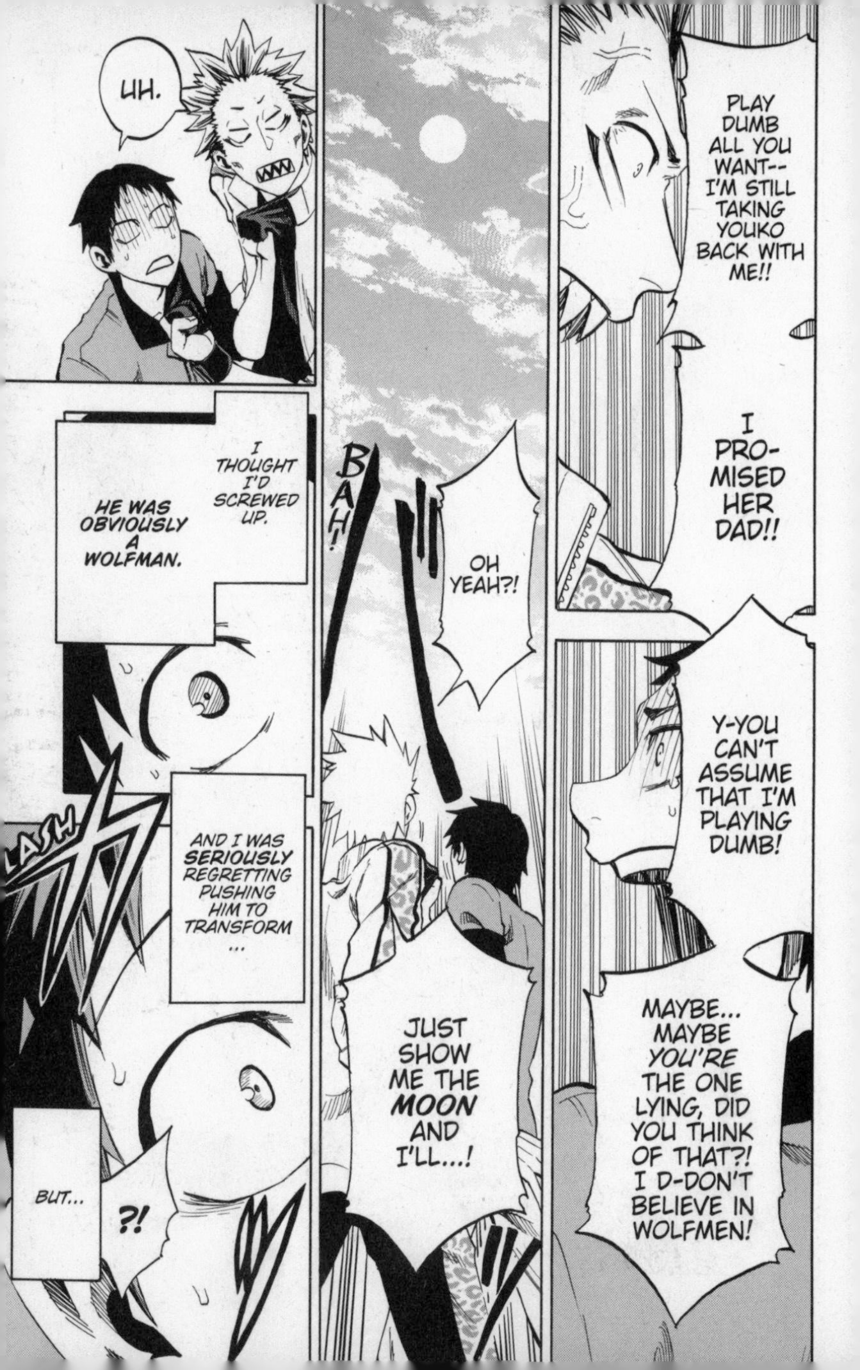
PLAY DUMB ALL YOU WANT-- I'M STILL TAKING YOUKO BACK WITH ME!!
I PROMISED HER DAD!!
Y-YOU CAN'T ASSUME THAT I'M PLAYING DUMB!
MAYBE... MAYBE YOU'RE THE ONE LYING, DID YOU THINK OF THAT?! I D-DON'T BELIEVE IN WOLFMEN!
OH YEAH?!
BAH!
JUST SHOW ME THE MOON AND I'LL...!
UH.
I THOUGHT I'D SCREWED UP.
HE WAS OBVIOUSLY A WOLFMAN.
AND I WAS SERIOUSLY REGRETTING PUSHING HIM TO TRANSFORM ...
LASH
BUT...
?!

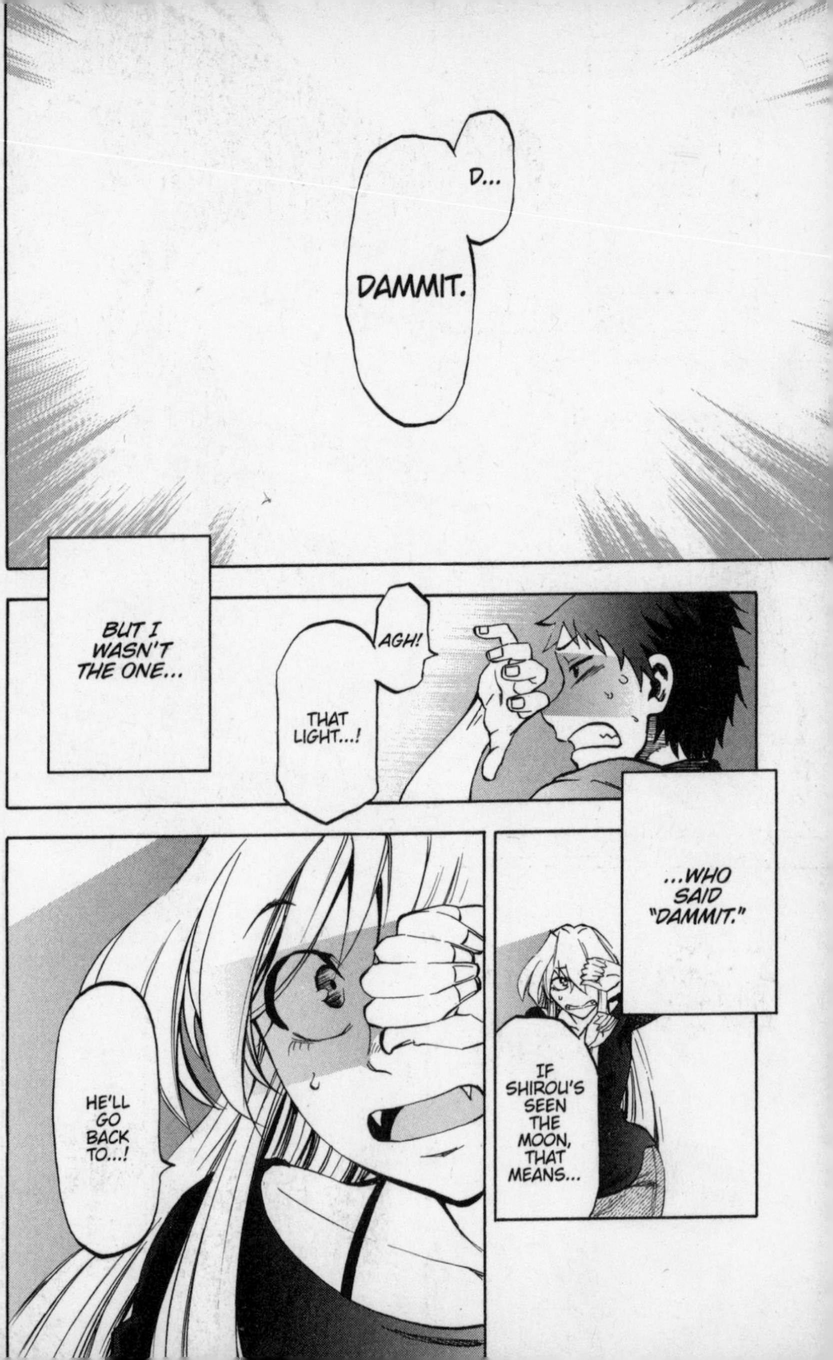
D...
DAMMIT.
AGH!
THAT LIGHT...!
BUT I WASN'T THE ONE...
...WHO SAID "DAMMIT."
IF SHIROU'S SEEN THE MOON, THAT MEANS...
HE'LL GO BACK TO...!

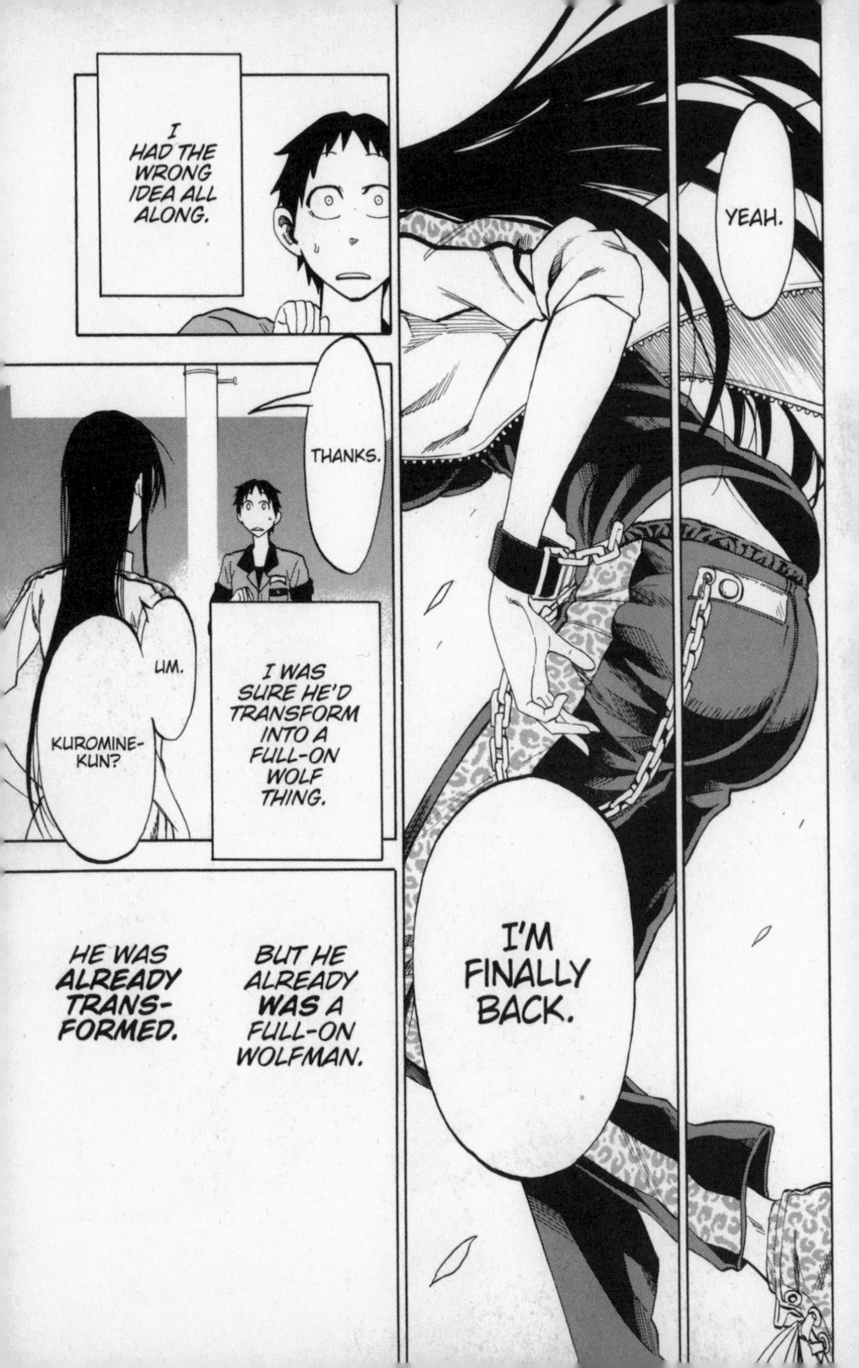
I HAD THE WRONG IDEA ALL ALONG.
I WAS SURE HE'D TRANSFORM INTO A FULL-ON WOLF THING.
UM.
KUROMINE-KUN?
THANKS.
BUT HE ALREADY WAS A FULL-ON WOLFMAN.
HE WAS ALREADY TRANS-FORMED.
YEAH.
I'M FINALLY BACK.

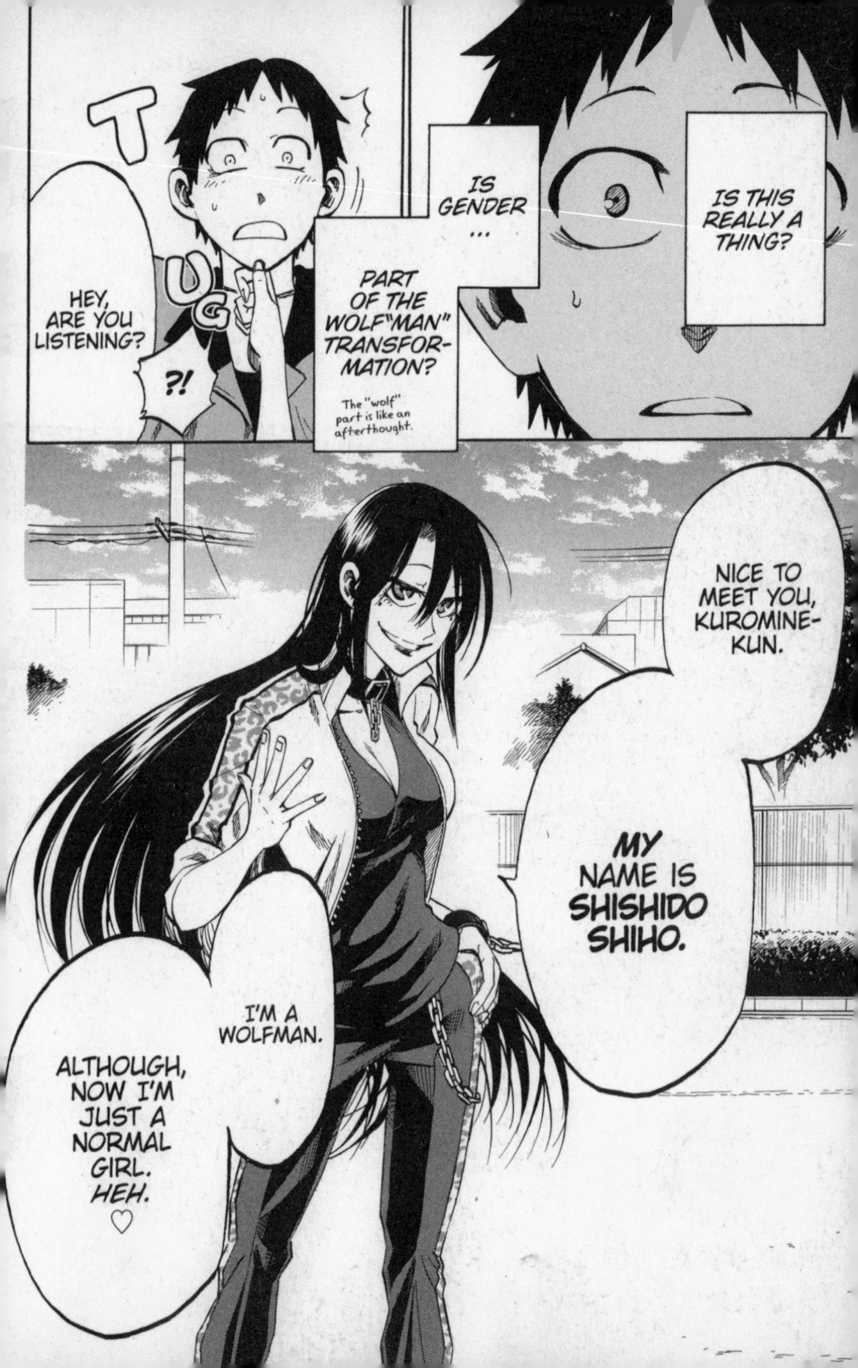
IS THIS REALLY A THING?
IS GENDER ... PART OF THE WOLF"MAN" TRANSFORMATION?
The "wolf" part is like an afterthought.
TUG
HEY, ARE YOU LISTENING?
?!
NICE TO MEET YOU, KUROMINE-KUN.
MY NAME IS SHISHIDO SHIHO.
I'M A WOLFMAN.
ALTHOUGH, NOW I'M JUST A NORMAL GIRL. HEH. ♡

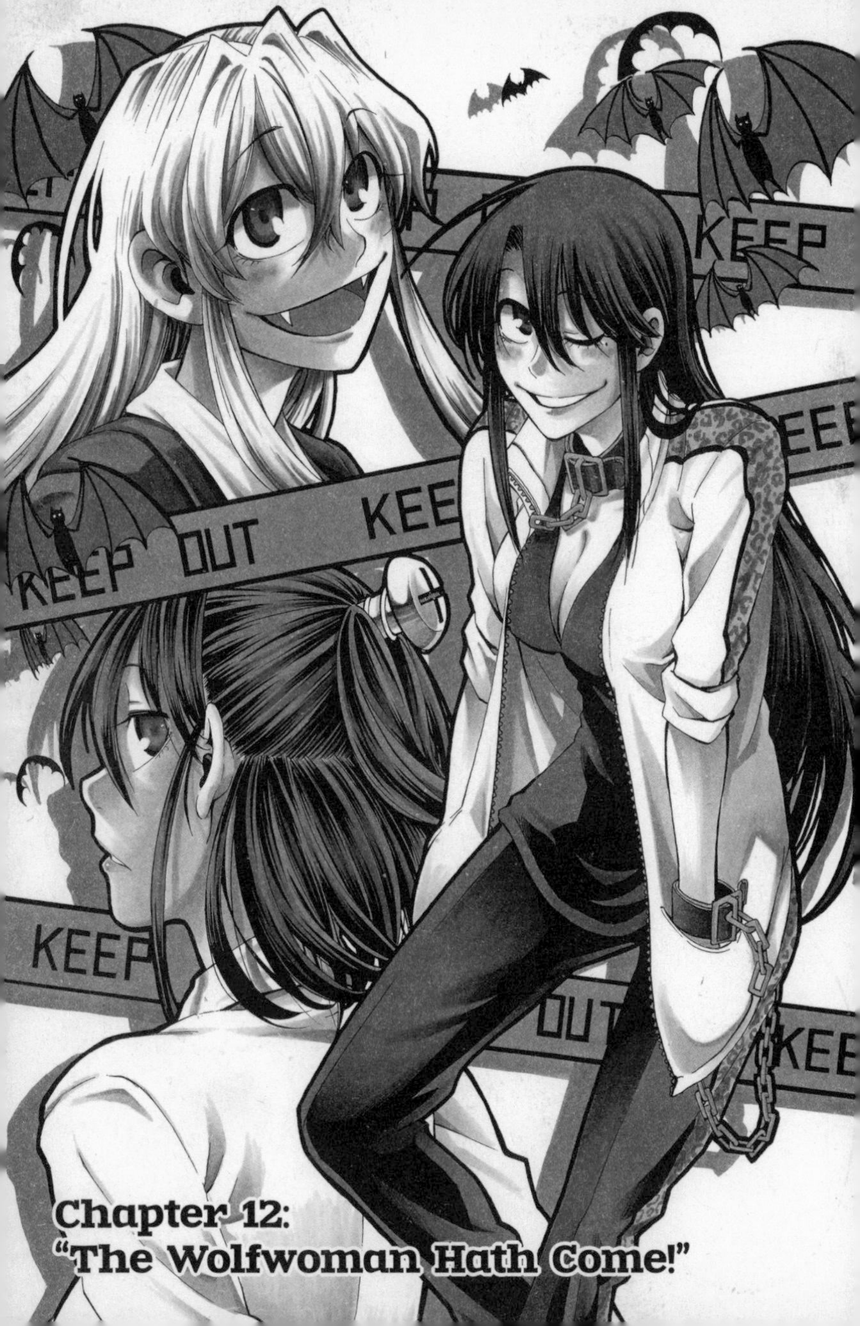
KEEP
KEEP OUT KEE
KEEP
OUT KEE

Chapter 12: "The Wolfwoman Hath Come!"

Bonus ①

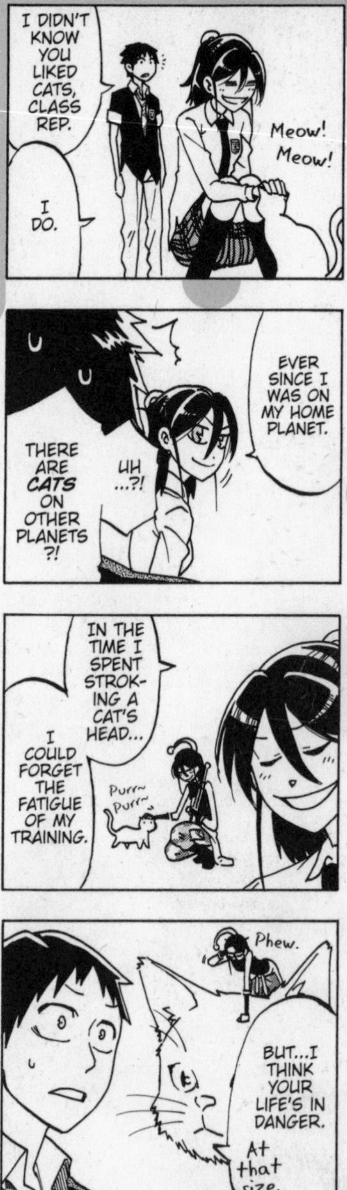
I DIDN'T KNOW YOU LIKED CATS, CLASS REP.
Meow! Meow!
I DO.
EVER SINCE I WAS ON MY HOME PLANET.
UH ...?!
THERE ARE CATS ON OTHER PLANETS ?!
IN THE TIME I SPENT STROKING A CAT'S HEAD...
I COULD FORGET THE FATIGUE OF MY TRAINING.
Purr~ Purr~
Phew.
BUT...I THINK YOUR LIFE'S IN DANGER.
At that size.

Bonus ②

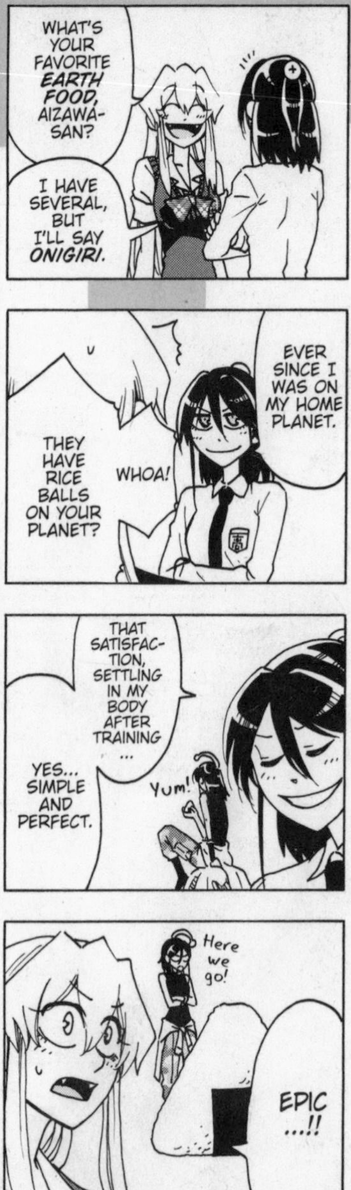
WHAT'S YOUR FAVORITE EARTH FOOD, AIZAWA-SAN?
I HAVE SEVERAL, BUT I'LL SAY ONIGIRI.
EVER SINCE I WAS ON MY HOME PLANET.
WHOA!
THEY HAVE RICE BALLS ON YOUR PLANET?
THAT SATISFACTION, SETTLING IN MY BODY AFTER TRAINING ...
Yum!
YES... SIMPLE AND PERFECT.
Here we go!
EPIC ...!!

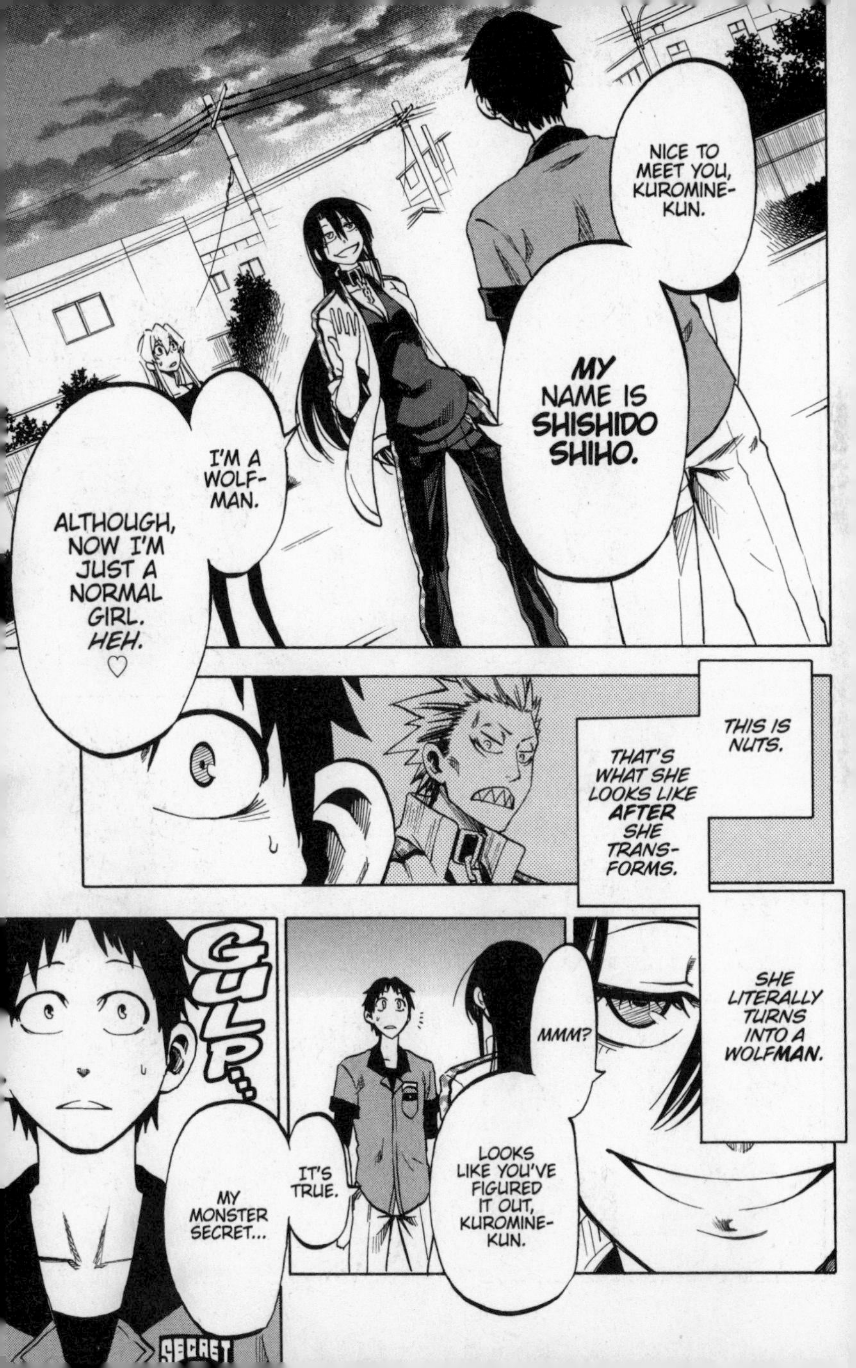
NICE TO MEET YOU, KUROMINE-KUN.
MY NAME IS SHISHIDO SHIHO.
I'M A WOLF-MAN.
ALTHOUGH, NOW I'M JUST A NORMAL GIRL. HEH. ♡
THIS IS NUTS.
THAT'S WHAT SHE LOOKS LIKE AFTER SHE TRANSFORMS.
SHE LITERALLY TURNS INTO A WOLFMAN.
MMM?
LOOKS LIKE YOU'VE FIGURED IT OUT, KUROMINE-KUN.
IT'S TRUE.
GULP...
MY MONSTER SECRET...
SECRET

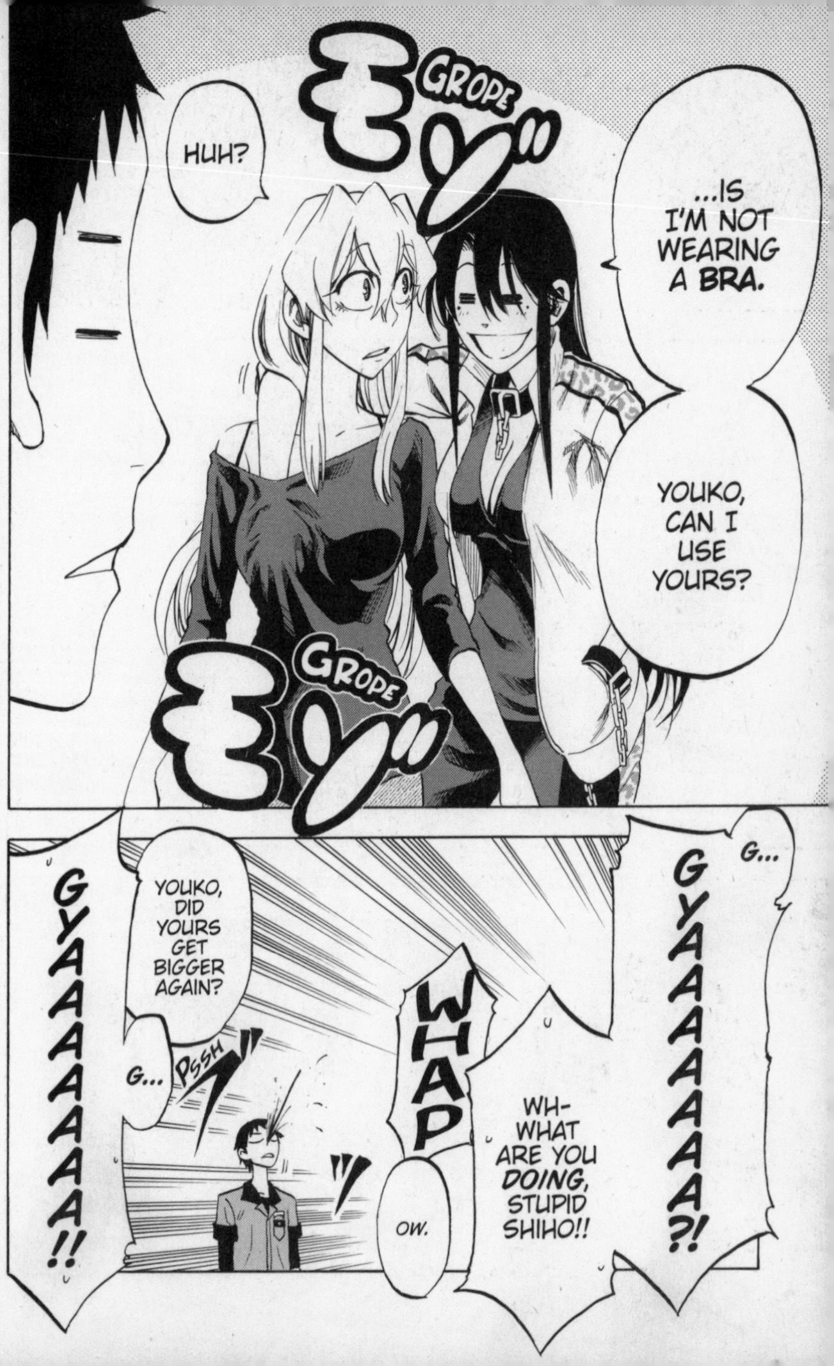
...IS I'M NOT WEARING A BRA.
YOUKO, CAN I USE YOURS?
GROPE
HUH?
GROPE
G...
GYAAAAAAAAA?!
WH- WHAT ARE YOU DOING, STUPID SHIHO!!
WHAP
OW.
YOUKO, DID YOURS GET BIGGER AGAIN?
G...
PSSH
GYAAAAAAAAAA!!

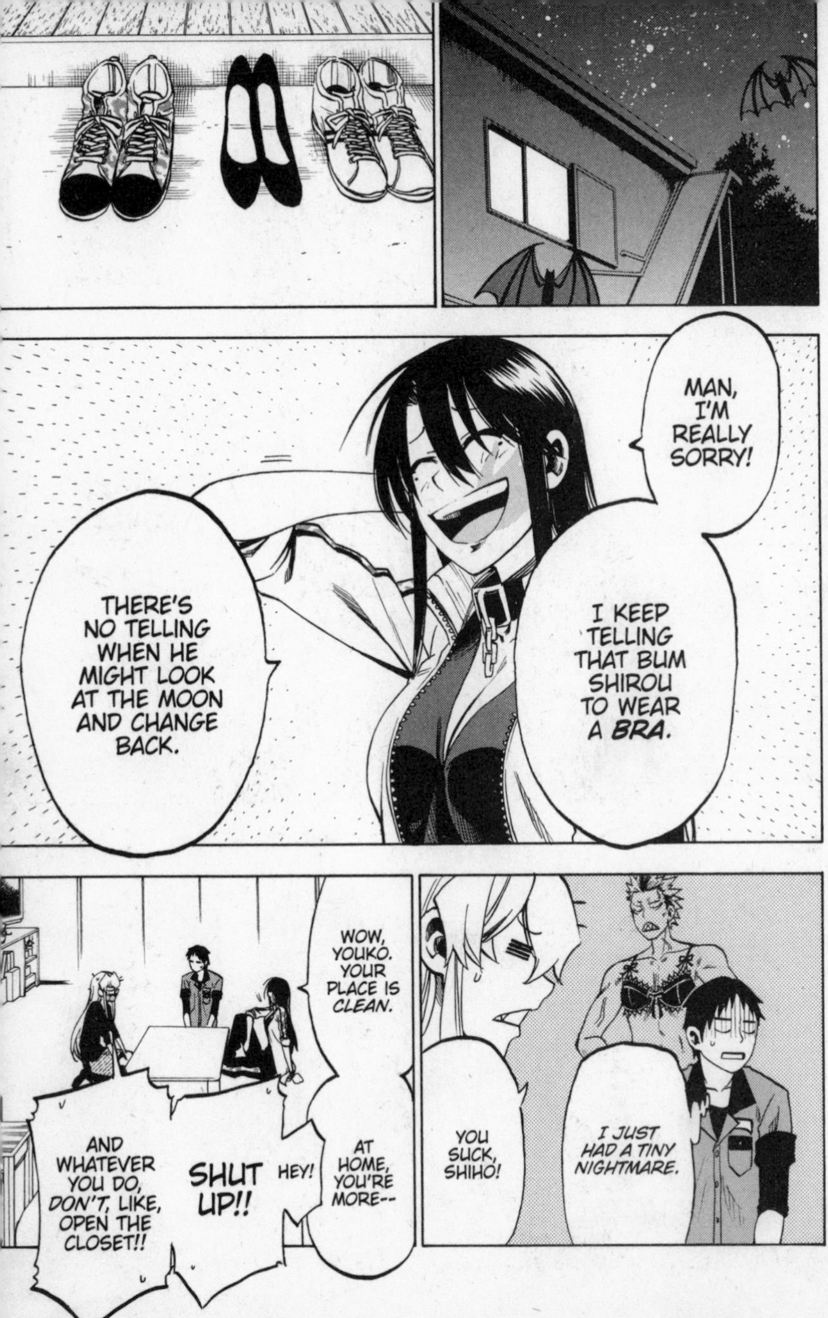
MAN, I'M REALLY SORRY!
I KEEP TELLING THAT BUM SHIROU TO WEAR A *BRA*.
THERE'S NO TELLING WHEN HE MIGHT LOOK AT THE MOON AND CHANGE BACK.
I JUST HAD A TINY NIGHTMARE.
YOU SUCK, SHIHO!
WOW, YOUKO. YOUR PLACE IS *CLEAN*.
AT HOME, YOU'RE MORE--
HEY!
SHUT UP!!
AND WHATEVER YOU DO, *DON'T*, LIKE, OPEN THE CLOSET!!

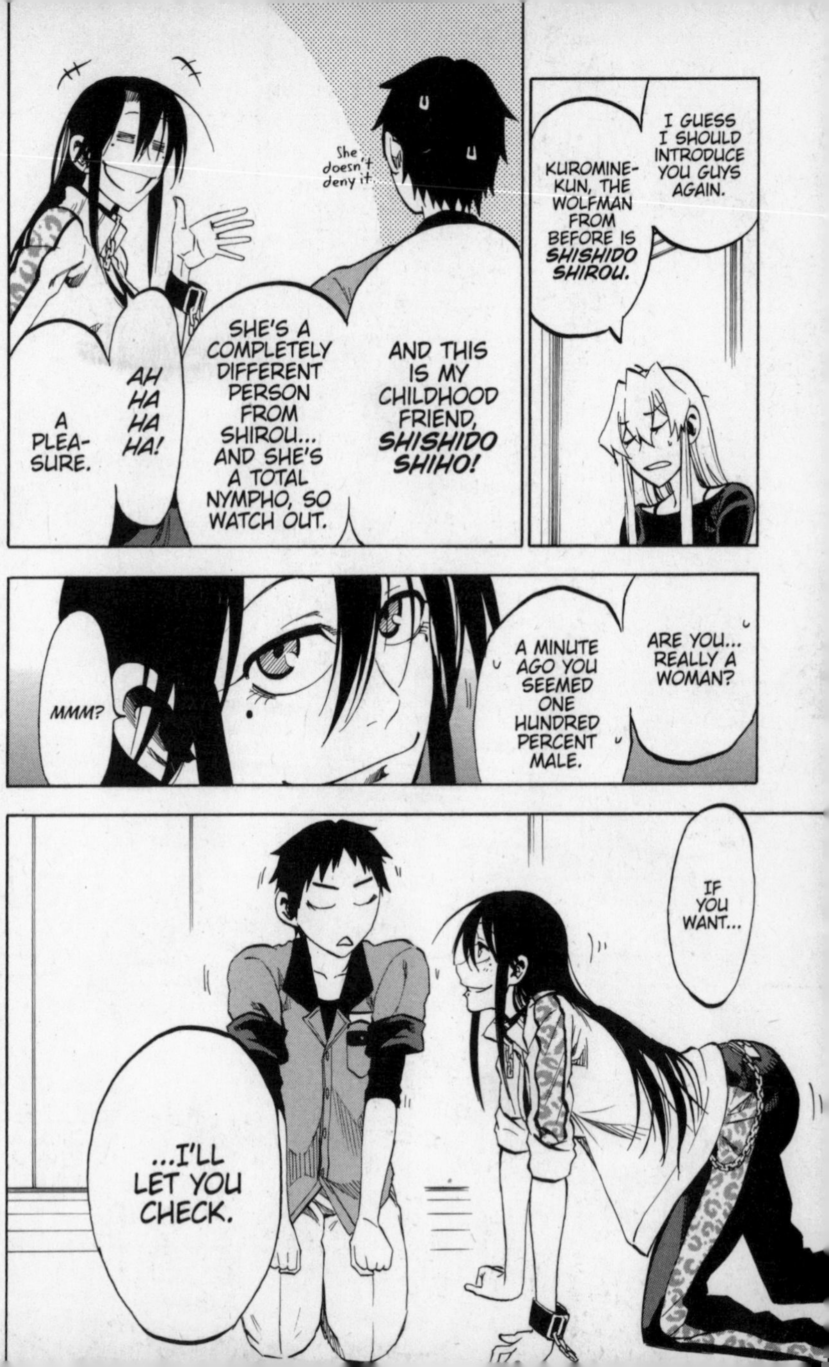
I GUESS I SHOULD INTRODUCE YOU GUYS AGAIN.
KUROMINE-KUN, THE WOLFMAN FROM BEFORE IS ***SHISHIDO SHIROU.***
AND THIS IS MY CHILDHOOD FRIEND, ***SHISHIDO SHIHO!***
She doesn't deny it.
SHE'S A COMPLETELY DIFFERENT PERSON FROM SHIROU... AND SHE'S A TOTAL NYMPHO, SO WATCH OUT.
AH HA HA HA!
A PLEASURE.
ARE YOU... REALLY A WOMAN?
A MINUTE AGO YOU SEEMED ONE HUNDRED PERCENT MALE.
MMM?
IF YOU WANT...
...I'LL LET YOU CHECK.

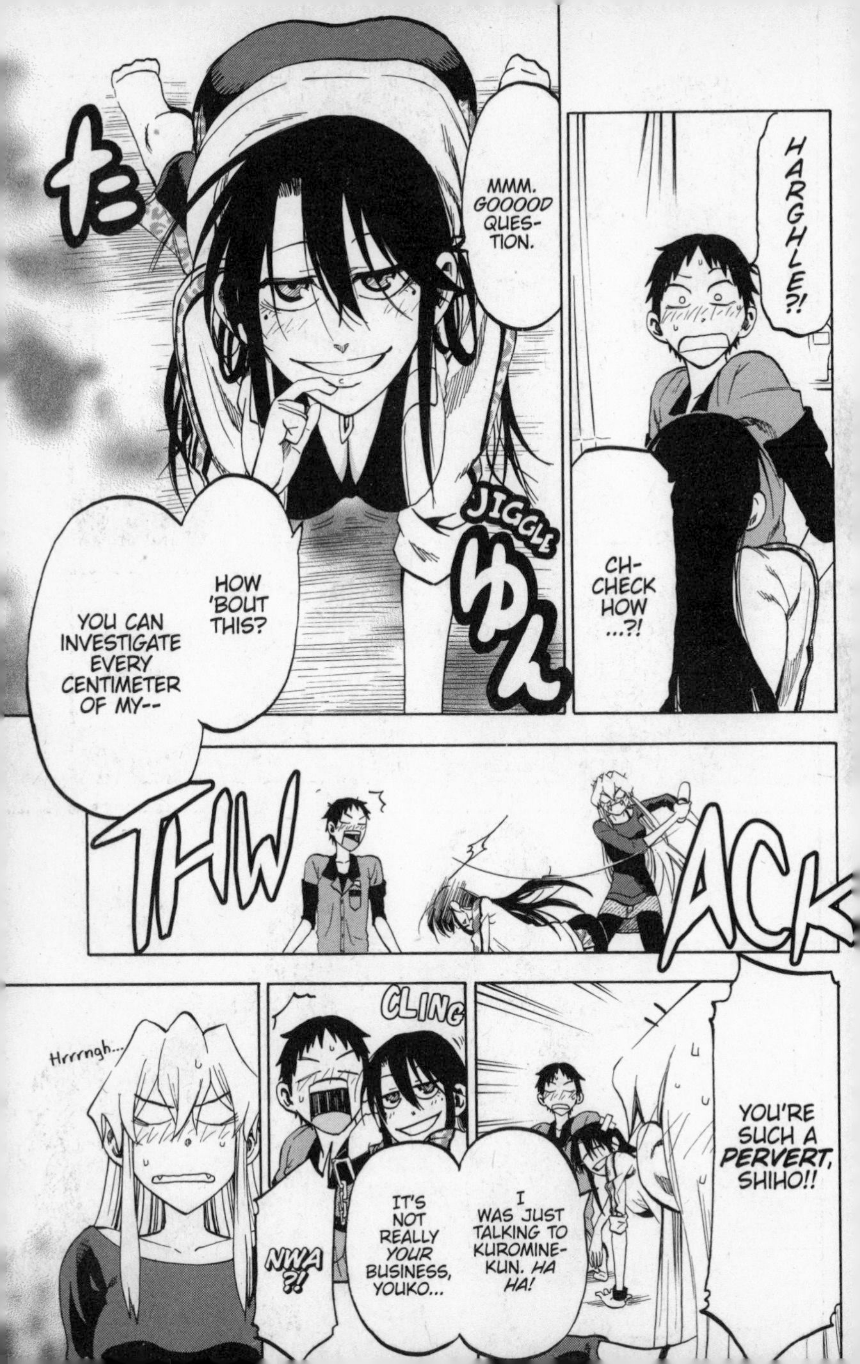
HARGHLE?!
CH-CHECK HOW...?!
MMM. GOOOOD QUESTION.
JIGGLE
HOW 'BOUT THIS?
YOU CAN INVESTIGATE EVERY CENTIMETER OF MY--
THWACK
YOU'RE SUCH A PERVERT, SHIHO!!
I WAS JUST TALKING TO KUROMINE-KUN. HA HA!
CLING
IT'S NOT REALLY YOUR BUSINESS, YOUKO...
NWA?!
Hrrrngh...

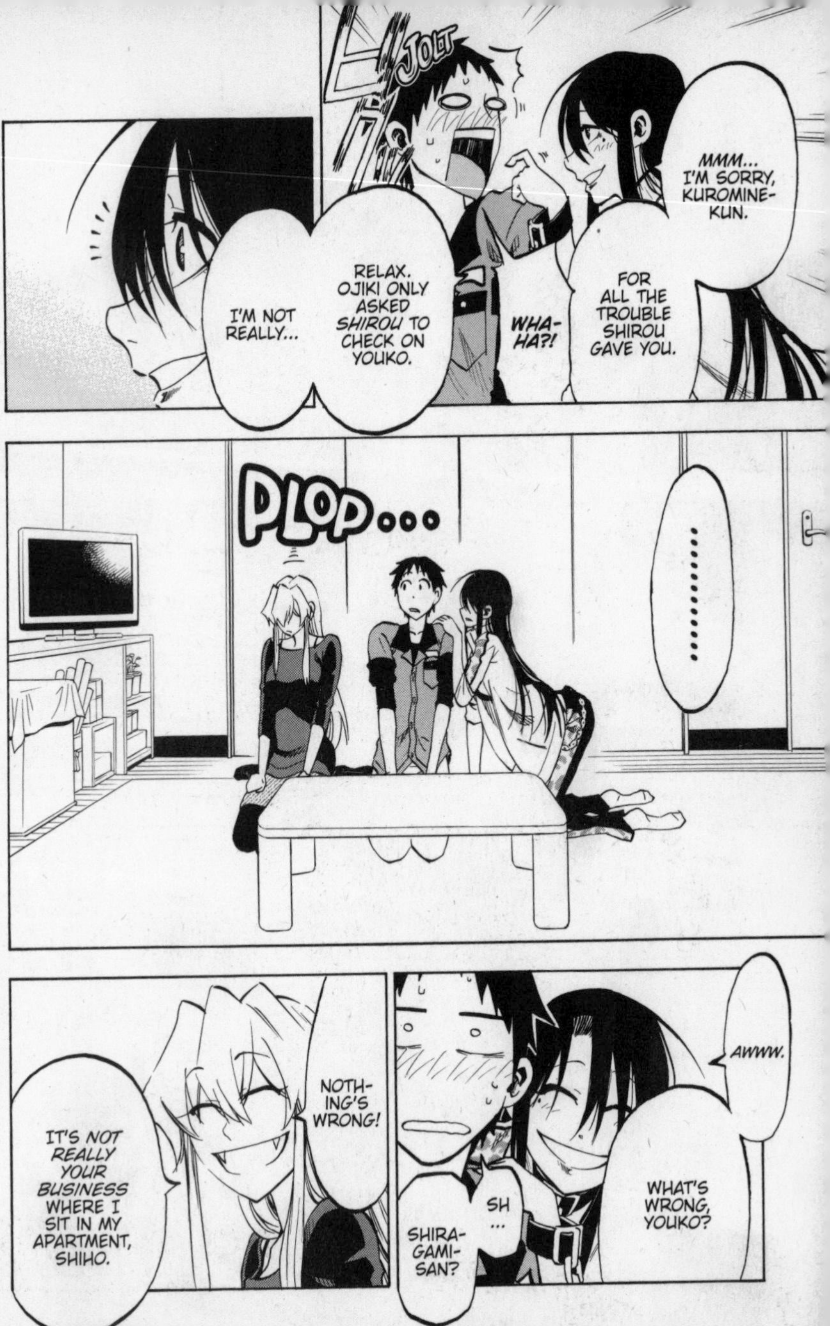
JOLT
MMM... I'M SORRY, KUROMINE-KUN.
FOR ALL THE TROUBLE SHIROU GAVE YOU.
WHA-HA?!
RELAX. OJIKI ONLY ASKED SHIROU TO CHECK ON YOUKO.
I'M NOT REALLY...
......
PLOP...
AWWW.
WHAT'S WRONG, YOUKO?
SH... SHIRA-GAMI-SAN?
NOTH-ING'S WRONG!
IT'S NOT REALLY YOUR BUSINESS WHERE I SIT IN MY APARTMENT, SHIHO.

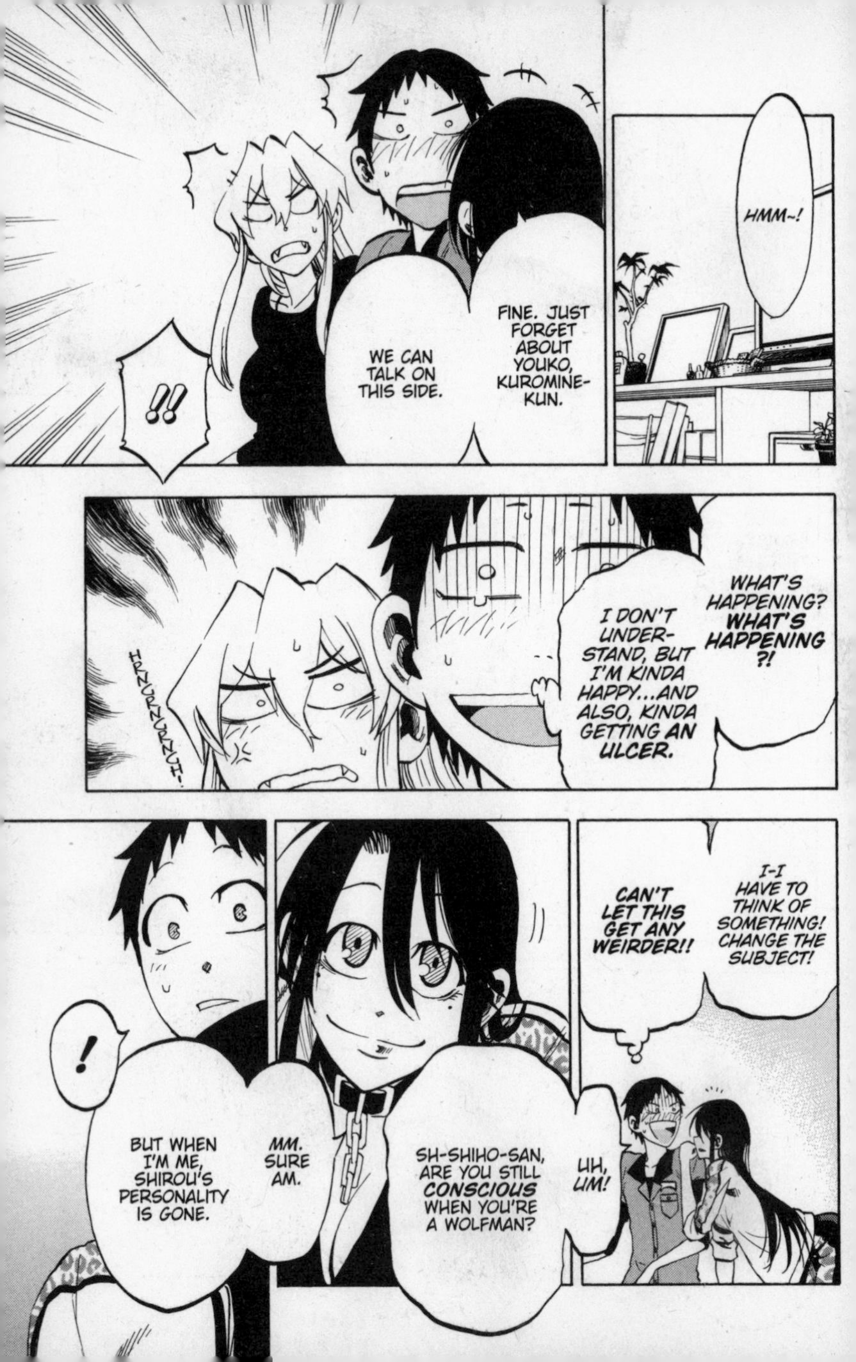
HMM~!
FINE. JUST FORGET ABOUT YOUKO, KUROMINE-KUN.
WE CAN TALK ON THIS SIDE.
!!
WHAT'S HAPPENING? WHAT'S HAPPENING?!
I DON'T UNDERSTAND, BUT I'M KINDA HAPPY...AND ALSO, KINDA GETTING AN ULCER.
HRNGRNGRNCH!
I-I HAVE TO THINK OF SOMETHING! CHANGE THE SUBJECT!
CAN'T LET THIS GET ANY WEIRDER!!
UH, UM!
SH-SHIHO-SAN, ARE YOU STILL CONSCIOUS WHEN YOU'RE A WOLFMAN?
MM. SURE AM.
!
BUT WHEN I'M ME, SHIROU'S PERSONALITY IS GONE.

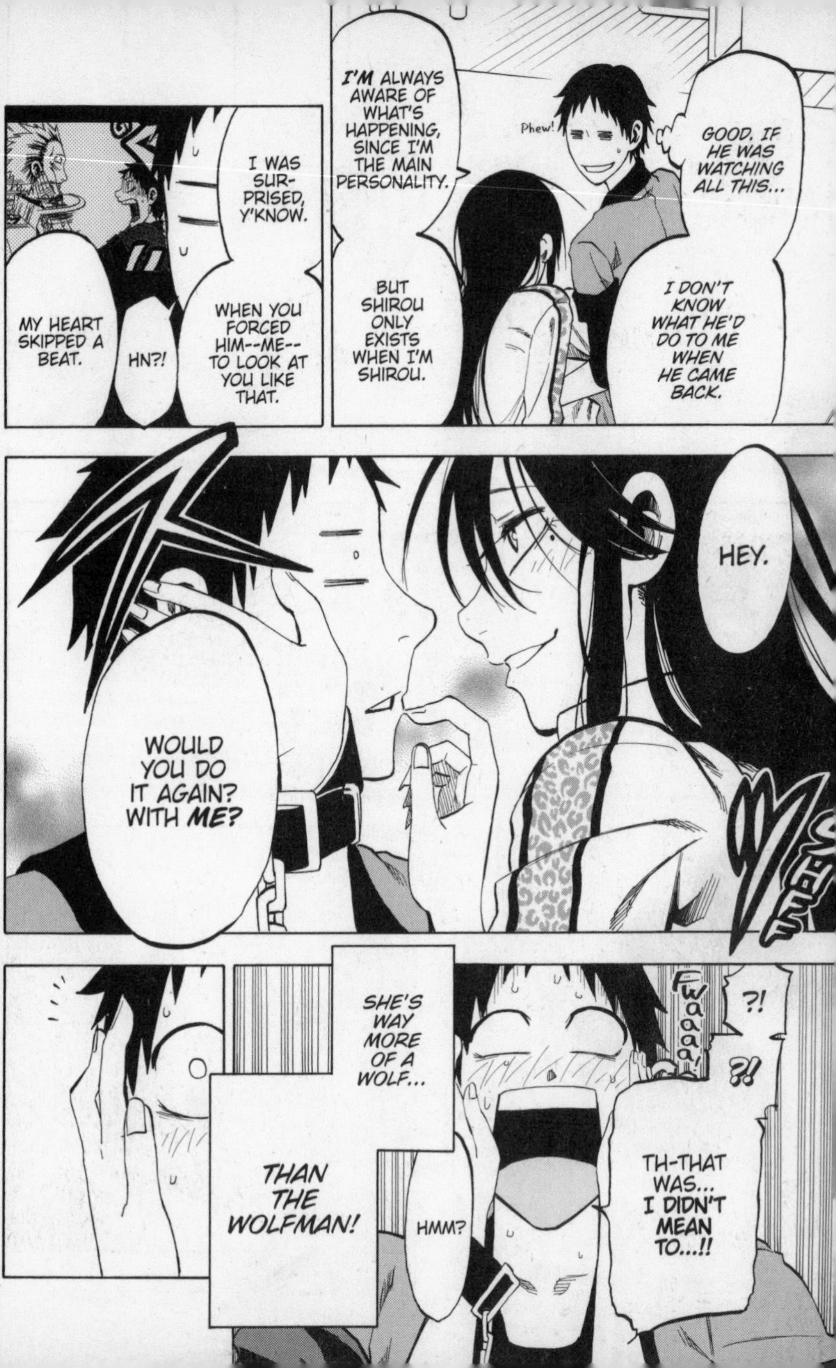
GOOD. IF HE WAS WATCHING ALL THIS...
I DON'T KNOW WHAT HE'D DO TO ME WHEN HE CAME BACK.
Phew!
I'M ALWAYS AWARE OF WHAT'S HAPPENING, SINCE I'M THE MAIN PERSONALITY.
BUT SHIROU ONLY EXISTS WHEN I'M SHIROU.
I WAS SURPRISED, Y'KNOW.
WHEN YOU FORCED HIM--ME--TO LOOK AT YOU LIKE THAT.
HN?!
MY HEART SKIPPED A BEAT.
HEY.
WOULD YOU DO IT AGAIN? WITH ME?
?!
?!!
Fwaaaa!
TH-THAT WAS... I DIDN'T MEAN TO...!!
HMM?
SHE'S WAY MORE OF A WOLF...
THAN THE WOLFMAN!

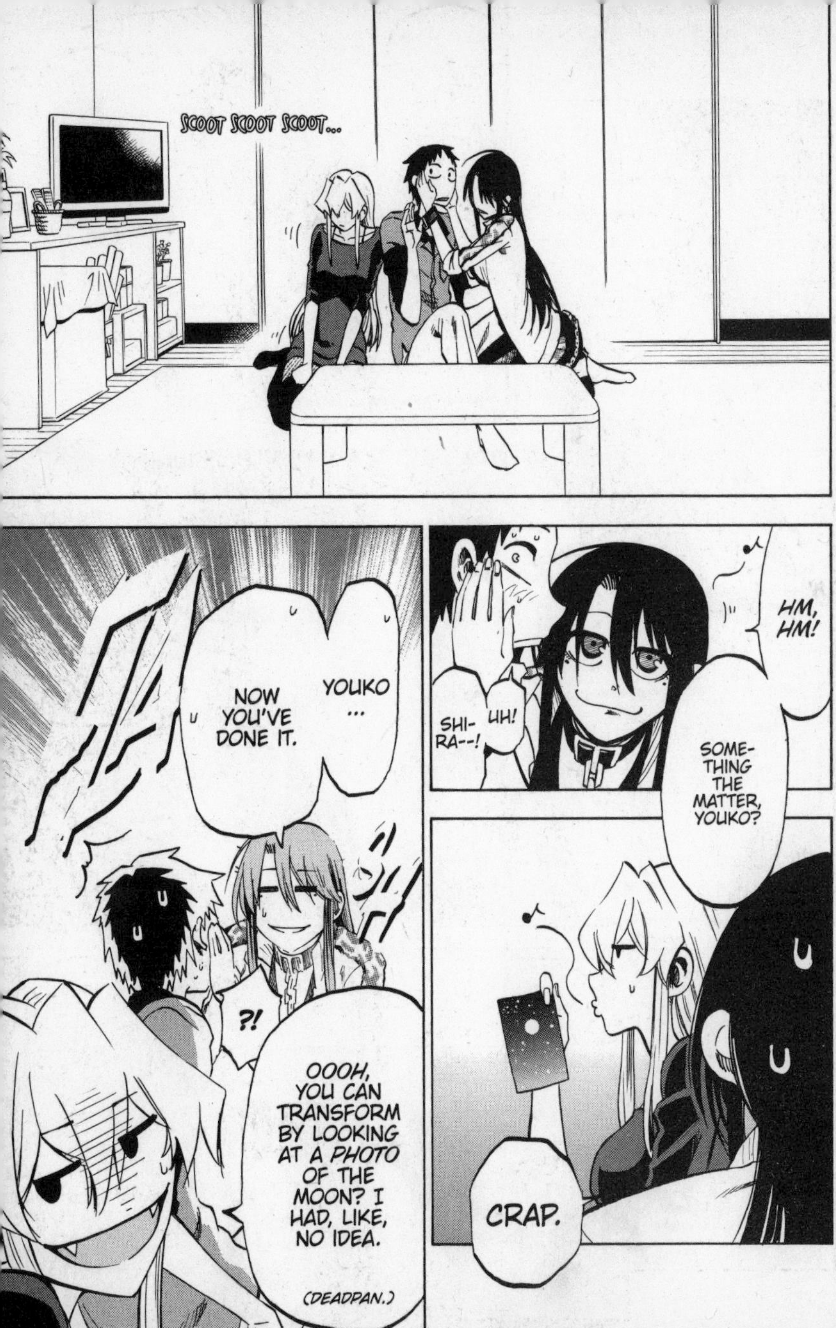
SCOOT SCOOT SCOOT...
HM, HM!
SHI- RA--!
UH!
SOME- THING THE MATTER, YOUKO?
CRAP.
YOUKO ...
NOW YOU'VE DONE IT.
?!
OOOH, YOU CAN TRANSFORM BY LOOKING AT A *PHOTO* OF THE MOON? I HAD, LIKE, NO IDEA.
(DEADPAN.)

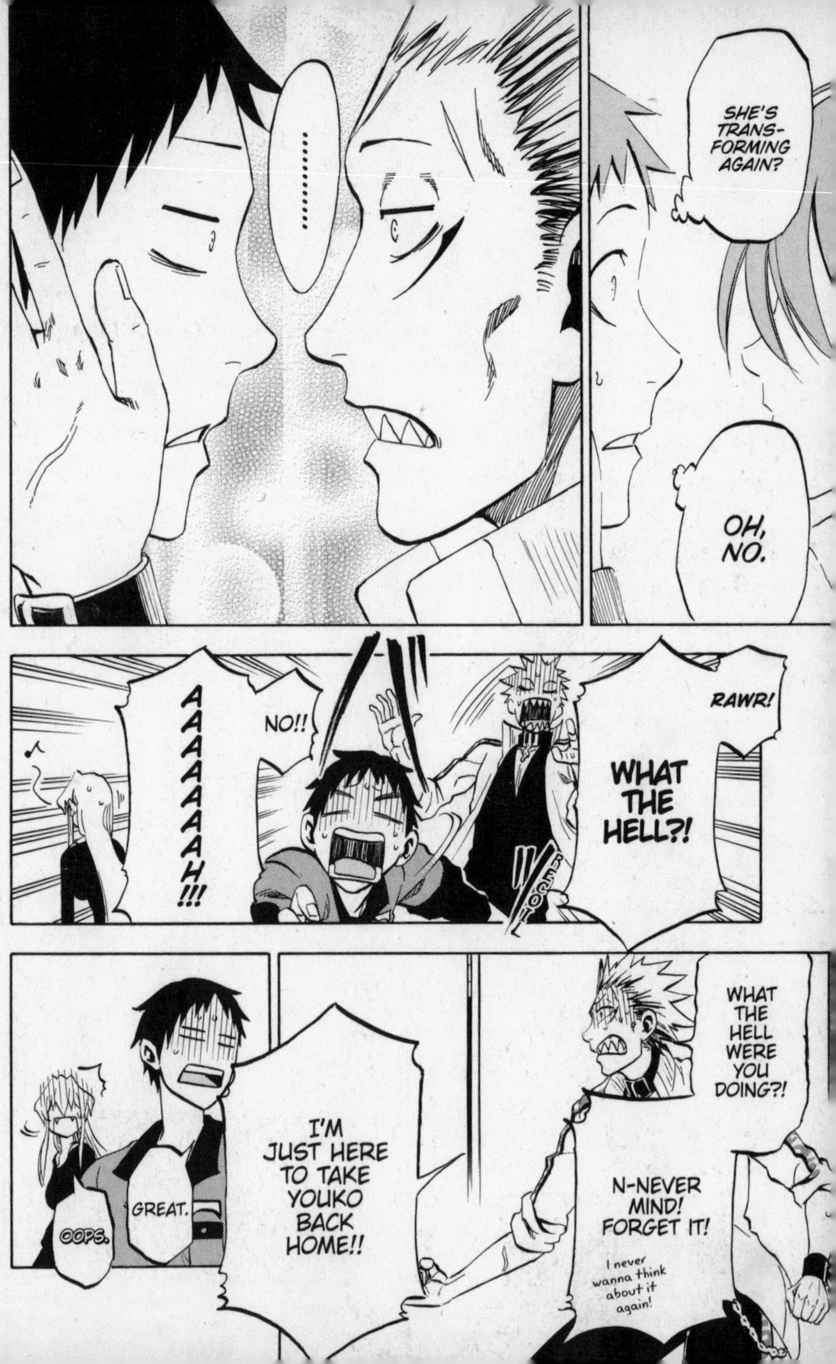
SHE'S TRANS-FORMING AGAIN?
OH, NO.
......
RAWR!
WHAT THE HELL?!
RECOIL
NO!!
AAAAAAAH!!!
WHAT THE HELL WERE YOU DOING?!
N-NEVER MIND! FORGET IT!
I never wanna think about it again!
I'M JUST HERE TO TAKE YOUKO BACK HOME!!
GREAT.
OOPS.

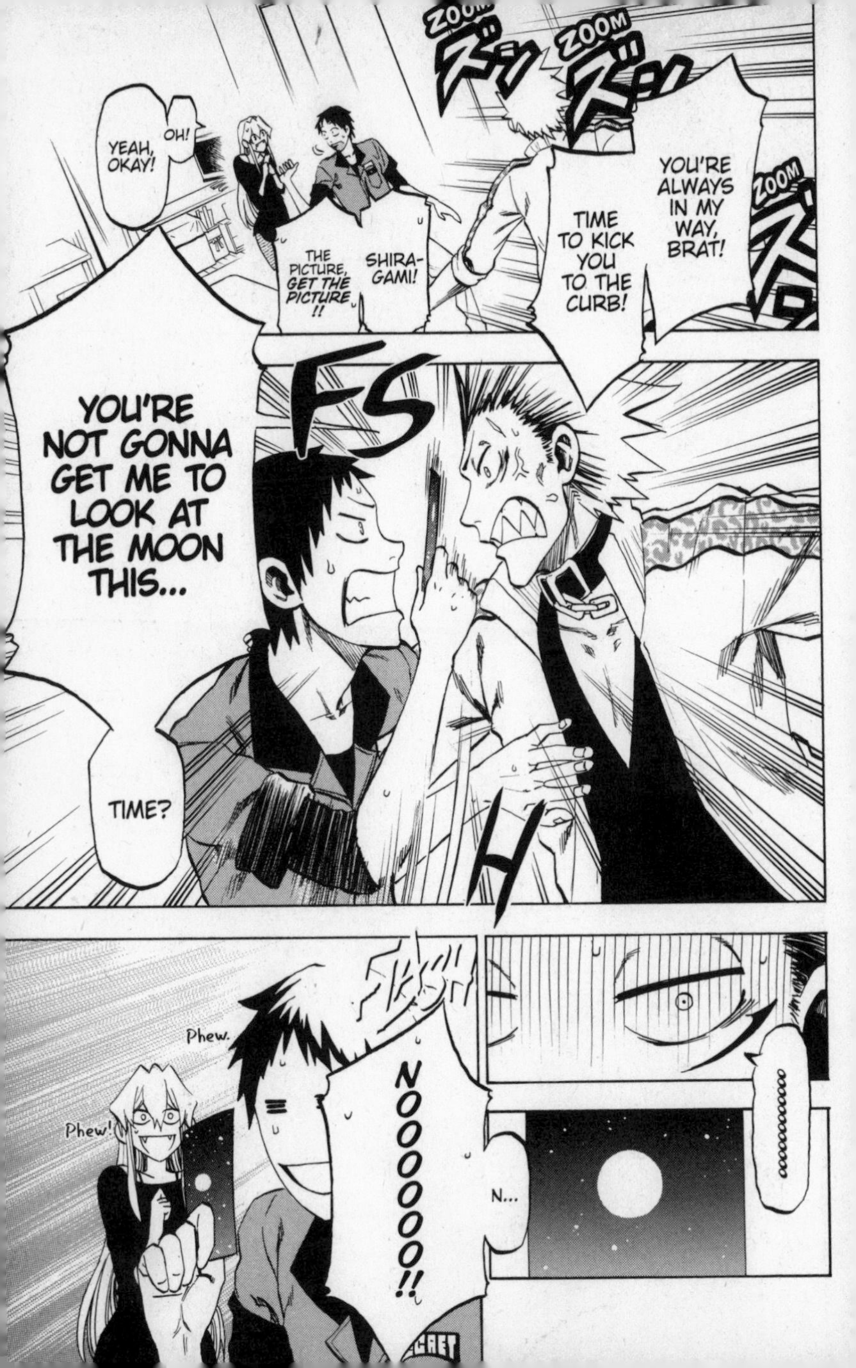
ZOOM
ZOOM
ZOOM
YOU'RE ALWAYS IN MY WAY, BRAT!
TIME TO KICK YOU TO THE CURB!
SHIRA-GAMI!
THE PICTURE, GET THE PICTURE!!
OH!
YEAH, OKAY!
FS
YOU'RE NOT GONNA GET ME TO LOOK AT THE MOON THIS...
TIME?
H
oooooooooooooo
N...
NOOOOOOOO!!
Phew.
Phew!

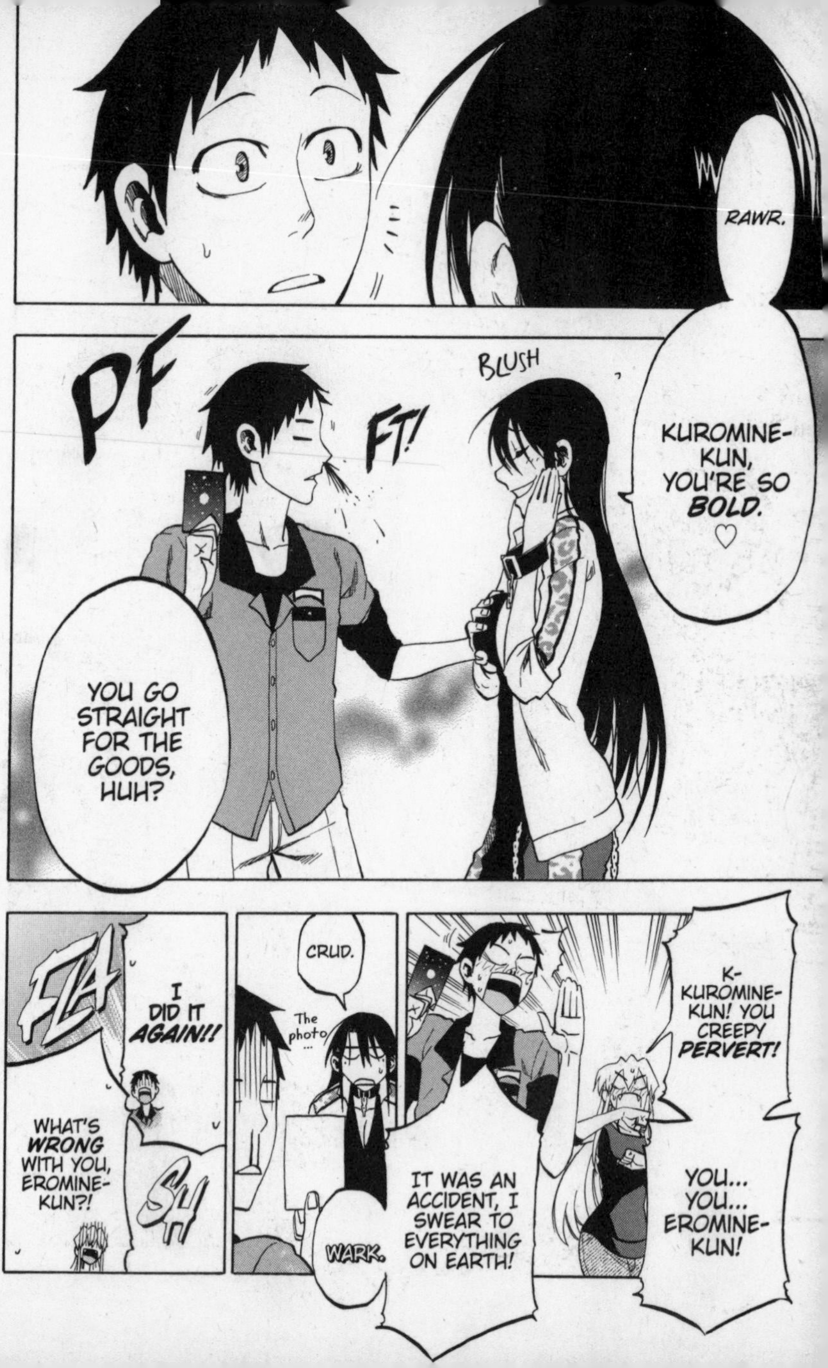

RAWR.
KUROMINE-KUN, YOU'RE SO BOLD. ♡
BLUSH
PF
FT!
YOU GO STRAIGHT FOR THE GOODS, HUH?
K-KUROMINE-KUN! YOU CREEPY PERVERT!
YOU... YOU... EROMINE-KUN!
CRUD.
The photo...
IT WAS AN ACCIDENT, I SWEAR TO EVERYTHING ON EARTH!
WARK.
ZA
I DID IT AGAIN!!
WHAT'S WRONG WITH YOU, EROMINE-KUN?!
SH

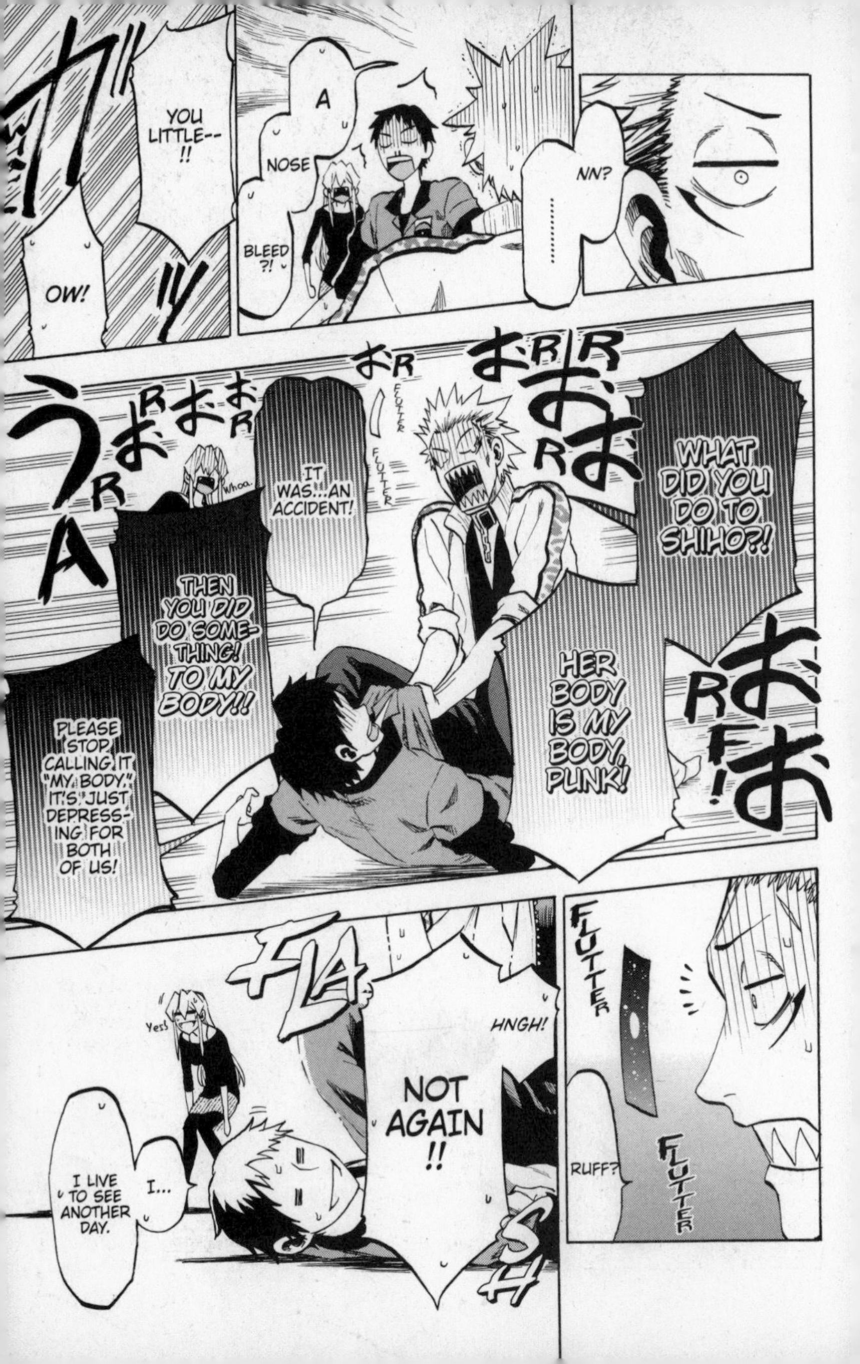
NN?
......
A NOSE BLEED?!
YOU LITTLE--!!
OW!
WHAT DID YOU DO TO SHIHO?!
HER BODY IS MY BODY, PUNK!
FLUTTER
FLUTTER
IT WAS...AN ACCIDENT!
Whoa.
THEN YOU DID DO SOMETHING! TO MY BODY!!
PLEASE STOP CALLING IT "MY BODY." IT'S JUST DEPRESSING FOR BOTH OF US!
FLUTTER
RUFF?
FLUTTER
FLA
HNGH!
NOT AGAIN!!
SH
Yes!
I...
I LIVE TO SEE ANOTHER DAY.

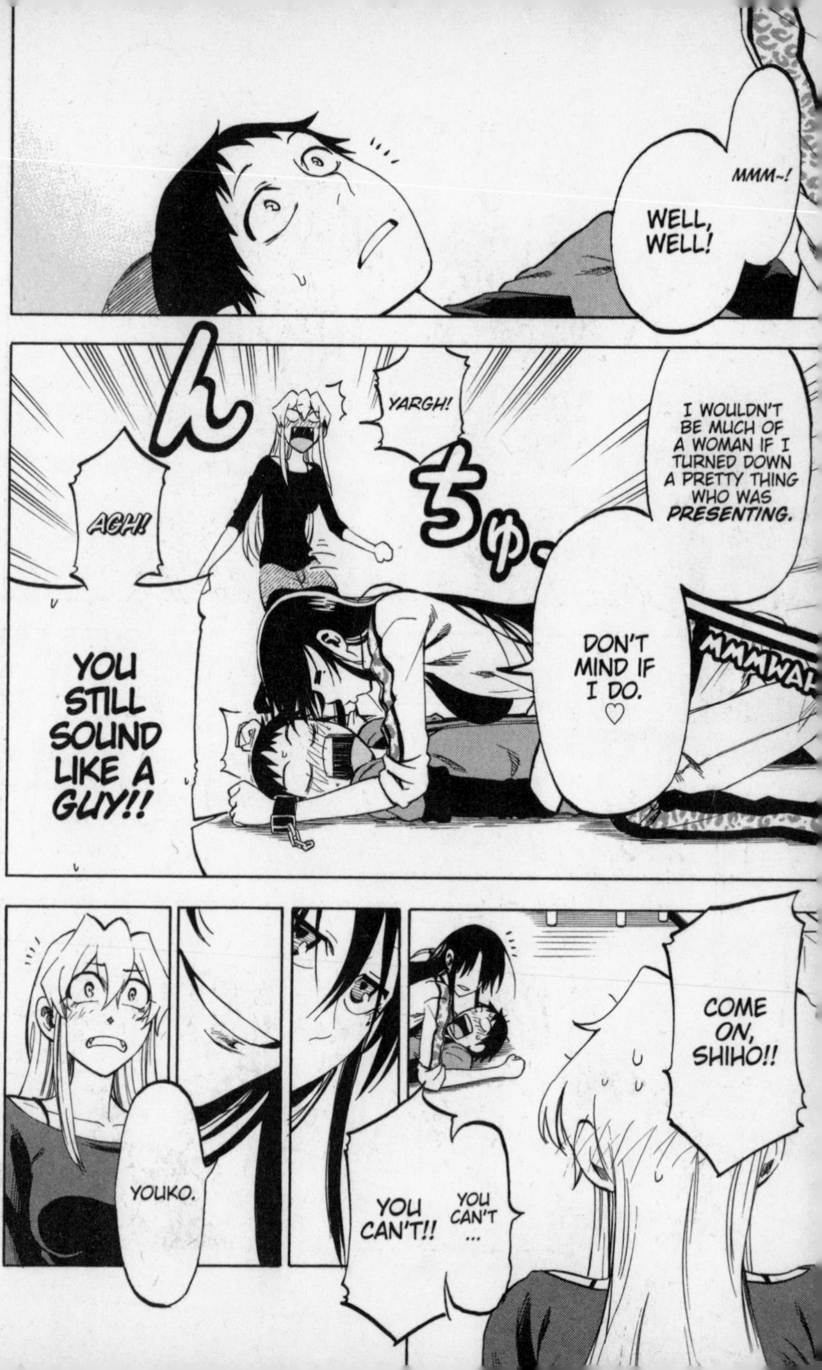
MMM~!
WELL, WELL!
I WOULDN'T BE MUCH OF A WOMAN IF I TURNED DOWN A PRETTY THING WHO WAS PRESENTING.
DON'T MIND IF I DO. ♡
MMMWAH
ちゅ
ん
YARGH!
AGH!
YOU STILL SOUND LIKE A GUY!!
COME ON, SHIHO!!
YOU CAN'T ...
YOU CAN'T!!
YOUKO.

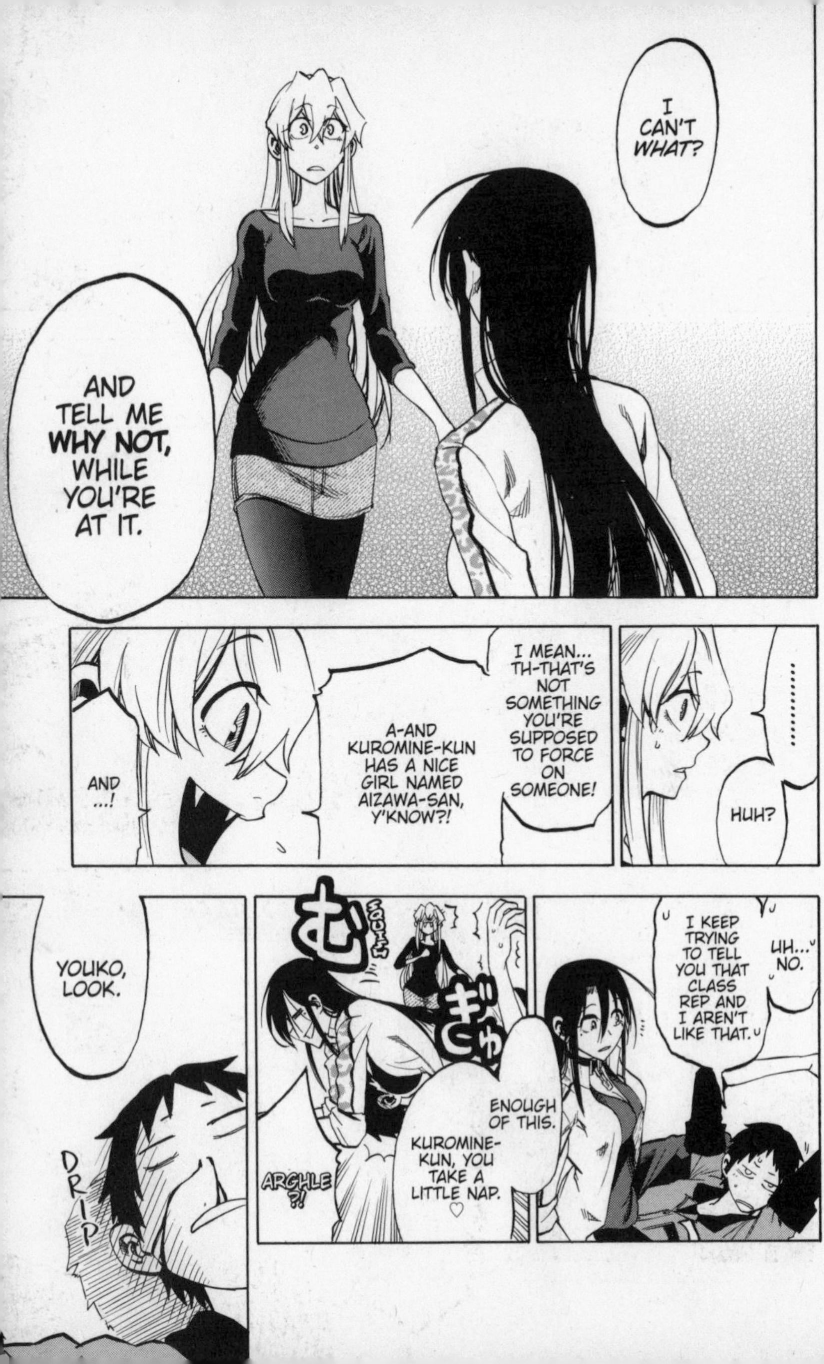
I CAN'T *WHAT?*
AND TELL ME **WHY NOT,** WHILE YOU'RE AT IT.
......
HUH?
I MEAN... TH-THAT'S NOT SOMETHING YOU'RE SUPPOSED TO FORCE ON SOMEONE!
A-AND KUROMINE-KUN HAS A NICE GIRL NAMED AIZAWA-SAN, Y'KNOW?!
AND ...!
I KEEP TRYING TO TELL YOU THAT CLASS REP AND I AREN'T LIKE THAT.
UH... NO.
ENOUGH OF THIS.
KUROMINE-KUN, YOU TAKE A LITTLE NAP. ♡
むぎゅ
SQUISH
ARGHLE ?!
YOUKO, LOOK.
DRIP

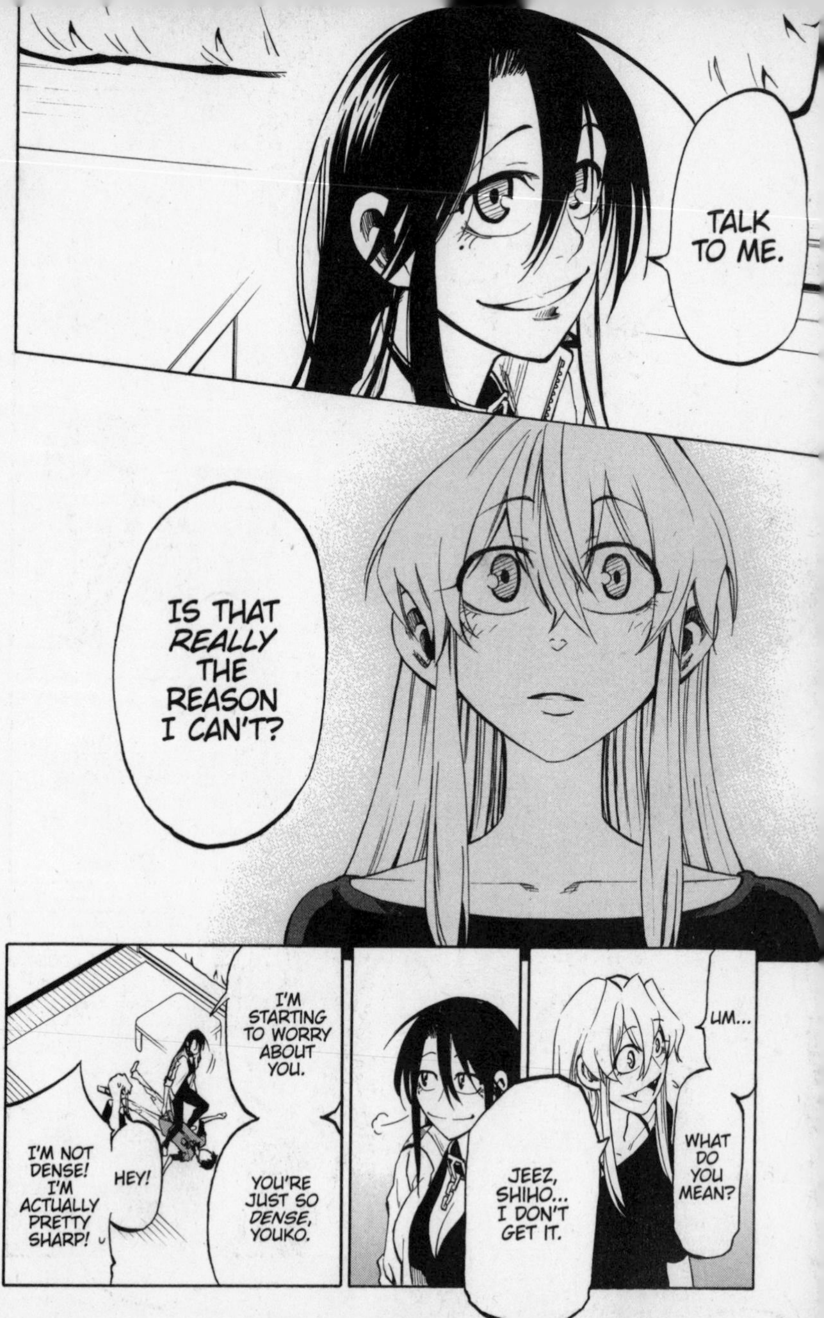
TALK TO ME.
IS THAT *REALLY* THE REASON I CAN'T?
UM...
WHAT DO YOU MEAN?
JEEZ, SHIHO... I DON'T GET IT.
I'M STARTING TO WORRY ABOUT YOU.
YOU'RE JUST SO *DENSE*, YOUKO.
HEY!
I'M NOT DENSE! I'M ACTUALLY PRETTY SHARP!

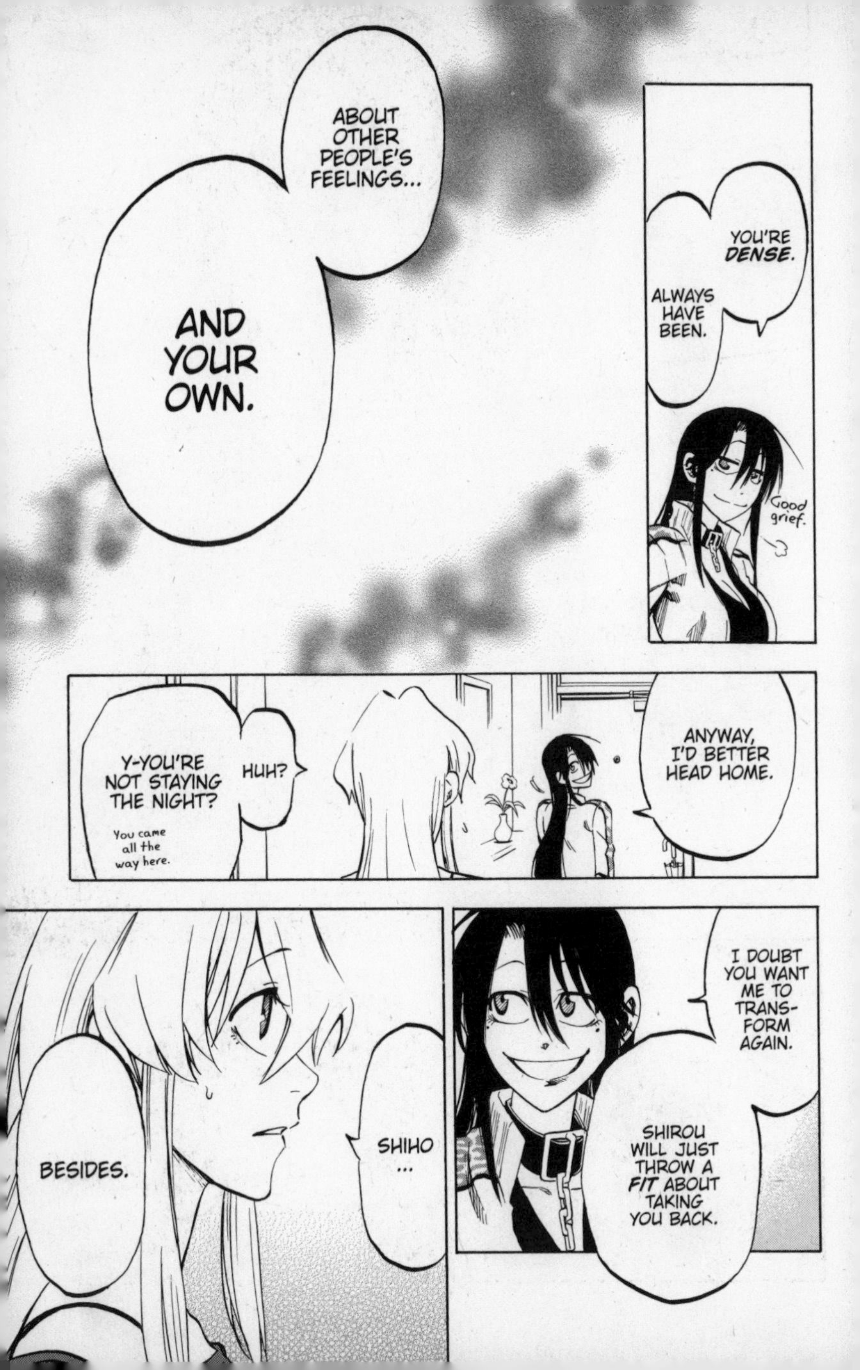
YOU'RE *DENSE*.
ALWAYS HAVE BEEN.
Good grief.
ABOUT OTHER PEOPLE'S FEELINGS...
AND YOUR OWN.
ANYWAY, I'D BETTER HEAD HOME.
HUH?
Y-YOU'RE NOT STAYING THE NIGHT?
You came all the way here.
I DOUBT YOU WANT ME TO TRANS-FORM AGAIN.
SHIROU WILL JUST THROW A *FIT* ABOUT TAKING YOU BACK.
SHIHO ...
BESIDES.

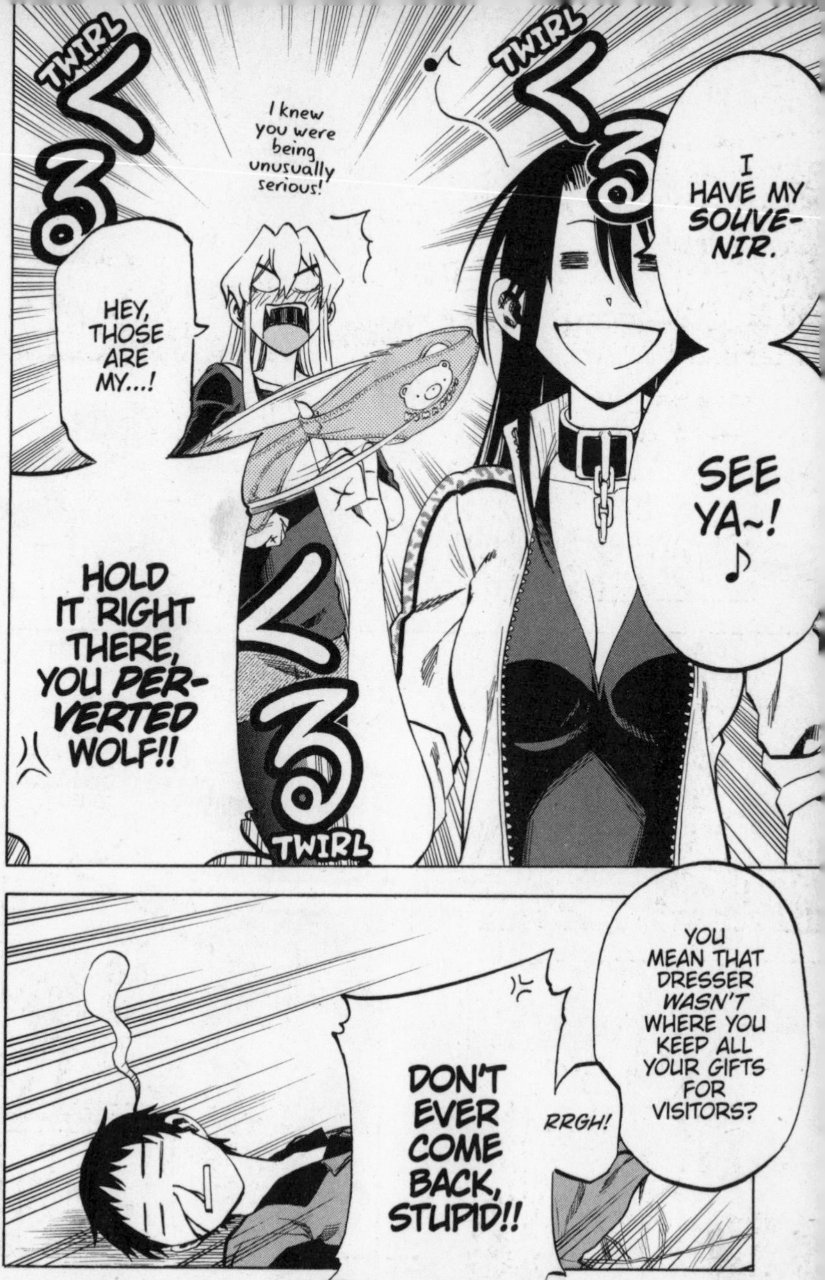
TWIRL
I HAVE MY SOUVENIR.
SEE YA~! ♪
I knew you were being unusually serious!
TWIRL
HEY, THOSE ARE MY...!
HOLD IT RIGHT THERE, YOU PERVERTED WOLF!!
TWIRL
YOU MEAN THAT DRESSER WASN'T WHERE YOU KEEP ALL YOUR GIFTS FOR VISITORS?
RRGH!
DON'T EVER COME BACK, STUPID!!

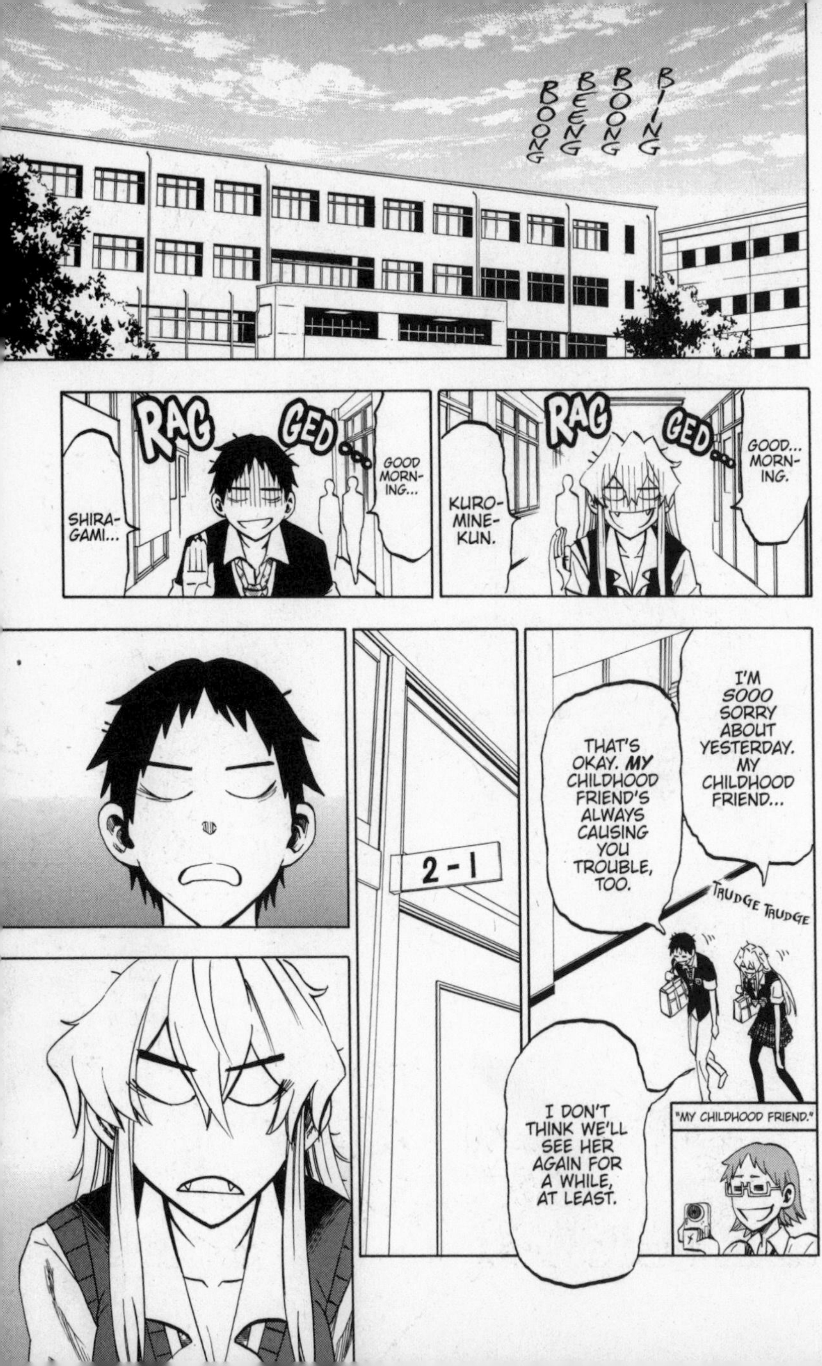
BIING
BOONG
BEENG
BOOONG
RAG GED...
GOOD... MORNING.
KUROMINE-KUN.
RAG GED...
GOOD MORNING...
SHIRAGAMI...
I'M SOOO SORRY ABOUT YESTERDAY. MY CHILDHOOD FRIEND...
THAT'S OKAY. MY CHILDHOOD FRIEND'S ALWAYS CAUSING YOU TROUBLE, TOO.
TRUDGE TRUDGE
I DON'T THINK WE'LL SEE HER AGAIN FOR A WHILE, AT LEAST.
"MY CHILDHOOD FRIEND."
2-1

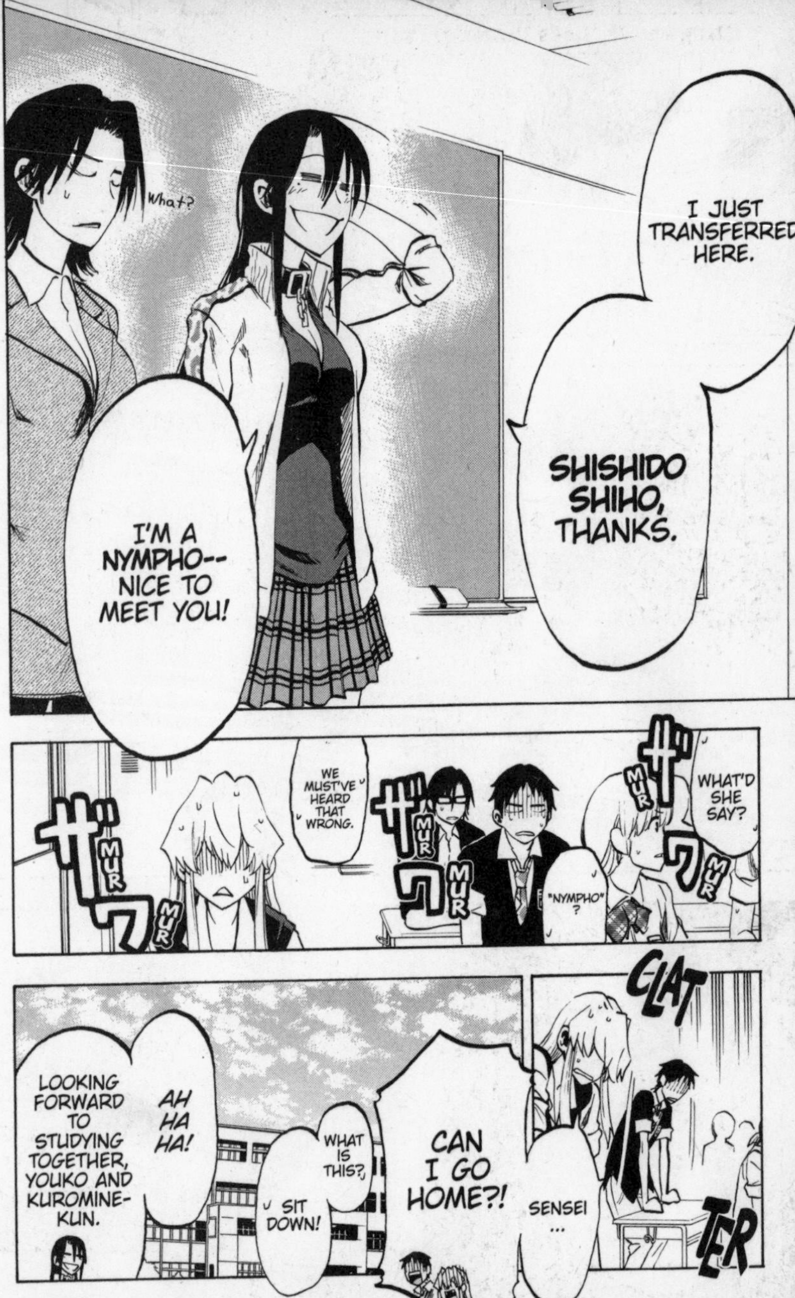
I JUST TRANSFERRED HERE.
SHISHIDO SHIHO, THANKS.
What?
I'M A NYMPHO-- NICE TO MEET YOU!
ザワ
MUR MUR
WHAT'D SHE SAY?
"NYMPHO"?
ザワ
MUR MUR
WE MUST'VE HEARD THAT WRONG.
ザワ
MUR MUR
CLATTER
SENSEI ...
CAN I GO HOME?!
WHAT IS THIS?
SIT DOWN!
AH HA HA!
LOOKING FORWARD TO STUDYING TOGETHER, YOUKO AND KUROMINE-KUN.

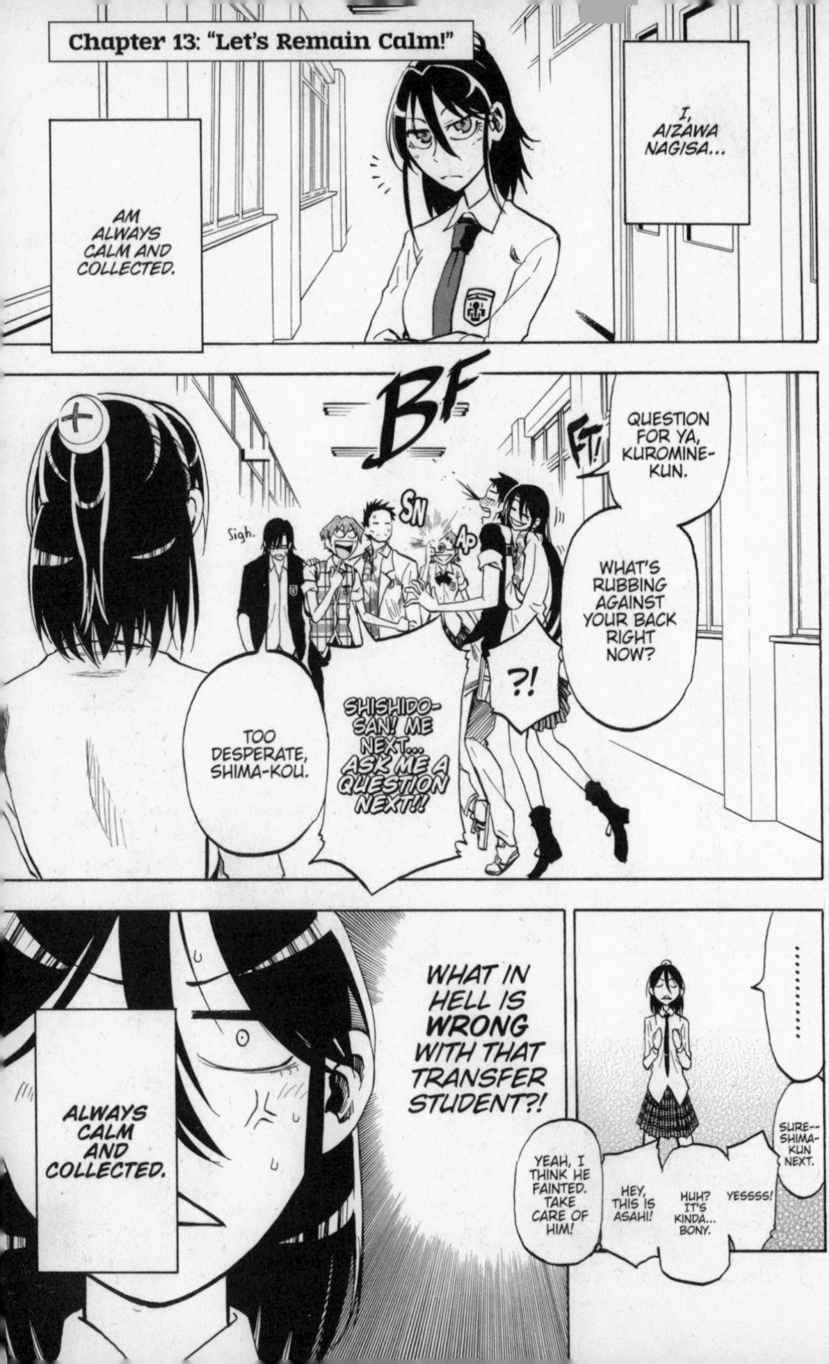
Chapter 13: "Let's Remain Calm!"
I, AIZAWA NAGISA...
AM ALWAYS CALM AND COLLECTED.
BFFT!
QUESTION FOR YA, KUROMINE-KUN.
WHAT'S RUBBING AGAINST YOUR BACK RIGHT NOW?
SN
AP
?!
SHISHIDO-SAN! ME NEXT... ASK ME A QUESTION NEXT!!
TOO DESPERATE, SHIMA-KOU.
Sigh.
......
SURE-- SHIMA-KUN NEXT.
YESSSS!
HUH? IT'S KINDA... BONY.
HEY, THIS IS ASAHI!
YEAH, I THINK HE FAINTED. TAKE CARE OF HIM!
WHAT IN HELL IS WRONG WITH THAT TRANSFER STUDENT?!
ALWAYS CALM AND COLLECTED.

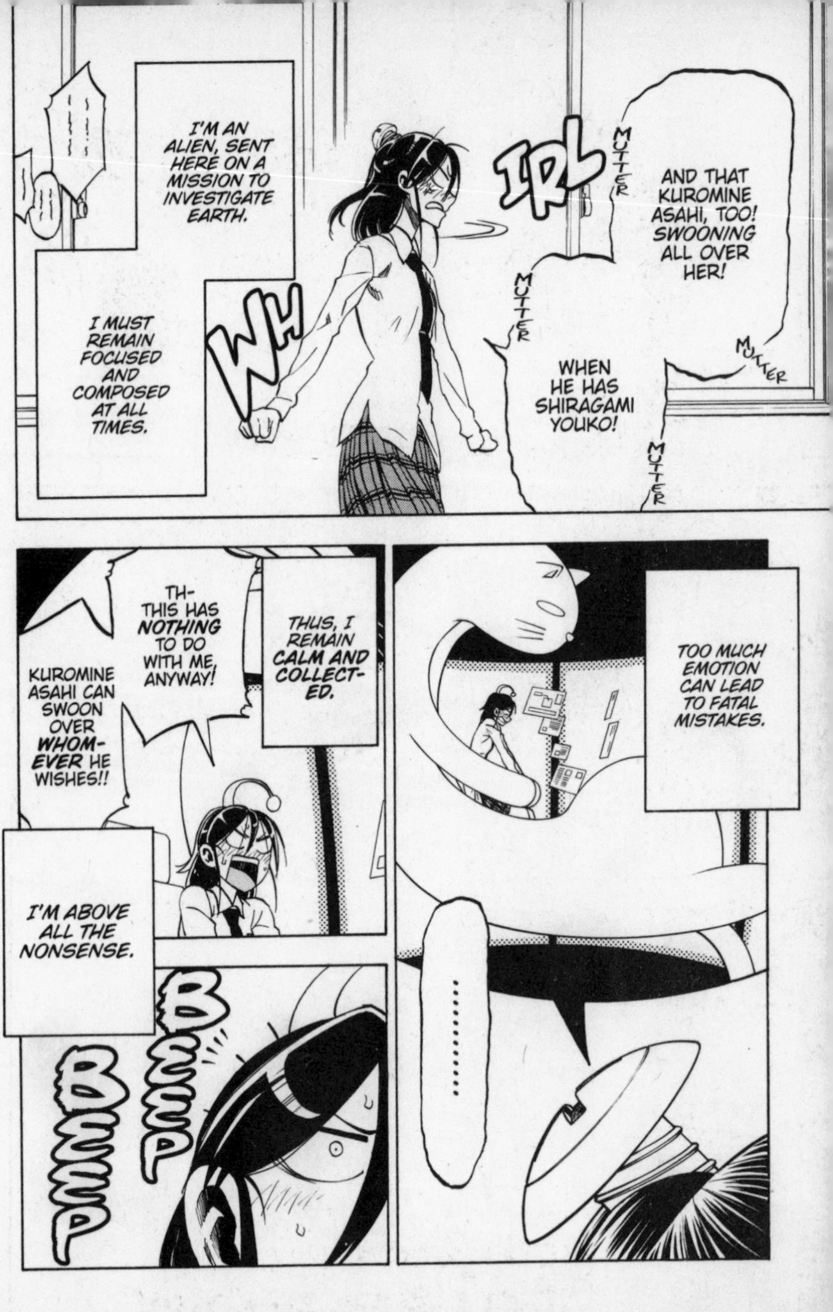

AND THAT KUROMINE ASAHI, TOO! SWOONING ALL OVER HER!
MUTTER
MUTTER
WHEN HE HAS SHIRAGAMI YOUKO!
MUTTER
MUTTER
IRL
WH
I'M AN ALIEN, SENT HERE ON A MISSION TO INVESTIGATE EARTH.
I MUST REMAIN FOCUSED AND COMPOSED AT ALL TIMES.
TOO MUCH EMOTION CAN LEAD TO FATAL MISTAKES.
....
THUS, I REMAIN CALM AND COLLECT-ED.
TH- THIS HAS NOTHING TO DO WITH ME, ANYWAY!
KUROMINE ASAHI CAN SWOON OVER WHOM-EVER HE WISHES!!
I'M ABOVE ALL THE NONSENSE.
BEEP
BEEP

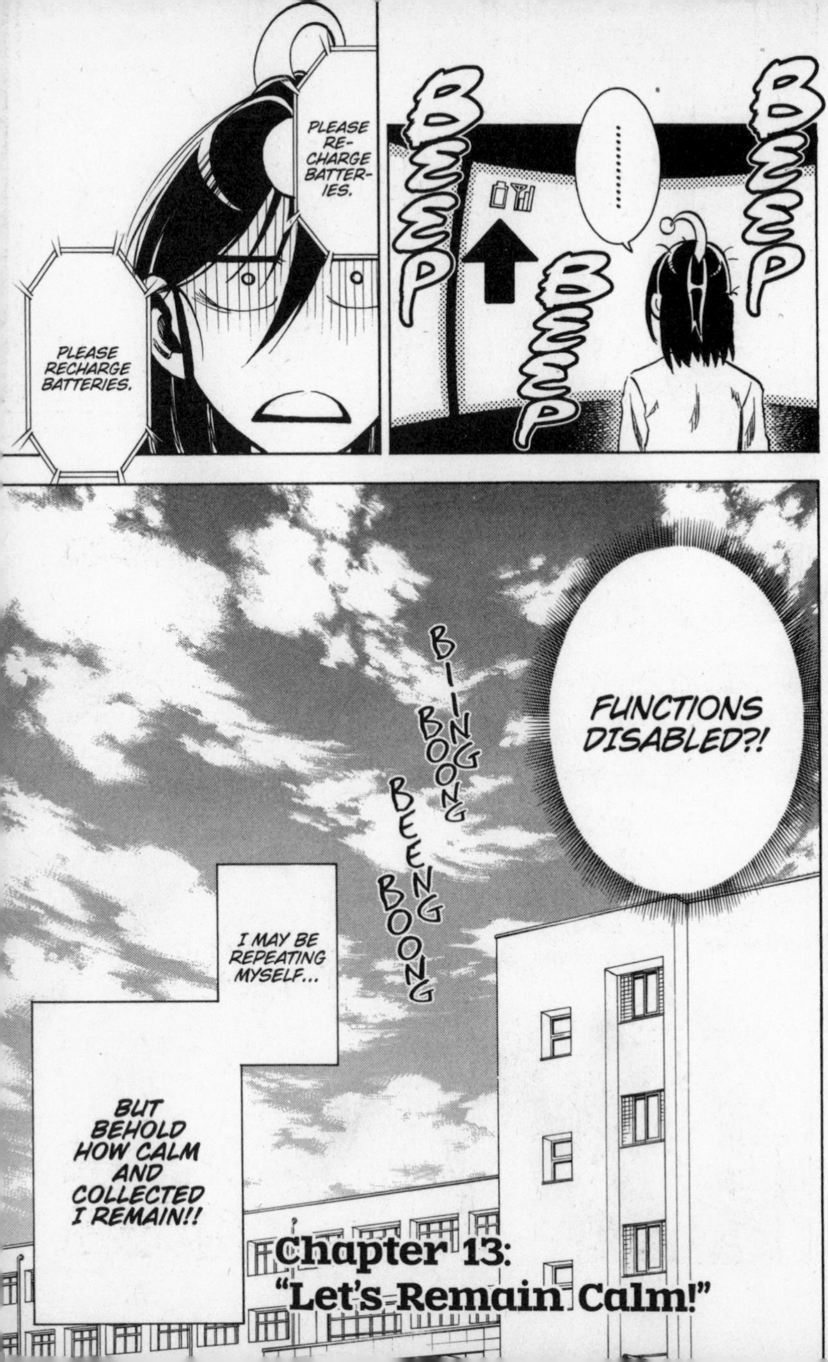
BEEP
......
BEEP
BEEP
PLEASE RE-CHARGE BATTER-IES.
PLEASE RECHARGE BATTERIES.
FUNCTIONS DISABLED?!
BIING BOONG BEENG BOONG
I MAY BE REPEATING MYSELF...
BUT BEHOLD HOW CALM AND COLLECTED I REMAIN!!
Chapter 13: "Let's Remain Calm!"

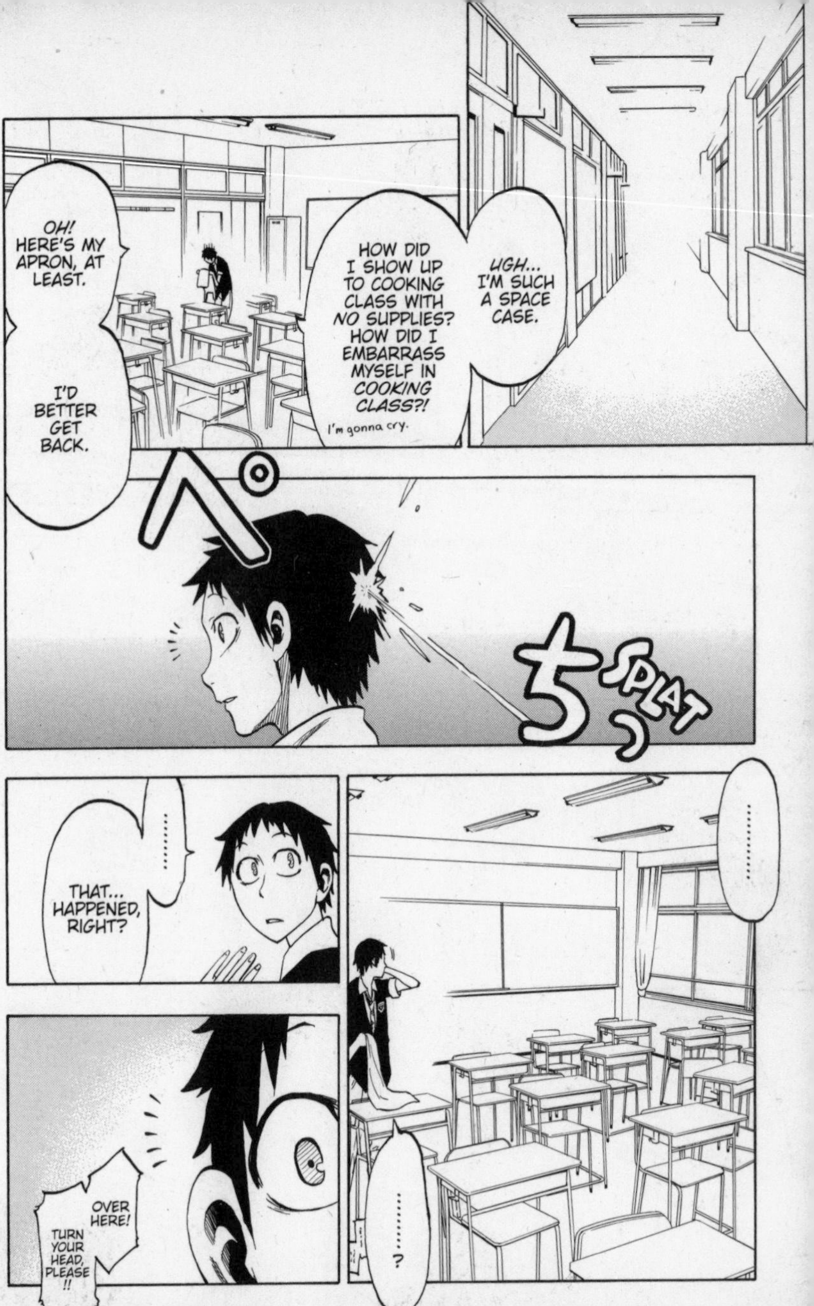
UGH... I'M SUCH A SPACE CASE.
HOW DID I SHOW UP TO COOKING CLASS WITH NO SUPPLIES? HOW DID I EMBARRASS MYSELF IN COOKING CLASS?!
I'm gonna cry.
OH! HERE'S MY APRON, AT LEAST.
I'D BETTER GET BACK.
SPLAT
......
......?
......
THAT... HAPPENED, RIGHT?
OVER HERE!
TURN YOUR HEAD, PLEASE!!

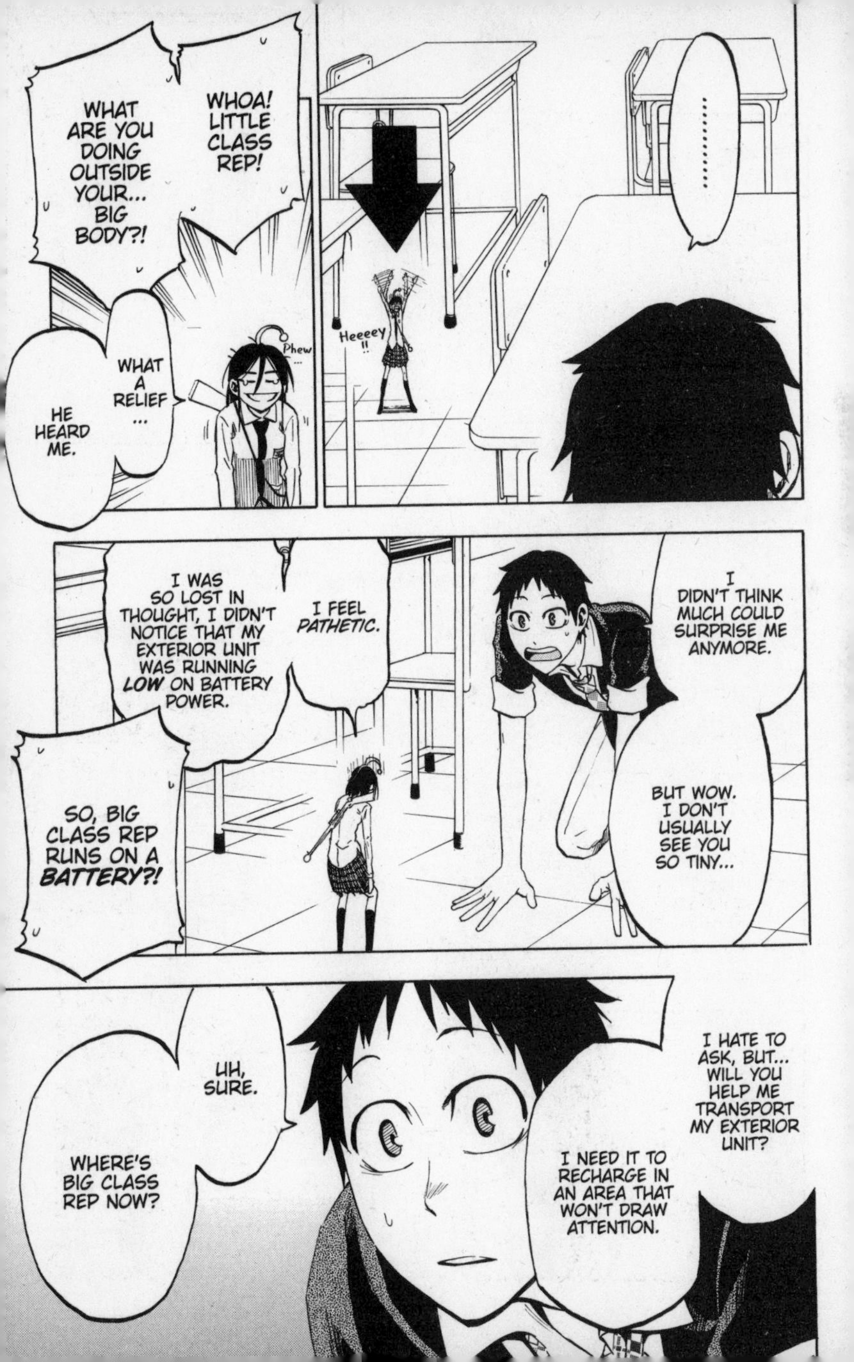
......
Heeeey!!
WHOA! LITTLE CLASS REP!
WHAT ARE YOU DOING OUTSIDE YOUR... BIG BODY?!
Phew...
WHAT A RELIEF...
HE HEARD ME.
I DIDN'T THINK MUCH COULD SURPRISE ME ANYMORE.
BUT WOW. I DON'T USUALLY SEE YOU SO TINY...
I FEEL *PATHETIC*.
I WAS SO LOST IN THOUGHT, I DIDN'T NOTICE THAT MY EXTERIOR UNIT WAS RUNNING ***LOW*** ON BATTERY POWER.
SO, BIG CLASS REP RUNS ON A ***BATTERY?!***
I HATE TO ASK, BUT... WILL YOU HELP ME TRANSPORT MY EXTERIOR UNIT?
I NEED IT TO RECHARGE IN AN AREA THAT WON'T DRAW ATTENTION.
UH, SURE.
WHERE'S BIG CLASS REP NOW?

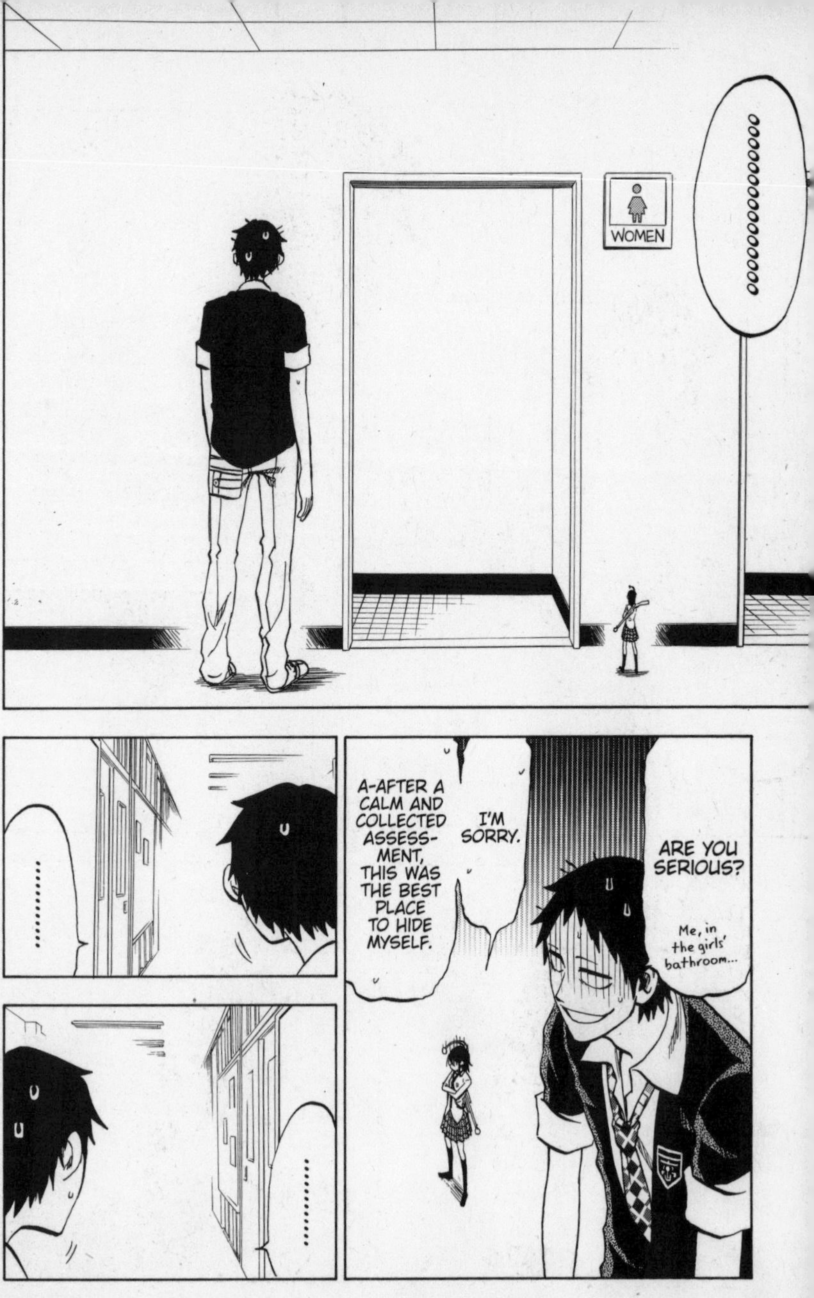
....
WOMEN
ARE YOU SERIOUS?
Me, in the girls' bathroom...
I'M SORRY.
A-AFTER A CALM AND COLLECTED ASSESS-MENT, THIS WAS THE BEST PLACE TO HIDE MYSELF.
....
....

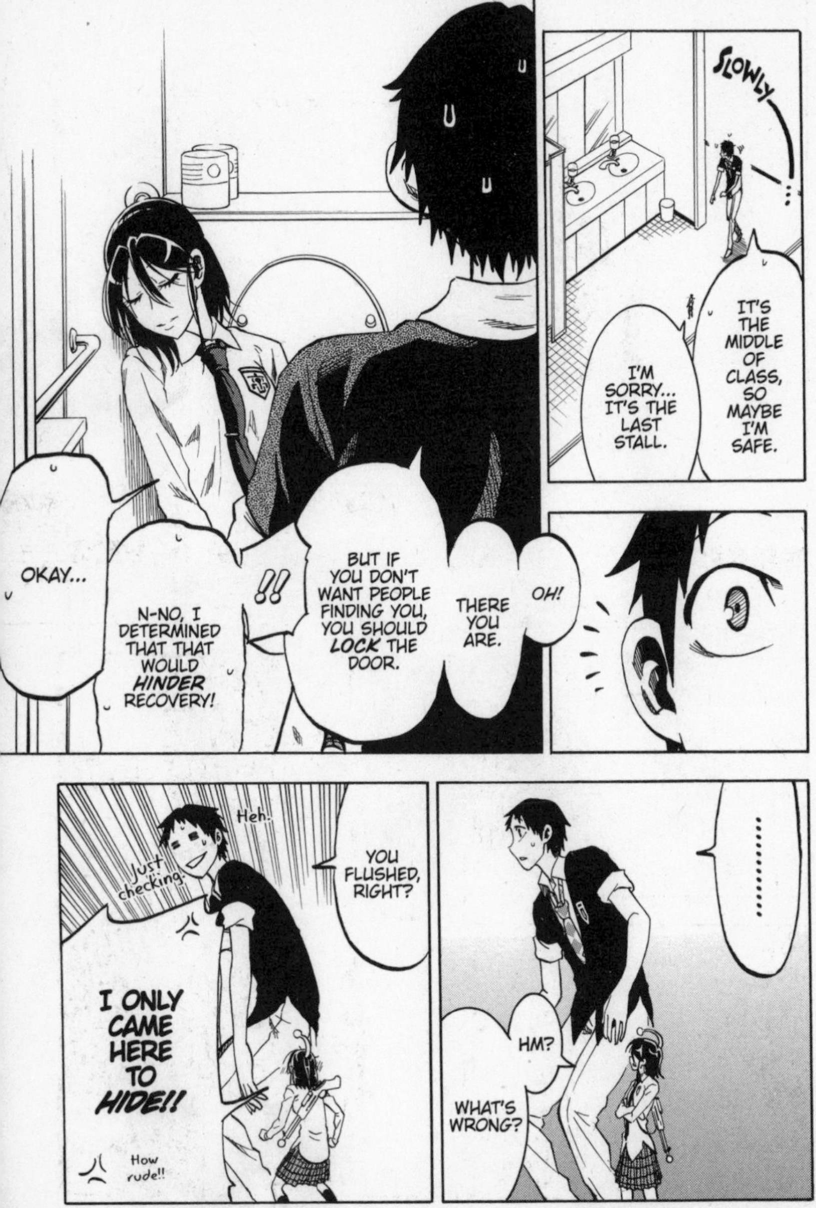
SLOWLY
IT'S THE MIDDLE OF CLASS, SO MAYBE I'M SAFE.
I'M SORRY... IT'S THE LAST STALL.
OH!
THERE YOU ARE.
BUT IF YOU DON'T WANT PEOPLE FINDING YOU, YOU SHOULD LOCK THE DOOR.
!!
N-NO, I DETERMINED THAT THAT WOULD HINDER RECOVERY!
OKAY...
......
HM?
WHAT'S WRONG?
YOU FLUSHED, RIGHT?
Heh.
Just checking.
I ONLY CAME HERE TO HIDE!!
How rude!!

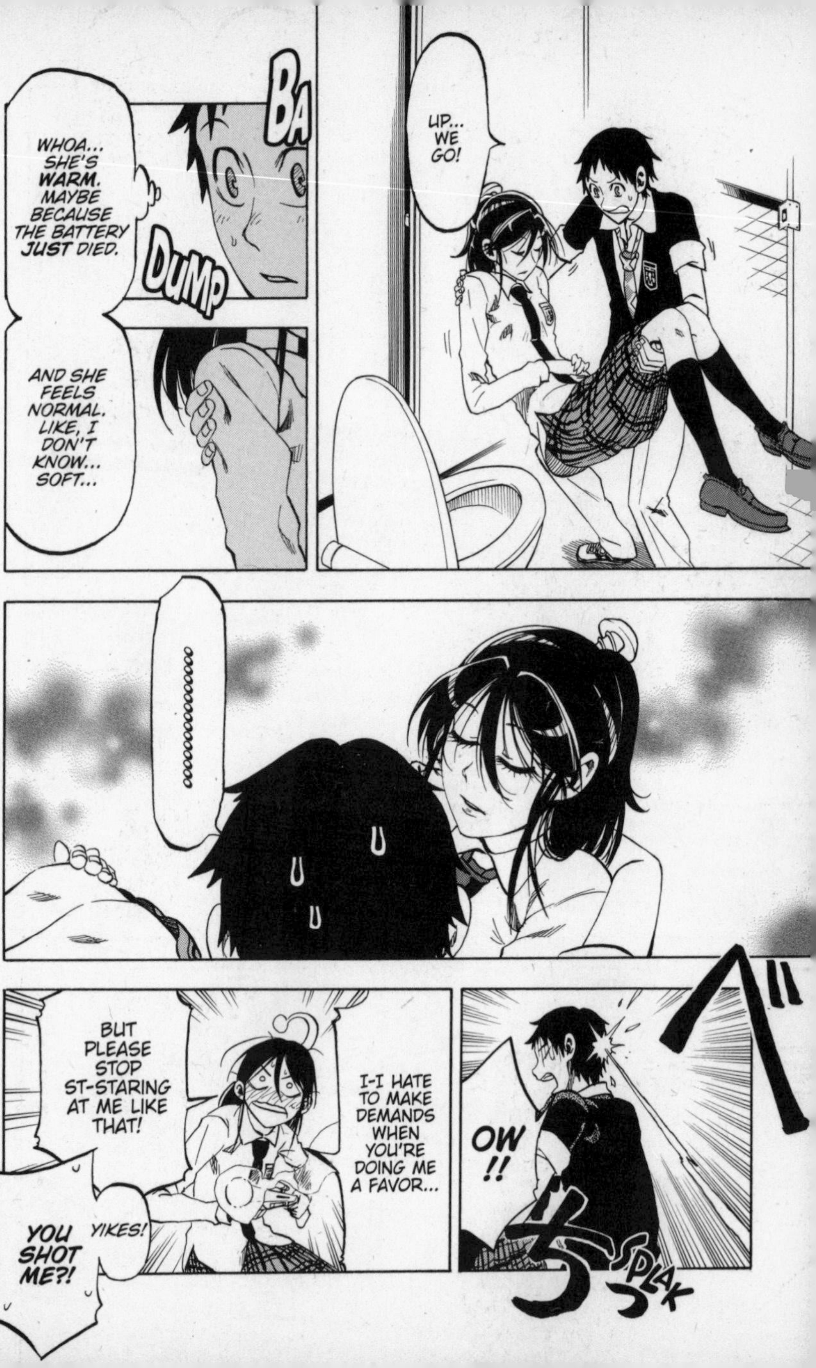
UP... WE GO!
BA
DUMP
WHOA... SHE'S WARM. MAYBE BECAUSE THE BATTERY JUST DIED.
AND SHE FEELS NORMAL. LIKE, I DON'T KNOW... SOFT...
....
OW!!
SPLAK
I-I HATE TO MAKE DEMANDS WHEN YOU'RE DOING ME A FAVOR...
BUT PLEASE STOP ST-STARING AT ME LIKE THAT!
YIKES!
YOU SHOT ME?!

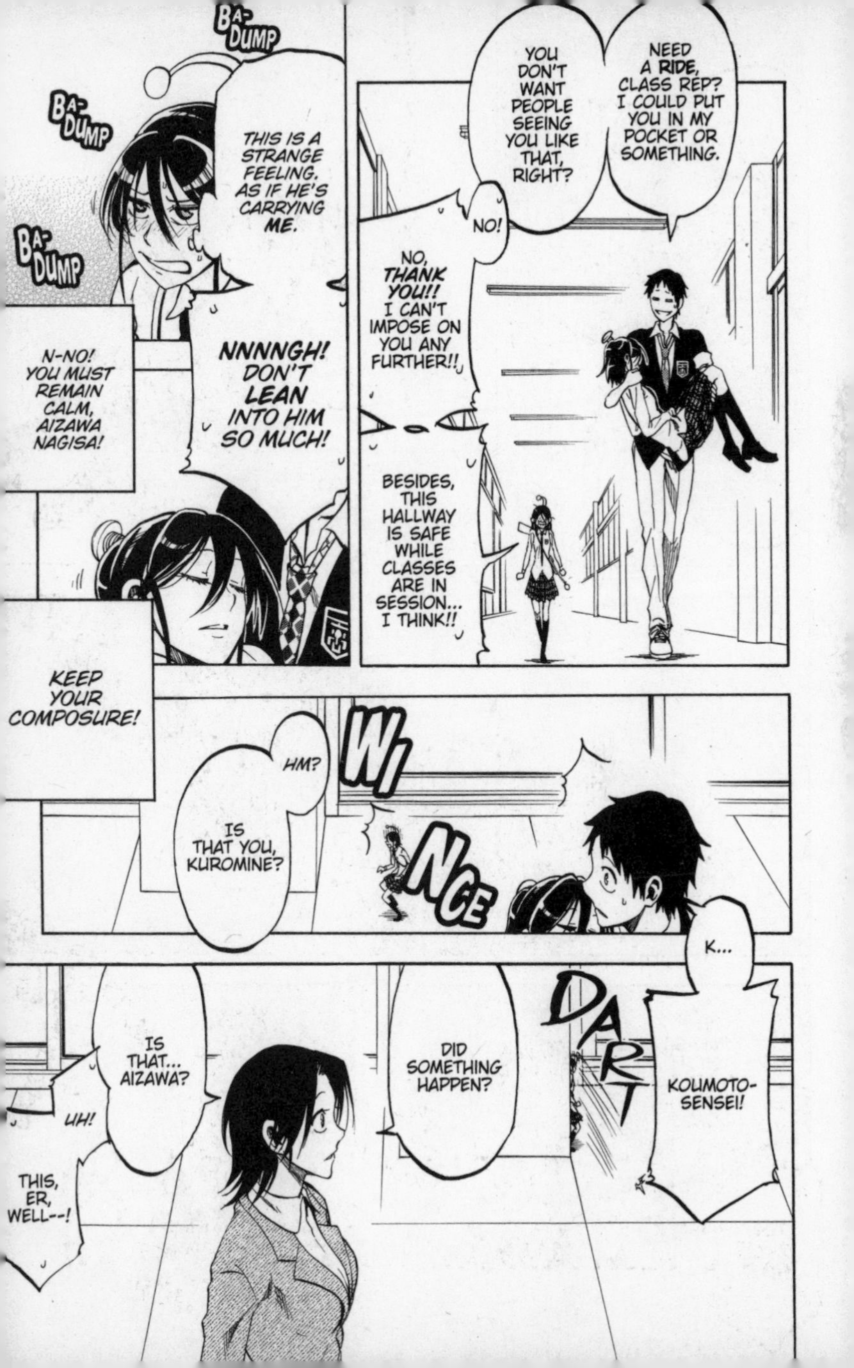
NEED A RIDE, CLASS REP? I COULD PUT YOU IN MY POCKET OR SOMETHING.
YOU DON'T WANT PEOPLE SEEING YOU LIKE THAT, RIGHT?
NO!
NO, THANK YOU!! I CAN'T IMPOSE ON YOU ANY FURTHER!!
BESIDES, THIS HALLWAY IS SAFE WHILE CLASSES ARE IN SESSION... I THINK!!
BA-DUMP
BA-DUMP
BA-DUMP
THIS IS A STRANGE FEELING. AS IF HE'S CARRYING ME.
N-NO! YOU MUST REMAIN CALM, AIZAWA NAGISA!
NNNNGH! DON'T LEAN INTO HIM SO MUCH!
KEEP YOUR COMPOSURE!
WINCE
HM?
IS THAT YOU, KUROMINE?
K...
KOUMOTO-SENSEI!
DART
DID SOMETHING HAPPEN?
IS THAT... AIZAWA?
UH!
THIS, ER, WELL--!

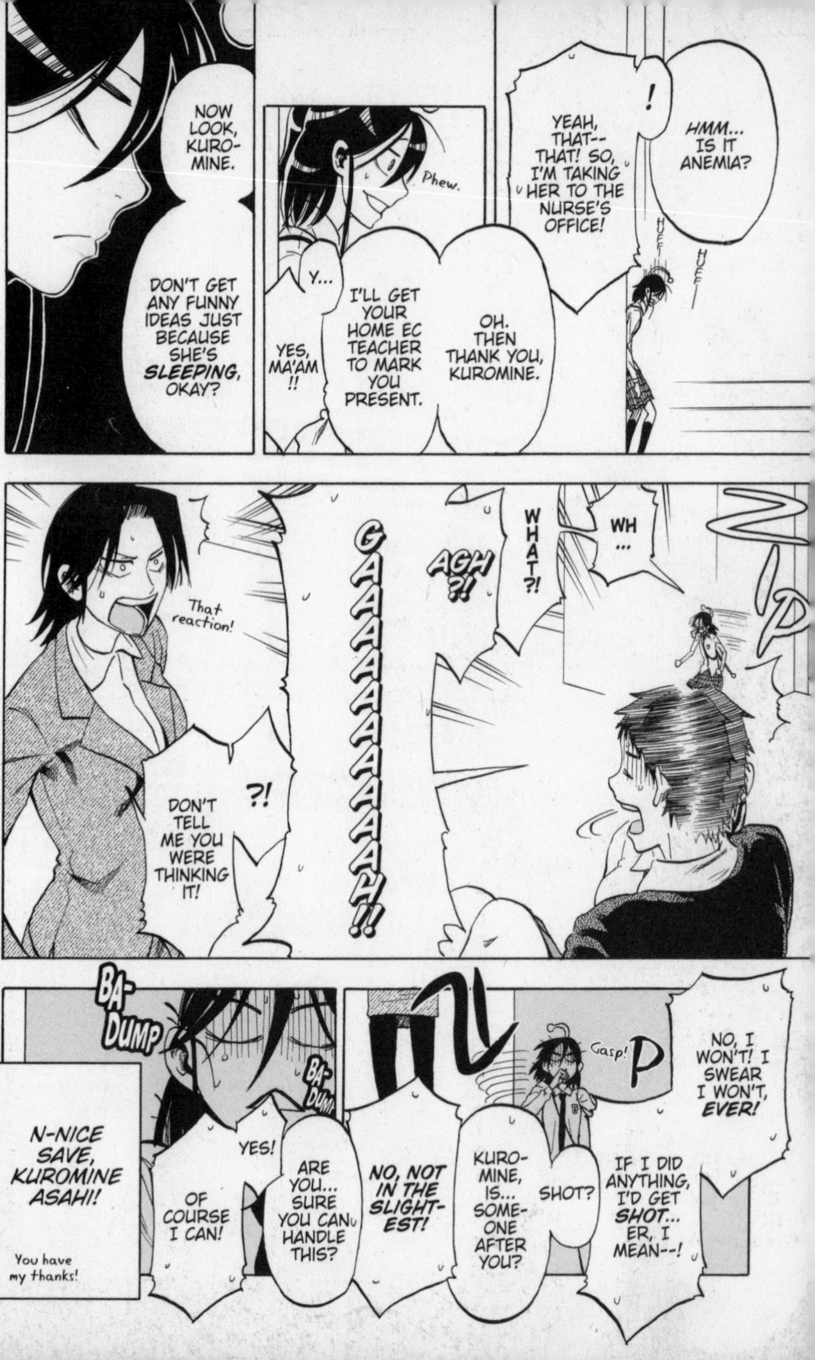
HMM... IS IT ANEMIA?
!
YEAH, THAT-- THAT! SO, I'M TAKING HER TO THE NURSE'S OFFICE!
HUFF HUFF
OH. THEN THANK YOU, KUROMINE.
I'LL GET YOUR HOME EC TEACHER TO MARK YOU PRESENT.
Phew.
Y...
YES, MA'AM!!
NOW LOOK, KUROMINE.
DON'T GET ANY FUNNY IDEAS JUST BECAUSE SHE'S SLEEPING, OKAY?
ZIP
WH...
WHAT?!
AGH?!
GAAAAAAAAAAAH!!
That reaction!
?!
DON'T TELL ME YOU WERE THINKING IT!
NO, I WON'T! I SWEAR I WON'T, EVER!
IF I DID ANYTHING, I'D GET SHOT... ER, I MEAN--!
P
Gasp!
SHOT?
KUROMINE, IS... SOMEONE AFTER YOU?
NO, NOT IN THE SLIGHTEST!
ARE YOU... SURE YOU CAN HANDLE THIS?
YES!
OF COURSE I CAN!
BA-DUMP
BA-DUMP
N-NICE SAVE, KUROMINE ASAHI!
You have my thanks!

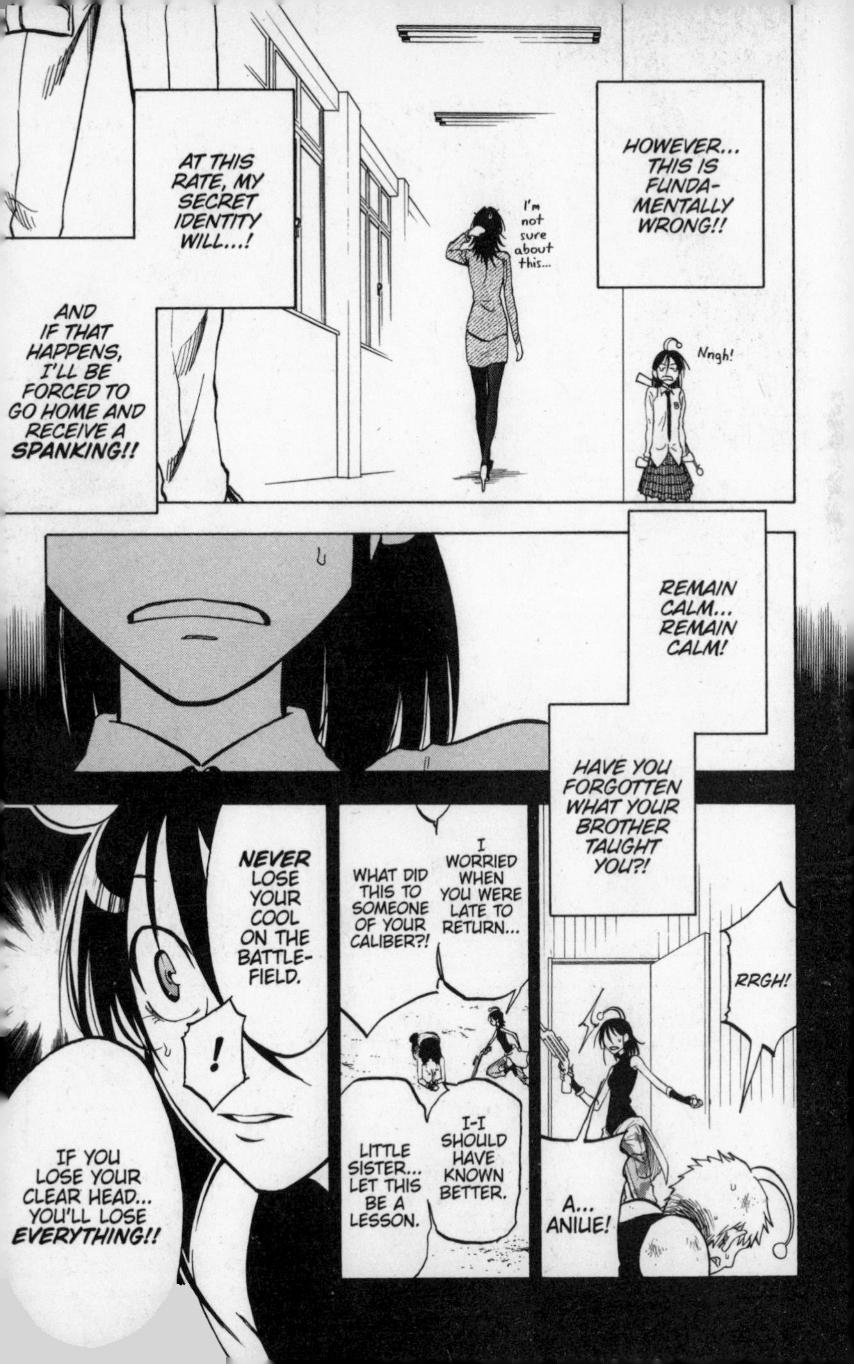
HOWEVER... THIS IS FUNDA-MENTALLY WRONG!!
Nngh!
I'm not sure about this...
AT THIS RATE, MY SECRET IDENTITY WILL...!
AND IF THAT HAPPENS, I'LL BE FORCED TO GO HOME AND RECEIVE A SPANKING!!
REMAIN CALM... REMAIN CALM!
HAVE YOU FORGOTTEN WHAT YOUR BROTHER TAUGHT YOU?!
RRGH!
A... ANIUE!
I WORRIED WHEN YOU WERE LATE TO RETURN...
WHAT DID THIS TO SOMEONE OF YOUR CALIBER?!
I-I SHOULD HAVE KNOWN BETTER.
LITTLE SISTER... LET THIS BE A LESSON.
NEVER LOSE YOUR COOL ON THE BATTLE-FIELD.
!
IF YOU LOSE YOUR CLEAR HEAD... YOU'LL LOSE EVERYTHING!!

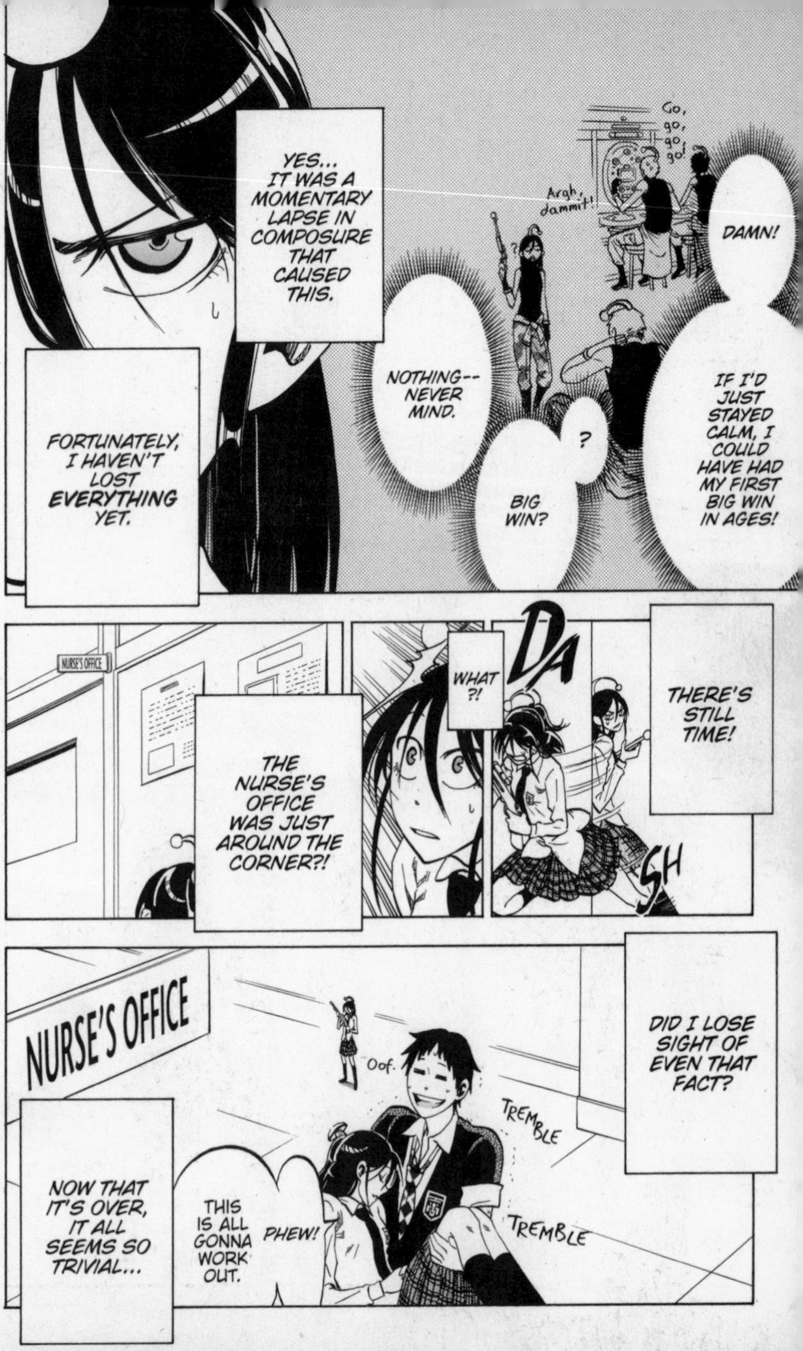
Go, go, go, go!
Argh, dammit!!
DAMN!
IF I'D JUST STAYED CALM, I COULD HAVE HAD MY FIRST BIG WIN IN AGES!
BIG WIN?
?
NOTHING-- NEVER MIND.
YES... IT WAS A MOMENTARY LAPSE IN COMPOSURE THAT CAUSED THIS.
FORTUNATELY, I HAVEN'T LOST EVERYTHING YET.
THERE'S STILL TIME!
DA
SH
WHAT?!
NURSE'S OFFICE
THE NURSE'S OFFICE WAS JUST AROUND THE CORNER?!
DID I LOSE SIGHT OF EVEN THAT FACT?
TREMBLE
TREMBLE
Oof.
NURSE'S OFFICE
PHEW!
THIS IS ALL GONNA WORK OUT.
NOW THAT IT'S OVER, IT ALL SEEMS SO TRIVIAL...

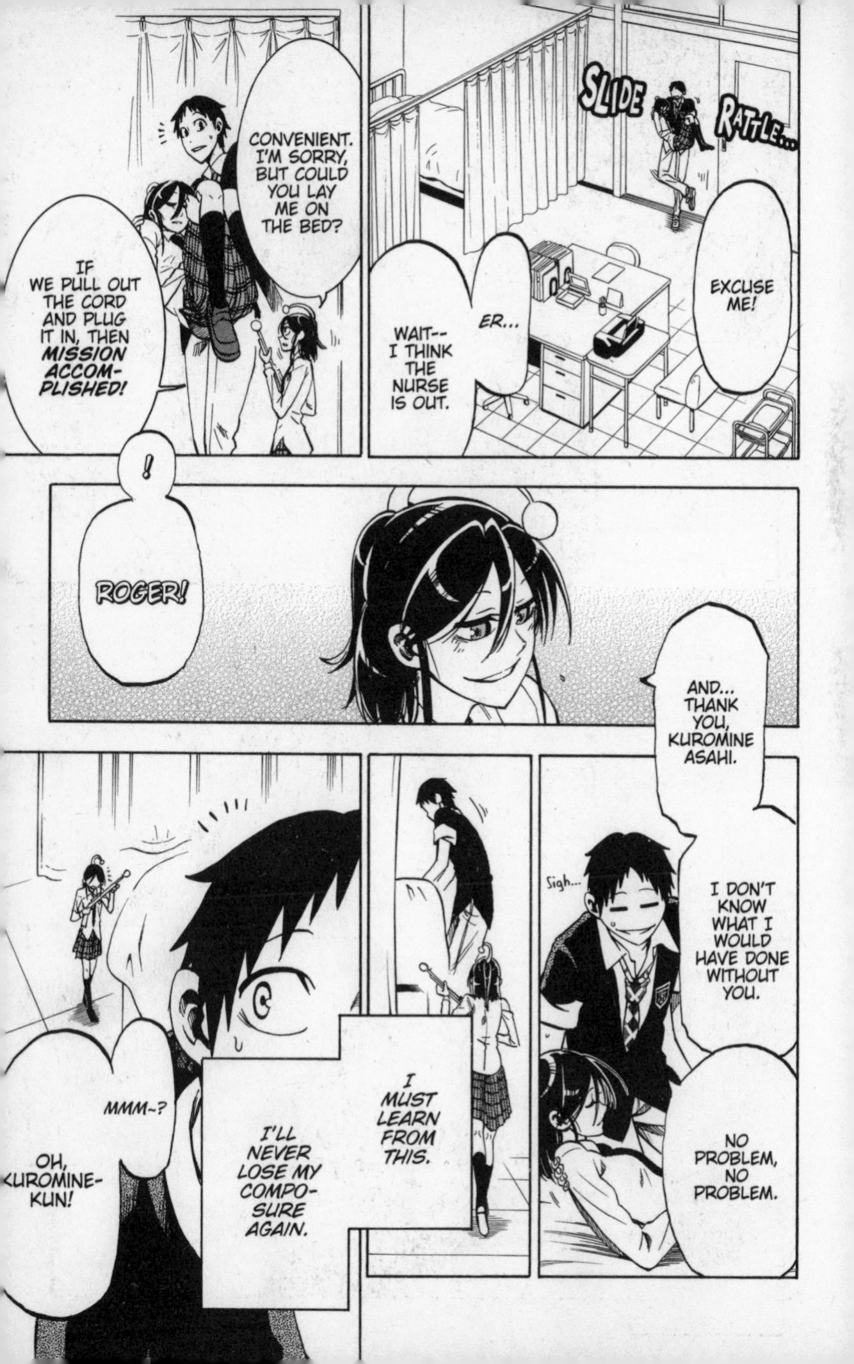
SLIDE
RATTLE...
EXCUSE ME!
ER...
WAIT-- I THINK THE NURSE IS OUT.
CONVENIENT. I'M SORRY, BUT COULD YOU LAY ME ON THE BED?
IF WE PULL OUT THE CORD AND PLUG IT IN, THEN *MISSION ACCOMPLISHED!*
!
ROGER!
AND... THANK YOU, KUROMINE ASAHI.
Sigh...
I DON'T KNOW WHAT I WOULD HAVE DONE WITHOUT YOU.
NO PROBLEM, NO PROBLEM.
I MUST LEARN FROM THIS.
I'LL NEVER LOSE MY COMPOSURE AGAIN.
MMM~?
OH, KUROMINE-KUN!

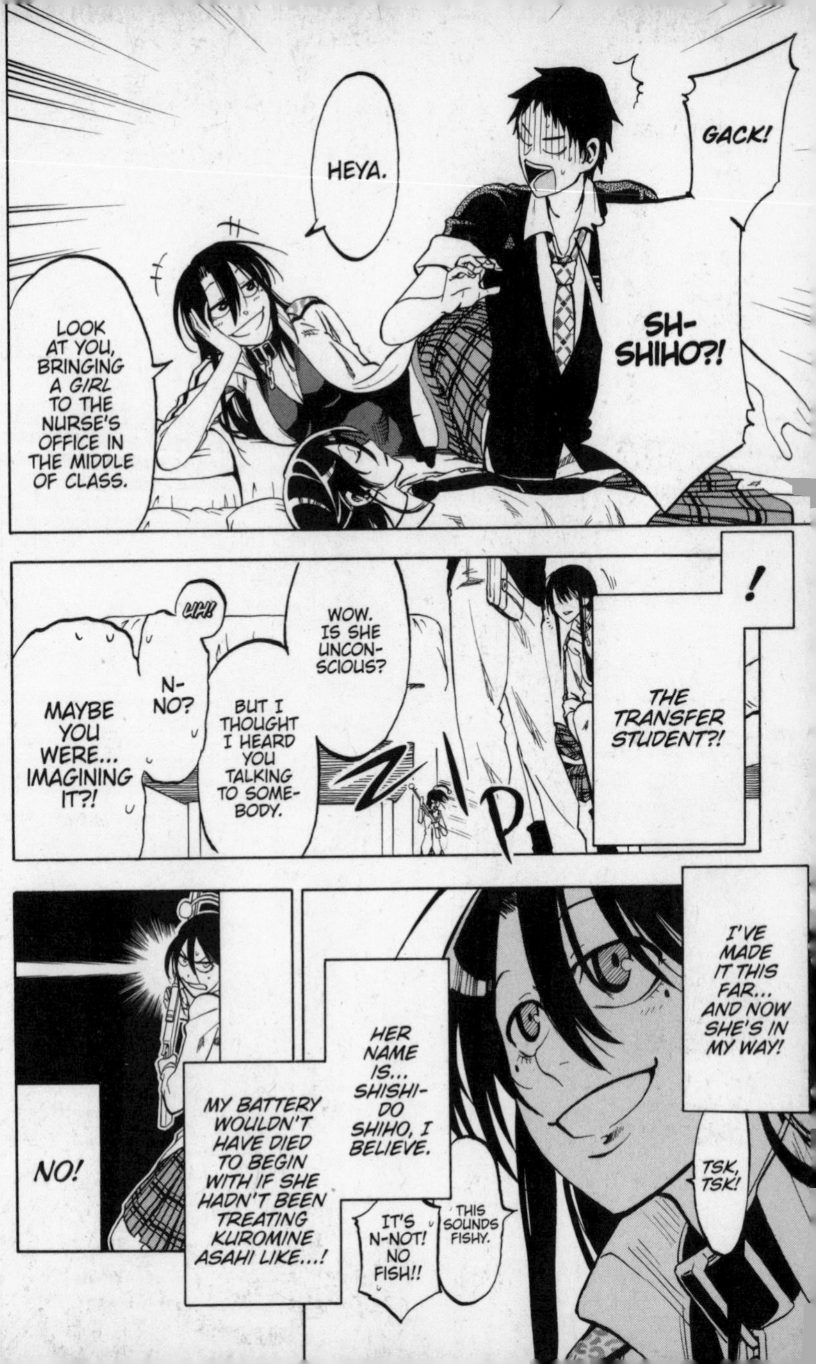
GACK!
HEYA.
SH-SHIHO?!
LOOK AT YOU, BRINGING A GIRL TO THE NURSE'S OFFICE IN THE MIDDLE OF CLASS.
!
THE TRANSFER STUDENT?!
WOW. IS SHE UNCONSCIOUS?
UH!
N-NO?
BUT I THOUGHT I HEARD YOU TALKING TO SOMEBODY.
ZIP
MAYBE YOU WERE... IMAGINING IT?!
I'VE MADE IT THIS FAR... AND NOW SHE'S IN MY WAY!
HER NAME IS... SHISHIDO SHIHO, I BELIEVE.
TSK, TSK!
MY BATTERY WOULDN'T HAVE DIED TO BEGIN WITH IF SHE HADN'T BEEN TREATING KUROMINE ASAHI LIKE...!
THIS SOUNDS FISHY.
IT'S N-NOT! NO FISH!!
NO!

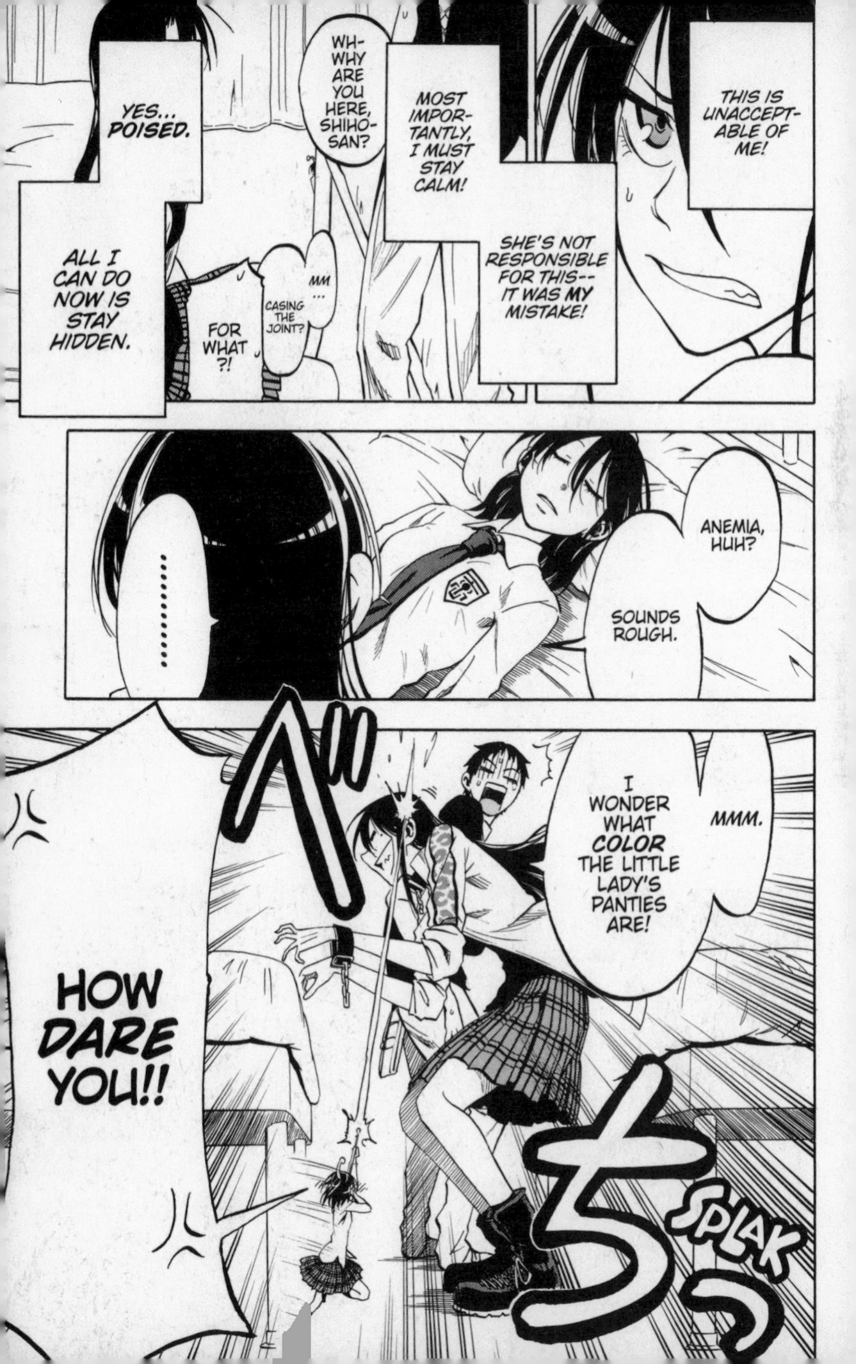
THIS IS UNACCEPTABLE OF ME!
SHE'S NOT RESPONSIBLE FOR THIS-- IT WAS MY MISTAKE!
MOST IMPORTANTLY, I MUST STAY CALM!
WH-WHY ARE YOU HERE, SHIHO-SAN?
MM... CASING THE JOINT?
FOR WHAT?!
YES... POISED.
ALL I CAN DO NOW IS STAY HIDDEN.
ANEMIA, HUH? SOUNDS ROUGH.
......
MMM.
I WONDER WHAT COLOR THE LITTLE LADY'S PANTIES ARE!
HOW DARE YOU!!
SPLAK

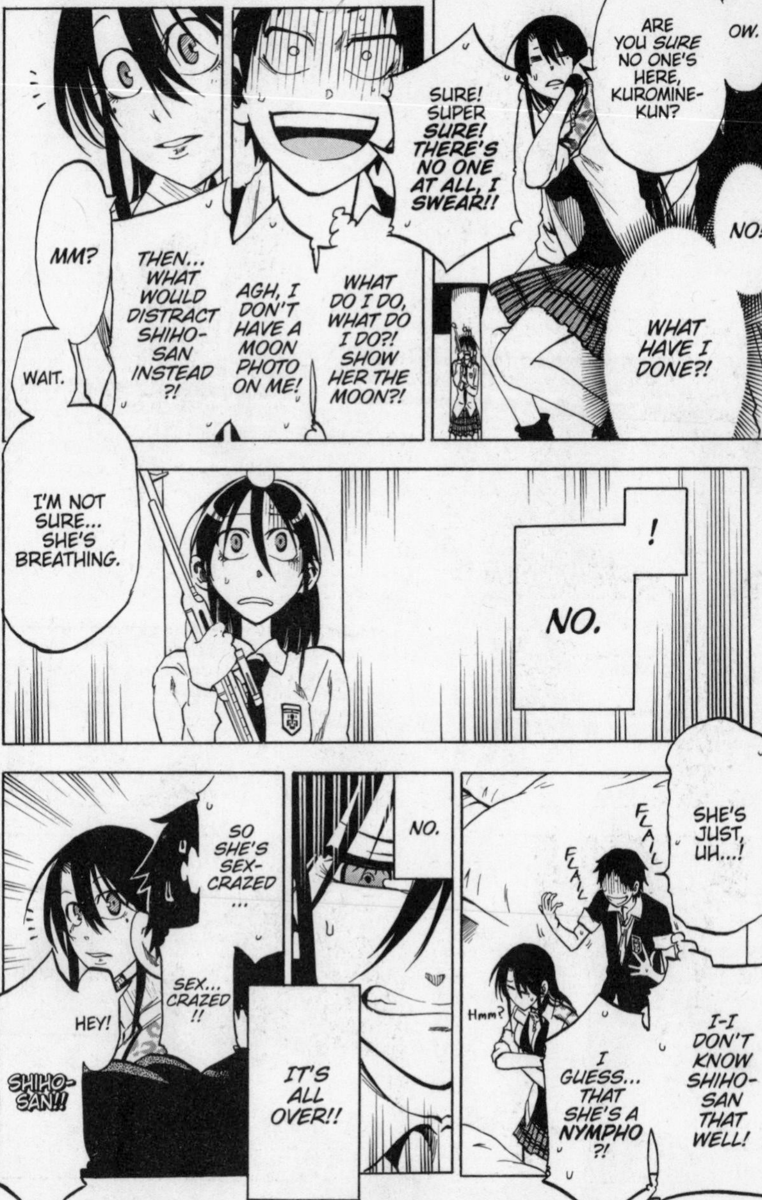

OW.
ARE YOU SURE NO ONE'S HERE, KUROMINE-KUN?
NO!
WHAT HAVE I DONE?!
SURE! SUPER SURE! THERE'S NO ONE AT ALL, I SWEAR!!
WHAT DO I DO, WHAT DO I DO?! SHOW HER THE MOON?!
AGH, I DON'T HAVE A MOON PHOTO ON ME!
THEN... WHAT WOULD DISTRACT SHIHO-SAN INSTEAD?!
MM?
WAIT.
!
NO.
I'M NOT SURE... SHE'S BREATHING.
SHE'S JUST, UH...!
FLAIL
FLAIL
I-I DON'T KNOW SHIHO-SAN THAT WELL!
Hmm?
I GUESS... THAT SHE'S A NYMPHO?!
NO.
IT'S ALL OVER!!
SO SHE'S SEX-CRAZED...
SEX... CRAZED!!
HEY!
SHIHO-SAN!!

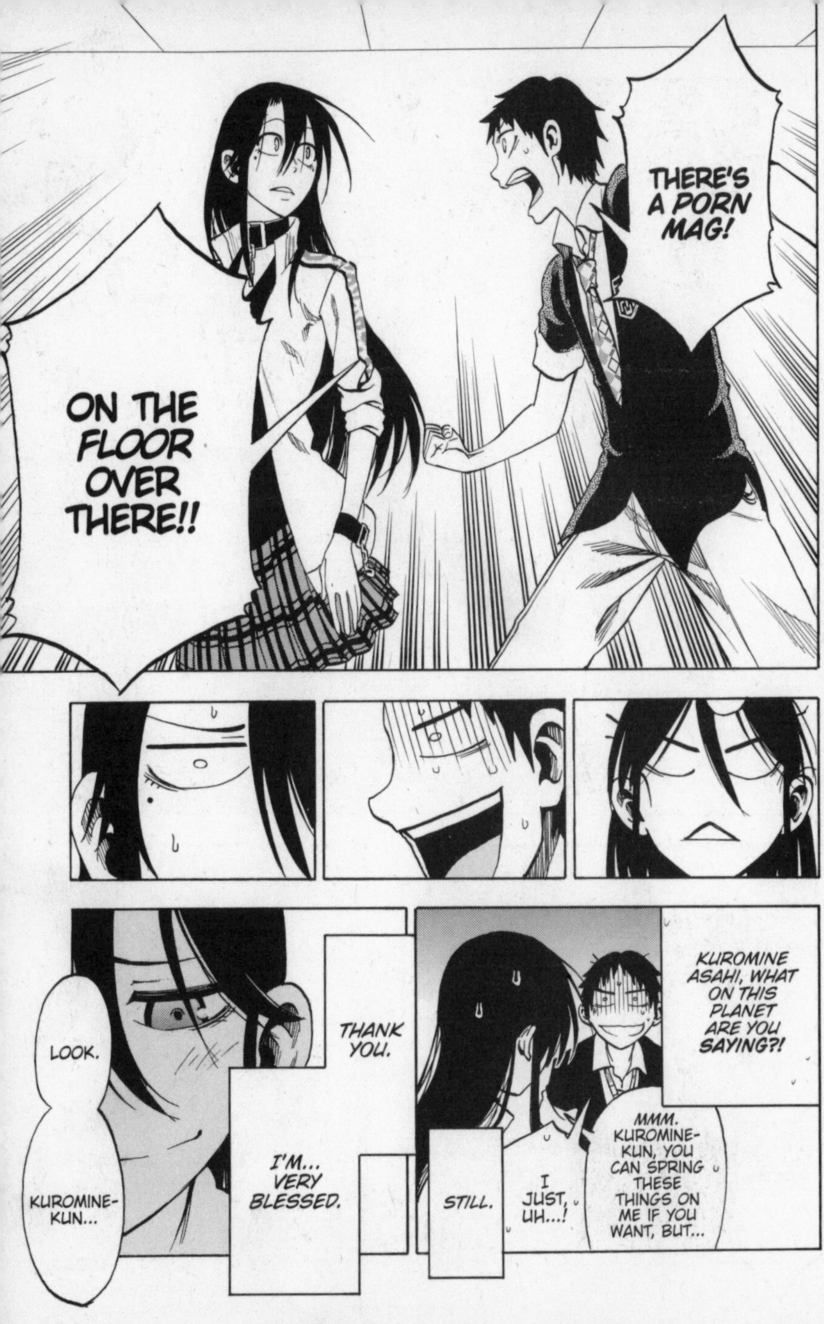
THERE'S A PORN MAG!
ON THE FLOOR OVER THERE!!
KUROMINE ASAHI, WHAT ON THIS PLANET ARE YOU SAYING?!
MMM. KUROMINE-KUN, YOU CAN SPRING THESE THINGS ON ME IF YOU WANT, BUT...
I JUST, UH...!
STILL.
THANK YOU.
LOOK.
I'M... VERY BLESSED.
KUROMINE-KUN...

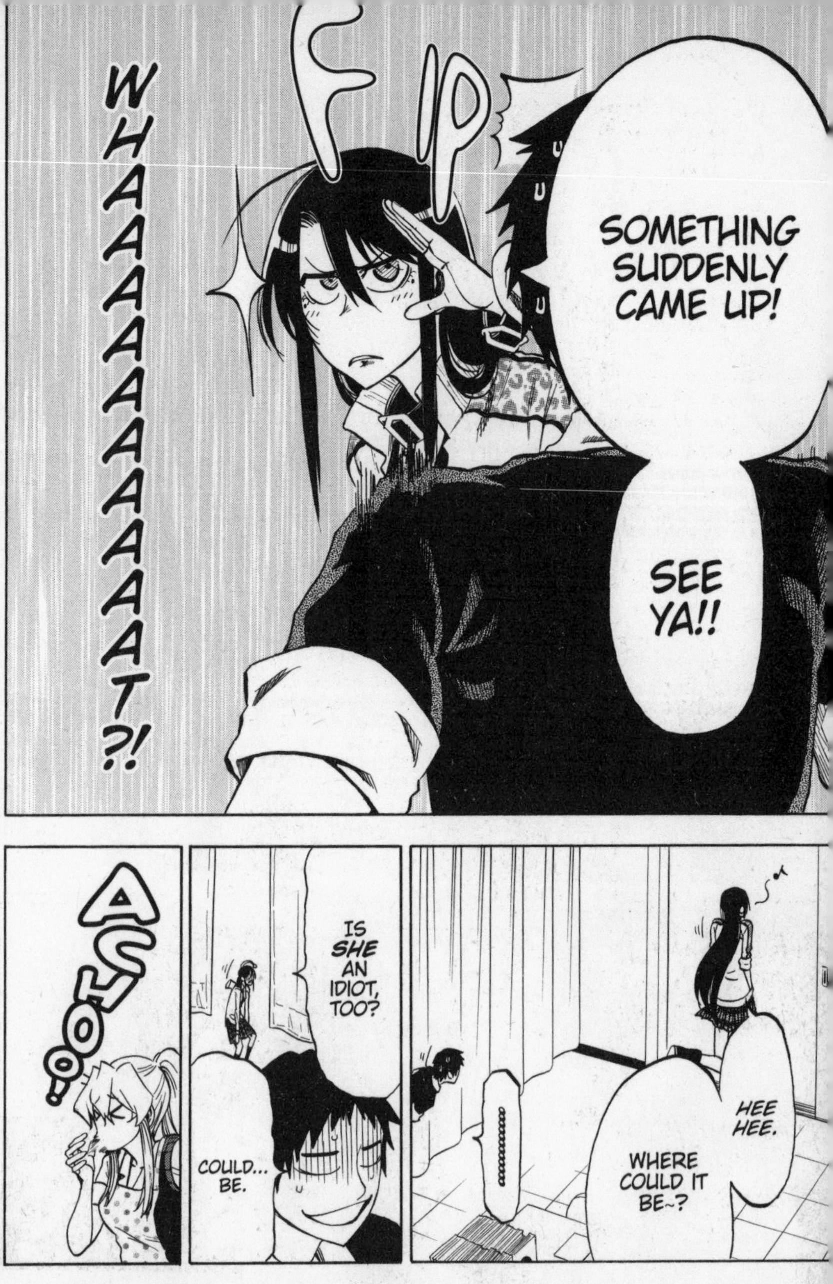
FLIP
SOMETHING SUDDENLY CAME UP!
SEE YA!!
WHAAAAAAAAAAAT?!
HEE HEE.
WHERE COULD IT BE~?
....
IS SHE AN IDIOT, TOO?
COULD... BE.
ACHOO!

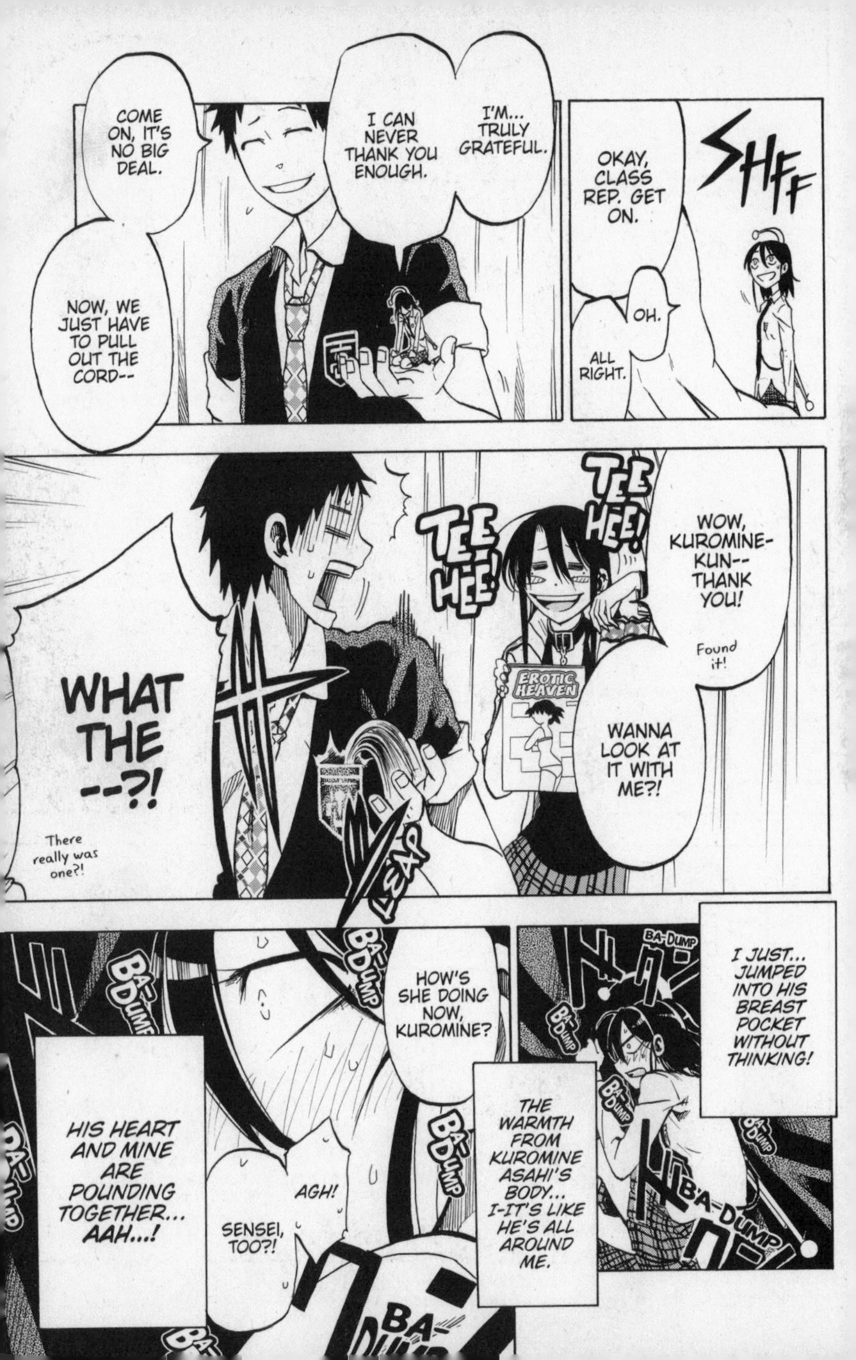
SHFF
OKAY, CLASS REP. GET ON.
OH.
ALL RIGHT.
I'M... TRULY GRATEFUL.
I CAN NEVER THANK YOU ENOUGH.
COME ON, IT'S NO BIG DEAL.
NOW, WE JUST HAVE TO PULL OUT THE CORD--
WOW, KUROMINE-KUN-- THANK YOU!
TEE HEE!
TEE HEE!
Found it!
EROTIC HEAVEN
WANNA LOOK AT IT WITH ME?!
WHAT THE --?!
There really was one?!
I JUST... JUMPED INTO HIS BREAST POCKET WITHOUT THINKING!
BA-DUMP
BA-DUMP
BA-DUMP
BA-DUMP
THE WARMTH FROM KUROMINE ASAHI'S BODY... I-IT'S LIKE HE'S ALL AROUND ME.
BA-DUMP
HOW'S SHE DOING NOW, KUROMINE?
BA-DUMP
AGH!
SENSEI, TOO?!
BA-DUMP
HIS HEART AND MINE ARE POUNDING TOGETHER... AAH...!

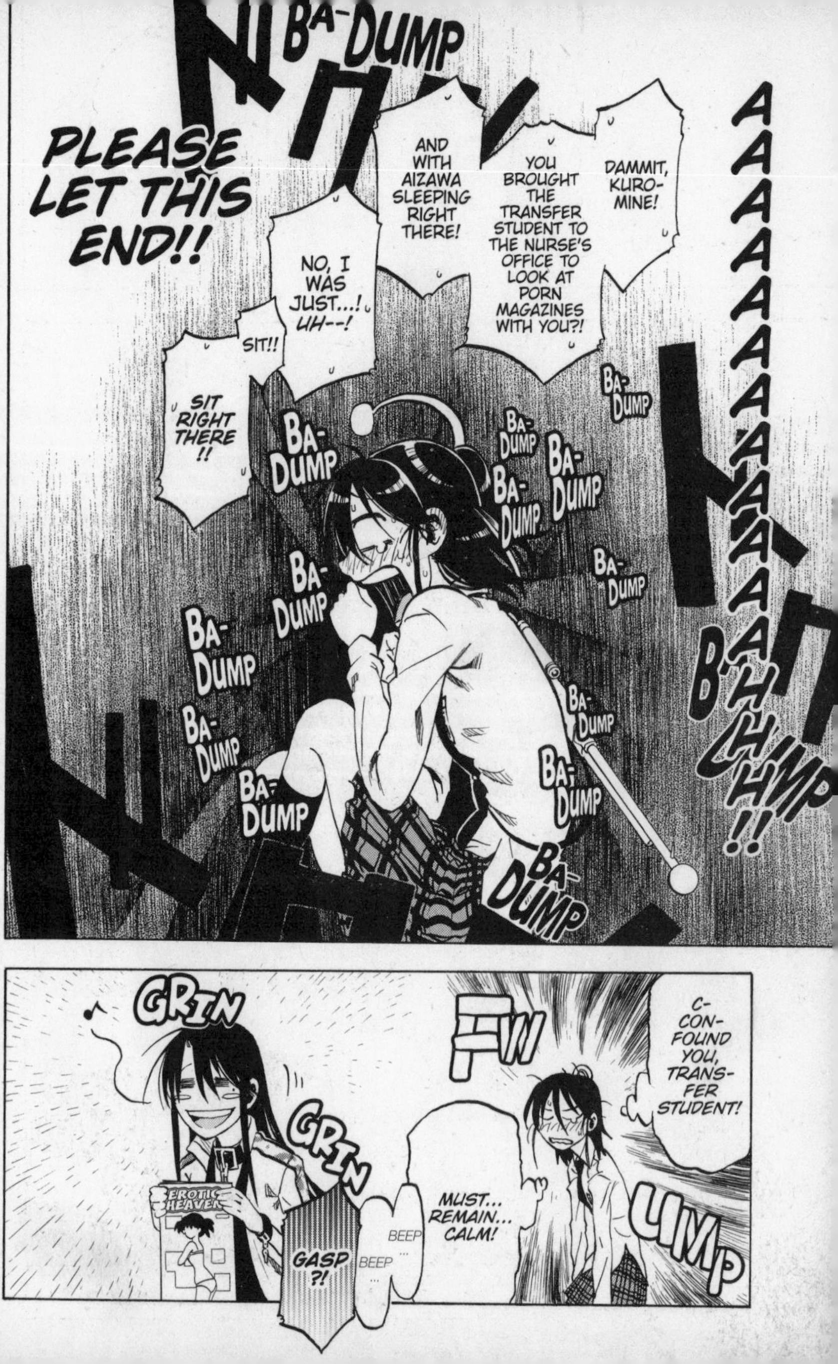

AAAAAAAAAAAAAAA
BAHUMP!!
DAMMIT, KURO-MINE!
YOU BROUGHT THE TRANSFER STUDENT TO THE NURSE'S OFFICE TO LOOK AT PORN MAGAZINES WITH YOU?!
AND WITH AIZAWA SLEEPING RIGHT THERE!
BA-DUMP
NO, I WAS JUST...! UH--!
SIT!!
SIT RIGHT THERE!!
PLEASE LET THIS END!!
BA-DUMP
BA-DUMP
BA-DUMP
BA-DUMP
BA-DUMP
BA-DUMP
BA-DUMP
BA-DUMP
BA-DUMP
BA-DUMP
BA-DUMP
BA-DUMP
BA-DUMP
BA-DUMP
C-CON-FOUND YOU, TRANS-FER STUDENT!
FW
LIMP
MUST... REMAIN... CALM!
BEEP... BEEP...
GASP?!
GRIN
GRIN
EROTIC HEAVEN

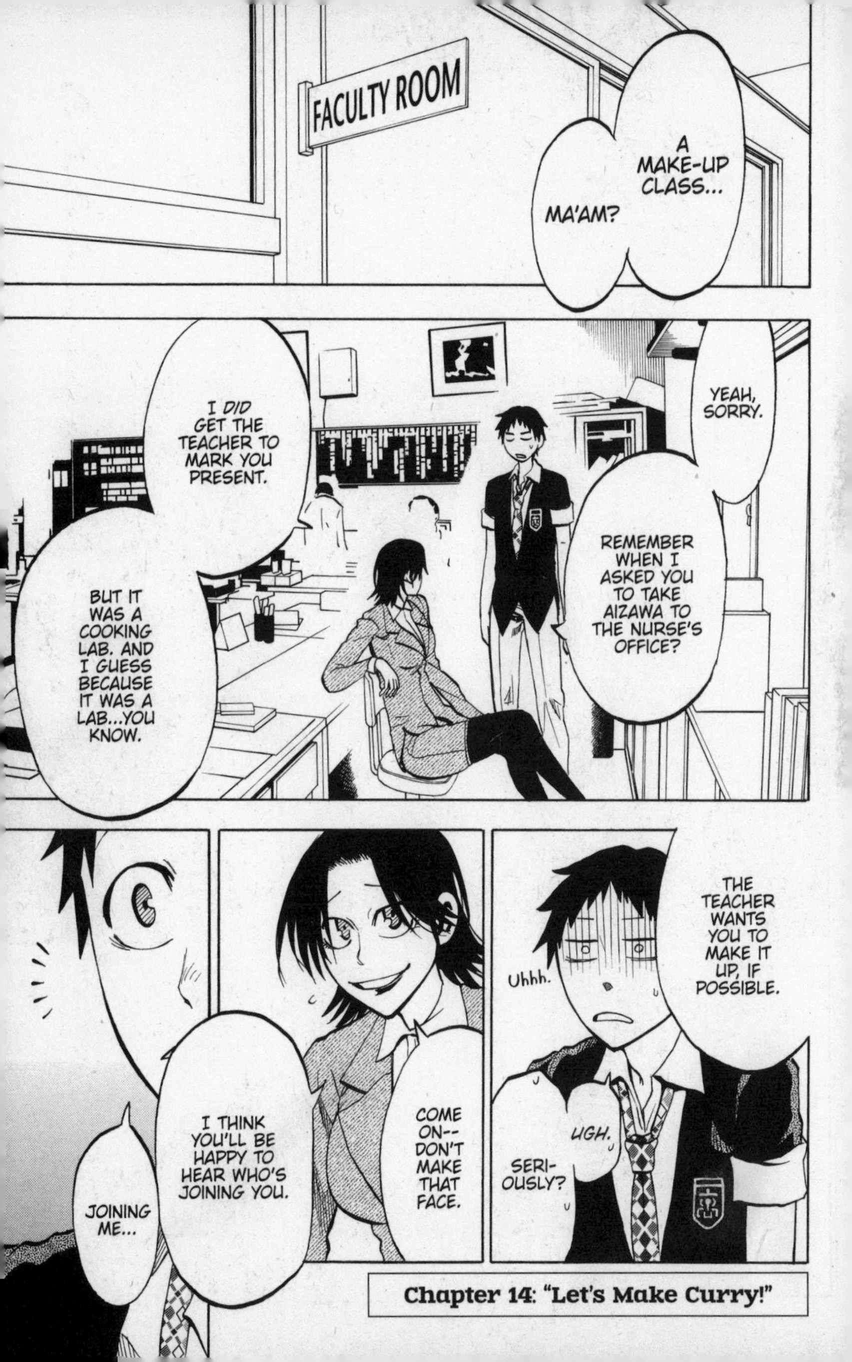
FACULTY ROOM
A MAKE-UP CLASS...
MA'AM?
YEAH, SORRY.
REMEMBER WHEN I ASKED YOU TO TAKE AIZAWA TO THE NURSE'S OFFICE?
I *DID* GET THE TEACHER TO MARK YOU PRESENT.
BUT IT WAS A COOKING LAB. AND I GUESS BECAUSE IT WAS A LAB...YOU KNOW.
THE TEACHER WANTS YOU TO MAKE IT UP, IF POSSIBLE.
Uhhh.
UGH.
SERIOUSLY?
COME ON-- DON'T MAKE THAT FACE.
I THINK YOU'LL BE HAPPY TO HEAR WHO'S JOINING YOU.
JOINING ME...

Chapter 14: "Let's Make Curry!"

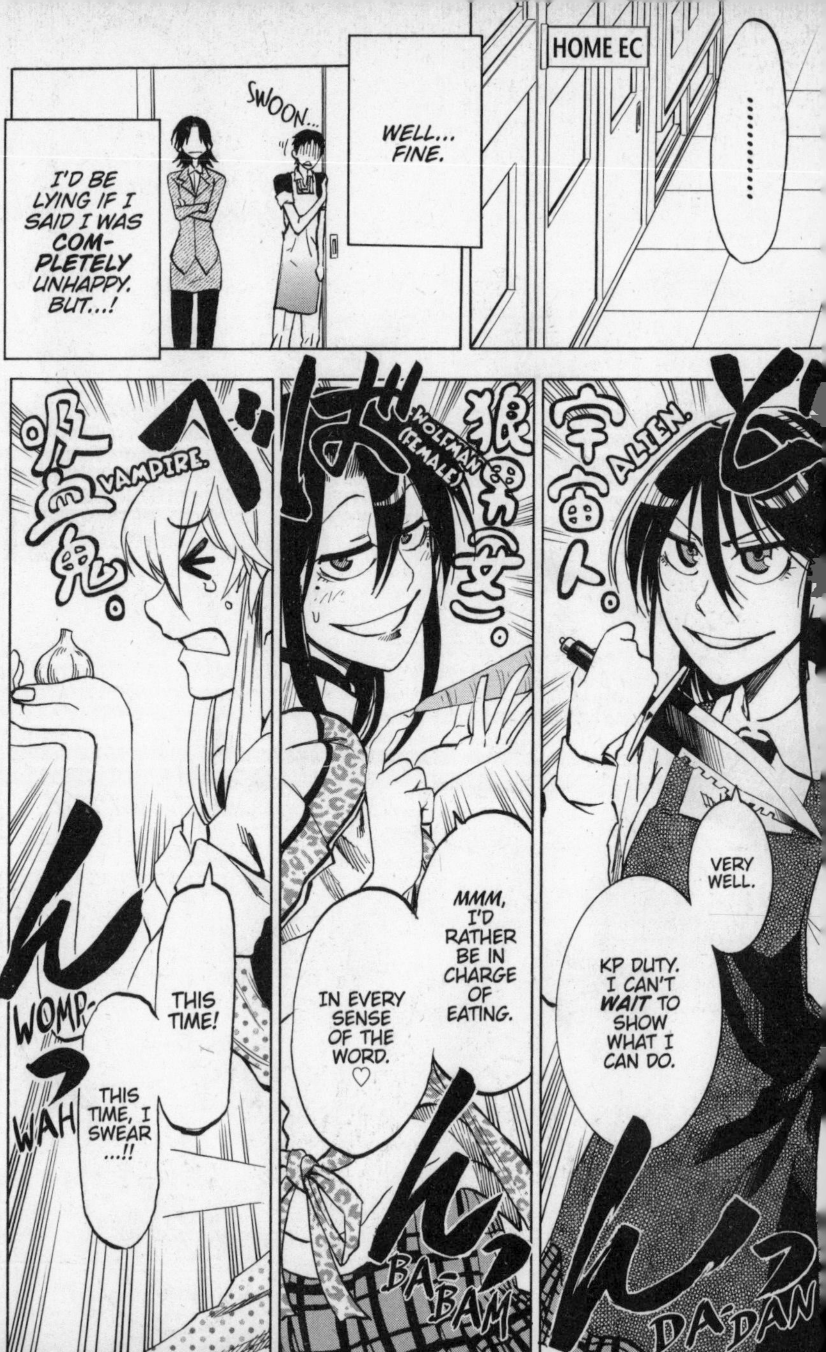
……
HOME EC
WELL… FINE.
SWOON…
I'D BE LYING IF I SAID I WAS COM-PLETELY UNHAPPY. BUT…!
宇宙人。
ALIEN.
VERY WELL.
KP DUTY. I CAN'T *WAIT* TO SHOW WHAT I CAN DO.
DA-DAN
狼男女。
WOLFMAN (FEMALE)
MMM, I'D RATHER BE IN CHARGE OF EATING.
IN EVERY SENSE OF THE WORD. ♡
BA-BAM
吸血鬼。
VAMPIRE.
THIS TIME!
THIS TIME, I SWEAR …!!
WOMP-WAH

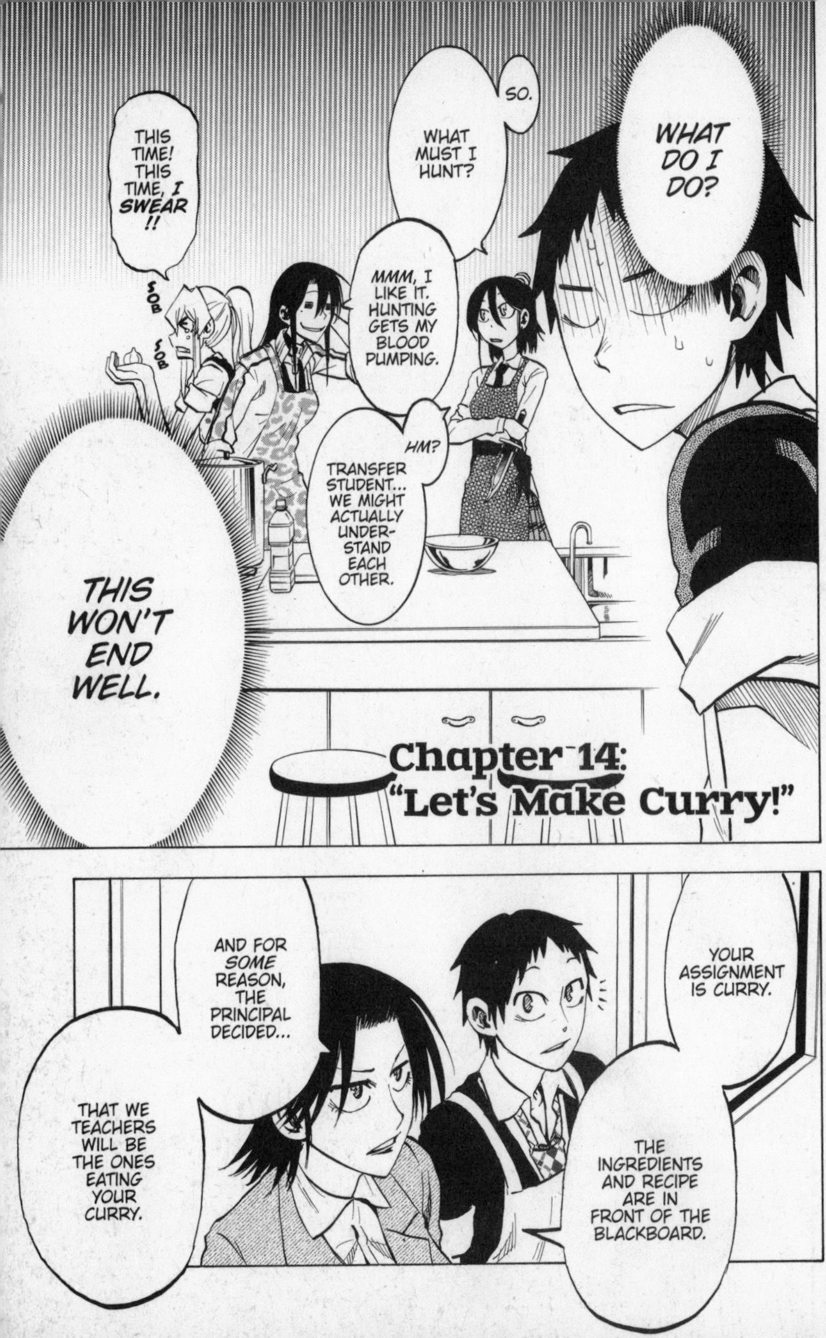
WHAT DO I DO?
SO.
WHAT MUST I HUNT?
THIS TIME! THIS TIME, I SWEAR!!
SOB SOB
MMM, I LIKE IT. HUNTING GETS MY BLOOD PUMPING.
HM?
TRANSFER STUDENT... WE MIGHT ACTUALLY UNDER-STAND EACH OTHER.
THIS WON'T END WELL.
Chapter 14: "Let's Make Curry!"
YOUR ASSIGNMENT IS CURRY.
THE INGREDIENTS AND RECIPE ARE IN FRONT OF THE BLACKBOARD.
AND FOR SOME REASON, THE PRINCIPAL DECIDED...
THAT WE TEACHERS WILL BE THE ONES EATING YOUR CURRY.

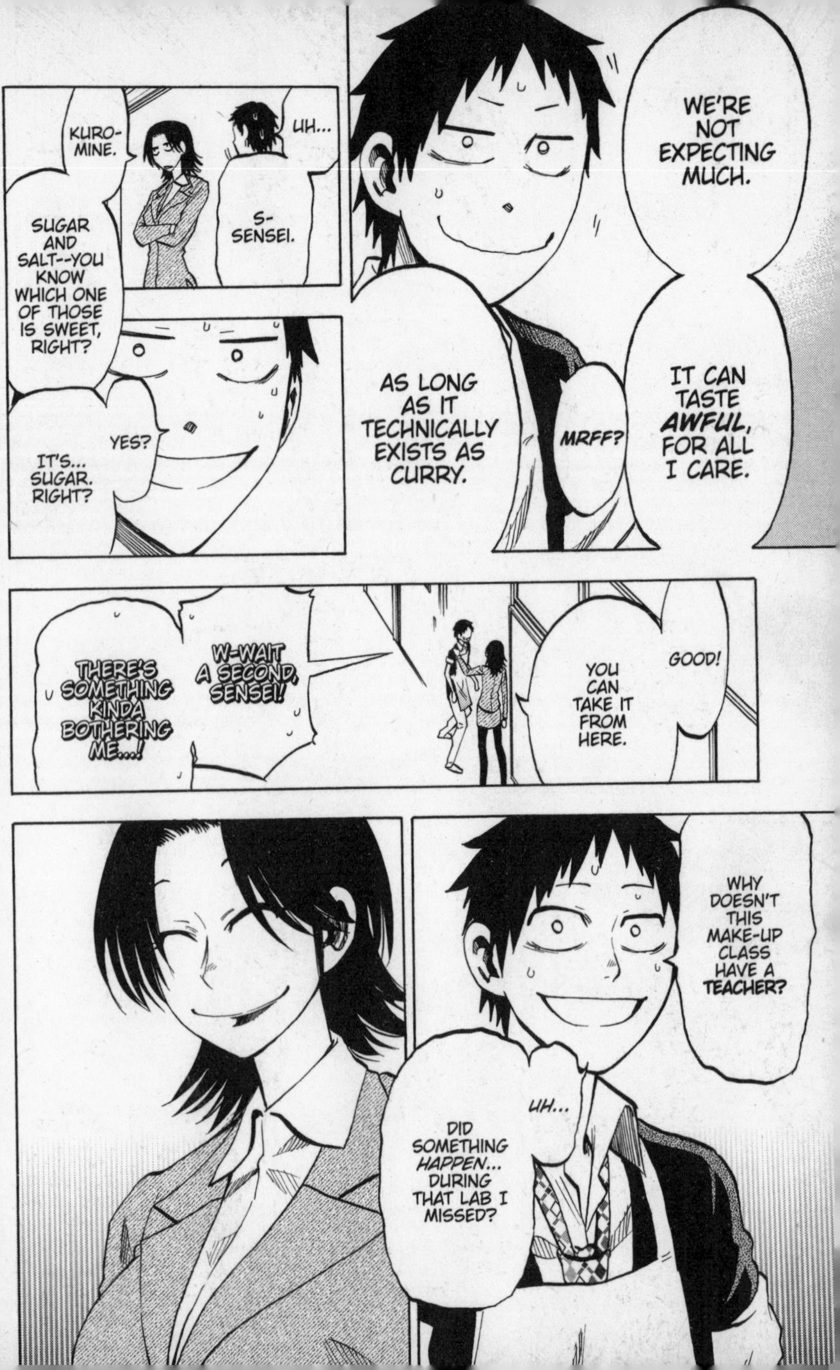
WE'RE NOT EXPECTING MUCH.
IT CAN TASTE **AWFUL**, FOR ALL I CARE.
MRFF?
AS LONG AS IT TECHNICALLY EXISTS AS CURRY.
UH...
S-SENSEI.
KURO-MINE.
SUGAR AND SALT--YOU KNOW WHICH ONE OF THOSE IS SWEET, RIGHT?
YES?
IT'S... SUGAR. RIGHT?
GOOD!
YOU CAN TAKE IT FROM HERE.
W-WAIT A SECOND, SENSEI!
THERE'S SOMETHING KINDA BOTHERING ME...!
WHY DOESN'T THIS MAKE-UP CLASS HAVE A **TEACHER**?
UH...
DID SOMETHING *HAPPEN*... DURING THAT LAB I MISSED?

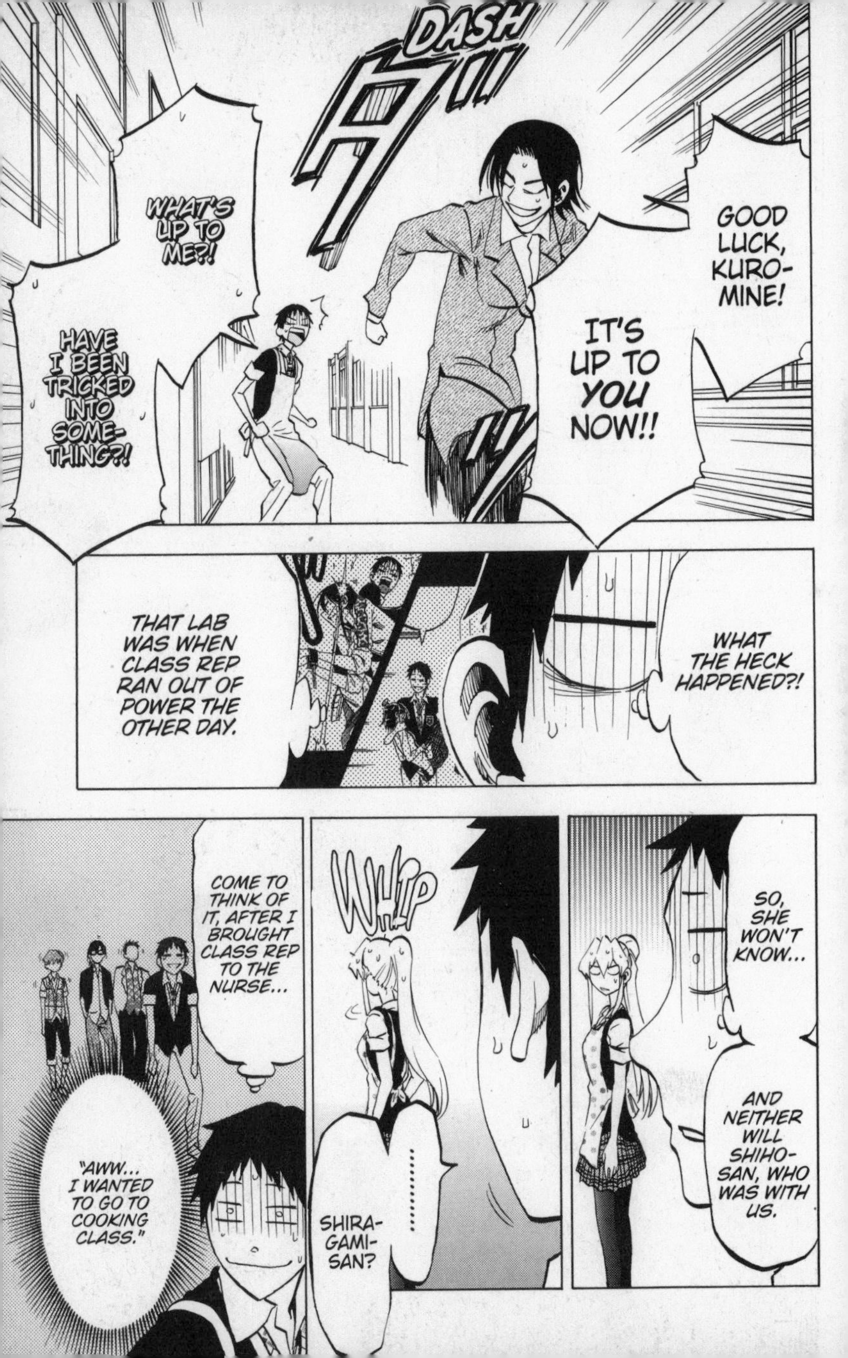
GOOD LUCK, KURO-MINE!
IT'S UP TO YOU NOW!!
DASH
WHAT'S UP TO ME?!
HAVE I BEEN TRICKED INTO SOME-THING?!
WHAT THE HECK HAPPENED?!
THAT LAB WAS WHEN CLASS REP RAN OUT OF POWER THE OTHER DAY.
SO, SHE WON'T KNOW...
AND NEITHER WILL SHIHO-SAN, WHO WAS WITH US.
WHIP
......
SHIRA-GAMI-SAN?
COME TO THINK OF IT, AFTER I BROUGHT CLASS REP TO THE NURSE...
"AWW... I WANTED TO GO TO COOKING CLASS."

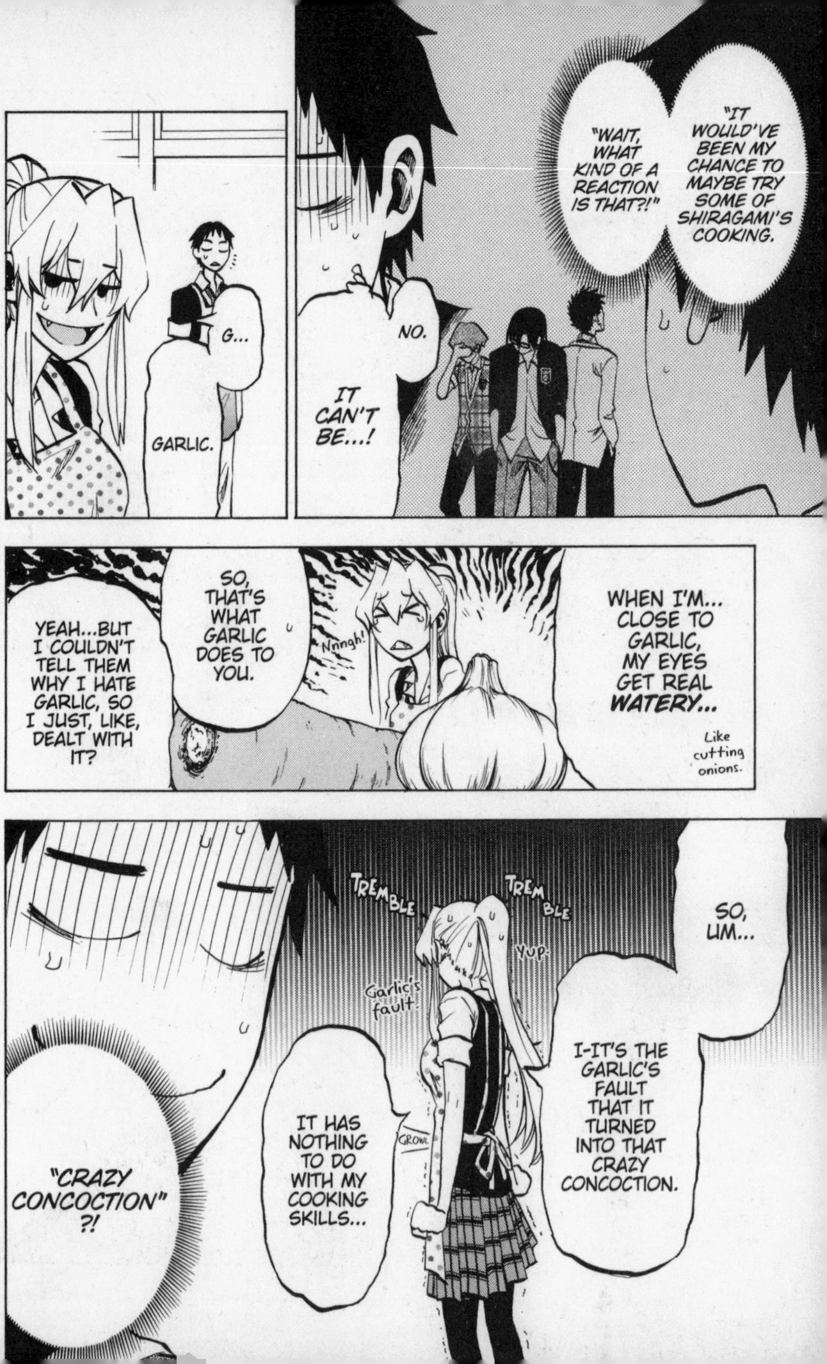
"IT WOULD'VE BEEN MY CHANCE TO MAYBE TRY SOME OF SHIRAGAMI'S COOKING.
"WAIT, WHAT KIND OF A REACTION IS THAT?!"
NO.
IT CAN'T BE...!
G...
GARLIC.
WHEN I'M... CLOSE TO GARLIC, MY EYES GET REAL WATERY...
Like cutting onions.
Nnngh!
SO, THAT'S WHAT GARLIC DOES TO YOU.
YEAH...BUT I COULDN'T TELL THEM WHY I HATE GARLIC, SO I JUST, LIKE, DEALT WITH IT?
SO, UM...
TREMBLE TREMBLE
YUP.
I-IT'S THE GARLIC'S FAULT THAT IT TURNED INTO THAT CRAZY CONCOCTION.
Garlic's fault.
GROWL
IT HAS NOTHING TO DO WITH MY COOKING SKILLS...
"CRAZY CONCOCTION" ?!

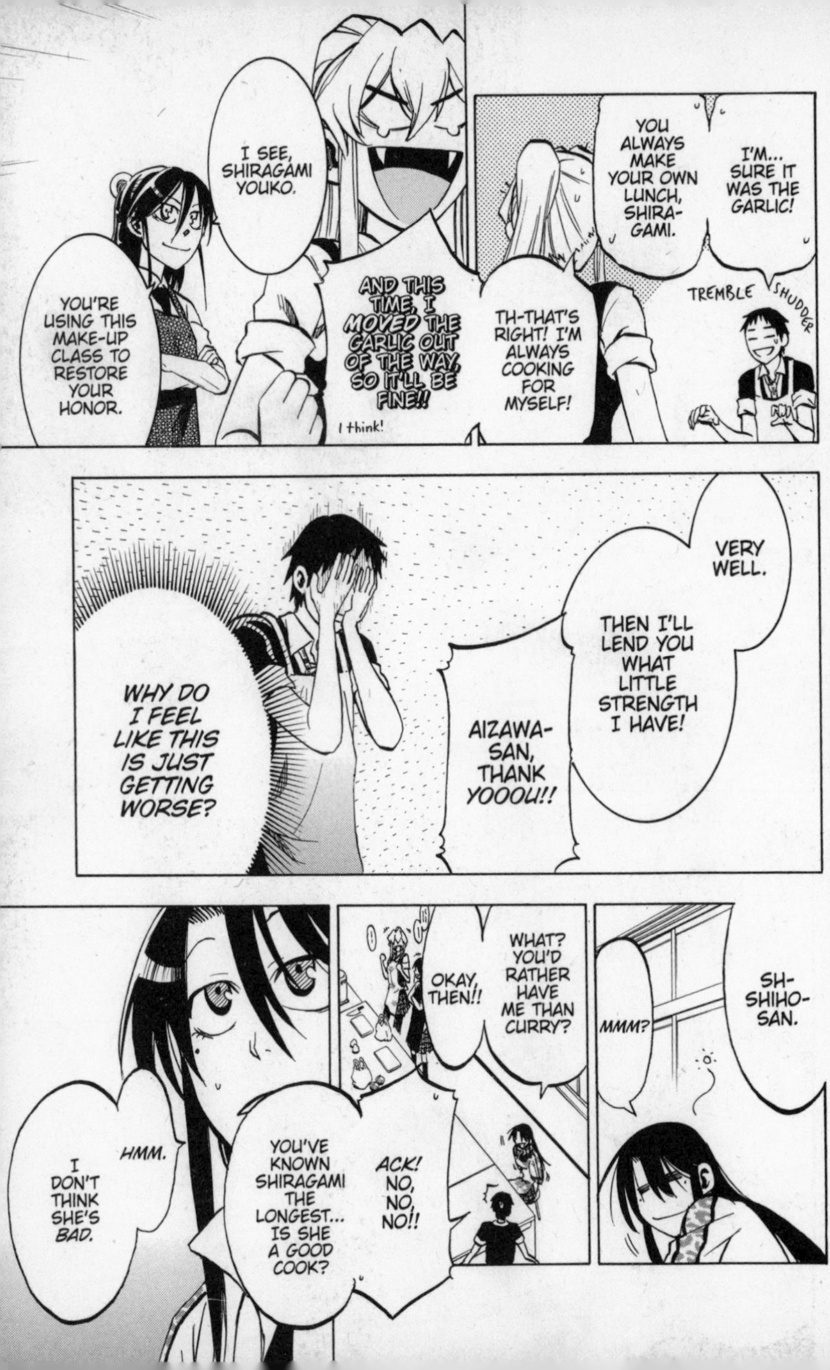
I'M... SURE IT WAS THE GARLIC!
YOU ALWAYS MAKE YOUR OWN LUNCH, SHIRAGAMI.
TREMBLE
SHUDDER
TH-THAT'S RIGHT! I'M ALWAYS COOKING FOR MYSELF!
I SEE, SHIRAGAMI YOUKO.
YOU'RE USING THIS MAKE-UP CLASS TO RESTORE YOUR HONOR.
AND THIS TIME, I *MOVED* THE GARLIC OUT OF THE WAY, SO IT'LL BE FINE!!
I think!
VERY WELL.
THEN I'LL LEND YOU WHAT LITTLE STRENGTH I HAVE!
AIZAWA-SAN, THANK *YOOOU!!*
WHY DO I FEEL LIKE THIS IS JUST GETTING WORSE?
SH-SHIHO-SAN.
MMM?
WHAT? YOU'D RATHER HAVE ME THAN CURRY?
OKAY, THEN!!
ACK! NO, NO, NO!!
YOU'VE KNOWN SHIRAGAMI THE LONGEST... IS SHE A GOOD COOK?
HMM.
I DON'T THINK SHE'S *BAD.*

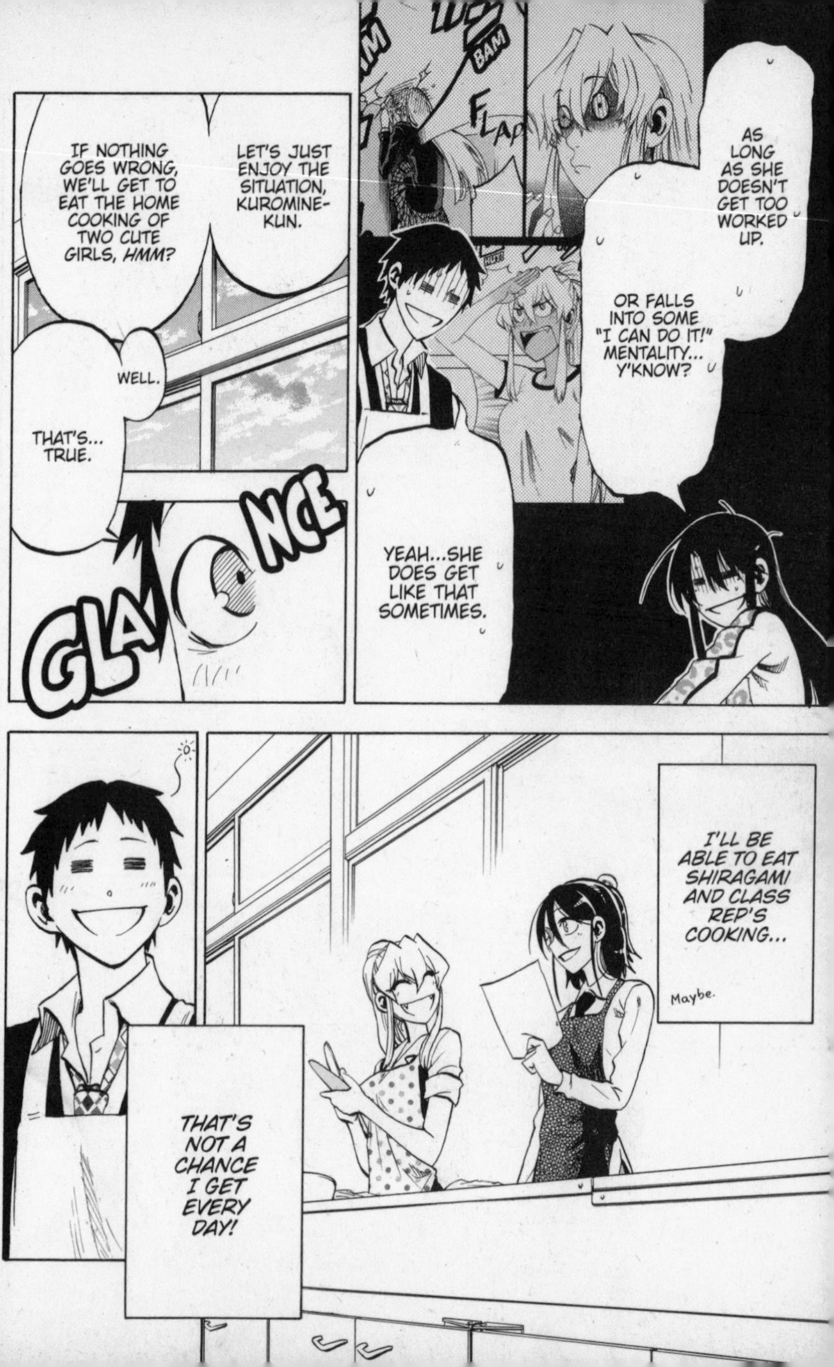
BAM
FLAP
AS LONG AS SHE DOESN'T GET TOO WORKED UP.
OR FALLS INTO SOME "I CAN DO IT!" MENTALITY... Y'KNOW?
YEAH...SHE DOES GET LIKE THAT SOMETIMES.
LET'S JUST ENJOY THE SITUATION, KUROMINE-KUN.
IF NOTHING GOES WRONG, WE'LL GET TO EAT THE HOME COOKING OF TWO CUTE GIRLS, *HMM?*
WELL.
THAT'S... TRUE.
GLANCE
I'LL BE ABLE TO EAT SHIRAGAMI AND CLASS REP'S COOKING...
Maybe.
THAT'S NOT A CHANCE I GET EVERY DAY!

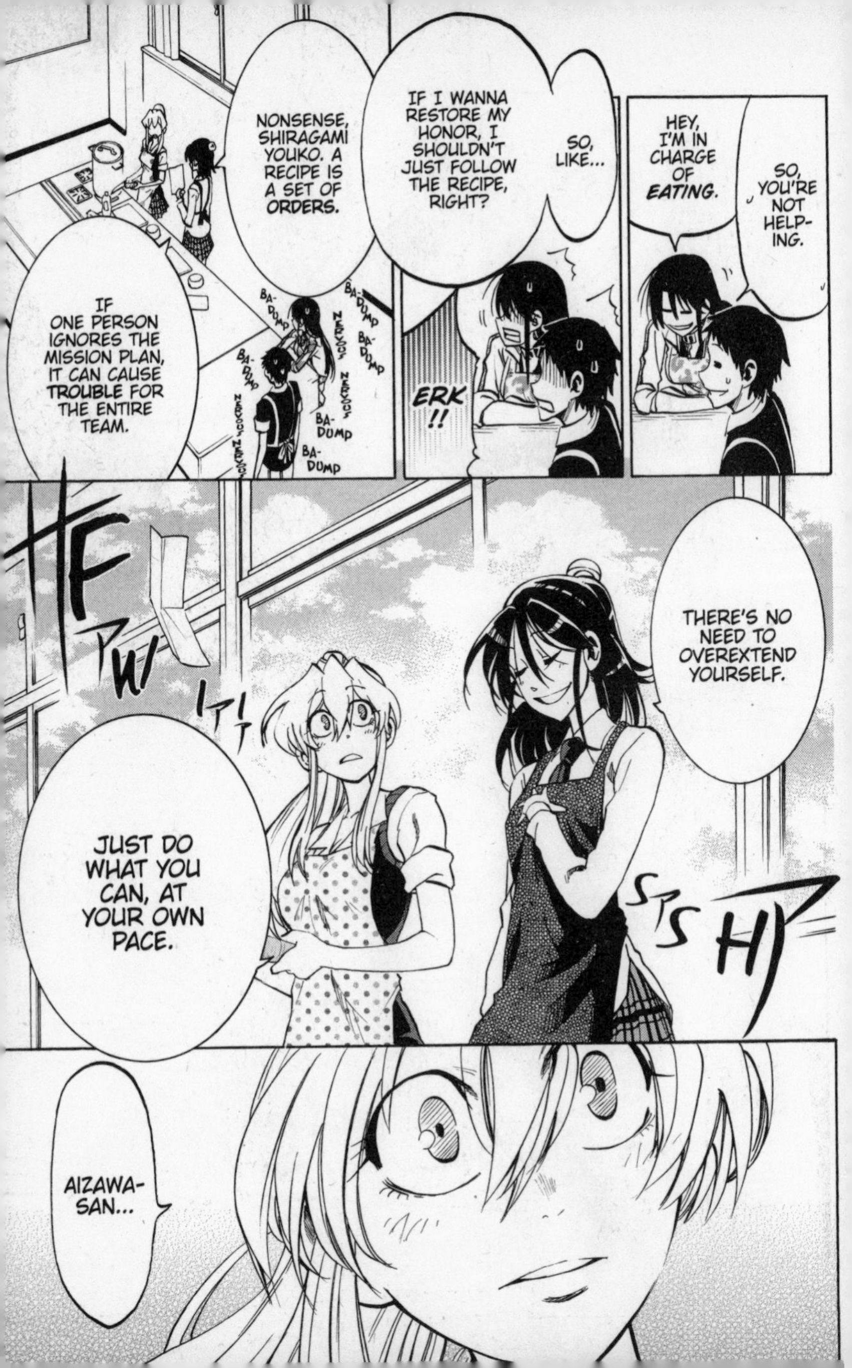
SO, YOU'RE NOT HELPING.
HEY, I'M IN CHARGE OF *EATING*.
SO, LIKE...
IF I WANNA RESTORE MY HONOR, I SHOULDN'T JUST FOLLOW THE RECIPE, RIGHT?
ERK !!
NONSENSE, SHIRAGAMI YOUKO. A RECIPE IS A SET OF ORDERS.
IF ONE PERSON IGNORES THE MISSION PLAN, IT CAN CAUSE TROUBLE FOR THE ENTIRE TEAM.
BA-DUMP
BA-DUMP
NERVOUS
BA-DUMP
NERVOUS
BA-DUMP
BA-DUMP
NERVOUS NERVOUS
THERE'S NO NEED TO OVEREXTEND YOURSELF.
JUST DO WHAT YOU CAN, AT YOUR OWN PACE.
AIZAWA-SAN...

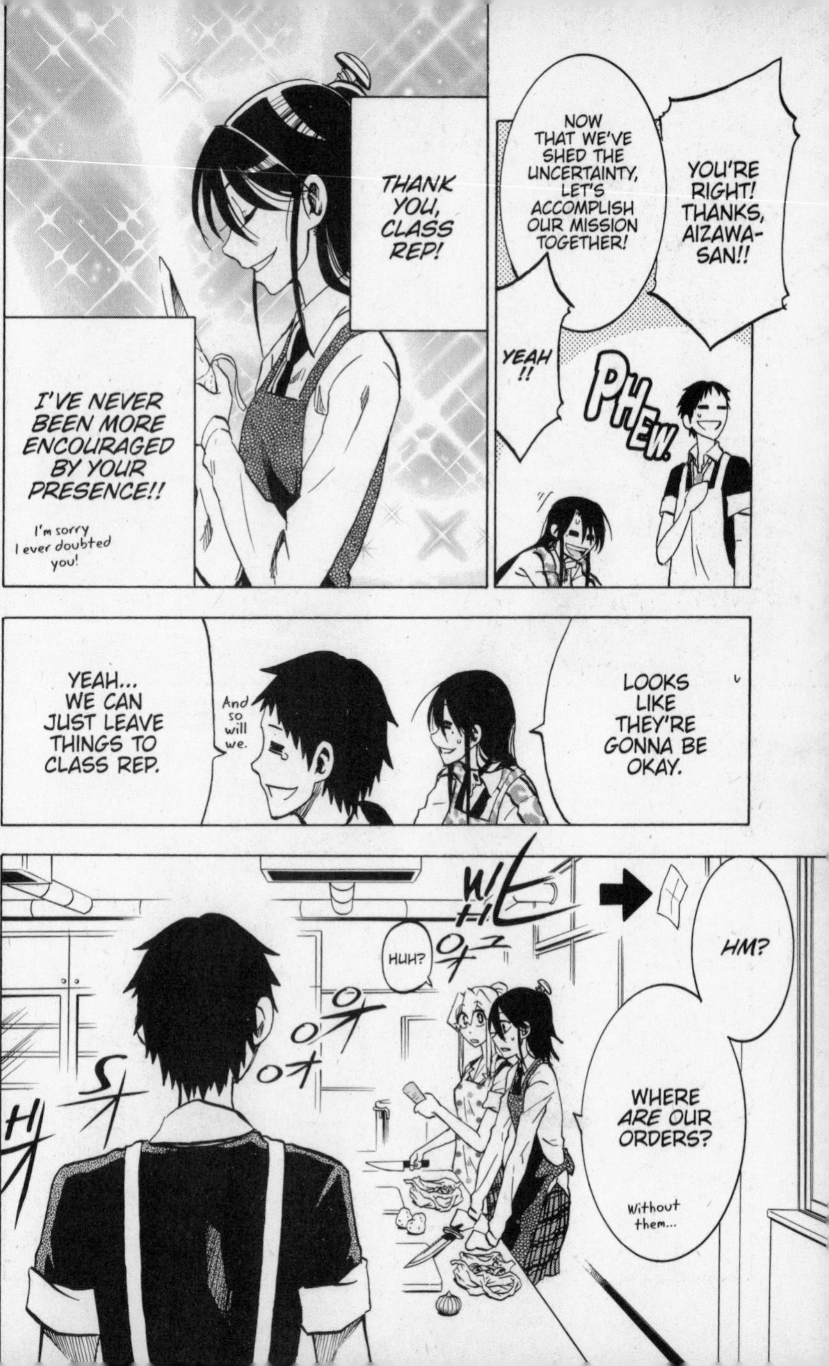
YOU'RE RIGHT! THANKS, AIZAWA-SAN!!
NOW THAT WE'VE SHED THE UNCERTAINTY, LET'S ACCOMPLISH OUR MISSION TOGETHER!
PHEW.
YEAH!!
THANK YOU, CLASS REP!
I'VE NEVER BEEN MORE ENCOURAGED BY YOUR PRESENCE!!
I'm sorry I ever doubted you!
LOOKS LIKE THEY'RE GONNA BE OKAY.
And so will we.
YEAH... WE CAN JUST LEAVE THINGS TO CLASS REP.
HM?
WHERE ARE OUR ORDERS?
Without them...
HUH?

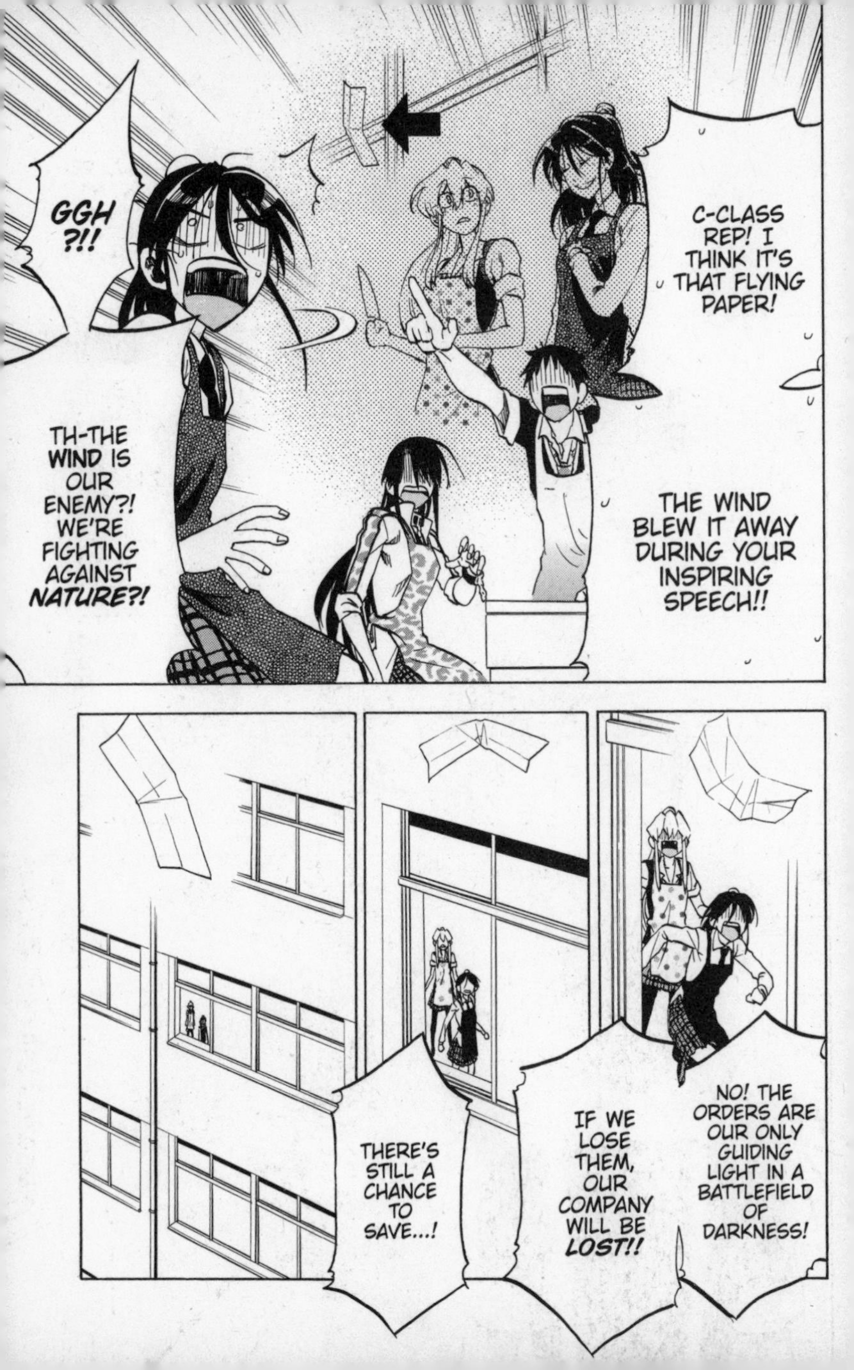
C-CLASS REP! I THINK IT'S THAT FLYING PAPER!
GGH ?!!
THE WIND BLEW IT AWAY DURING YOUR INSPIRING SPEECH!!
TH-THE WIND IS OUR ENEMY?! WE'RE FIGHTING AGAINST NATURE?!
NO! THE ORDERS ARE OUR ONLY GUIDING LIGHT IN A BATTLEFIELD OF DARKNESS!
IF WE LOSE THEM, OUR COMPANY WILL BE LOST!!
THERE'S STILL A CHANCE TO SAVE...!

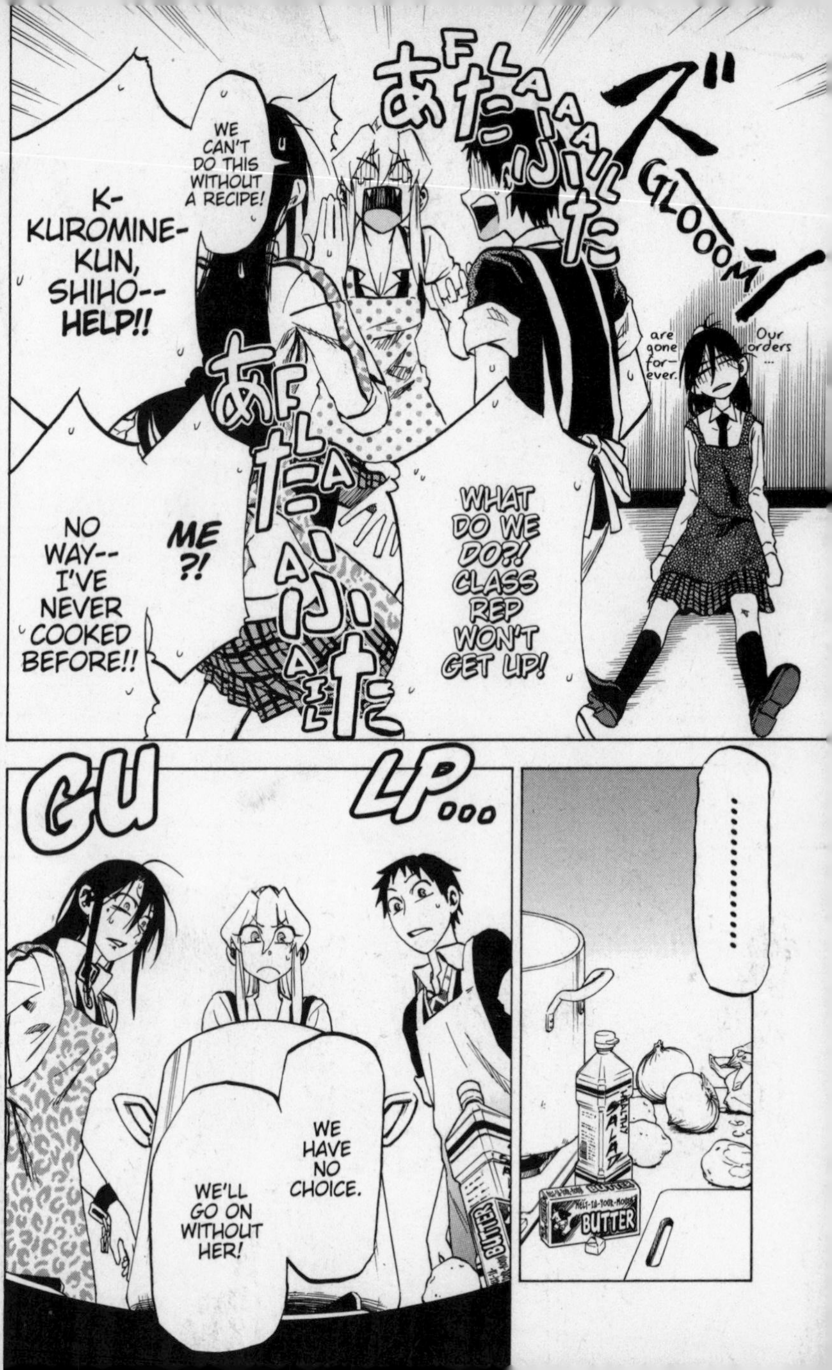
ズーン
GLOOOM
Our orders...
are gone forever.
あたふた
FLAAAIL
WE CAN'T DO THIS WITHOUT A RECIPE!
K-KUROMINE-KUN, SHIHO--HELP!!
WHAT DO WE DO?! CLASS REP WON'T GET UP!
あたふた
FLAAAIL
ME?!
NO WAY-- I'VE NEVER COOKED BEFORE!!
......
SALAD
BUTTER
GULP...
WE HAVE NO CHOICE.
WE'LL GO ON WITHOUT HER!

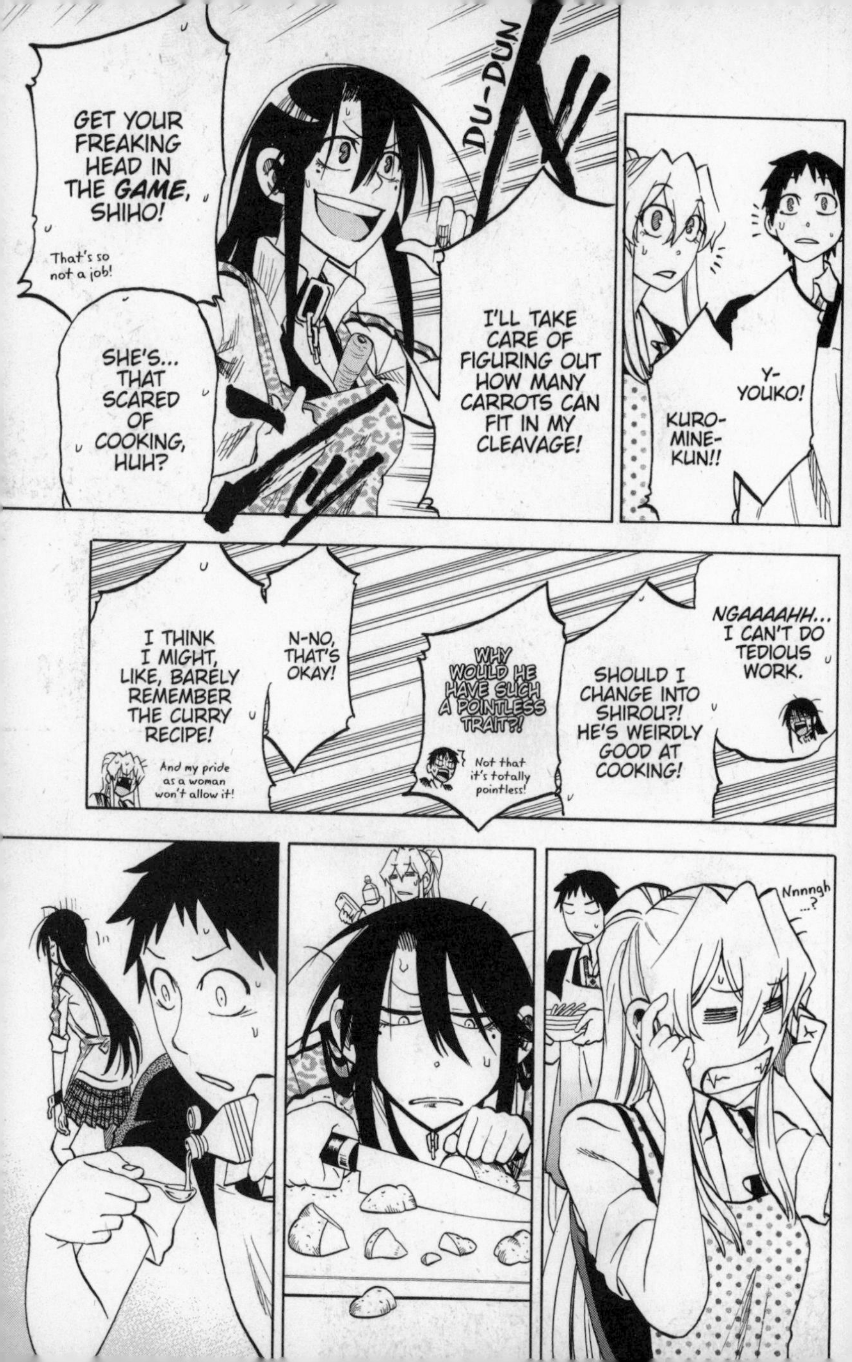
Y-YOUKO!
KURO-MINE-KUN!!
DU-DUN
I'LL TAKE CARE OF FIGURING OUT HOW MANY CARROTS CAN FIT IN MY CLEAVAGE!
GET YOUR FREAKING HEAD IN THE GAME, SHIHO!
That's so not a job!
SHE'S... THAT SCARED OF COOKING, HUH?
NGAAAAHH... I CAN'T DO TEDIOUS WORK.
SHOULD I CHANGE INTO SHIROU?! HE'S WEIRDLY GOOD AT COOKING!
WHY WOULD HE HAVE SUCH A POINTLESS TRAIT?!
Not that it's totally pointless!
N-NO, THAT'S OKAY!
I THINK I MIGHT, LIKE, BARELY REMEMBER THE CURRY RECIPE!
And my pride as a woman won't allow it!
Nnnngh ...?

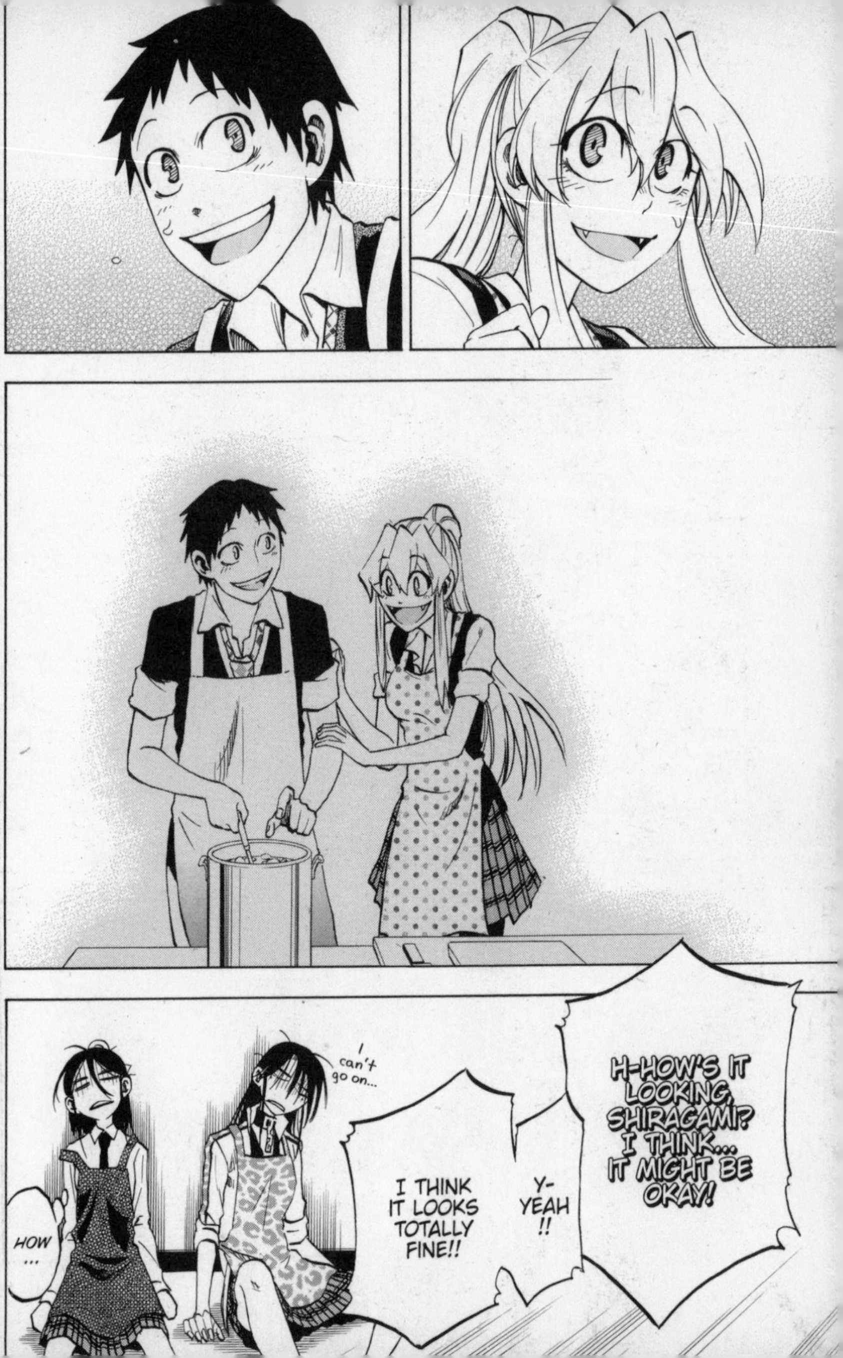
H-HOW'S IT LOOKING, SHIRAGAMI? I THINK... IT MIGHT BE OKAY!
Y-YEAH!!
I THINK IT LOOKS TOTALLY FINE!!
I can't go on...
HOW...

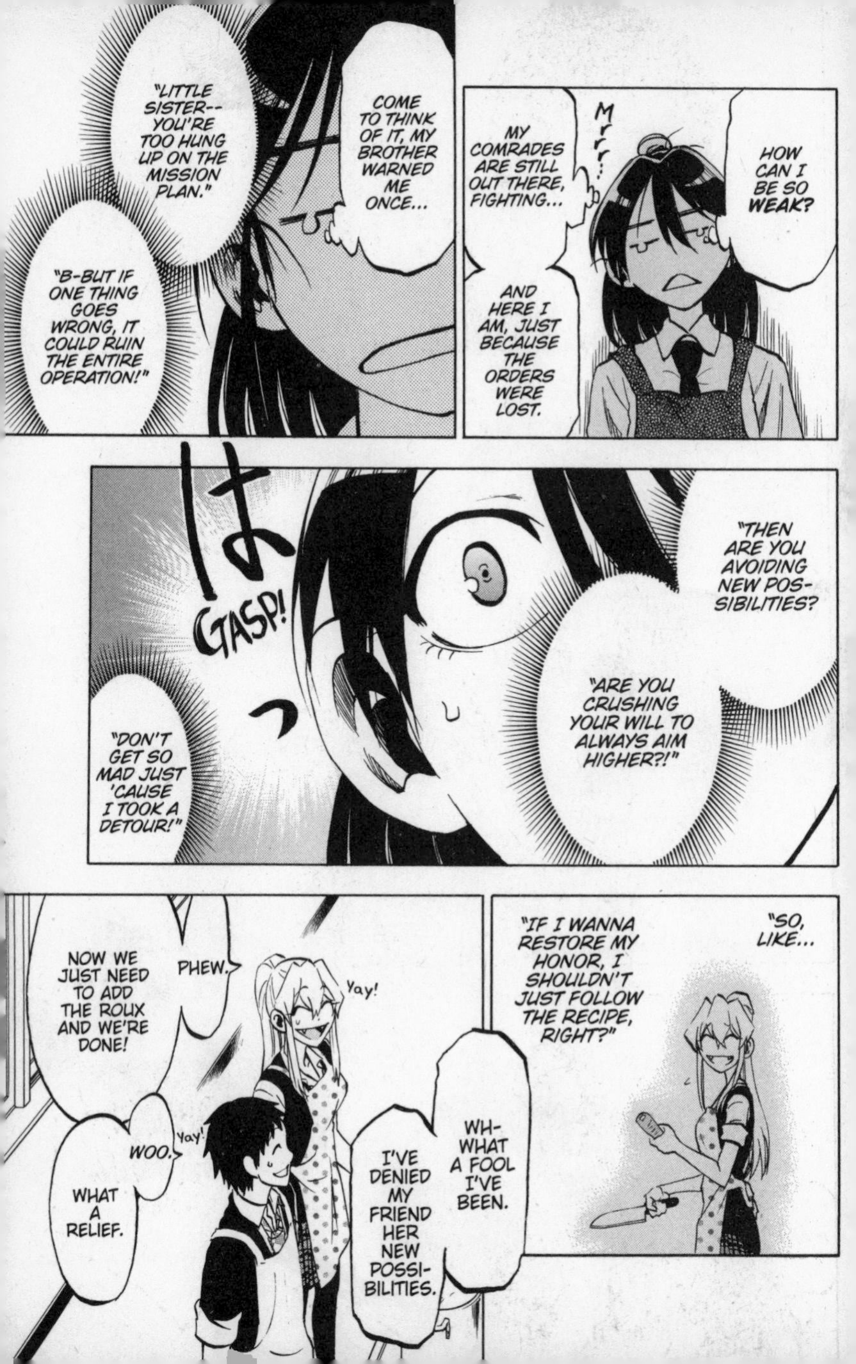
HOW CAN I BE SO WEAK?
Mrrr...
MY COMRADES ARE STILL OUT THERE, FIGHTING...
AND HERE I AM, JUST BECAUSE THE ORDERS WERE LOST.
COME TO THINK OF IT, MY BROTHER WARNED ME ONCE...
"LITTLE SISTER-- YOU'RE TOO HUNG UP ON THE MISSION PLAN."
"B-BUT IF ONE THING GOES WRONG, IT COULD RUIN THE ENTIRE OPERATION!"
"THEN ARE YOU AVOIDING NEW POS-SIBILITIES?
"ARE YOU CRUSHING YOUR WILL TO ALWAYS AIM HIGHER?!"
は
GASP!
"DON'T GET SO MAD JUST 'CAUSE I TOOK A DETOUR!"
"SO, LIKE...
"IF I WANNA RESTORE MY HONOR, I SHOULDN'T JUST FOLLOW THE RECIPE, RIGHT?"
WH-WHAT A FOOL I'VE BEEN.
I'VE DENIED MY FRIEND HER NEW POSSI-BILITIES.
Yay!
PHEW.
NOW WE JUST NEED TO ADD THE ROUX AND WE'RE DONE!
WOO.
Yay!
WHAT A RELIEF.

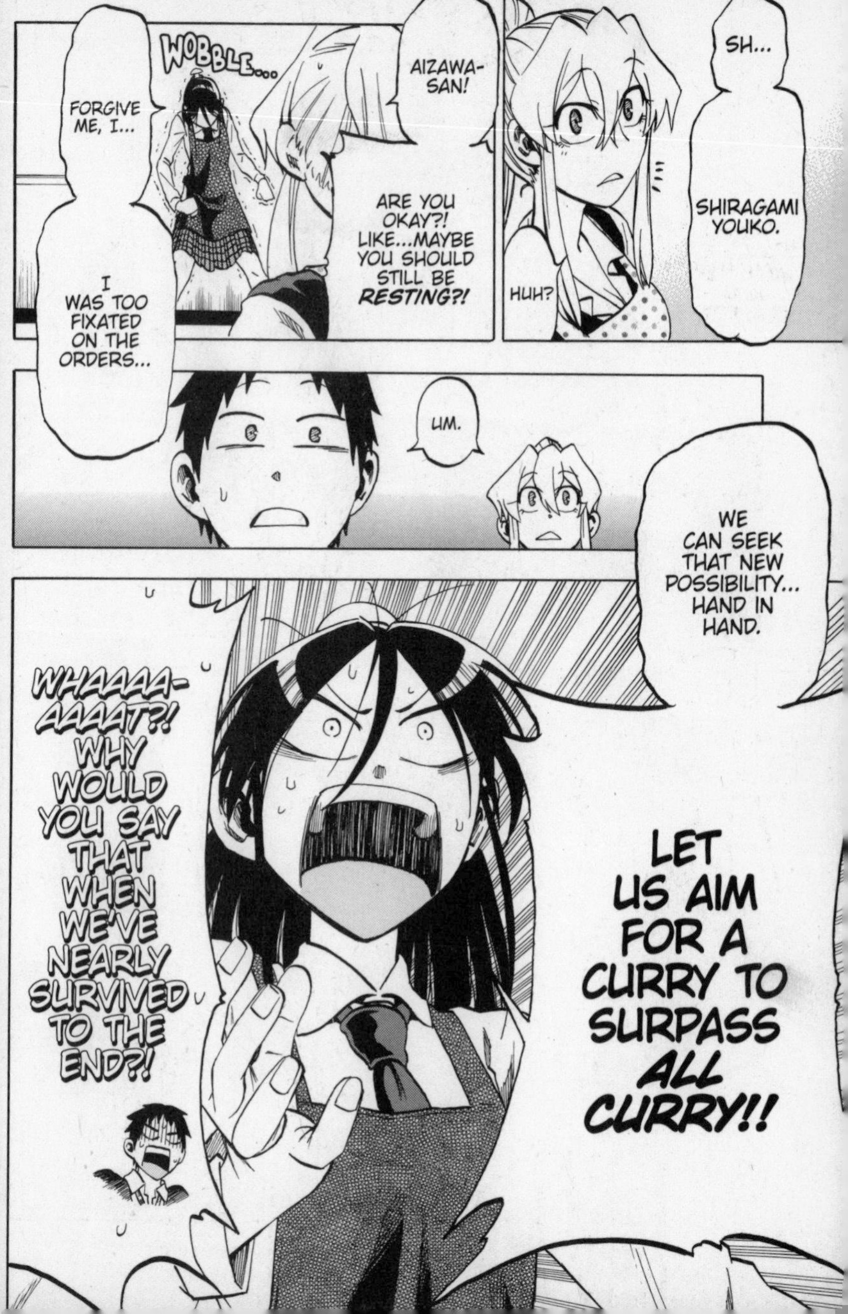
SH...
SHIRAGAMI YOUKO.
HUH?
AIZAWA-SAN!
ARE YOU OKAY?! LIKE...MAYBE YOU SHOULD STILL BE RESTING?!
WOBBLE...
FORGIVE ME, I...
I WAS TOO FIXATED ON THE ORDERS...
UM.
WE CAN SEEK THAT NEW POSSIBILITY... HAND IN HAND.
LET US AIM FOR A CURRY TO SURPASS ALL CURRY!!
WHAAAAA-AAAAT?! WHY WOULD YOU SAY THAT WHEN WE'VE NEARLY SURVIVED TO THE END?!

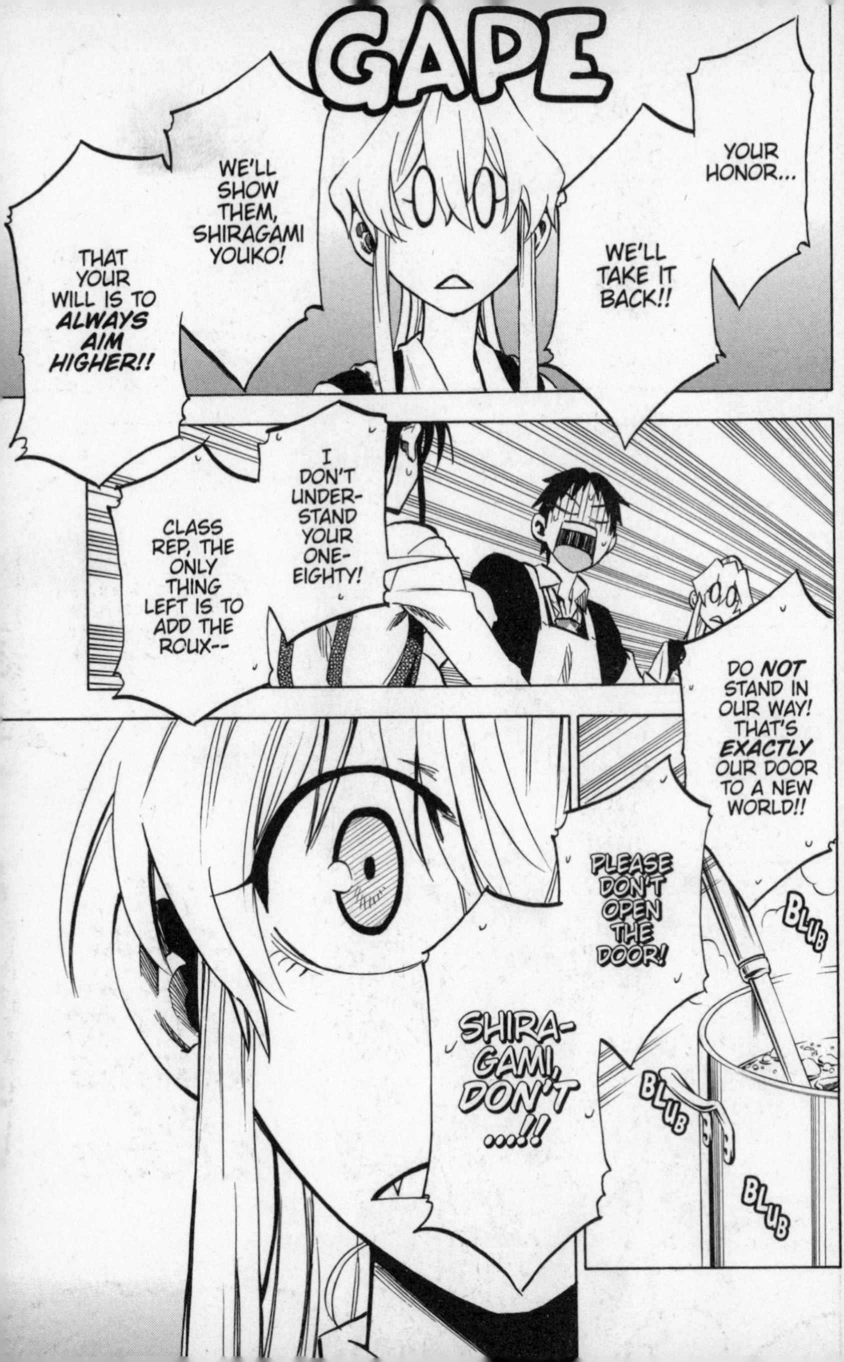
GAPE
YOUR HONOR...
WE'LL TAKE IT BACK!!
WE'LL SHOW THEM, SHIRAGAMI YOUKO!
THAT YOUR WILL IS TO ALWAYS AIM HIGHER!!
I DON'T UNDERSTAND YOUR ONE-EIGHTY!
CLASS REP, THE ONLY THING LEFT IS TO ADD THE ROUX--
DO NOT STAND IN OUR WAY! THAT'S EXACTLY OUR DOOR TO A NEW WORLD!!
PLEASE DON'T OPEN THE DOOR!
BLUB
BLUB
BLUB
SHIRAGAMI, DON'T ...!!

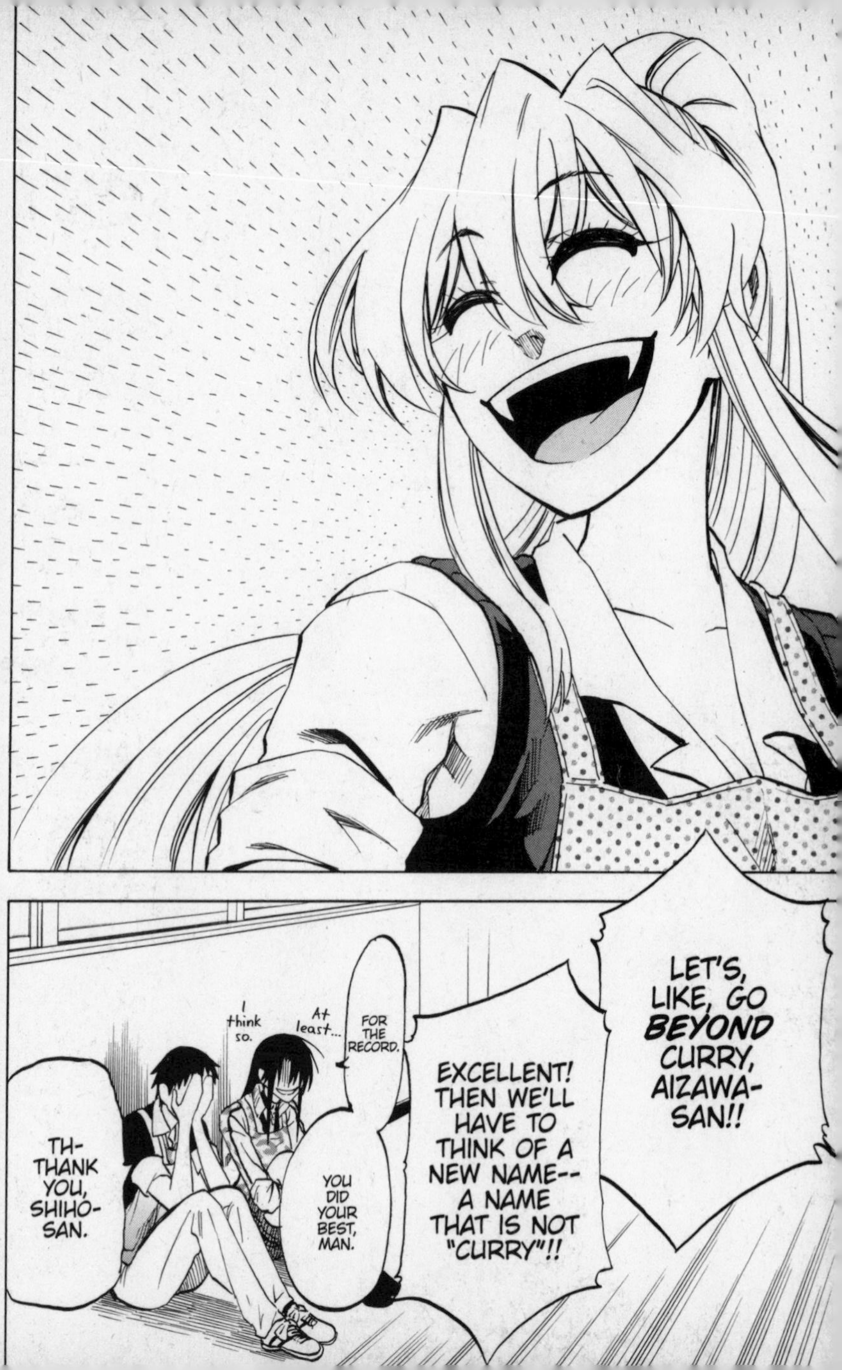
LET'S, LIKE, GO *BEYOND* CURRY, AIZAWA-SAN!!
EXCELLENT! THEN WE'LL HAVE TO THINK OF A NEW NAME-- A NAME THAT IS NOT "CURRY"!!
FOR THE RECORD.
At least...
YOU DID YOUR BEST, MAN.
I think so.
TH-THANK YOU, SHIHO-SAN.

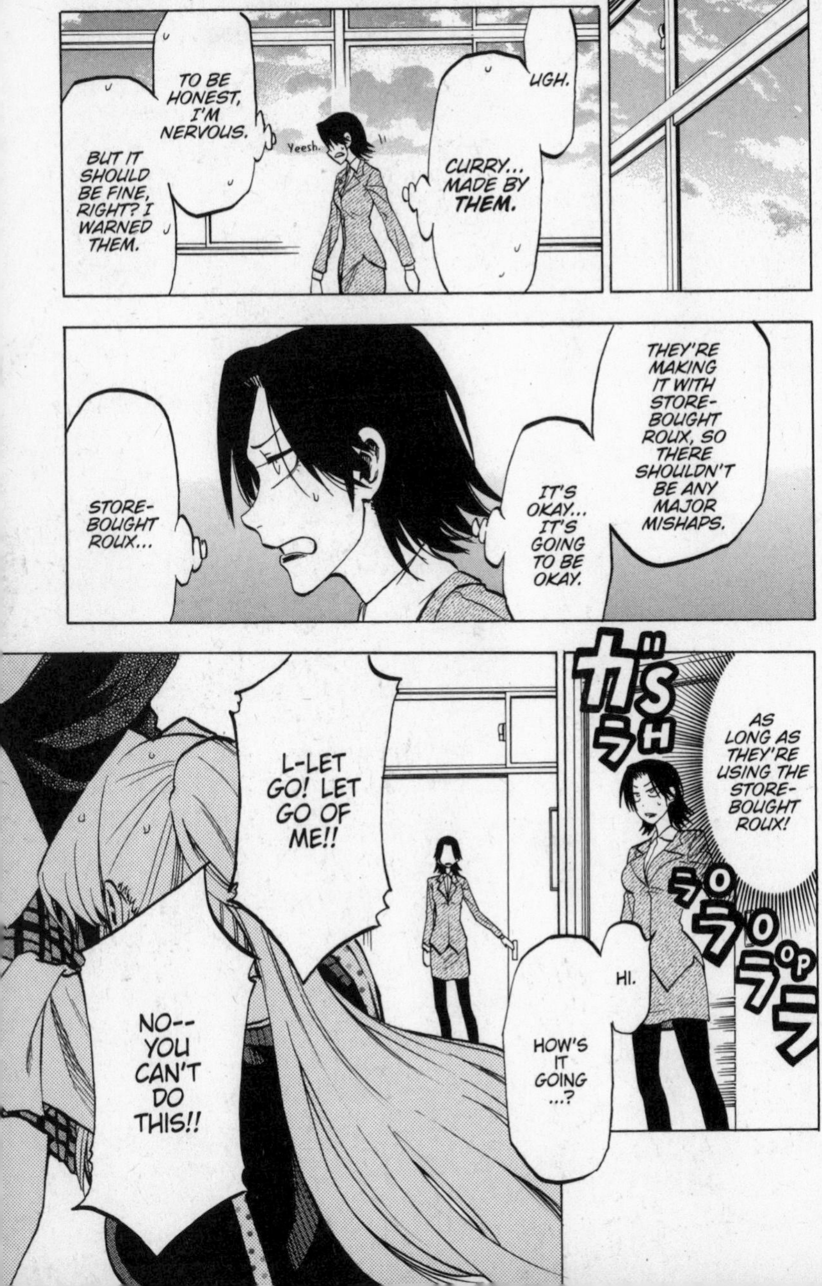
UGH.
CURRY... MADE BY THEM.
Yeesh.
TO BE HONEST, I'M NERVOUS.
BUT IT SHOULD BE FINE, RIGHT? I WARNED THEM.
THEY'RE MAKING IT WITH STORE-BOUGHT ROUX, SO THERE SHOULDN'T BE ANY MAJOR MISHAPS.
IT'S OKAY... IT'S GOING TO BE OKAY.
STORE-BOUGHT ROUX...
AS LONG AS THEY'RE USING THE STORE-BOUGHT ROUX!
ガラ SH
ラOラOラOPラ
HI.
HOW'S IT GOING ...?
L-LET GO! LET GO OF ME!!
NO-- YOU CAN'T DO THIS!!

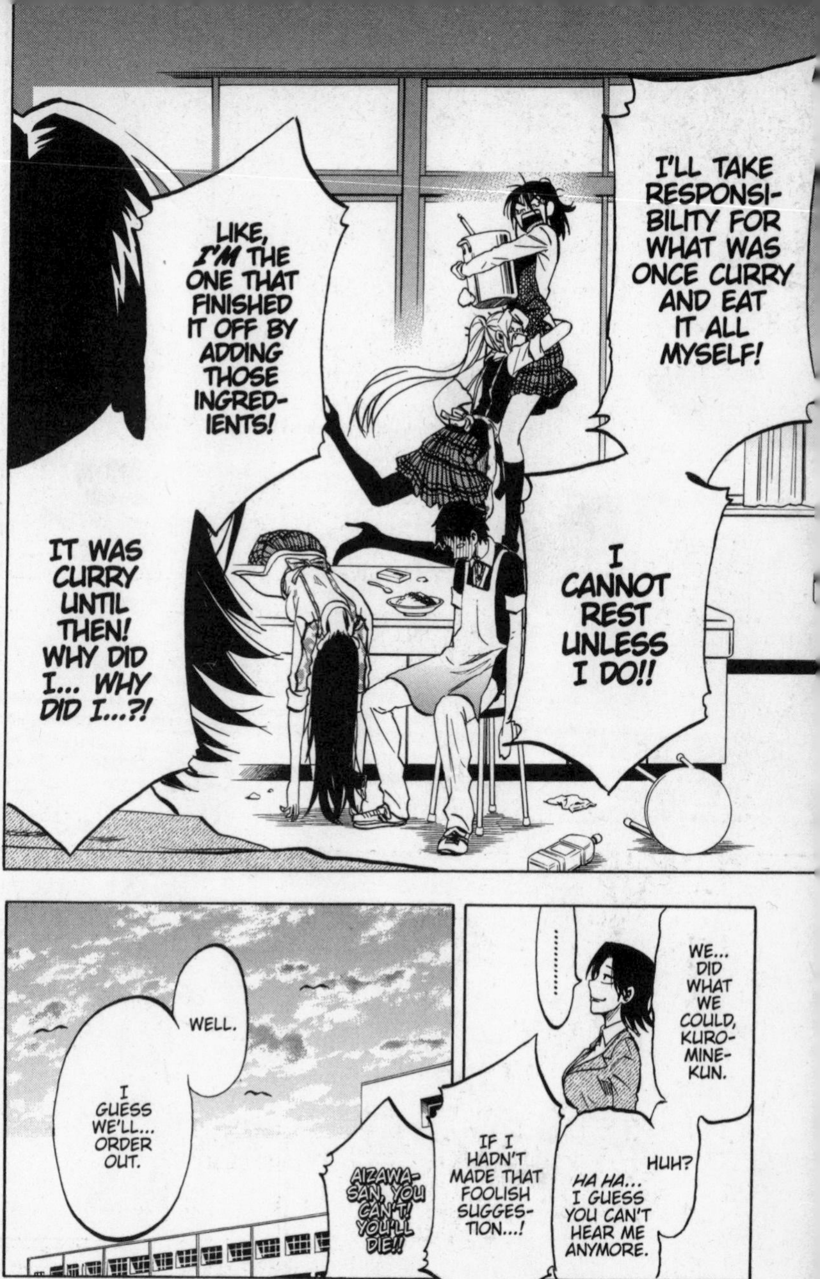
I'LL TAKE RESPONSIBILITY FOR WHAT WAS ONCE CURRY AND EAT IT ALL MYSELF!
I CANNOT REST UNLESS I DO!!
LIKE, *I'M* THE ONE THAT FINISHED IT OFF BY ADDING THOSE INGREDIENTS!
IT WAS CURRY UNTIL THEN! WHY DID I... WHY DID I...?!
......
WE... DID WHAT WE COULD, KUROMINE-KUN.
HUH?
HA HA... I GUESS YOU CAN'T HEAR ME ANYMORE.
IF I HADN'T MADE THAT FOOLISH SUGGESTION...!
AIZAWA-SAN, YOU CAN'T! YOU'LL DIE!!
WELL.
I GUESS WE'LL... ORDER OUT.

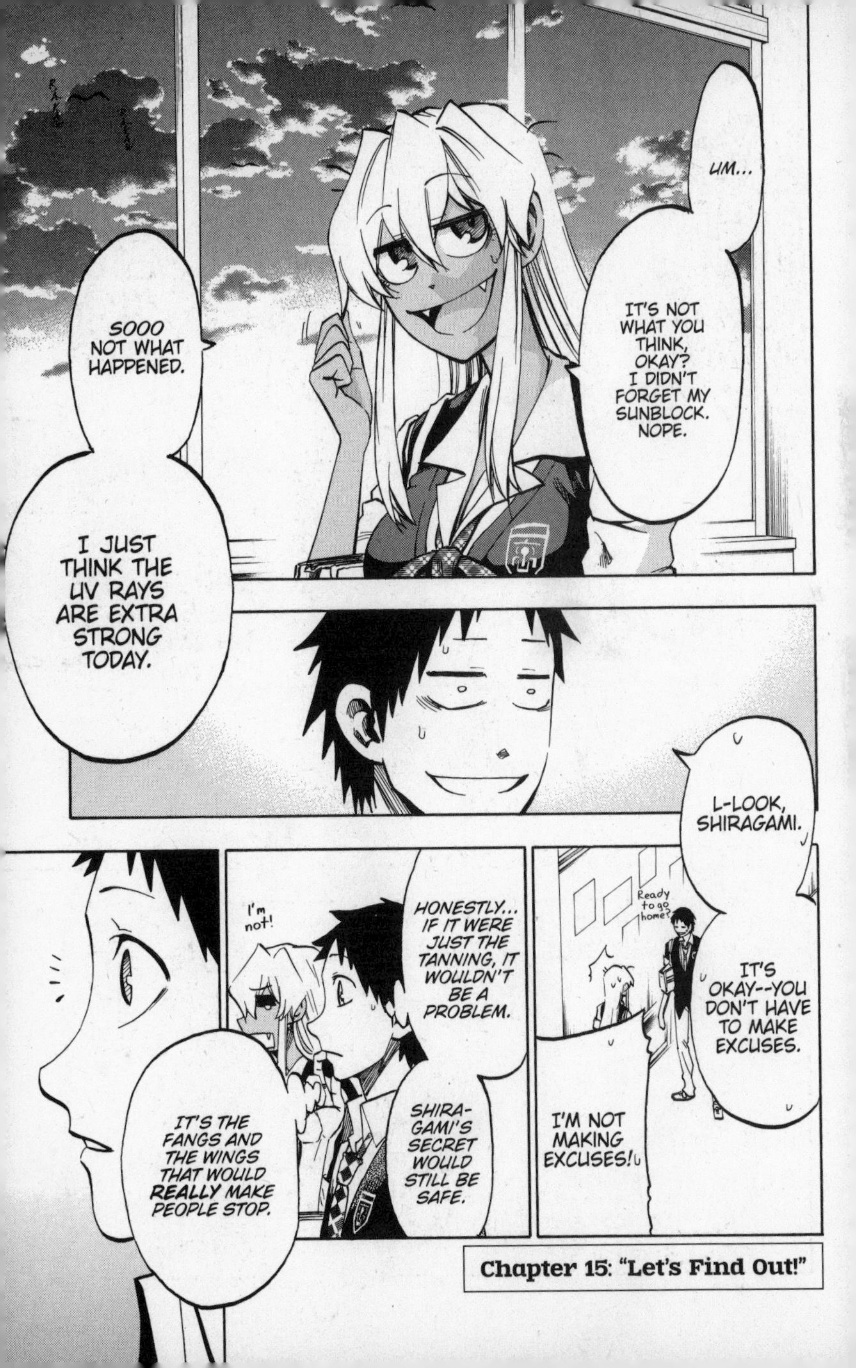
UM...
IT'S NOT WHAT YOU THINK, OKAY? I DIDN'T FORGET MY SUNBLOCK. NOPE.
SOOO NOT WHAT HAPPENED.
I JUST THINK THE UV RAYS ARE EXTRA STRONG TODAY.
L-LOOK, SHIRAGAMI.
Ready to go home?
IT'S OKAY--YOU DON'T HAVE TO MAKE EXCUSES.
I'M NOT MAKING EXCUSES!
HONESTLY... IF IT WERE JUST THE TANNING, IT WOULDN'T BE A PROBLEM.
I'm not!
SHIRAGAMI'S SECRET WOULD STILL BE SAFE.
IT'S THE FANGS AND THE WINGS THAT WOULD REALLY MAKE PEOPLE STOP.

Chapter 15: "Let's Find Out!"

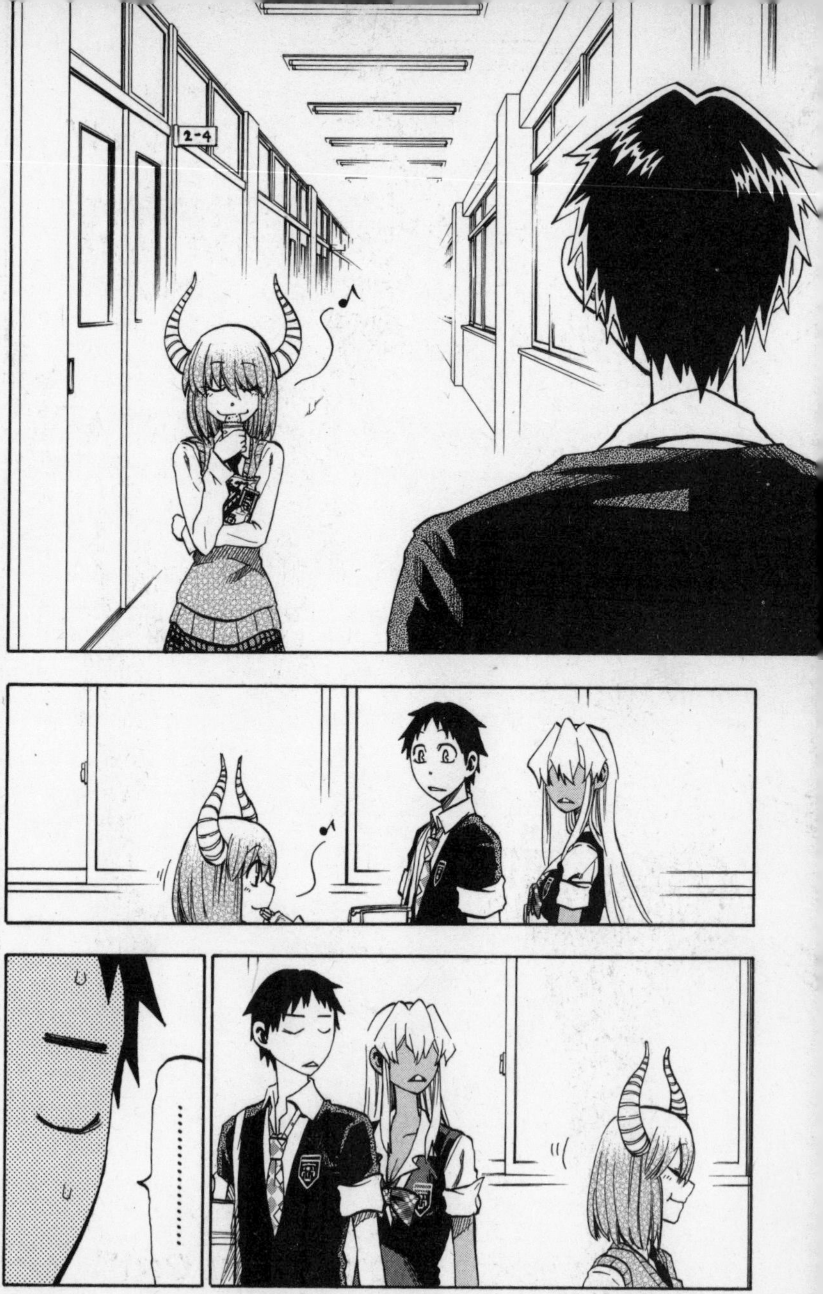
2-4

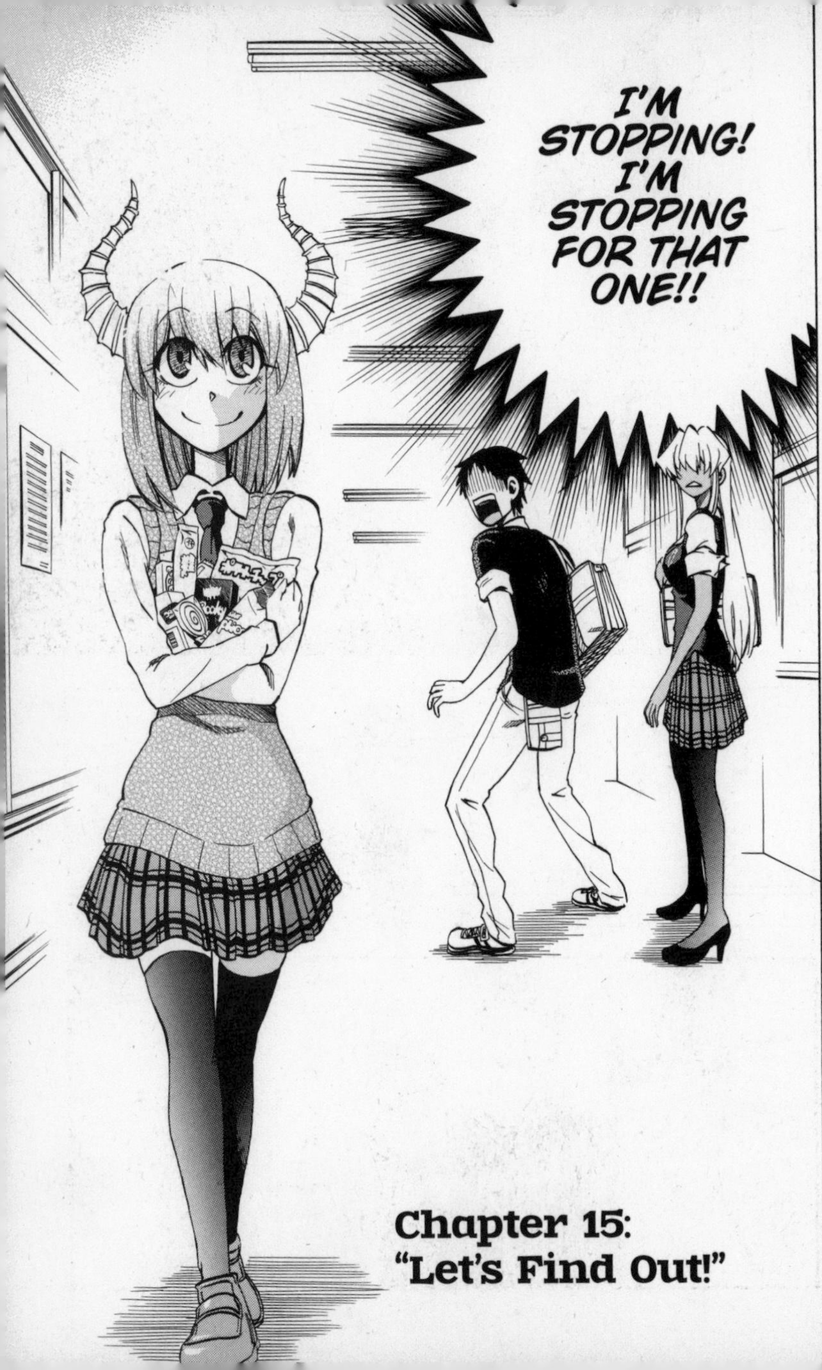
I'M STOPPING! I'M STOPPING FOR THAT ONE!!
Chapter 15:
"Let's Find Out!"

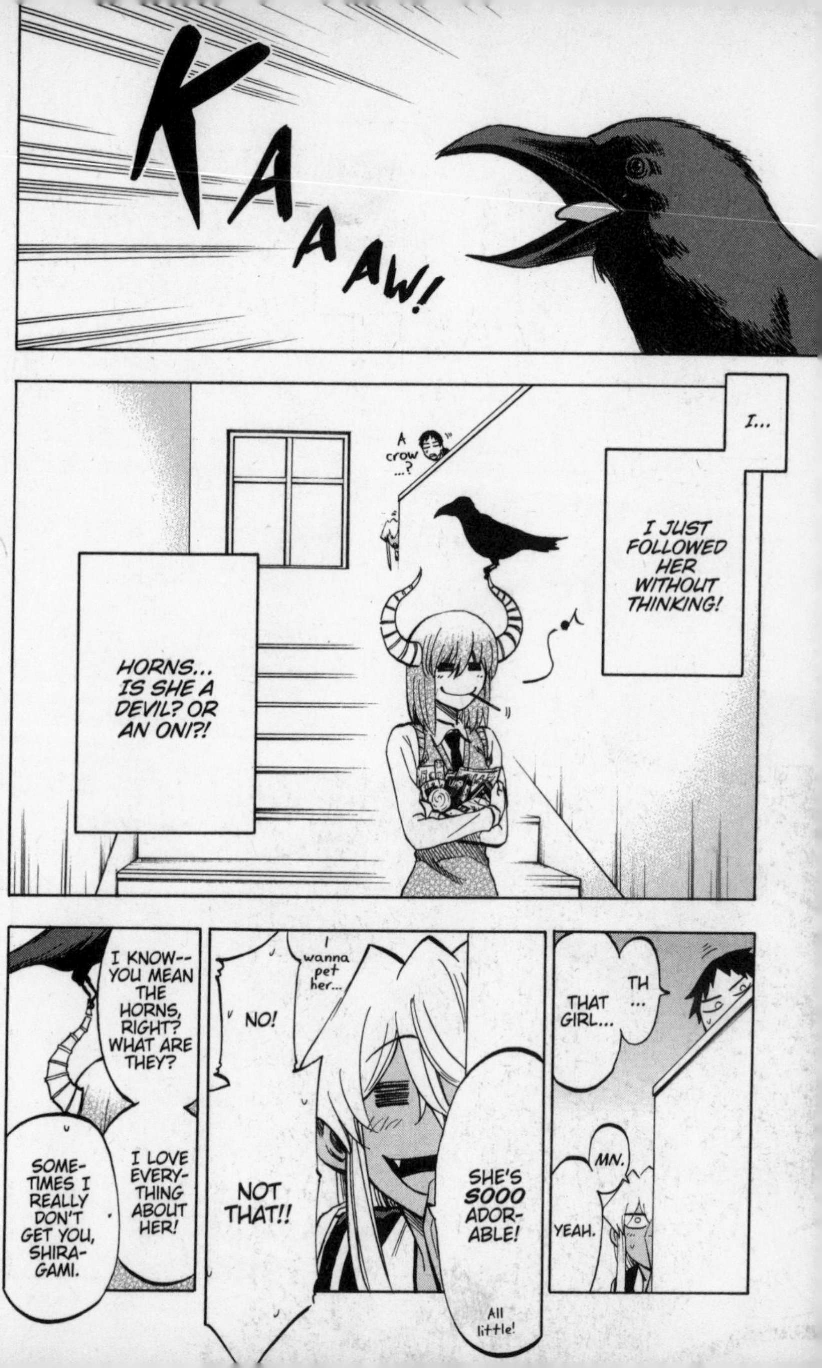
KAAAAW!
I...
I JUST FOLLOWED HER WITHOUT THINKING!
A crow ...?
HORNS... IS SHE A DEVIL? OR AN ONI?!
TH ...
THAT GIRL...
MN.
YEAH.
I wanna pet her...
NO!
SHE'S SOOO ADORABLE!
All little!
NOT THAT!!
I KNOW-- YOU MEAN THE HORNS, RIGHT? WHAT ARE THEY?
I LOVE EVERYTHING ABOUT HER!
SOMETIMES I REALLY DON'T GET YOU, SHIRAGAMI.

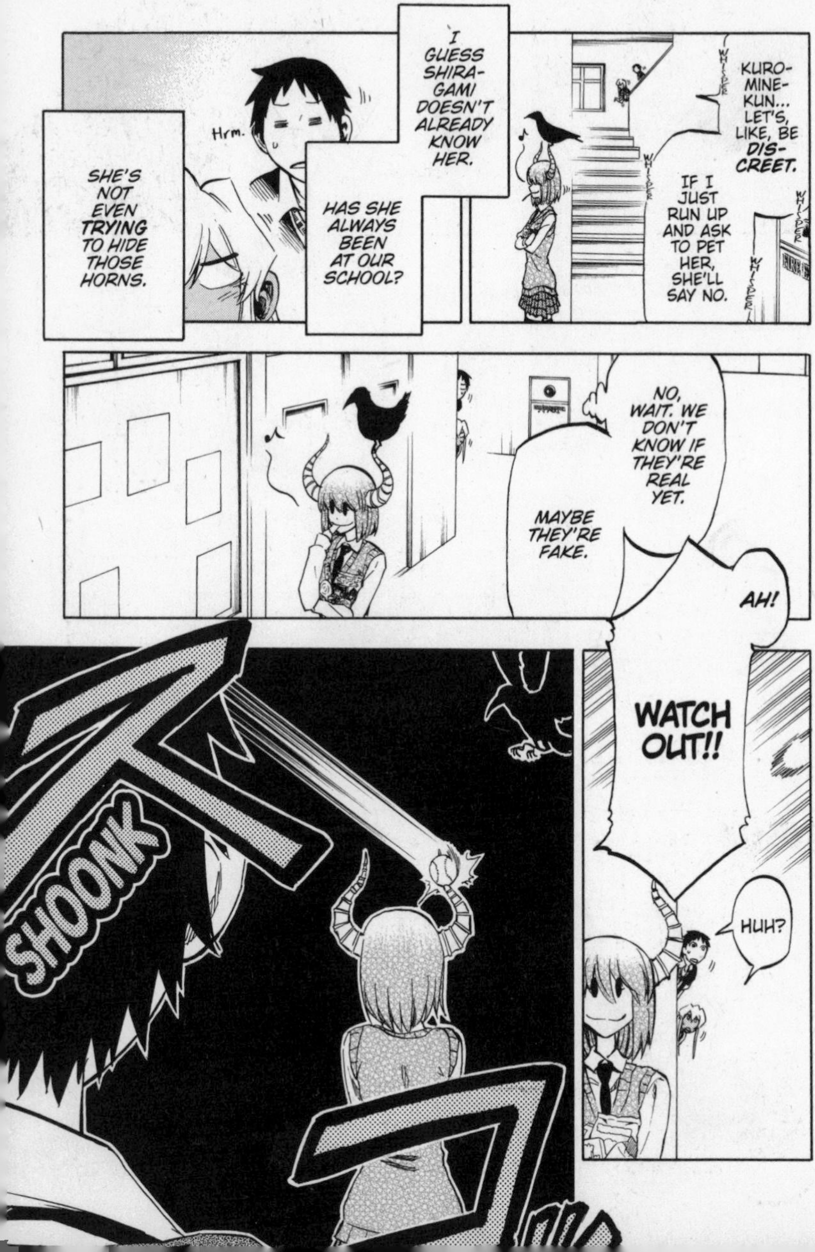
WHISPER
KURO-MINE-KUN... LET'S, LIKE, BE DIS-CREET.
WHISPER
IF I JUST RUN UP AND ASK TO PET HER, SHE'LL SAY NO.
WHISPER
WHISPER
I GUESS SHIRA-GAMI DOESN'T ALREADY KNOW HER.
HAS SHE ALWAYS BEEN AT OUR SCHOOL?
Hrm.
SHE'S NOT EVEN TRYING TO HIDE THOSE HORNS.
NO, WAIT. WE DON'T KNOW IF THEY'RE REAL YET.
MAYBE THEY'RE FAKE.
AH!
WATCH OUT!!
HUH?
SHOONK

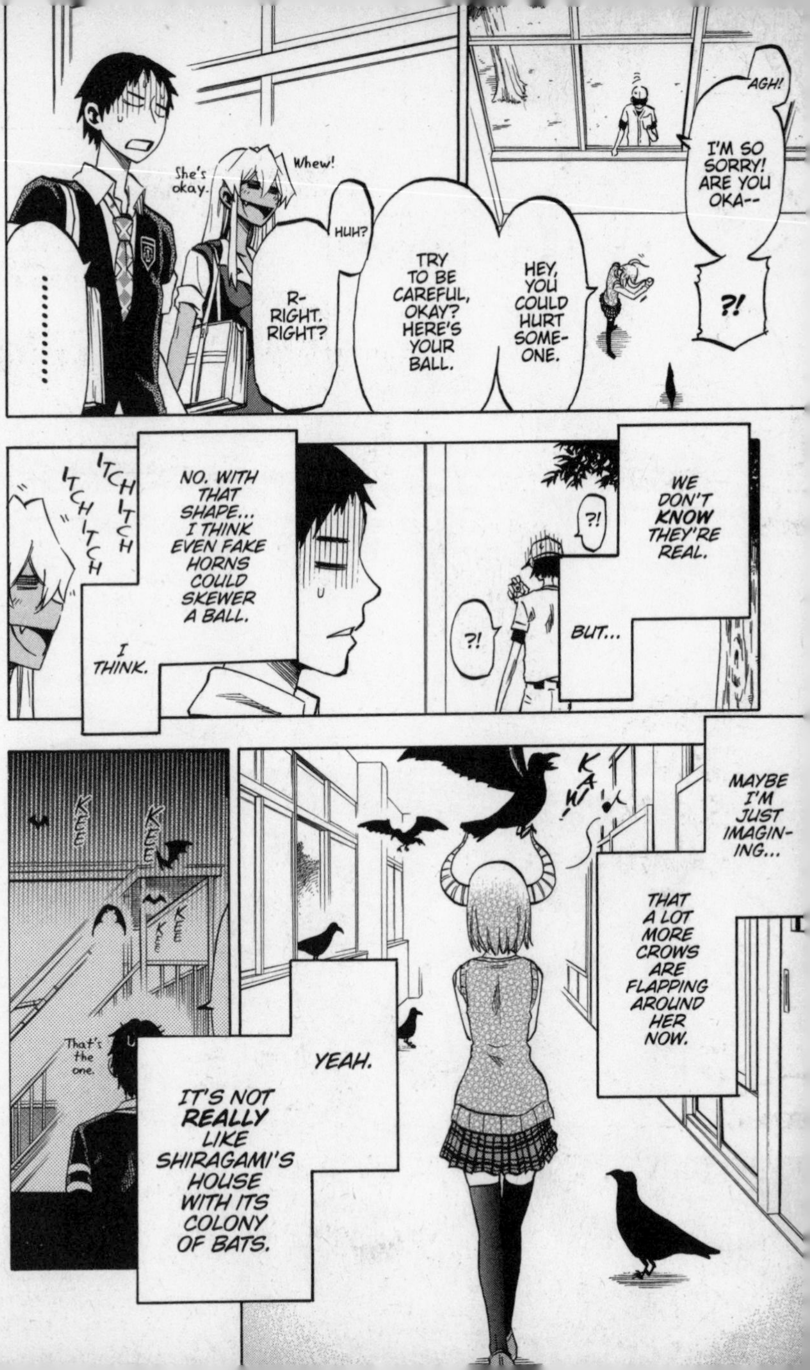
AGH!
I'M SO SORRY! ARE YOU OKA--
?!
HEY, YOU COULD HURT SOME-ONE.
TRY TO BE CAREFUL, OKAY? HERE'S YOUR BALL.
HUH?
R- RIGHT. RIGHT?
Whew!
She's okay.
......
?!
WE DON'T KNOW THEY'RE REAL.
?!
BUT...
NO. WITH THAT SHAPE... I THINK EVEN FAKE HORNS COULD SKEWER A BALL.
ITCH ITCH
ITCH ITCH
I THINK.
MAYBE I'M JUST IMAGIN-ING...
KAW!
THAT A LOT MORE CROWS ARE FLAPPING AROUND HER NOW.
YEAH.
IT'S NOT REALLY LIKE SHIRAGAMI'S HOUSE WITH ITS COLONY OF BATS.
KEE KEE
KEE KEE
That's the one.

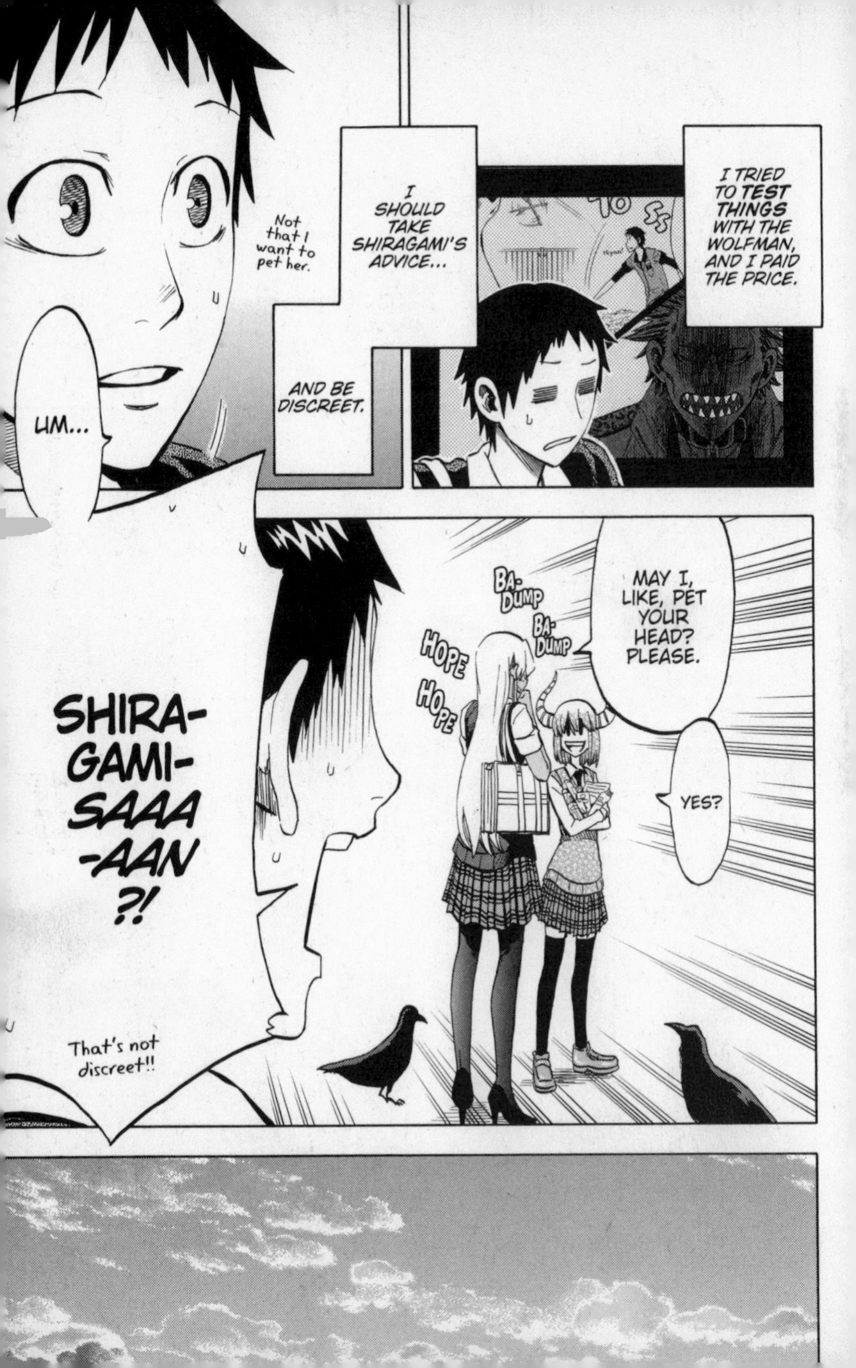
I TRIED TO TEST THINGS WITH THE WOLFMAN, AND I PAID THE PRICE.
I SHOULD TAKE SHIRAGAMI'S ADVICE...
AND BE DISCREET.
Not that I want to pet her.
UM...
MAY I, LIKE, PET YOUR HEAD? PLEASE.
BA-DUMP
BA-DUMP
HOPE
HOPE
YES?
SHIRA-GAMI-SAAAA-AAN?!
That's not discreet!!

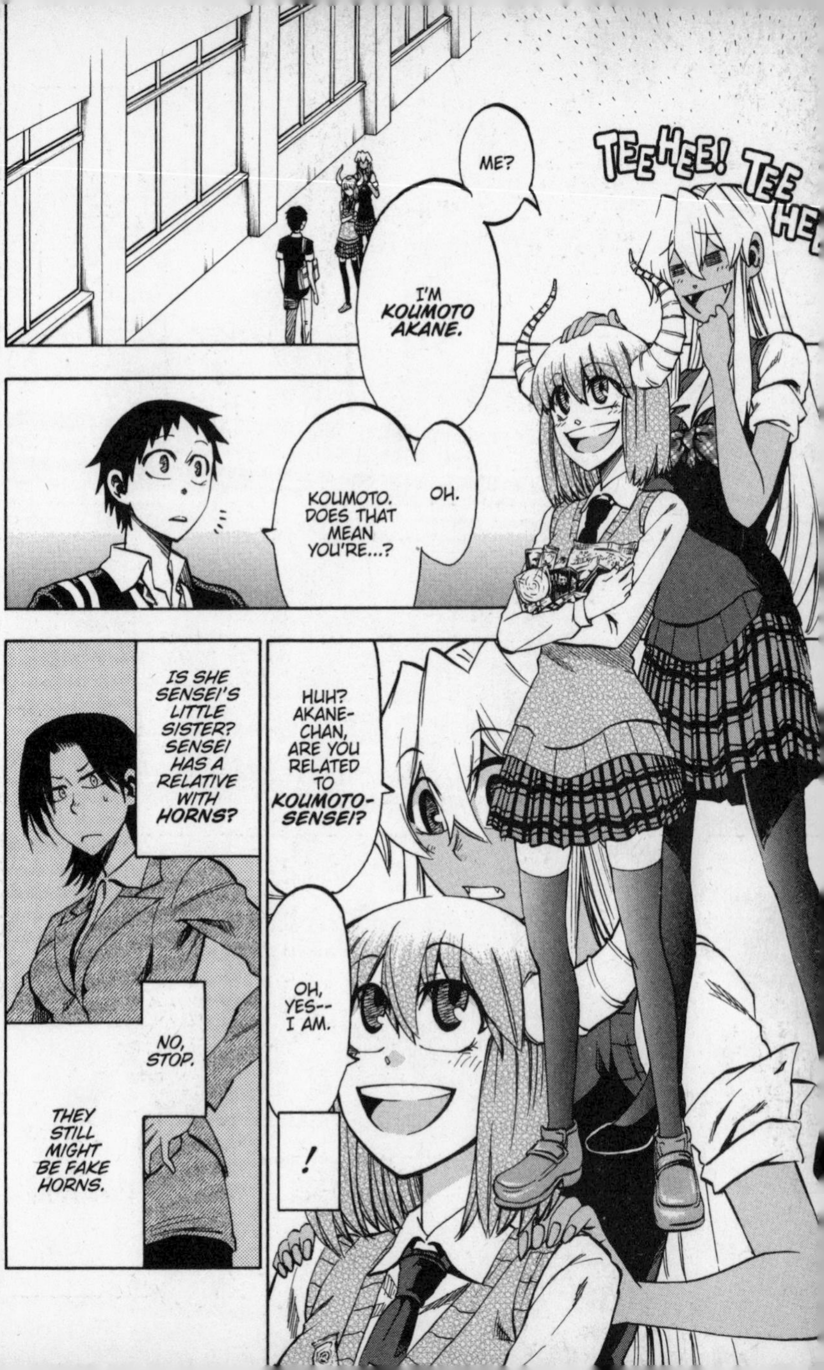
TEE HEE! TEE HE
ME?
I'M KOUMOTO AKANE.
OH.
KOUMOTO. DOES THAT MEAN YOU'RE...?
HUH? AKANE-CHAN, ARE YOU RELATED TO KOUMOTO-SENSEI?
OH, YES-- I AM.
!
IS SHE SENSEI'S LITTLE SISTER? SENSEI HAS A RELATIVE WITH HORNS?
NO, STOP.
THEY STILL MIGHT BE FAKE HORNS.

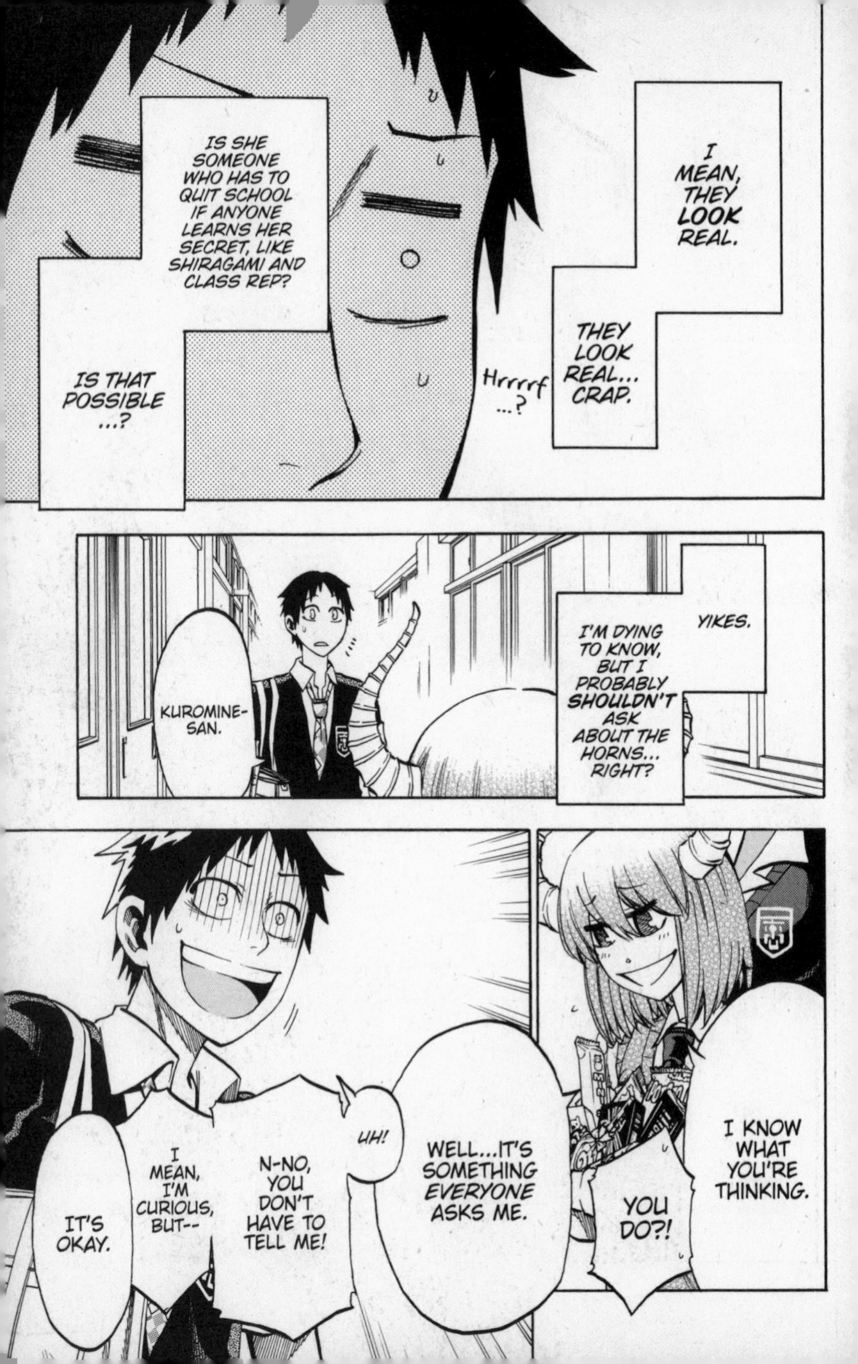

I MEAN, THEY LOOK REAL.
THEY LOOK REAL... CRAP.
Hrrrrf ...?
IS SHE SOMEONE WHO HAS TO QUIT SCHOOL IF ANYONE LEARNS HER SECRET, LIKE SHIRAGAMI AND CLASS REP?
IS THAT POSSIBLE ...?
YIKES.
I'M DYING TO KNOW, BUT I PROBABLY SHOULDN'T ASK ABOUT THE HORNS... RIGHT?
KUROMINE-SAN.
I KNOW WHAT YOU'RE THINKING.
YOU DO?!
WELL...IT'S SOMETHING EVERYONE ASKS ME.
UH!
N-NO, YOU DON'T HAVE TO TELL ME!
I MEAN, I'M CURIOUS, BUT--
IT'S OKAY.

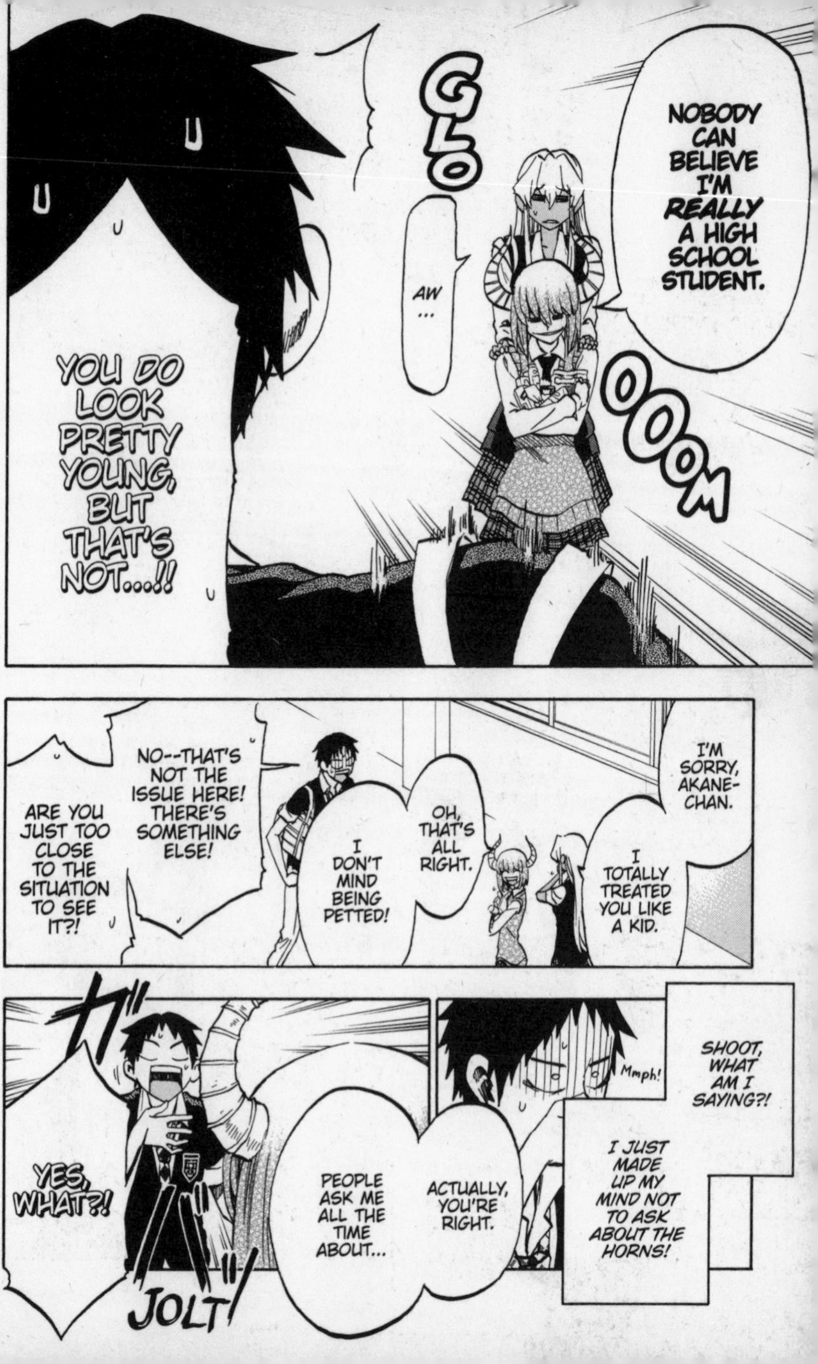
NOBODY CAN BELIEVE I'M *REALLY* A HIGH SCHOOL STUDENT.
GLOOOOM
AW...
YOU DO LOOK PRETTY YOUNG, BUT THAT'S NOT...!!
I'M SORRY, AKANE-CHAN.
I TOTALLY TREATED YOU LIKE A KID.
OH, THAT'S ALL RIGHT.
I DON'T MIND BEING PETTED!
NO--THAT'S NOT THE ISSUE HERE! THERE'S SOMETHING ELSE!
ARE YOU JUST TOO CLOSE TO THE SITUATION TO SEE IT?!
SHOOT, WHAT AM I SAYING?!
Mmph!
I JUST MADE UP MY MIND NOT TO ASK ABOUT THE HORNS!
ACTUALLY, YOU'RE RIGHT.
PEOPLE ASK ME ALL THE TIME ABOUT...
YES, WHAT?!
JOLT

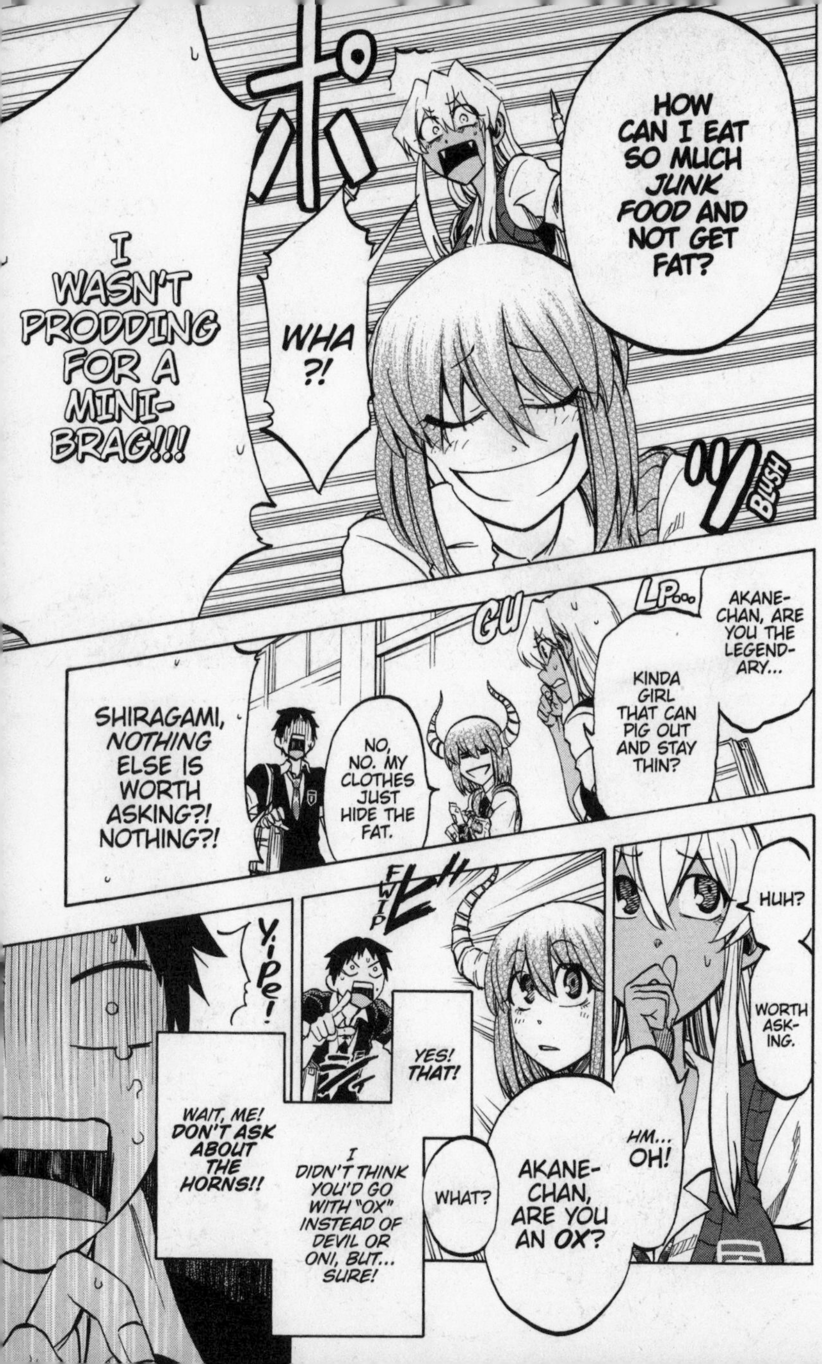
HOW CAN I EAT SO MUCH JUNK FOOD AND NOT GET FAT?
BLUSH
WHA ?!
ポ
I WASN'T PRODDING FOR A MINI-BRAG!!!
AKANE-CHAN, ARE YOU THE LEGENDARY...
GU
LP...
KINDA GIRL THAT CAN PIG OUT AND STAY THIN?
NO, NO. MY CLOTHES JUST HIDE THE FAT.
SHIRAGAMI, NOTHING ELSE IS WORTH ASKING?! NOTHING?!
HUH?
WORTH ASK-ING.
HM... OH!
AKANE-CHAN, ARE YOU AN OX?
WHAT?
FWIP
YES! THAT!
I DIDN'T THINK YOU'D GO WITH "OX" INSTEAD OF DEVIL OR ONI, BUT... SURE!
Yipe!
WAIT, ME! DON'T ASK ABOUT THE HORNS!!

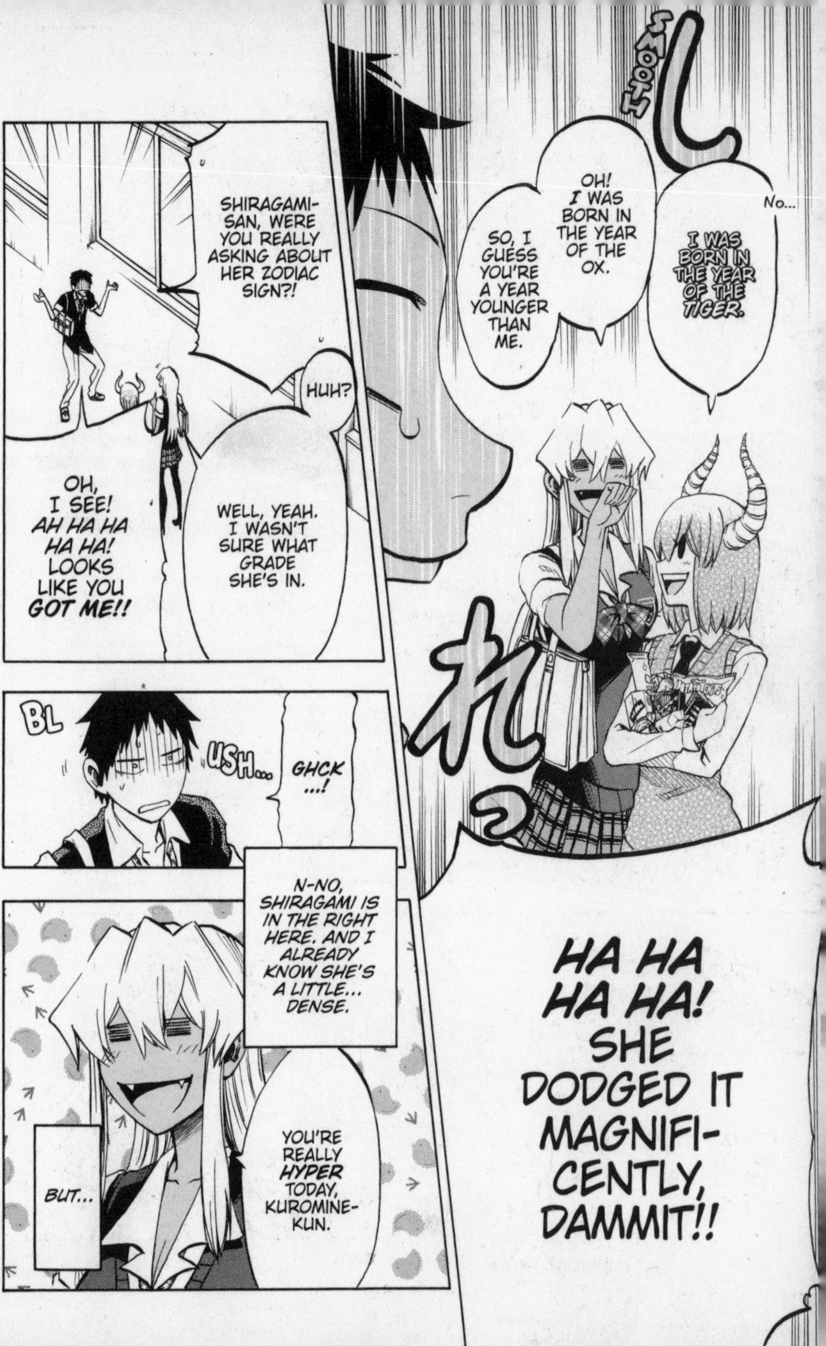
SMOOTH
OH! I WAS BORN IN THE YEAR OF THE OX.
SO, I GUESS YOU'RE A YEAR YOUNGER THAN ME.
No...
I WAS BORN IN THE YEAR OF THE TIGER.
HA HA HA HA! SHE DODGED IT MAGNIFI-CENTLY, DAMMIT!!
SHIRAGAMI-SAN, WERE YOU REALLY ASKING ABOUT HER ZODIAC SIGN?!
HUH?
WELL, YEAH. I WASN'T SURE WHAT GRADE SHE'S IN.
OH, I SEE! AH HA HA HA HA! LOOKS LIKE YOU GOT ME!!
BL
USH...
GHCK ...!
N-NO, SHIRAGAMI IS IN THE RIGHT HERE. AND I ALREADY KNOW SHE'S A LITTLE... DENSE.
YOU'RE REALLY HYPER TODAY, KUROMINE-KUN.
BUT...

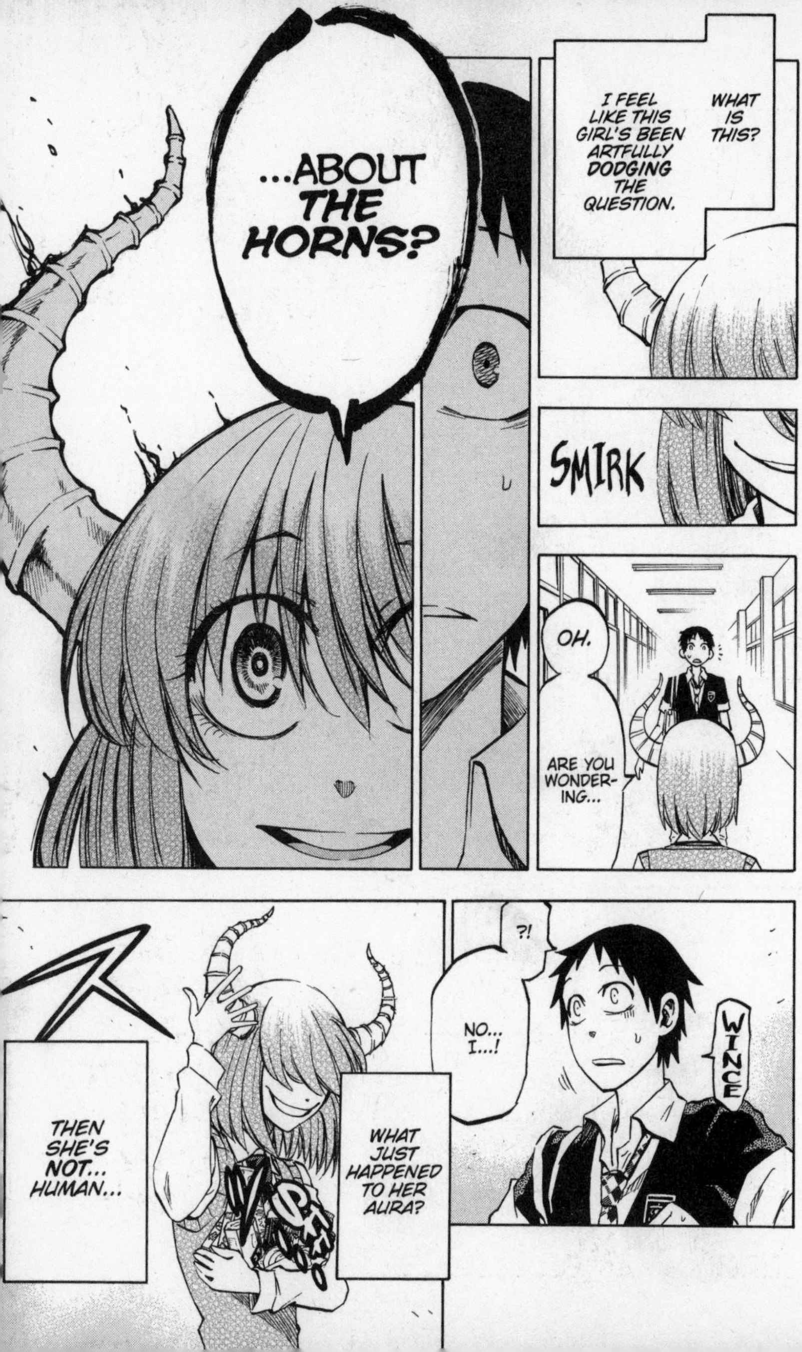
WHAT IS THIS?
I FEEL LIKE THIS GIRL'S BEEN ARTFULLY DODGING THE QUESTION.
SMIRK
OH.
ARE YOU WONDERING...
...ABOUT THE HORNS?
?!
WINCE
NO... I...!
WHAT JUST HAPPENED TO HER AURA?
THEN SHE'S NOT... HUMAN...

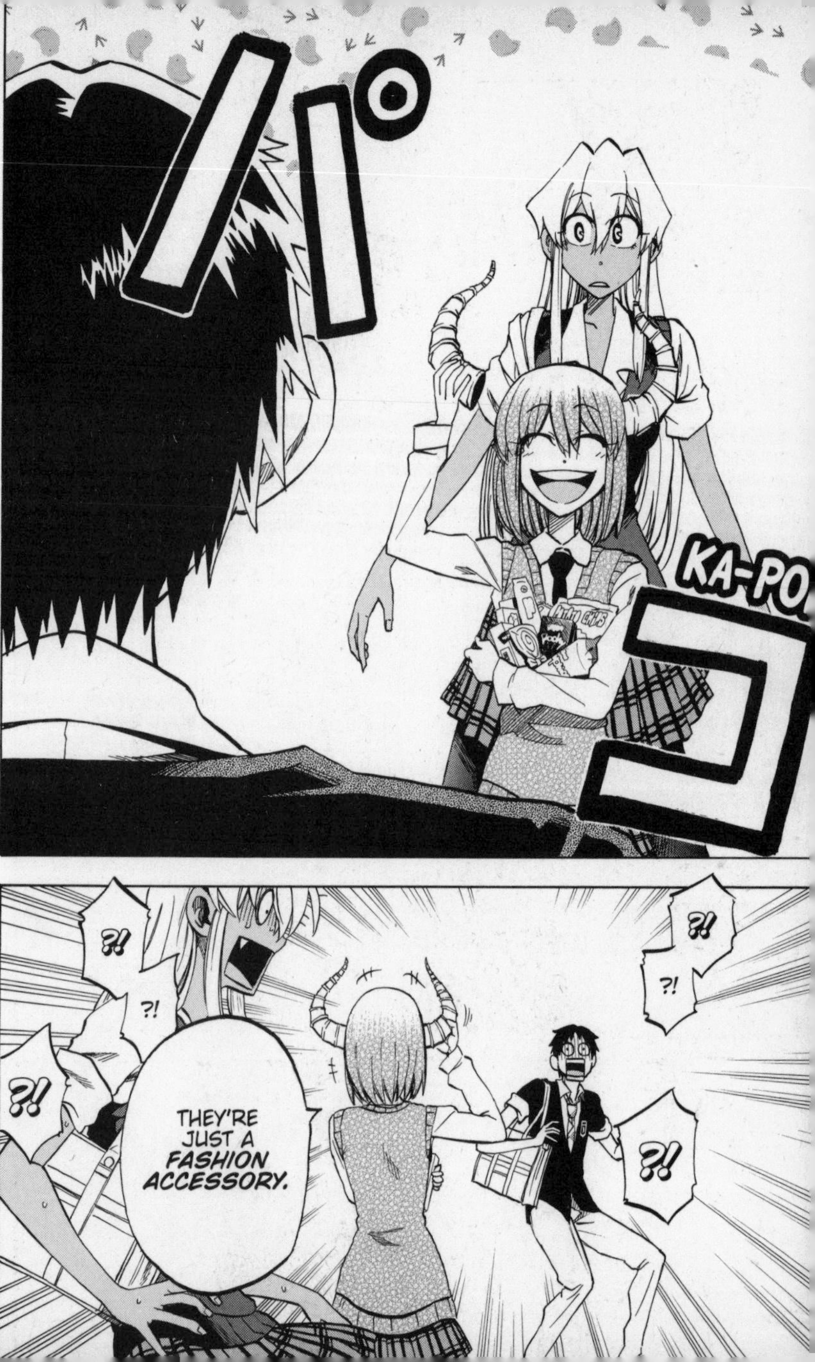
KA-PO
?!
?!
?!
THEY'RE JUST A FASHION ACCESSORY.
?!
?!
?!

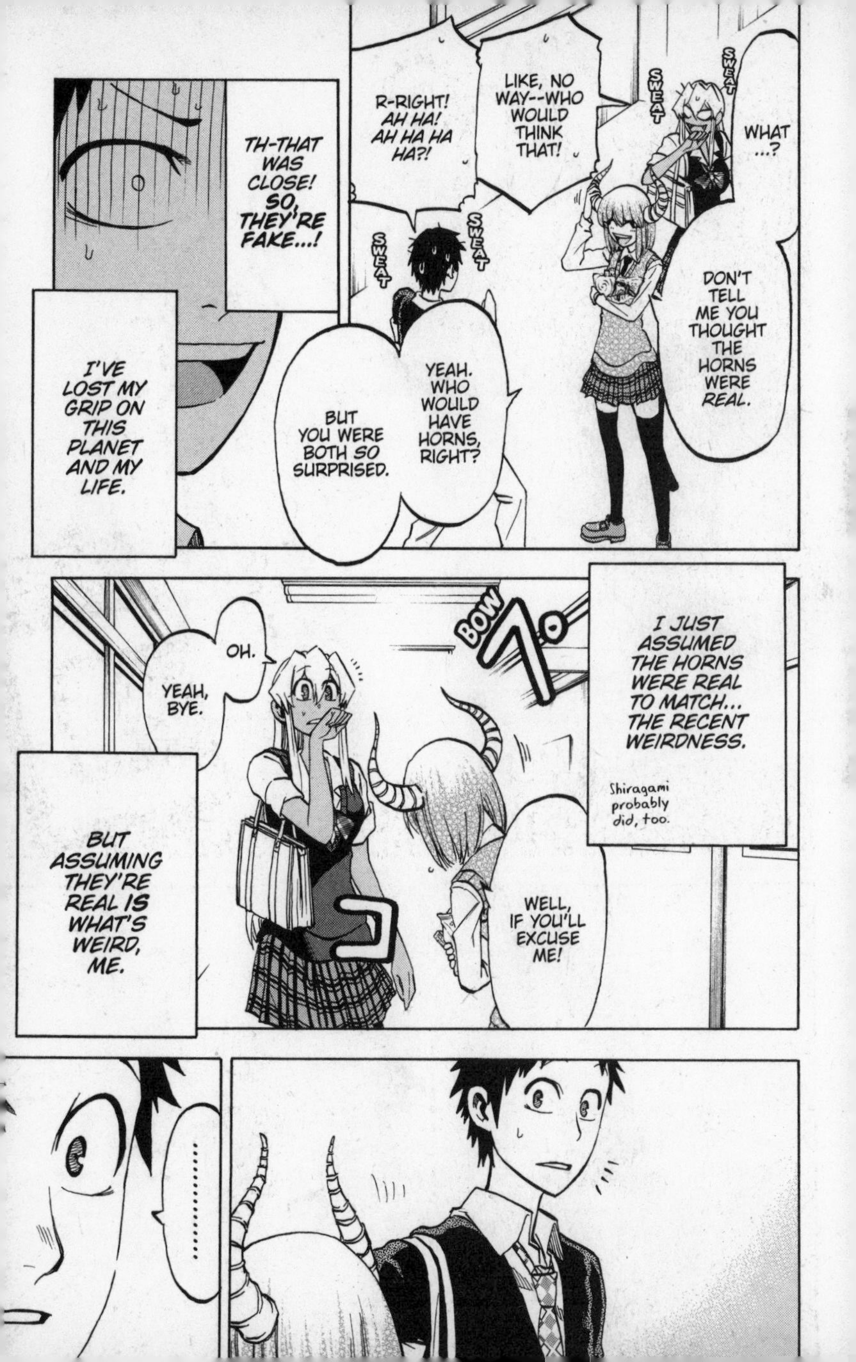
SWEAT
WHAT ...?
SWEAT
LIKE, NO WAY--WHO WOULD THINK THAT!
R-RIGHT! AH HA! AH HA HA HA?!
SWEAT
SWEAT
DON'T TELL ME YOU THOUGHT THE HORNS WERE REAL.
YEAH. WHO WOULD HAVE HORNS, RIGHT?
BUT YOU WERE BOTH SO SURPRISED.
TH-THAT WAS CLOSE! SO, THEY'RE FAKE...!
I'VE LOST MY GRIP ON THIS PLANET AND MY LIFE.
I JUST ASSUMED THE HORNS WERE REAL TO MATCH... THE RECENT WEIRDNESS.
Shiragami probably did, too.
BOW
WELL, IF YOU'LL EXCUSE ME!
OH.
YEAH, BYE.
BUT ASSUMING THEY'RE REAL IS WHAT'S WEIRD, ME.
......

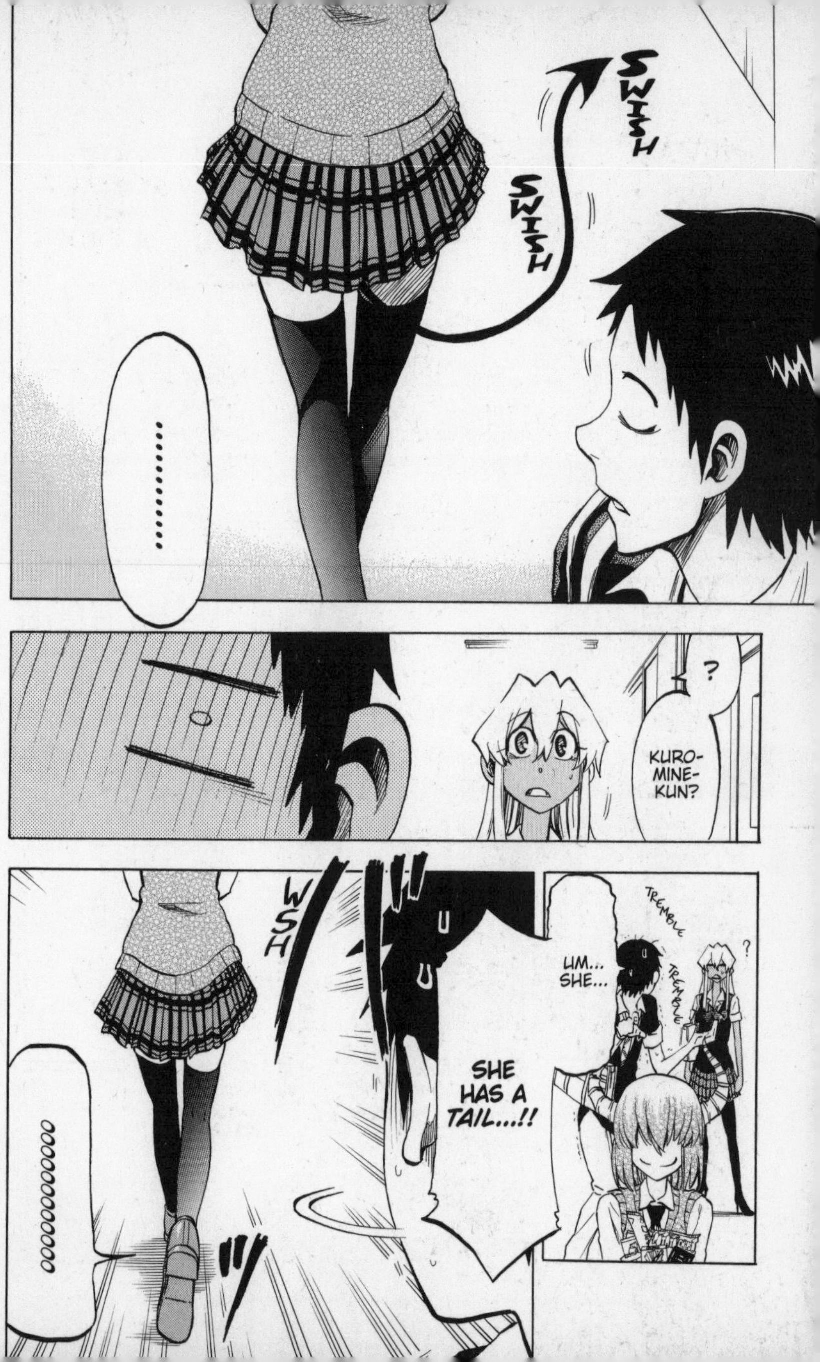
SWISH
SWISH
......
?
KURO-MINE-KUN?
TREMBLE
TREMBLE
?
UM... SHE...
SHE HAS A TAIL...!!
WSH
OOOOOOOOOOOO

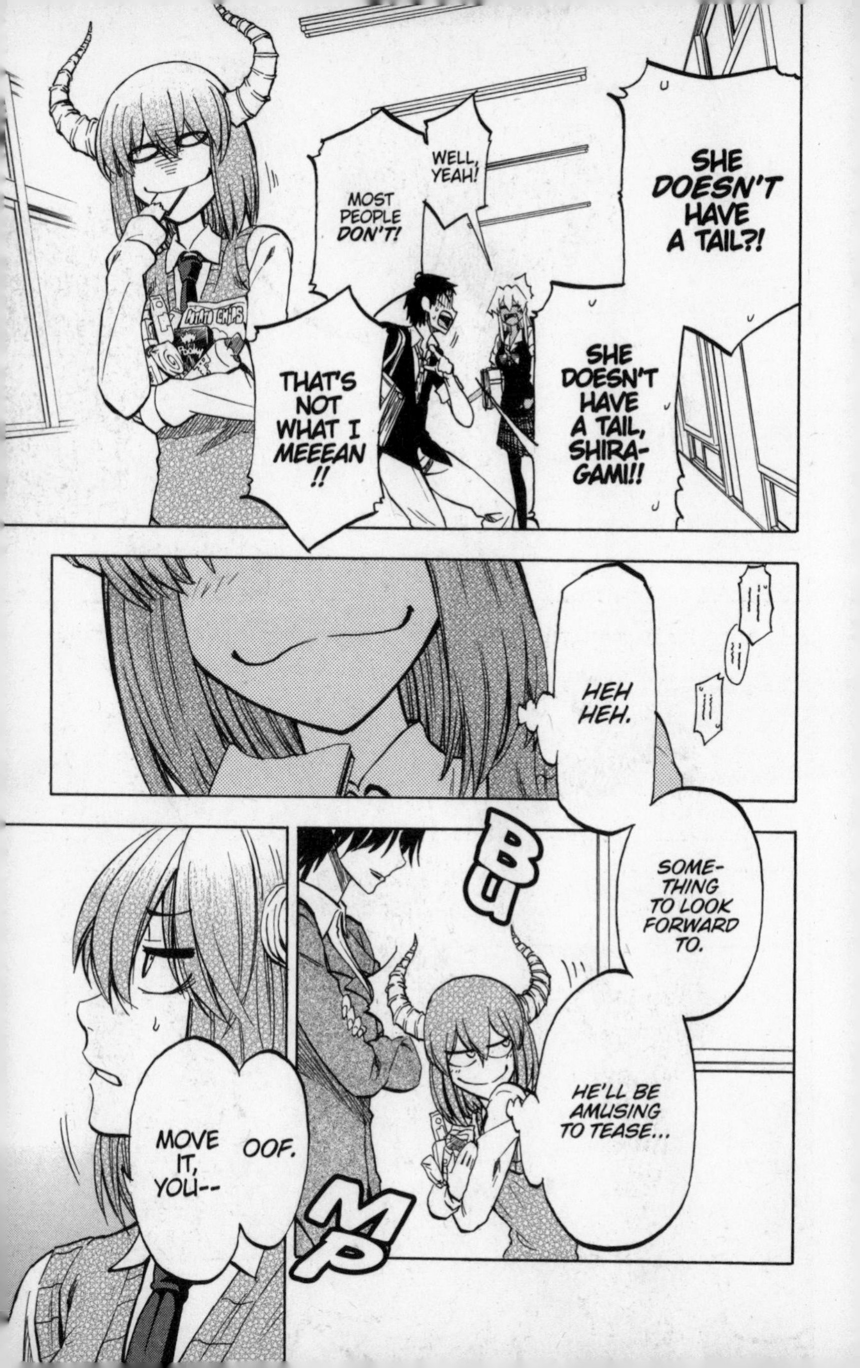
SHE DOESN'T HAVE A TAIL?!
WELL, YEAH!
MOST PEOPLE DON'T!
SHE DOESN'T HAVE A TAIL, SHIRA-GAMI!!
THAT'S NOT WHAT I MEEEAN!!
HEH HEH.
SOME-THING TO LOOK FORWARD TO.
BU
HE'LL BE AMUSING TO TEASE...
MP
OOF.
MOVE IT, YOU--

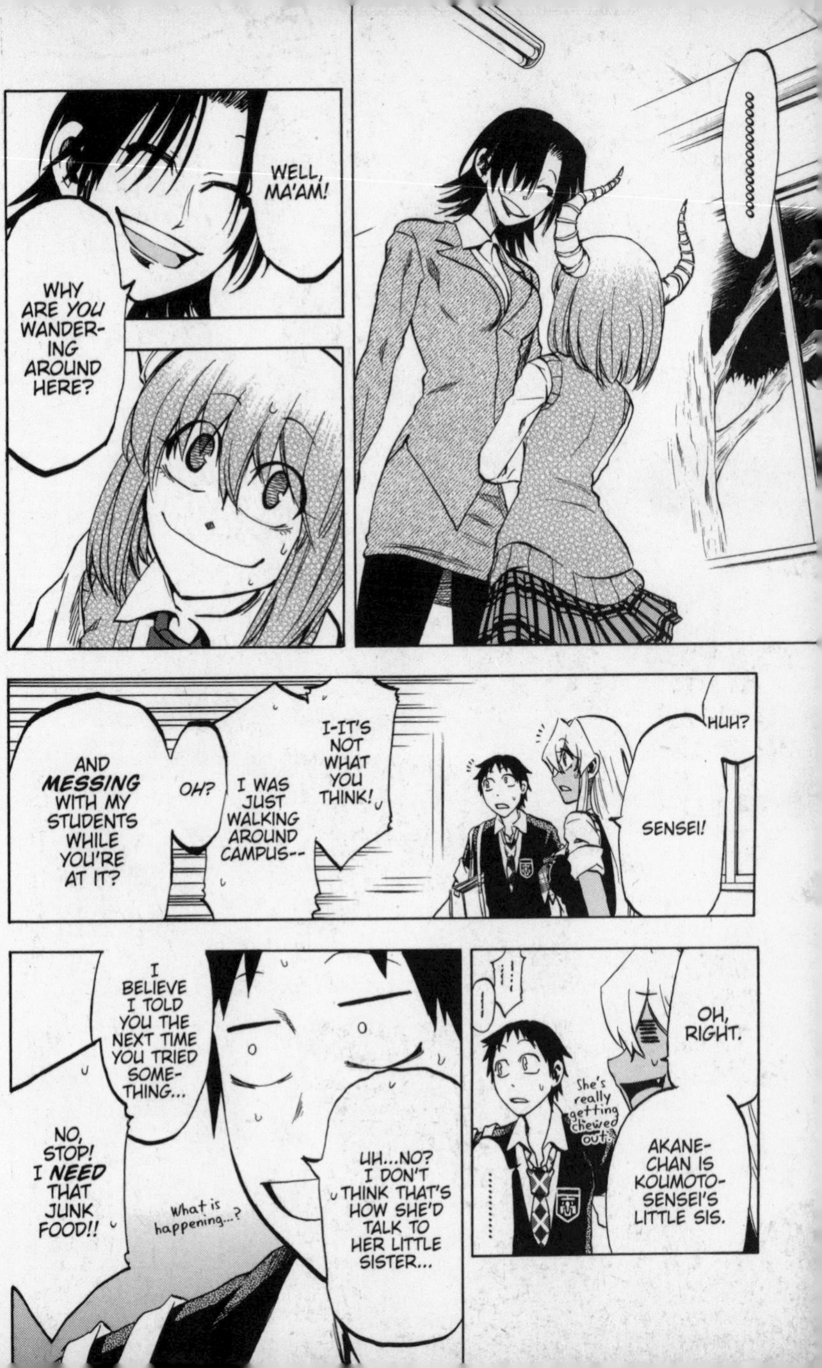
....
WELL, MA'AM!
WHY ARE *YOU* WANDERING AROUND HERE?
HUH?
SENSEI!
I-IT'S NOT WHAT YOU THINK!
I WAS JUST WALKING AROUND CAMPUS--
OH?
AND ***MESSING*** WITH MY STUDENTS WHILE YOU'RE AT IT?
OH, RIGHT.
AKANE-CHAN IS KOUMOTO-SENSEI'S LITTLE SIS.
She's really getting chewed out.
......
......!
......
UH...NO? I DON'T THINK THAT'S HOW SHE'D TALK TO HER LITTLE SISTER...
I BELIEVE I TOLD YOU THE NEXT TIME YOU TRIED SOMETHING...
NO, STOP! I ***NEED*** THAT JUNK FOOD!!
What is happening...?

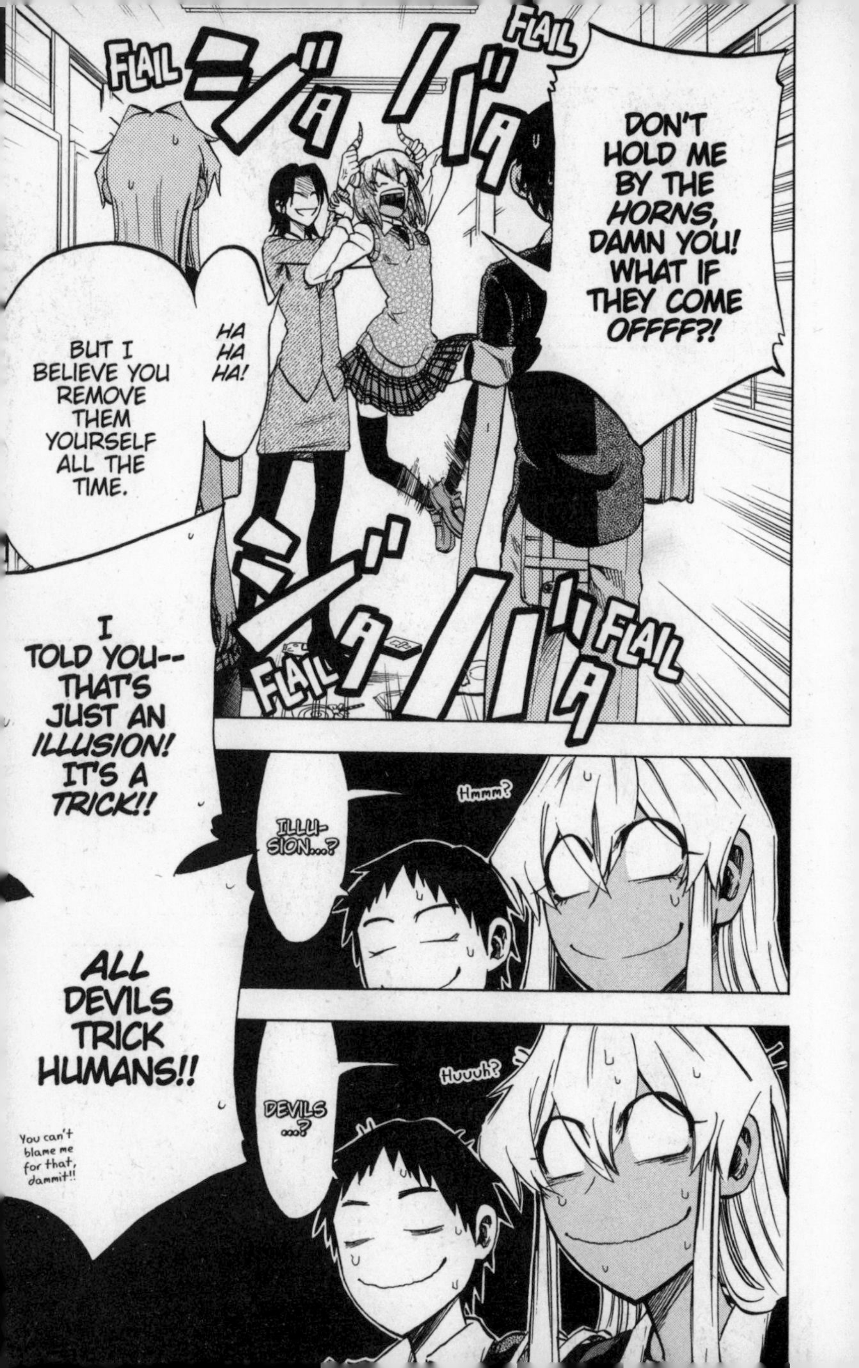
FLAIL
DON'T HOLD ME BY THE *HORNS,* DAMN YOU! WHAT IF THEY COME OFFFF?!
FLAIL
HA HA HA!
BUT I BELIEVE YOU REMOVE THEM YOURSELF ALL THE TIME.
FLAIL
FLAIL
I TOLD YOU-- THAT'S JUST AN *ILLUSION!* IT'S A *TRICK!!*
Hmmm?
ILLU-SION...?
ALL DEVILS TRICK HUMANS!!
Huuuh?
DEVILS ...?
You can't blame me for that, dammit!!

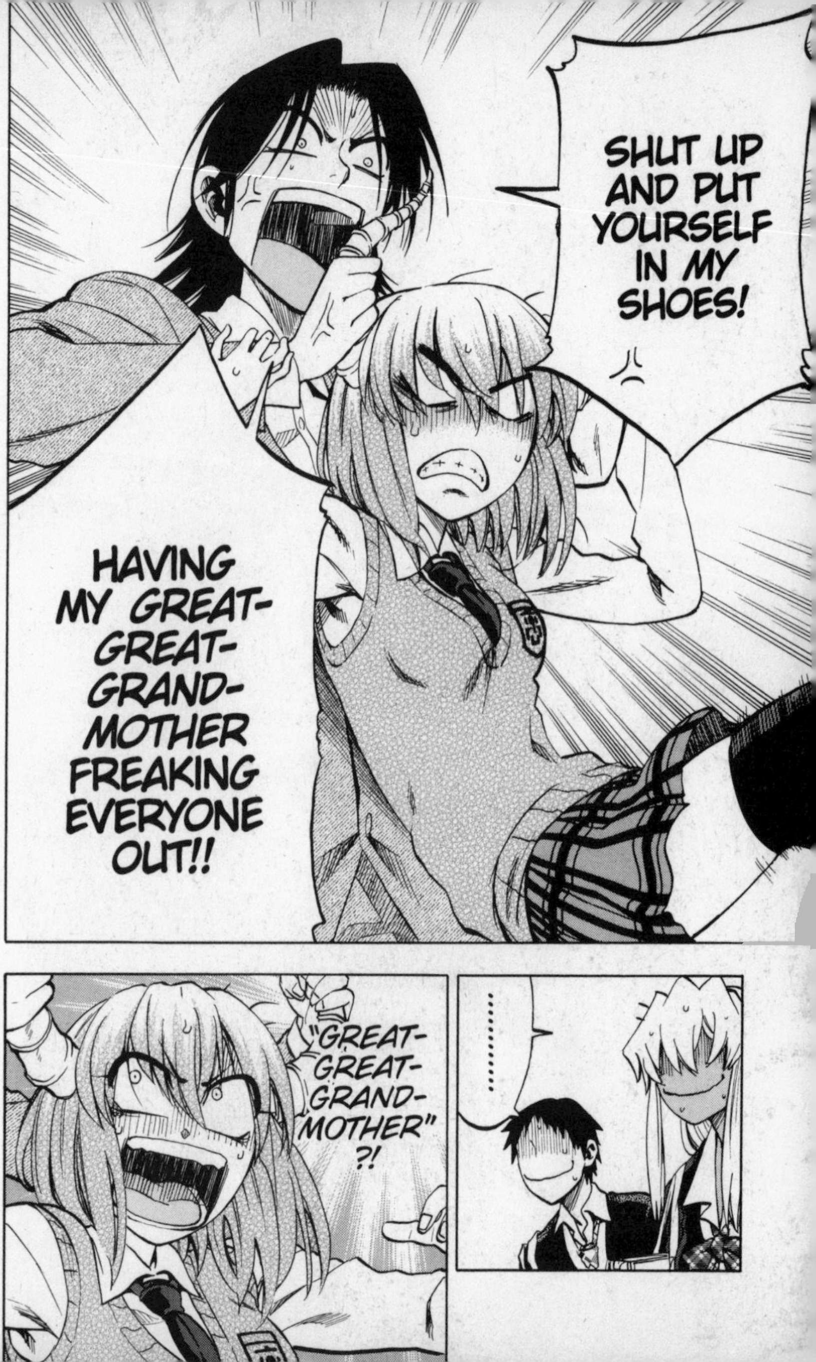
SHUT UP AND PUT YOURSELF IN MY SHOES!
HAVING MY GREAT-GREAT-GRANDMOTHER FREAKING EVERYONE OUT!!
......
"GREAT-GREAT-GRANDMOTHER"?!

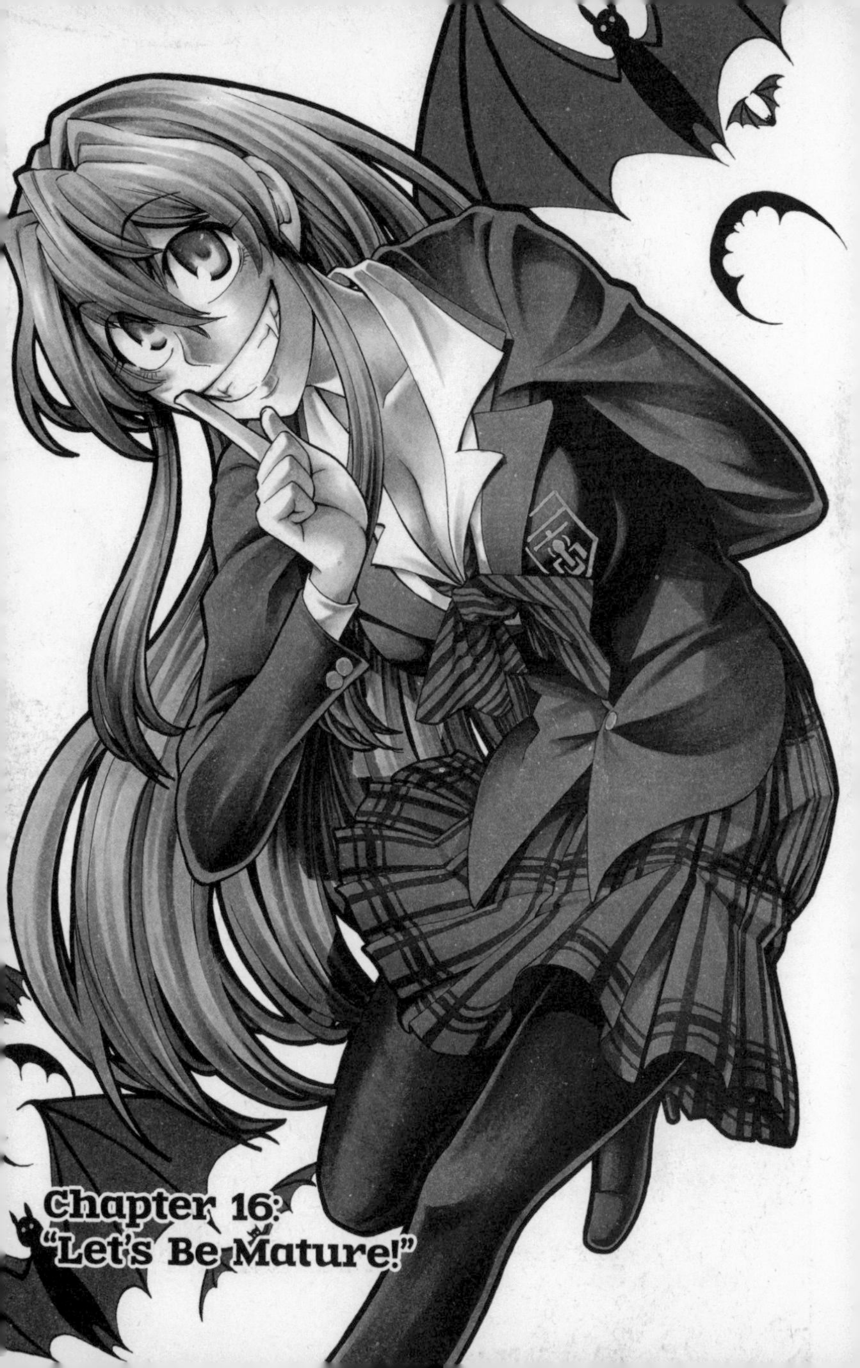
Chapter 16:
"Let's Be Mature!"

Bonus ③

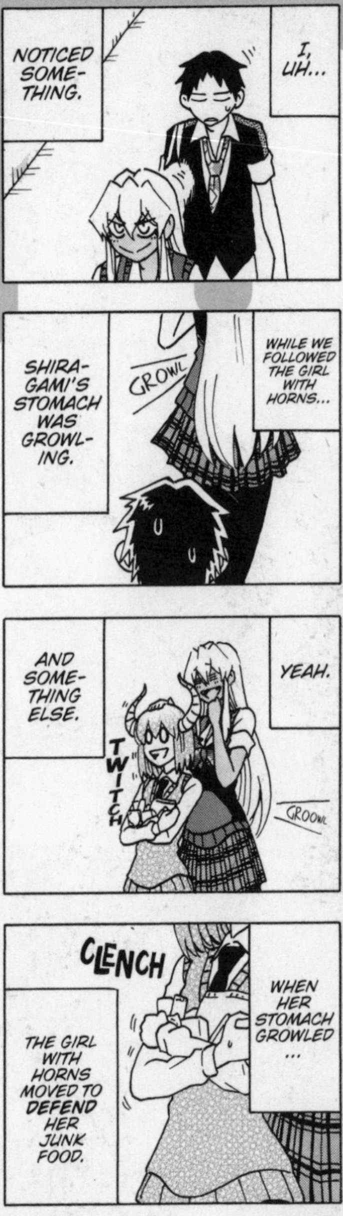
I, UH...
NOTICED SOMETHING.
WHILE WE FOLLOWED THE GIRL WITH HORNS...
GROWL
SHIRAGAMI'S STOMACH WAS GROWLING.
YEAH.
AND SOMETHING ELSE.
TWITCH
GROOWL
WHEN HER STOMACH GROWLED...
CLENCH
THE GIRL WITH HORNS MOVED TO DEFEND HER JUNK FOOD.

Bonus ④

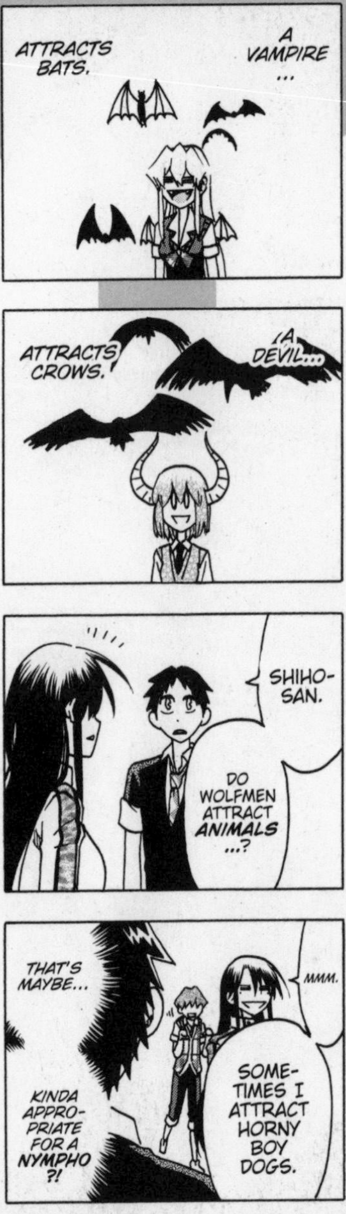
A VAMPIRE...
ATTRACTS BATS.
A DEVIL...
ATTRACTS CROWS.
SHIHO-SAN.
DO WOLFMEN ATTRACT ANIMALS...?
MMM.
SOMETIMES I ATTRACT HORNY BOY DOGS.
THAT'S MAYBE...
KINDA APPROPRIATE FOR A NYMPHO?!

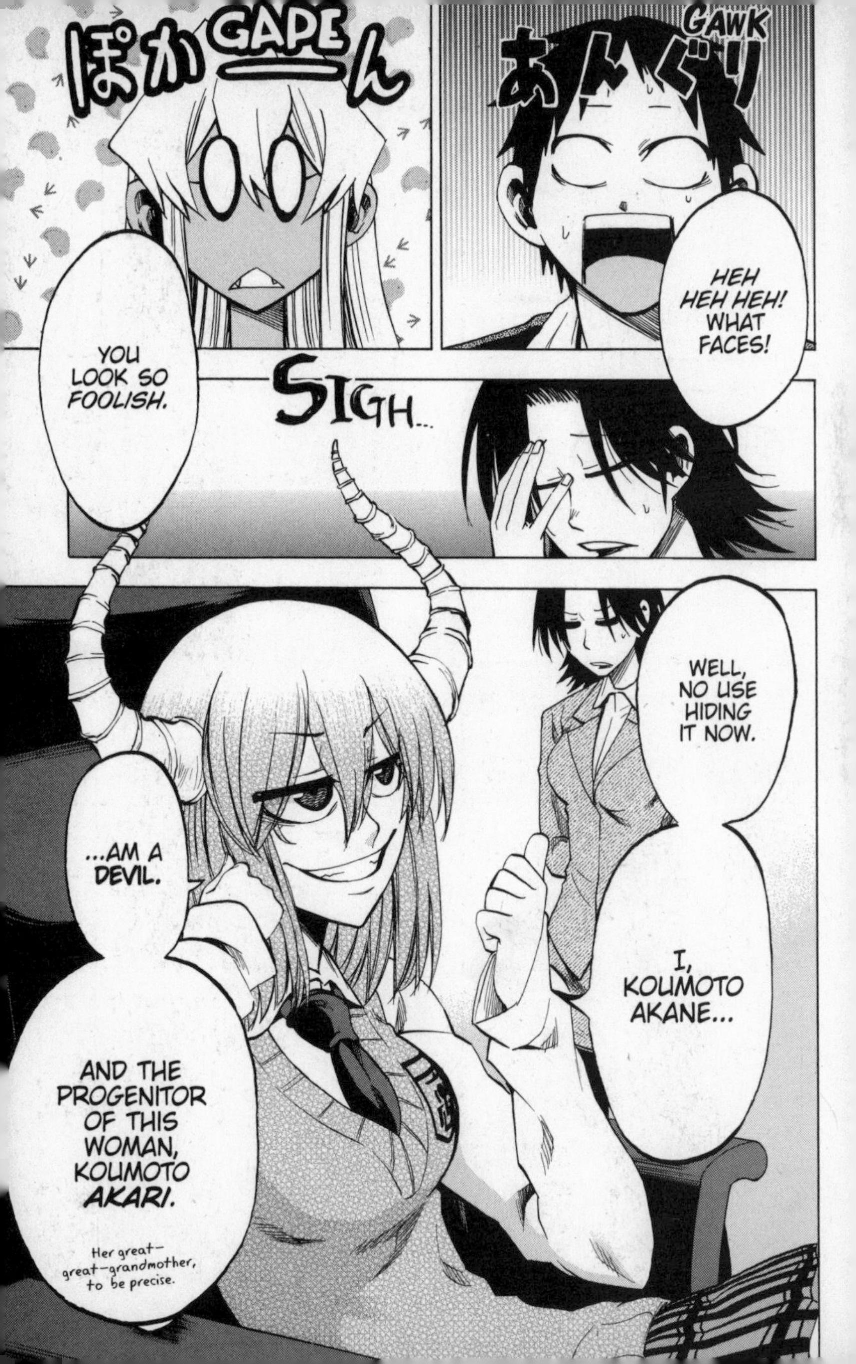
GAWK
あんぐり
HEH HEH HEH! WHAT FACES!
ぽかーん
GAPE
YOU LOOK SO FOOLISH.
SIGH...
WELL, NO USE HIDING IT NOW.
I, KOUMOTO AKANE...
...AM A DEVIL.
AND THE PROGENITOR OF THIS WOMAN, KOUMOTO AKARI.
Her great-great-grandmother, to be precise.

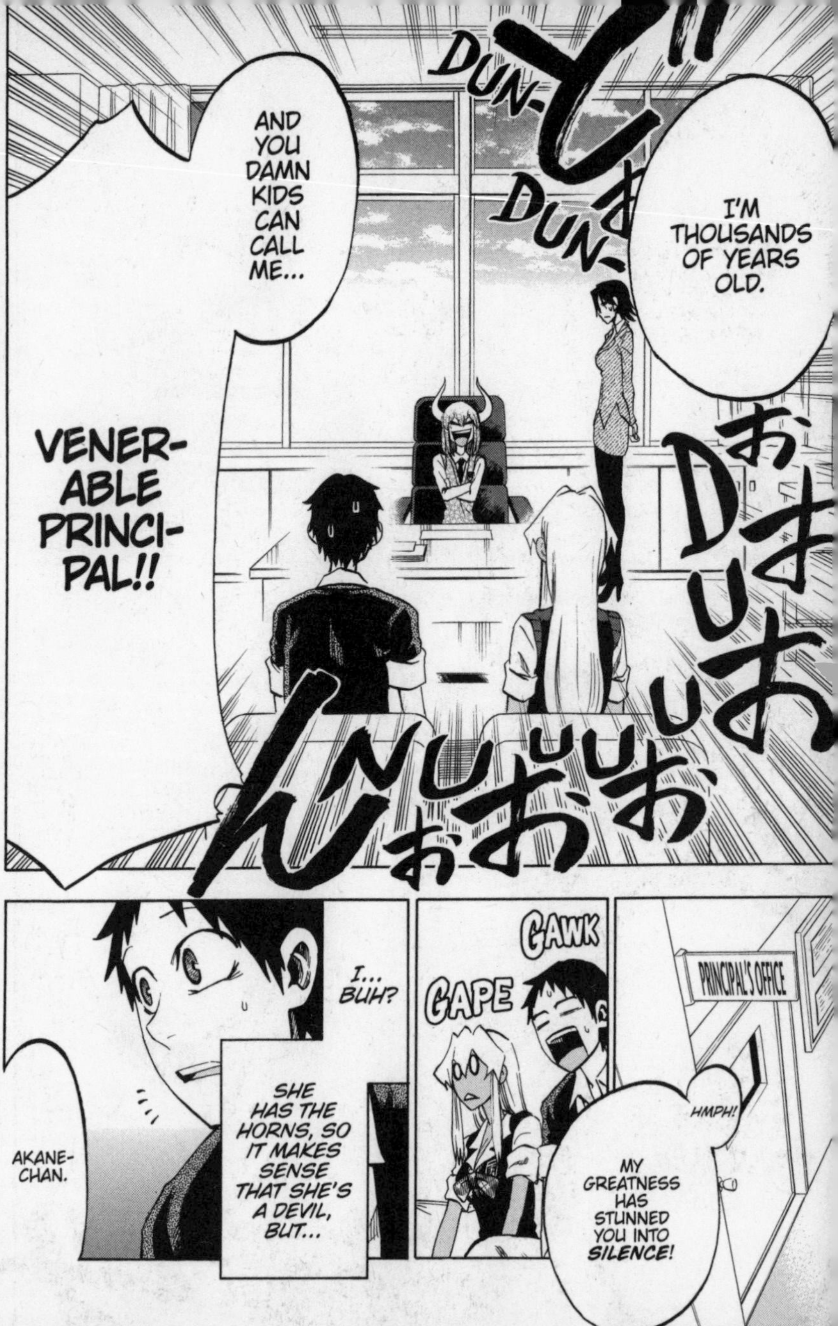
I'M THOUSANDS OF YEARS OLD.
DUN- DUN-
AND YOU DAMN KIDS CAN CALL ME...
VENERABLE PRINCIPAL!!
PRINCIPAL'S OFFICE
HMPH!
MY GREATNESS HAS STUNNED YOU INTO SILENCE!
GAWK
GAPE
I... BUH?
SHE HAS THE HORNS, SO IT MAKES SENSE THAT SHE'S A DEVIL, BUT...
AKANE-CHAN.

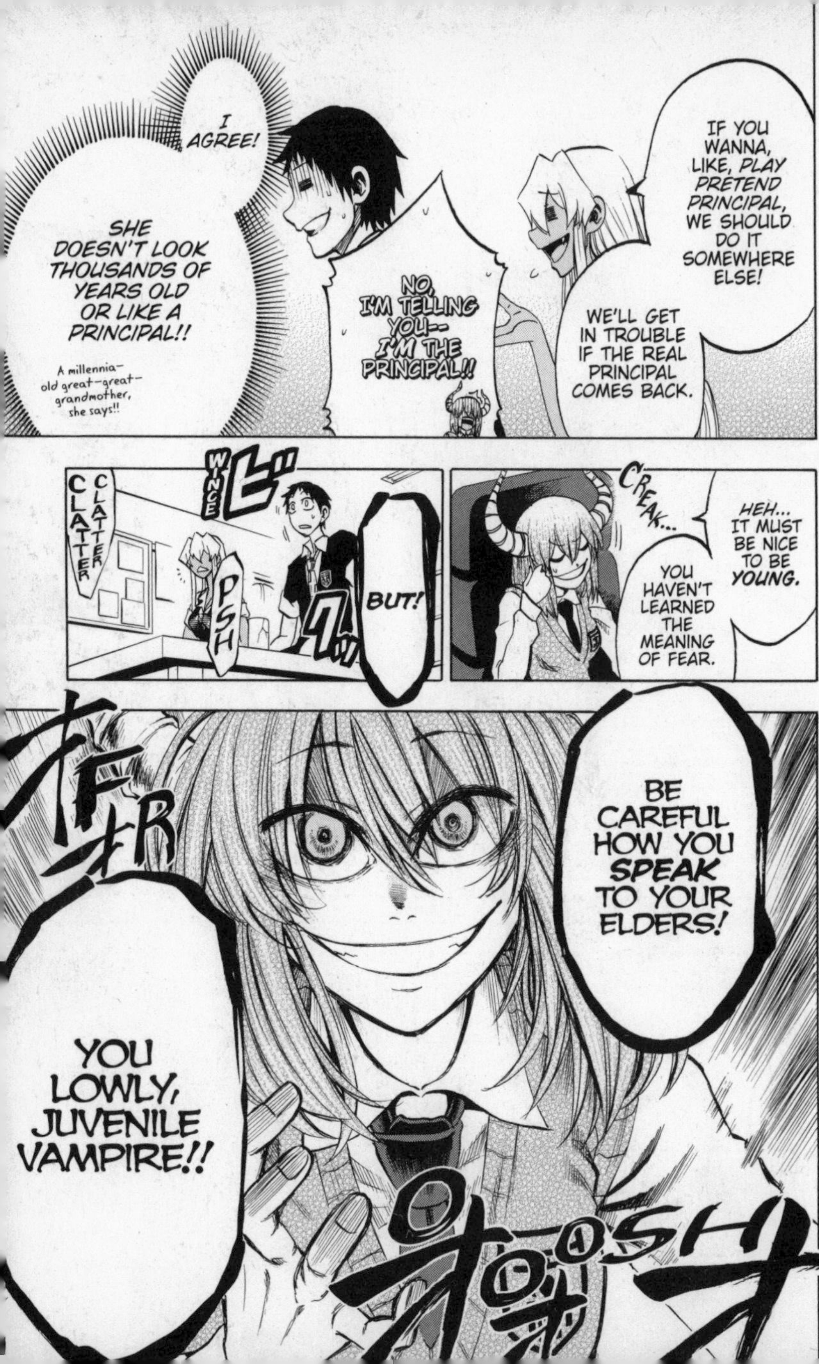
IF YOU WANNA, LIKE, PLAY PRETEND PRINCIPAL, WE SHOULD DO IT SOMEWHERE ELSE!
WE'LL GET IN TROUBLE IF THE REAL PRINCIPAL COMES BACK.
NO, I'M TELLING YOU-- I'M THE PRINCIPAL!!
I AGREE!
SHE DOESN'T LOOK THOUSANDS OF YEARS OLD OR LIKE A PRINCIPAL!!
A millennia-old great-great-grandmother, she says!!
CREAK...
HEH... IT MUST BE NICE TO BE YOUNG.
YOU HAVEN'T LEARNED THE MEANING OF FEAR.
BUT!
WINCE
PSH
CLATTER CLATTER
BE CAREFUL HOW YOU SPEAK TO YOUR ELDERS!
FR
YOU LOWLY, JUVENILE VAMPIRE!!
WOOSH

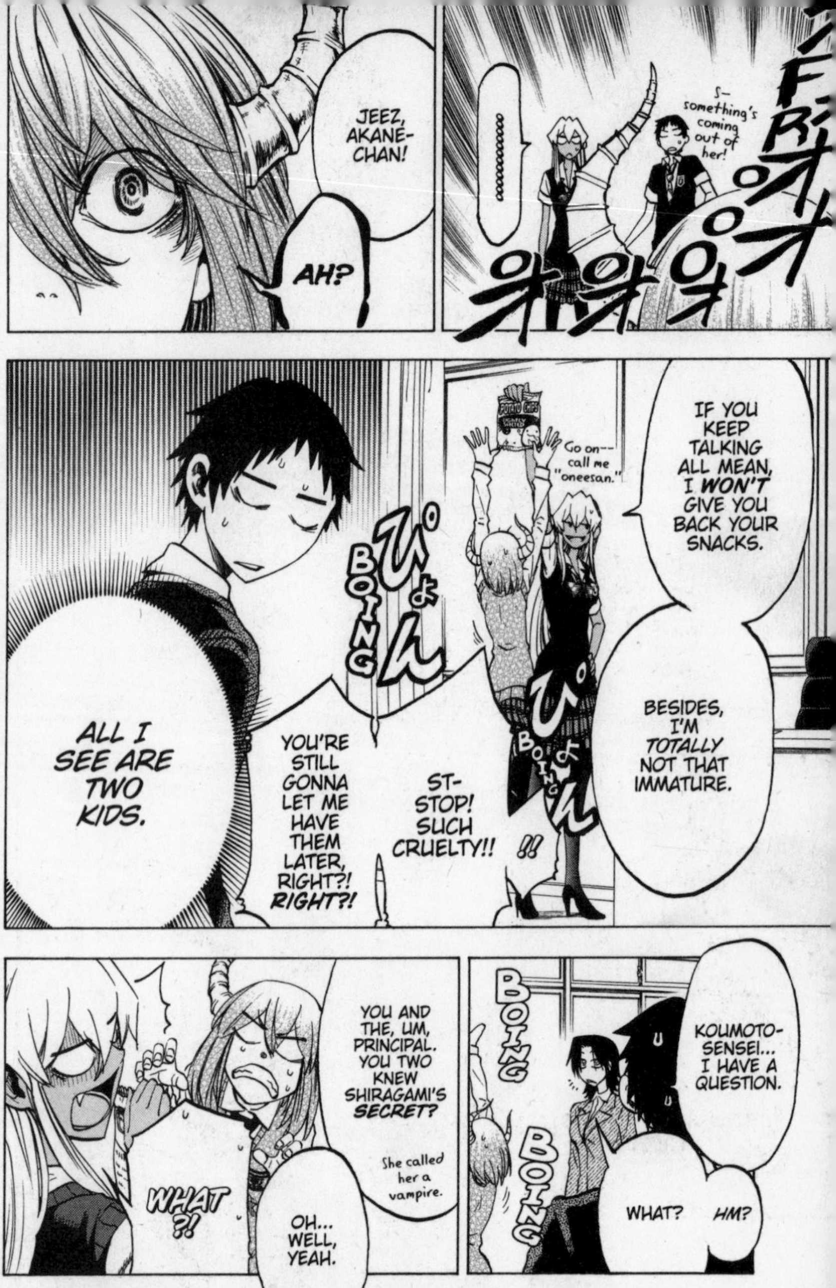
FR
S-something's coming out of her!
....
JEEZ, AKANE-CHAN!
AH?
IF YOU KEEP TALKING ALL MEAN, I WON'T GIVE YOU BACK YOUR SNACKS.
Go on-- call me "oneesan."
POTATO CHIPS
BESIDES, I'M TOTALLY NOT THAT IMMATURE.
ぴょん BOING
!!
ST-STOP! SUCH CRUELTY!!
YOU'RE STILL GONNA LET ME HAVE THEM LATER, RIGHT?! RIGHT?!
ぴょん BOING
ALL I SEE ARE TWO KIDS.
KOUMOTO-SENSEI... I HAVE A QUESTION.
BOING
BOING
HM?
WHAT?
YOU AND THE, UM, PRINCIPAL. YOU TWO KNEW SHIRAGAMI'S SECRET?
She called her a vampire.
OH... WELL, YEAH.
WHAT?!

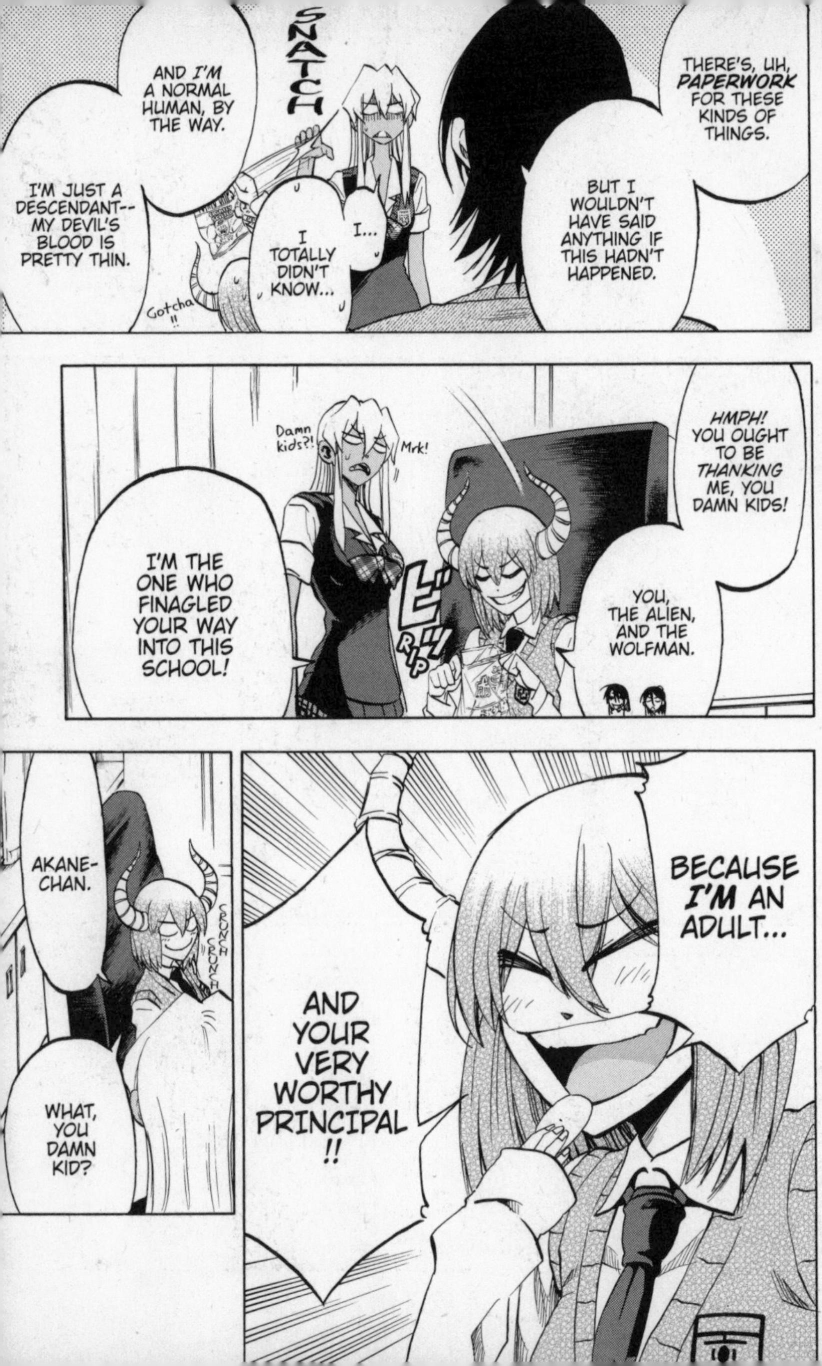
THERE'S, UH, *PAPERWORK* FOR THESE KINDS OF THINGS.
BUT I WOULDN'T HAVE SAID ANYTHING IF THIS HADN'T HAPPENED.
SNATCH
I...
I TOTALLY DIDN'T KNOW...
AND *I'M* A NORMAL HUMAN, BY THE WAY.
I'M JUST A DESCENDANT-- MY DEVIL'S BLOOD IS PRETTY THIN.
Gotcha!!
HMPH! YOU OUGHT TO BE *THANKING* ME, YOU DAMN KIDS!
YOU, THE ALIEN, AND THE WOLFMAN.
ビッ
RIP
Mrk!
Damn kids?!
I'M THE ONE WHO FINAGLED YOUR WAY INTO THIS SCHOOL!
BECAUSE *I'M* AN ADULT...
AND YOUR VERY WORTHY PRINCIPAL!!
AKANE-CHAN.
CRUNCH CRUNCH
WHAT, YOU DAMN KID?

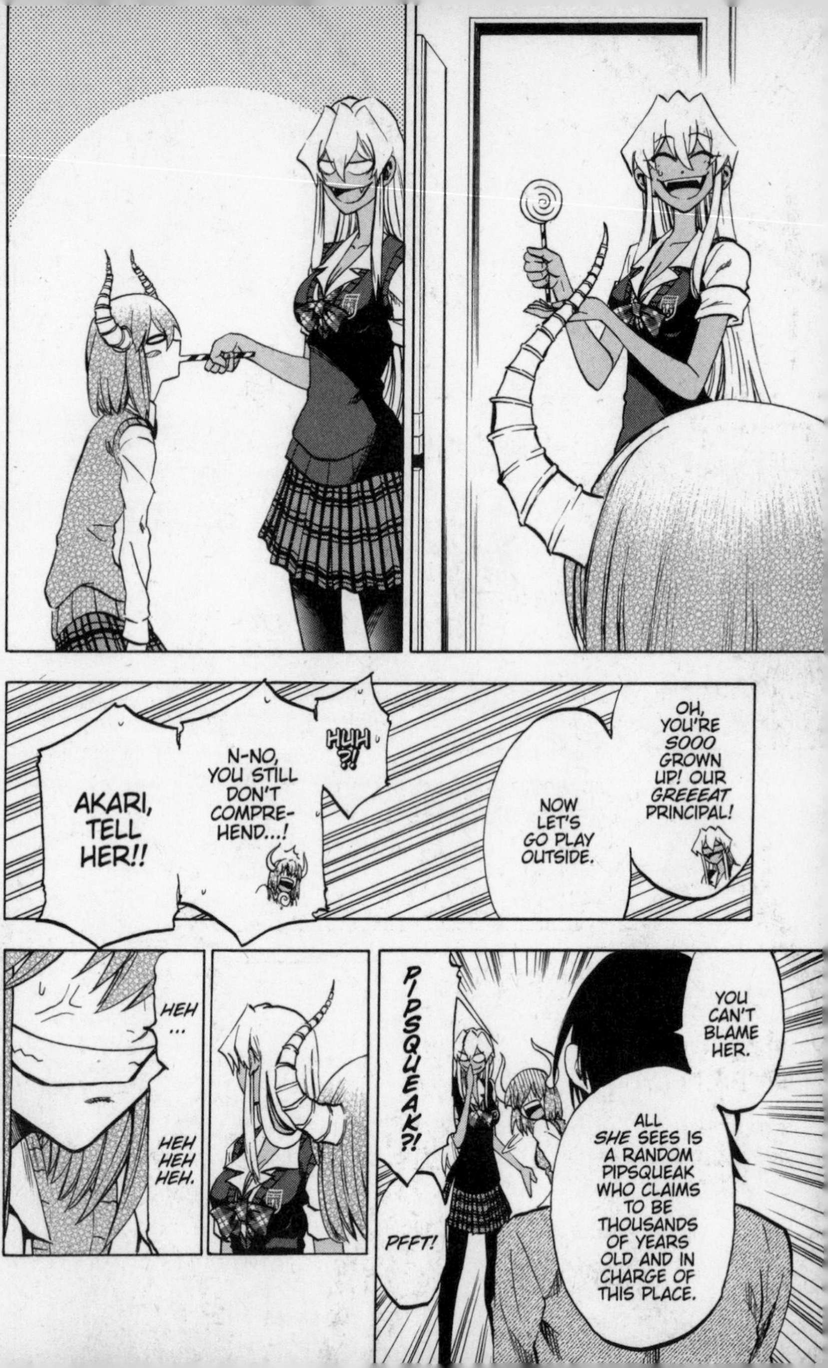
OH, YOU'RE SOOO GROWN UP! OUR GREEEAT PRINCIPAL!
NOW LET'S GO PLAY OUTSIDE.
HUH ?!
N-NO, YOU STILL DON'T COMPRE-HEND...!
AKARI, TELL HER!!
YOU CAN'T BLAME HER.
ALL SHE SEES IS A RANDOM PIPSQUEAK WHO CLAIMS TO BE THOUSANDS OF YEARS OLD AND IN CHARGE OF THIS PLACE.
PIPSQUEAK?!
PFFT!
HEH...
HEH HEH HEH.

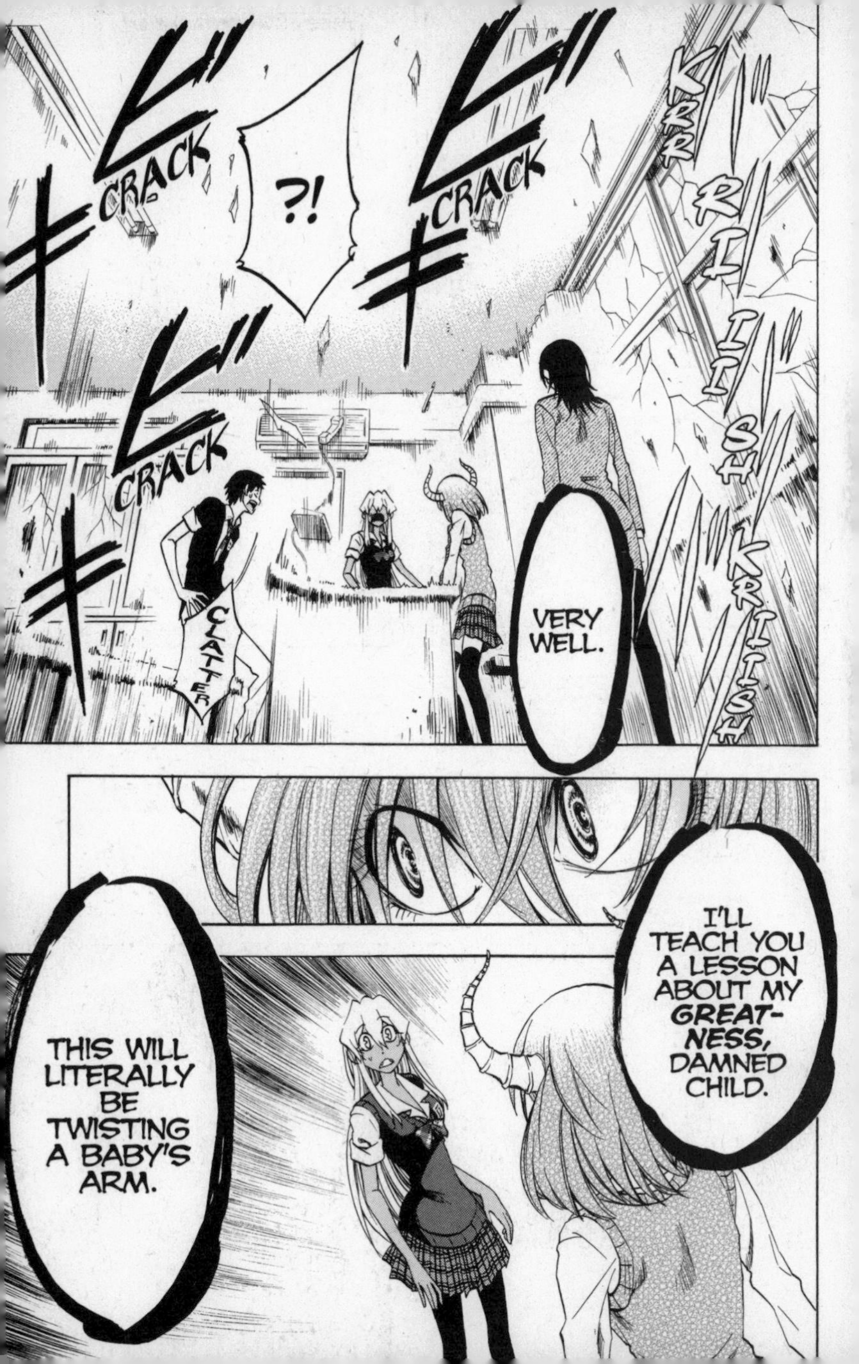

KRRRIIISH
KRIIISH
CRACK
?!
CRACK
CRACK
CLATTER
VERY WELL.
I'LL TEACH YOU A LESSON ABOUT MY GREAT-NESS, DAMNED CHILD.
THIS WILL LITERALLY BE TWISTING A BABY'S ARM.

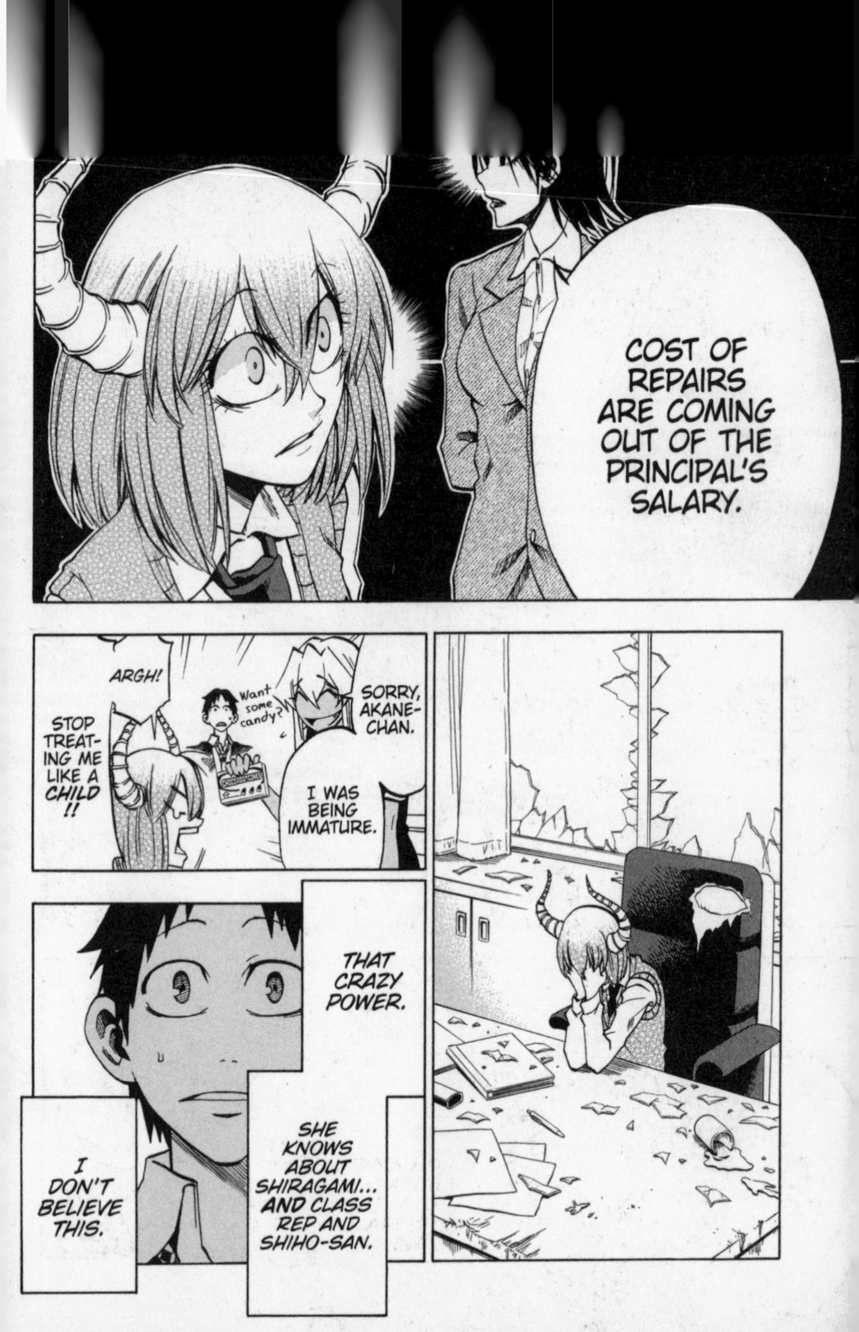
COST OF REPAIRS ARE COMING OUT OF THE PRINCIPAL'S SALARY.
SORRY, AKANE-CHAN.
I WAS BEING IMMATURE.
Want some candy?
ARGH!
STOP TREATING ME LIKE A CHILD!!
THAT CRAZY POWER.
SHE KNOWS ABOUT SHIRAGAMI... AND CLASS REP AND SHIHO-SAN.
I DON'T BELIEVE THIS.

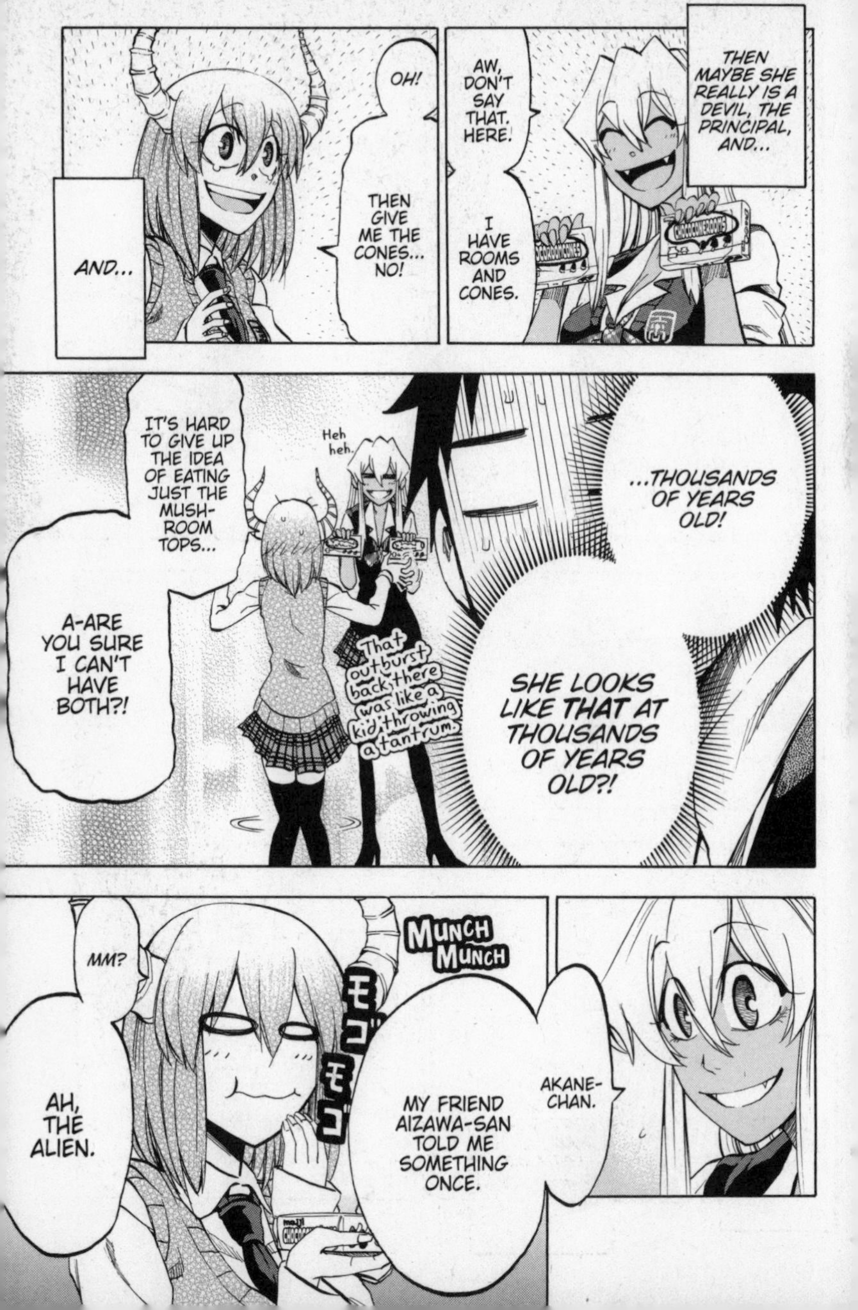
THEN MAYBE SHE REALLY IS A DEVIL, THE PRINCIPAL, AND...
AW, DON'T SAY THAT. HERE.
I HAVE ROOMS AND CONES.
OH!
THEN GIVE ME THE CONES... NO!
AND...
...THOUSANDS OF YEARS OLD!
SHE LOOKS LIKE THAT AT THOUSANDS OF YEARS OLD?!
Heh heh.
IT'S HARD TO GIVE UP THE IDEA OF EATING JUST THE MUSH-ROOM TOPS...
That outburst back there was like a kid throwing a tantrum.
A-ARE YOU SURE I CAN'T HAVE BOTH?!
AKANE-CHAN.
MY FRIEND AIZAWA-SAN TOLD ME SOMETHING ONCE.
MUNCH MUNCH
モゴモゴ
MM?
AH, THE ALIEN.

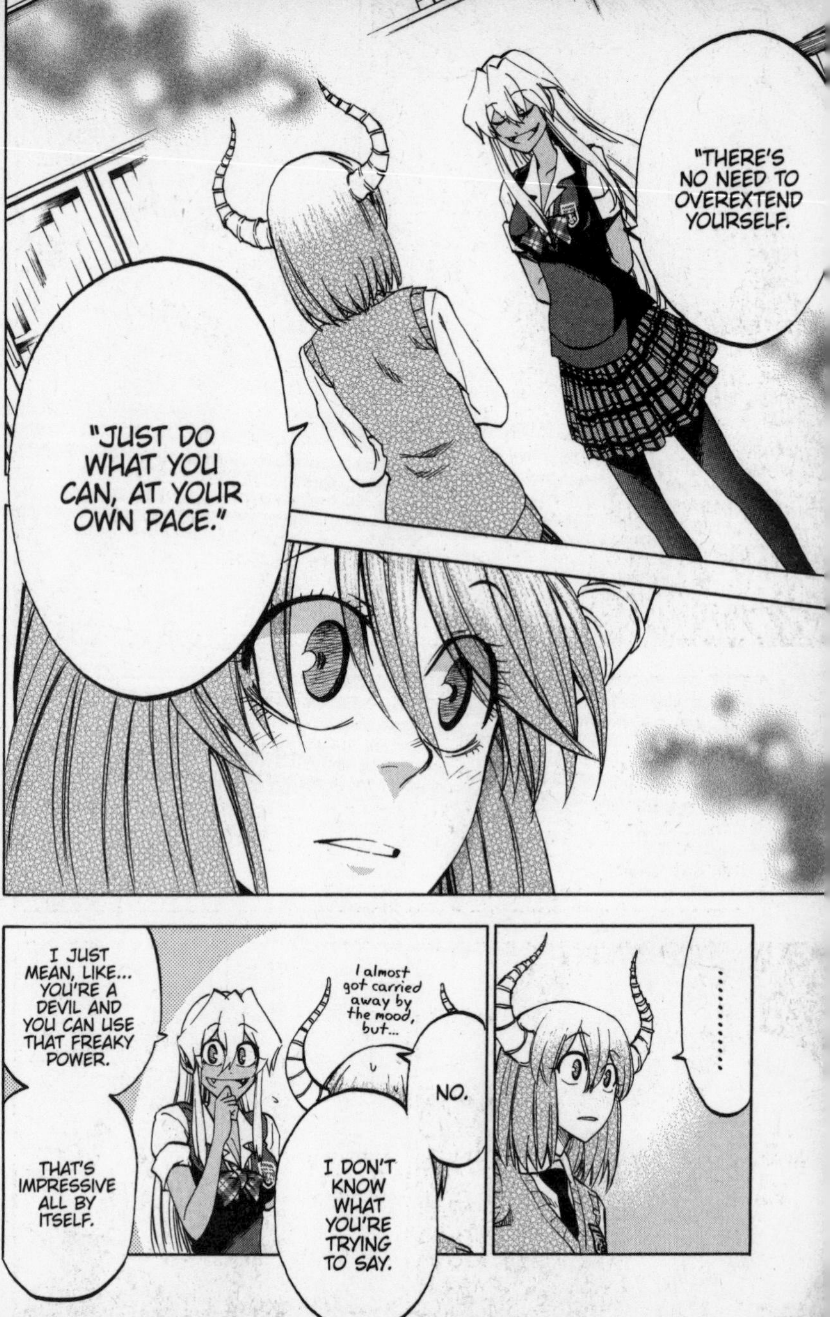
"THERE'S NO NEED TO OVEREXTEND YOURSELF.
"JUST DO WHAT YOU CAN, AT YOUR OWN PACE."
....
I almost got carried away by the mood, but...
NO.
I DON'T KNOW WHAT YOU'RE TRYING TO SAY.
I JUST MEAN, LIKE... YOU'RE A DEVIL AND YOU CAN USE THAT FREAKY POWER.
THAT'S IMPRESSIVE ALL BY ITSELF.

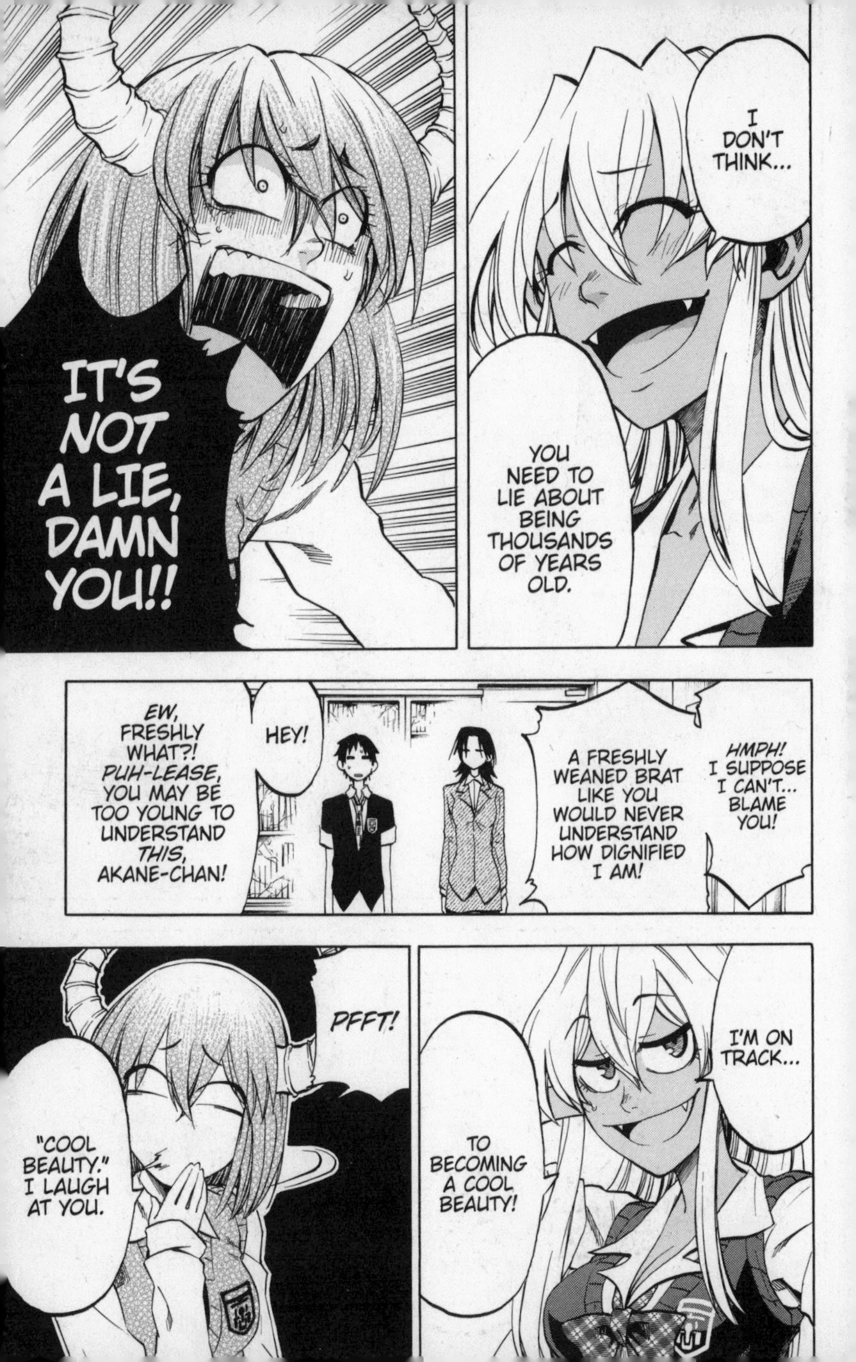
I DON'T THINK...
YOU NEED TO LIE ABOUT BEING THOUSANDS OF YEARS OLD.
IT'S *NOT* A LIE, DAMN YOU!!
HMPH! I SUPPOSE I CAN'T... BLAME YOU!
A FRESHLY WEANED BRAT LIKE YOU WOULD NEVER UNDERSTAND HOW DIGNIFIED I AM!
HEY!
EW, FRESHLY WHAT?! *PUH-LEASE*, YOU MAY BE TOO YOUNG TO UNDERSTAND *THIS*, AKANE-CHAN!
I'M ON TRACK...
TO BECOMING A COOL BEAUTY!
PFFT!
"COOL BEAUTY." I LAUGH AT YOU.

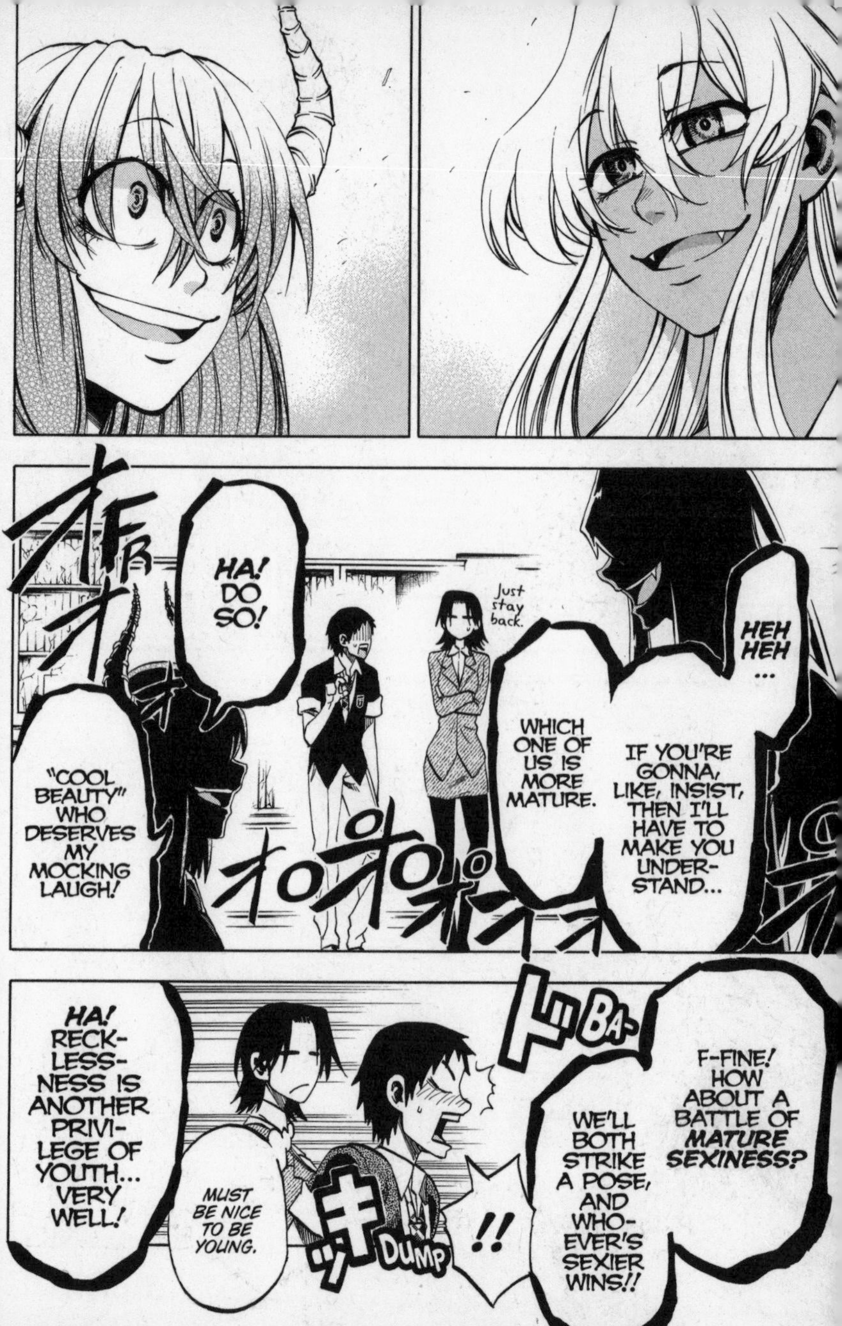
HEH HEH...
IF YOU'RE GONNA, LIKE, INSIST, THEN I'LL HAVE TO MAKE YOU UNDER-STAND...
WHICH ONE OF US IS MORE MATURE.
Just stay back.
HA! DO SO!
"COOL BEAUTY" WHO DESERVES MY MOCKING LAUGH!
BA-
F-FINE! HOW ABOUT A BATTLE OF MATURE SEXINESS?
WE'LL BOTH STRIKE A POSE, AND WHO-EVER'S SEXIER WINS!!
!!
DUMP
MUST BE NICE TO BE YOUNG.
HA! RECK-LESS-NESS IS ANOTHER PRIVI-LEGE OF YOUTH... VERY WELL!

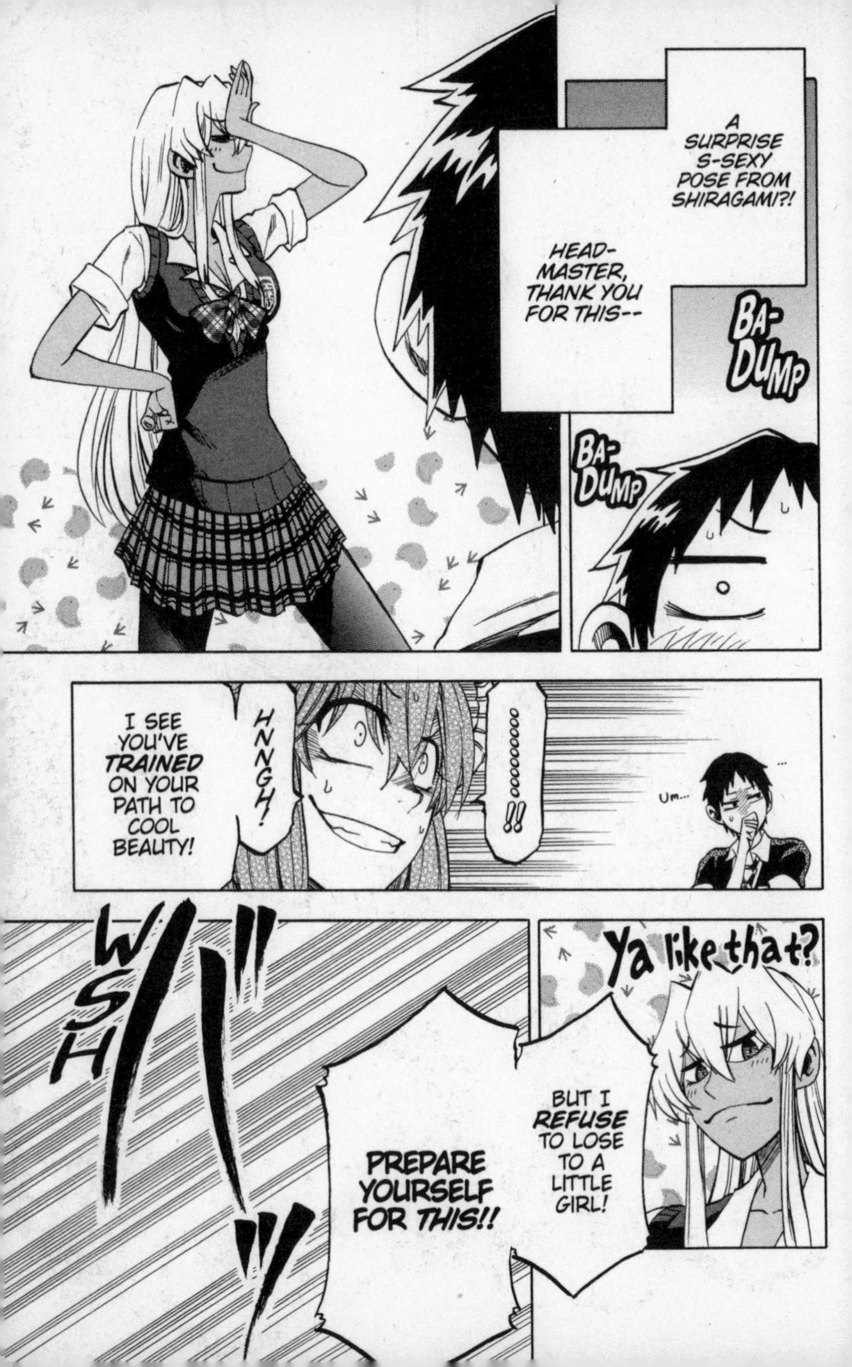
A SURPRISE S-SEXY POSE FROM SHIRAGAMI?!
HEAD-MASTER, THANK YOU FOR THIS--
BA-DUMP
BA-DUMP
...
Um...
OOOOOOOO!!
HNNGH!
I SEE YOU'VE TRAINED ON YOUR PATH TO COOL BEAUTY!
Ya like that?
BUT I REFUSE TO LOSE TO A LITTLE GIRL!
PREPARE YOURSELF FOR THIS!!
WSH

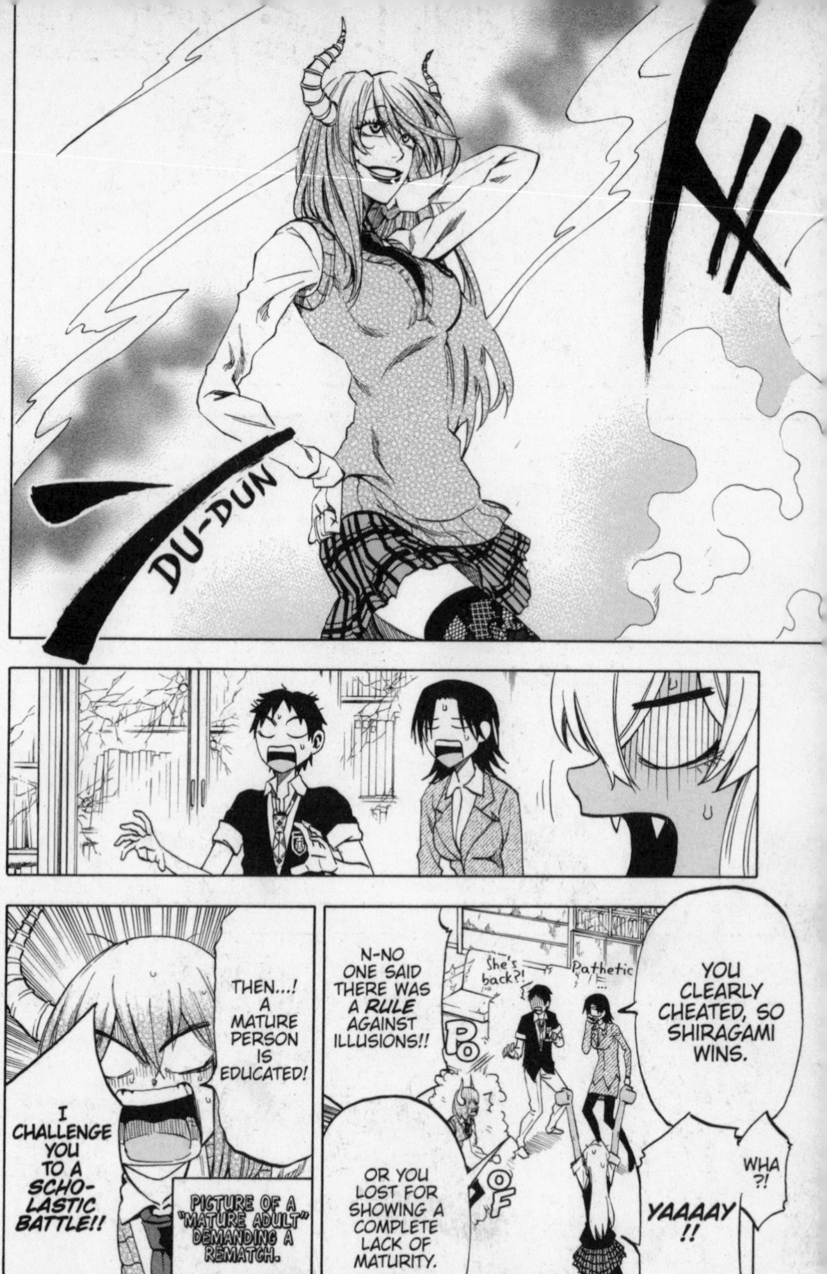
DU-DUN
YOU CLEARLY CHEATED, SO SHIRAGAMI WINS.
WHA ?!
YAAAAY !!
Pathetic ...
She's back?!
N-NO ONE SAID THERE WAS A RULE AGAINST ILLUSIONS!!
POOF
OR YOU LOST FOR SHOWING A COMPLETE LACK OF MATURITY.
THEN...! A MATURE PERSON IS EDUCATED!
I CHALLENGE YOU TO A SCHO-LASTIC BATTLE!!
PICTURE OF A "MATURE ADULT" DEMANDING A REMATCH.

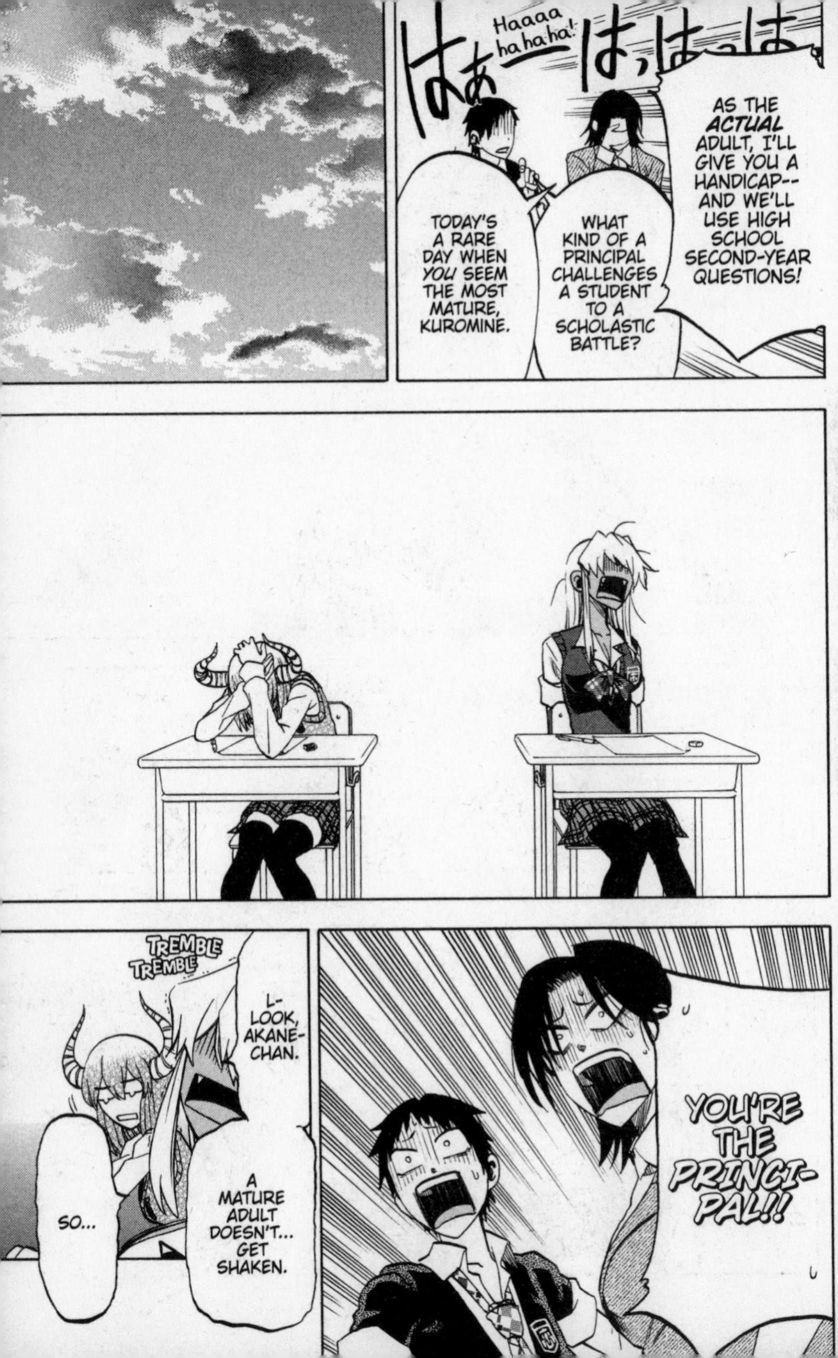
Haaaa ha ha ha!
はぁーはっはっは
AS THE ACTUAL ADULT, I'LL GIVE YOU A HANDICAP-- AND WE'LL USE HIGH SCHOOL SECOND-YEAR QUESTIONS!
WHAT KIND OF A PRINCIPAL CHALLENGES A STUDENT TO A SCHOLASTIC BATTLE?
TODAY'S A RARE DAY WHEN YOU SEEM THE MOST MATURE, KUROMINE.
YOU'RE THE PRINCI-PAL!!
TREMBLE TREMBLE
L-LOOK, AKANE-CHAN.
A MATURE ADULT DOESN'T... GET SHAKEN.
SO...

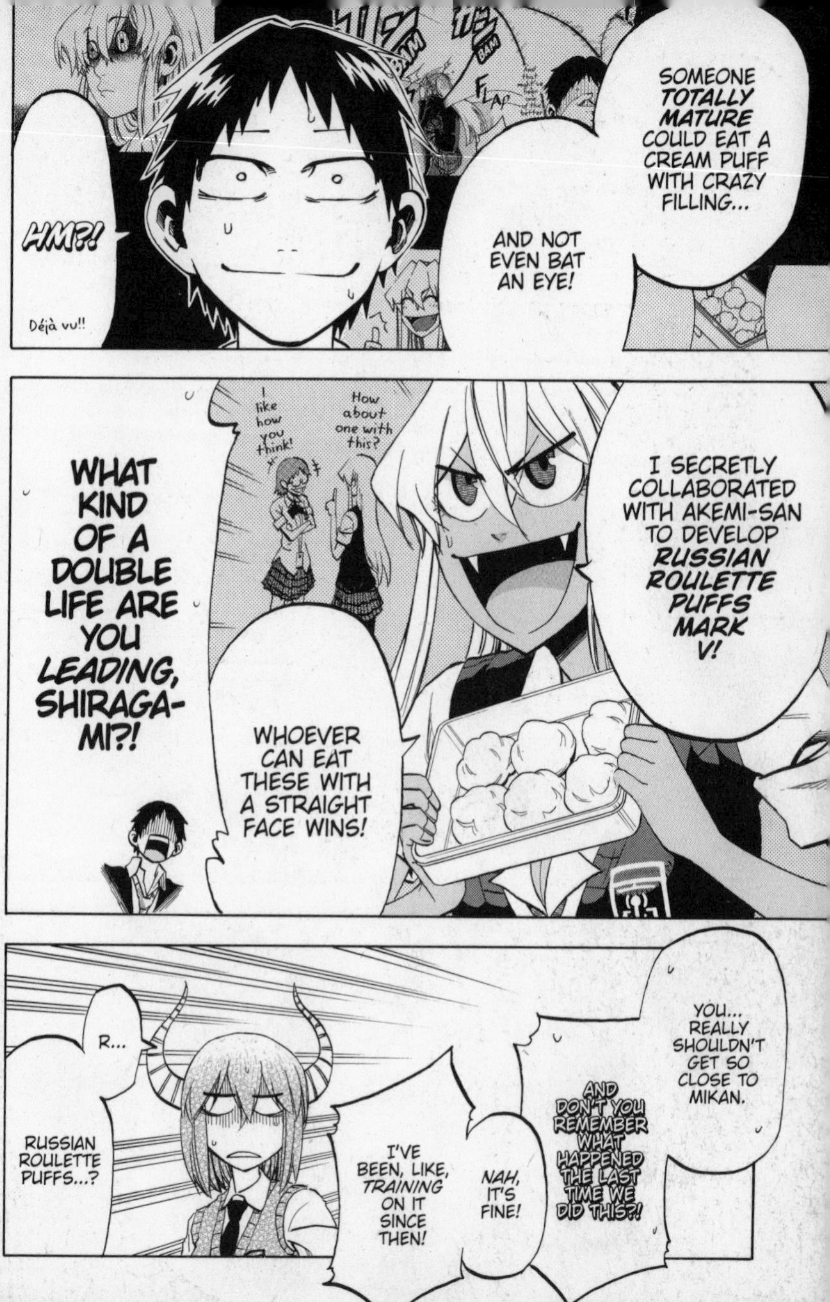
SOMEONE TOTALLY MATURE COULD EAT A CREAM PUFF WITH CRAZY FILLING...
AND NOT EVEN BAT AN EYE!
HM?!
Déjà vu!!
I SECRETLY COLLABORATED WITH AKEMI-SAN TO DEVELOP RUSSIAN ROULETTE PUFFS MARK V!
How about one with this?
I like how you think!
WHOEVER CAN EAT THESE WITH A STRAIGHT FACE WINS!
WHAT KIND OF A DOUBLE LIFE ARE YOU LEADING, SHIRAGAMI?!
YOU... REALLY SHOULDN'T GET SO CLOSE TO MIKAN.
AND DON'T YOU REMEMBER WHAT HAPPENED THE LAST TIME WE DID THIS?!
NAH, IT'S FINE!
I'VE BEEN, LIKE, TRAINING ON IT SINCE THEN!
R...
RUSSIAN ROULETTE PUFFS...?

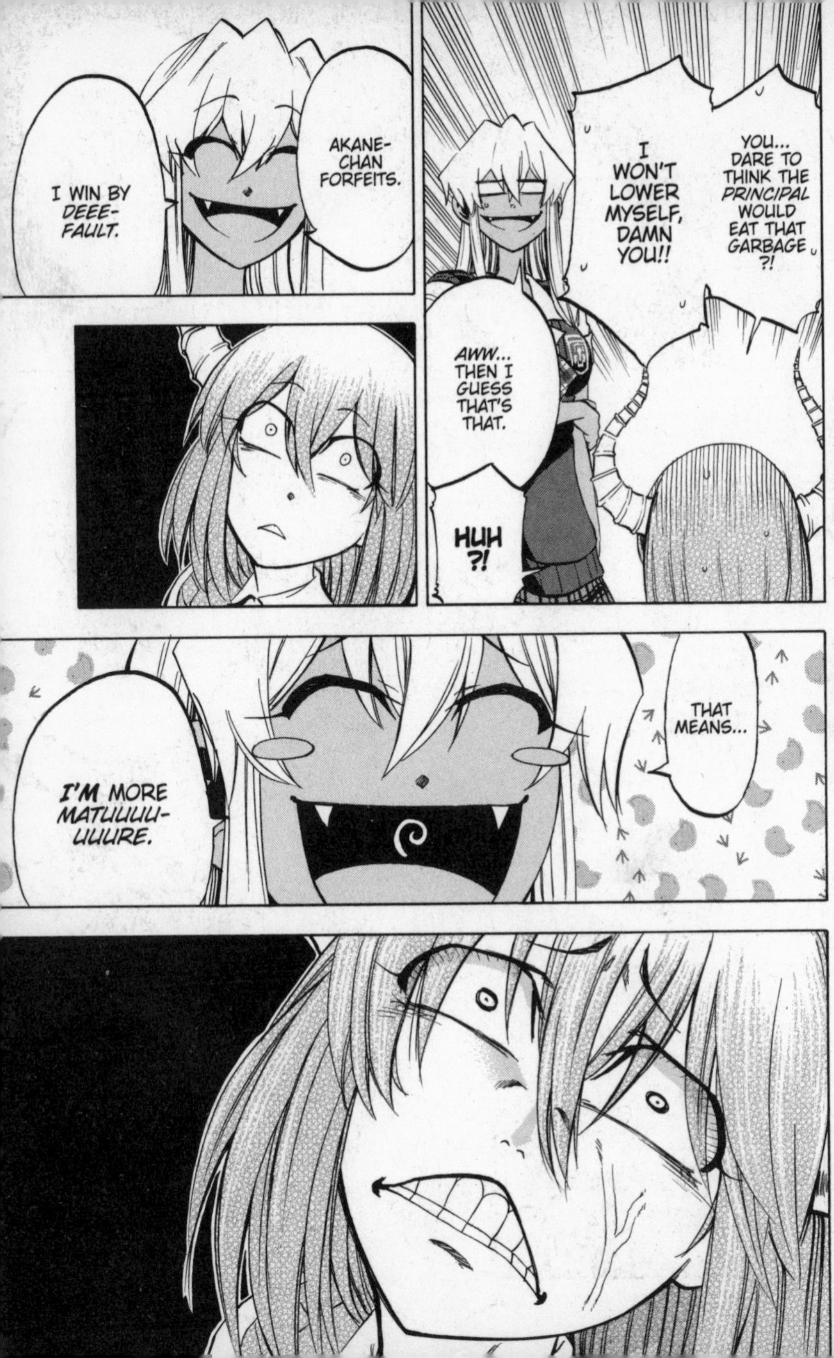
YOU... DARE TO THINK THE *PRINCIPAL* WOULD EAT THAT GARBAGE?!
I WON'T LOWER MYSELF, DAMN YOU!!
AWW... THEN I GUESS THAT'S THAT.
HUH?!
AKANE-CHAN FORFEITS.
I WIN BY *DEEE-FAULT.*
THAT MEANS...
I'M MORE *MATUUUUU-UUURE.*

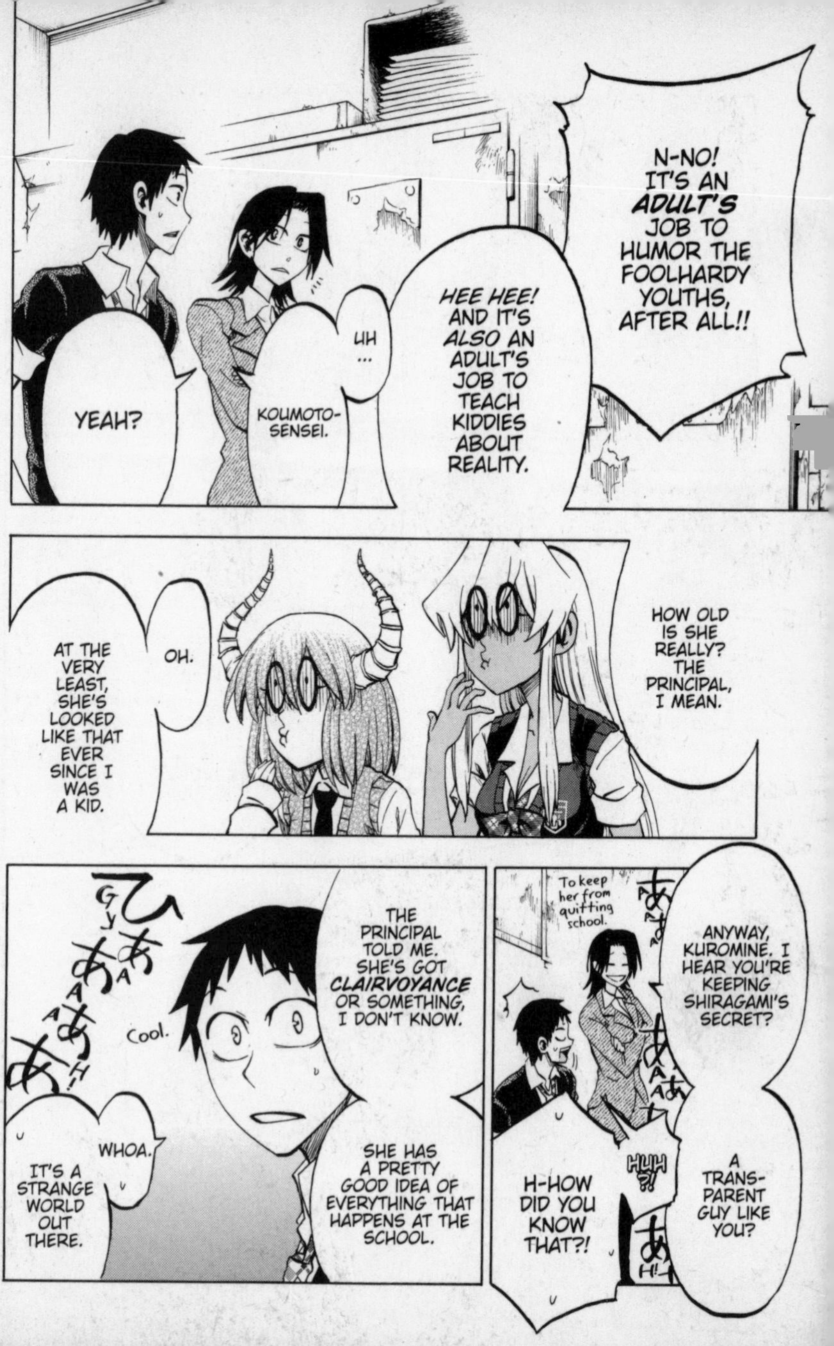
N-NO! IT'S AN ADULT'S JOB TO HUMOR THE FOOLHARDY YOUTHS, AFTER ALL!!
HEE HEE! AND IT'S ALSO AN ADULT'S JOB TO TEACH KIDDIES ABOUT REALITY.
UH ...
KOUMOTO-SENSEI.
YEAH?
HOW OLD IS SHE REALLY? THE PRINCIPAL, I MEAN.
OH.
AT THE VERY LEAST, SHE'S LOOKED LIKE THAT EVER SINCE I WAS A KID.
ANYWAY, KUROMINE. I HEAR YOU'RE KEEPING SHIRAGAMI'S SECRET?
To keep her from quitting school.
A TRANSPARENT GUY LIKE YOU?
HUH ?!
H-HOW DID YOU KNOW THAT?!
THE PRINCIPAL TOLD ME. SHE'S GOT CLAIRVOYANCE OR SOMETHING, I DON'T KNOW.
SHE HAS A PRETTY GOOD IDEA OF EVERYTHING THAT HAPPENS AT THE SCHOOL.
Cool.
WHOA.
IT'S A STRANGE WORLD OUT THERE.

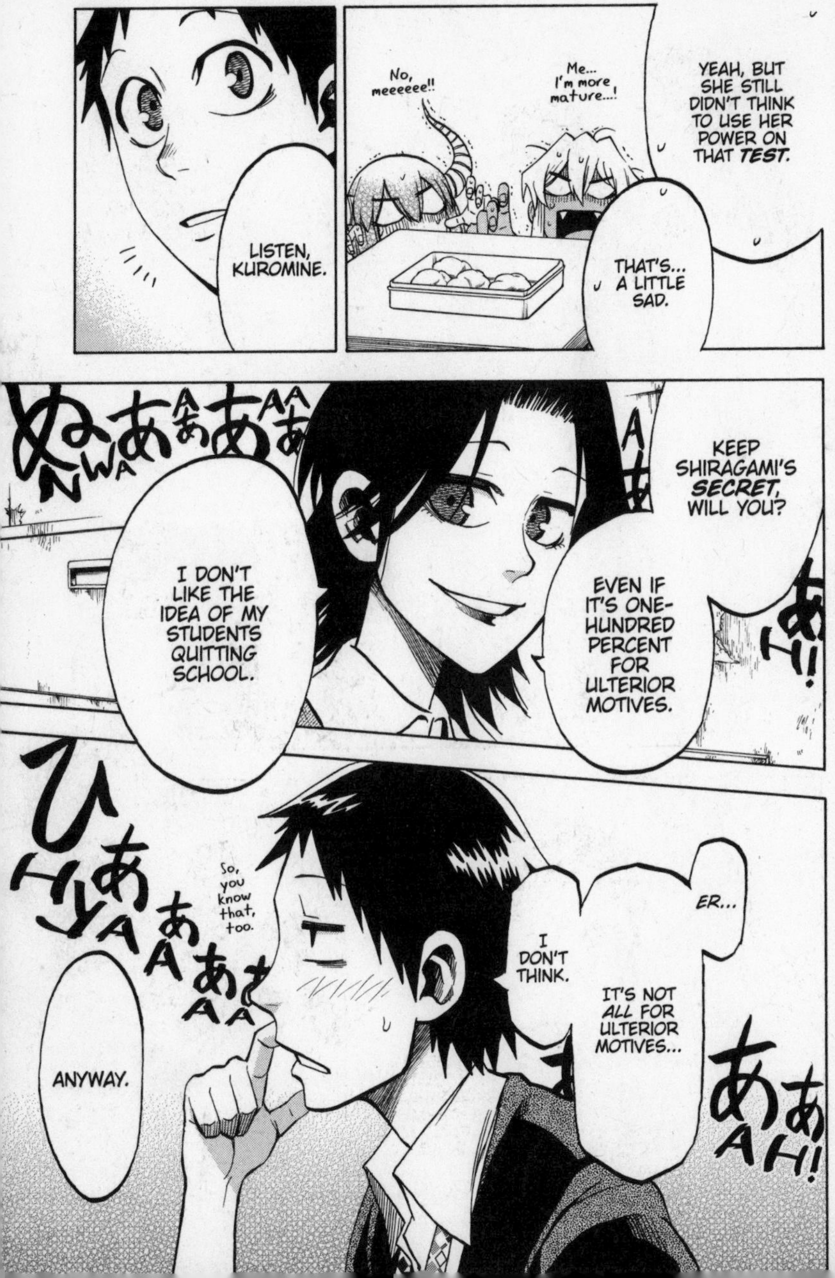
YEAH, BUT SHE STILL DIDN'T THINK TO USE HER POWER ON THAT *TEST*.
Me... I'm more mature...!
No, meeeeee!!
THAT'S... A LITTLE SAD.
LISTEN, KUROMINE.
KEEP SHIRAGAMI'S *SECRET*, WILL YOU?
EVEN IF IT'S ONE-HUNDRED PERCENT FOR ULTERIOR MOTIVES.
I DON'T LIKE THE IDEA OF MY STUDENTS QUITTING SCHOOL.
ぬあああああ NWAAAA
あ AH!
ER...
I DON'T THINK.
IT'S NOT *ALL* FOR ULTERIOR MOTIVES...
So, you know that, too.
ANYWAY.
ひああああ HYAAAA
ああ AH!

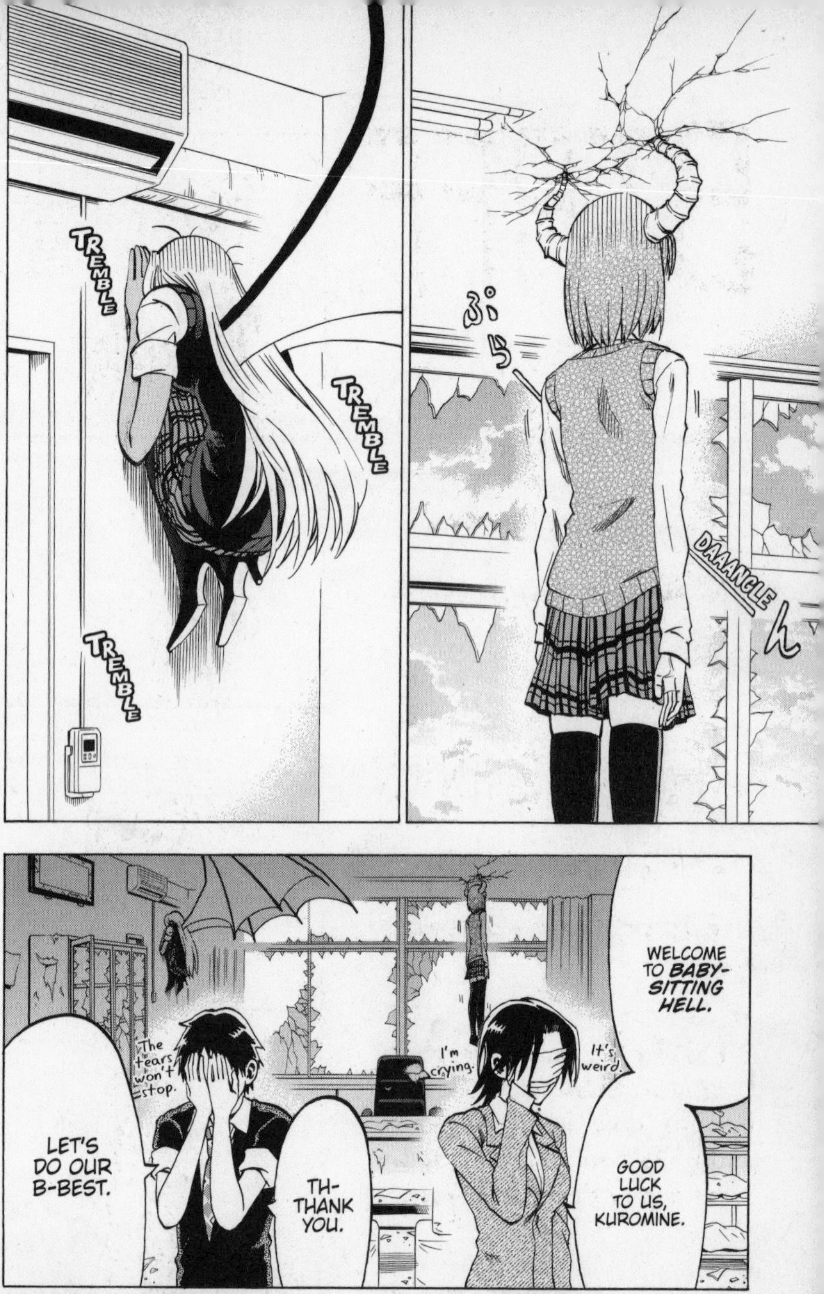

ふら
DAAANGLE ん
TREMBLE
TREMBLE
TREMBLE
WELCOME TO BABY-SITTING HELL.
GOOD LUCK TO US, KUROMINE.
It's weird.
I'm crying.
TH-THANK YOU.
The tears won't stop.
LET'S DO OUR B-BEST.

My Monster Secret
Volume 2 / End

STAFF.

SHIHO-SAN'S SEXY SUGGES-TIONS.

- Akutsu-san

- Shuumeigiku-san

- Seijun Suzuki-san

- Hiroki Minemura-san

- Junko Yamada-san

(in syllabary order)

SPECIAL THANKS

- Youhei Yamashita-san

Editor: Mukawa-san

I give my thanks to those of you holding this book right now and everyone who let me and this work be a part of their lives.

Eiji Masuda

GROOOWL

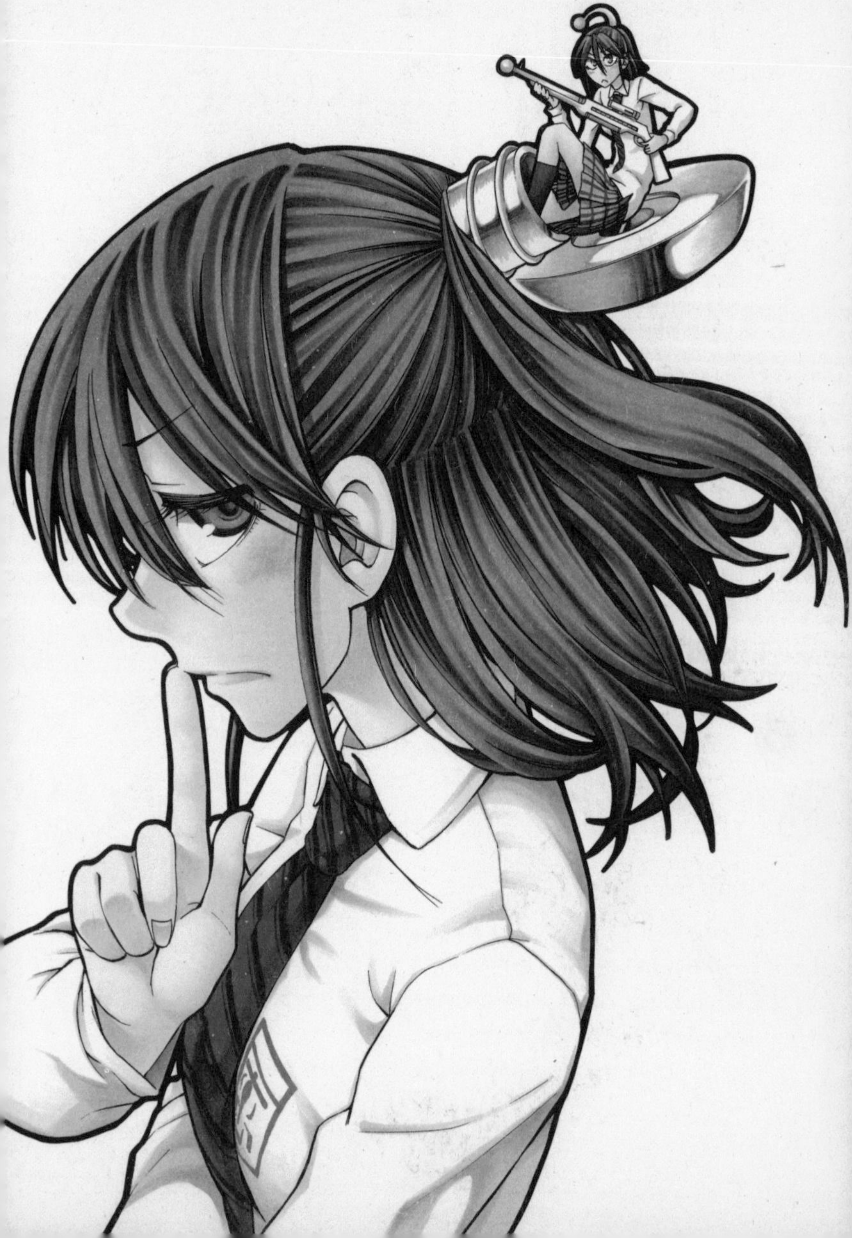

I am ...
an Alien